# Research Methods
# for Social Work

*We would like to dedicate this book to our children, Bradford,*
*Evan, and Elliott, as they provided us with the emotional support*
*we needed while writing this book. We also like to dedicate this book to the late*
*Phyllis W. Rodgers, the mother of Antoinette Y. Farmer, and the late Lawrence and*
*Dorothy Farmer, the parents of G. Lawrence Farmer.*

Sara Miller McCune founded SAGE Publishing in 1965 to support the dissemination of usable knowledge and educate a global community. SAGE publishes more than 1000 journals and over 600 new books each year, spanning a wide range of subject areas. Our growing selection of library products includes archives, data, case studies and video. SAGE remains majority owned by our founder and after her lifetime will become owned by a charitable trust that secures the company's continued independence.

Los Angeles | London | New Delhi | Singapore | Washington DC | Melbourne

# Research Methods for Social Work

## A Problem-Based Approach

**Antoinette Y. Farmer**

*Rutgers, The State University of New Jersey*

**G. Lawrence Farmer**

*Fordham University*

Los Angeles | London | New Delhi
Singapore | Washington DC | Melbourne

FOR INFORMATION:

SAGE Publications, Inc.
2455 Teller Road
Thousand Oaks, California 91320
E-mail: order@sagepub.com

SAGE Publications Ltd.
1 Oliver's Yard
55 City Road
London EC1Y 1SP
United Kingdom

SAGE Publications India Pvt. Ltd.
B 1/I 1 Mohan Cooperative Industrial Area
Mathura Road, New Delhi 110 044
India

SAGE Publications Asia-Pacific Pte. Ltd.
18 Cross Street #10–10/11/12
China Square Central
Singapore 048423

Acquisitions Editor:   Josh Perigo
Content Development Editor:   Alissa Nance
Marketing Manager:   Zina Craft
Production Editor:   Veronica Stapleton Hooper
Copy Editor:   Terri Lee Paulsen
Typesetter:   C&M Digitals (P) Ltd.
Proofreader:   Sally Jaskold
Indexer:   Sheila Hill
Cover Designer:   Dally Verghese

Printed in the United States of America

*Library of Congress Cataloging-in-Publication Data*

Names: Rodgers-Farmer, Antoinette Y., author. | Farmer, G. Lawrence, author.

Title: Research methods for social work : a problem-based approach / Antoinette Y. Farmer, Rutgers—The State University of New Jersey. G. Lawrence Farmer, Fordham University.

Description: Thousand Oaks, Calif. : SAGE, [2021] | Includes bibliographical references and index.

Identifiers: LCCN 2019037241 | ISBN 9781506345307 (paperback) | ISBN 9781506345321 (epub) | ISBN 9781506345314 (epub) | ISBN 9781506345291 (pdf)

Subjects: LCSH: Social service—Research—Methodology.

Classification: LCC HV11 .R525 2021 | DDC 361.3/20721—dc23
LC record available at https://lccn.loc.gov/2019037241

This book is printed on acid-free paper.

20 21 22 23 24 10 9 8 7 6 5 4 3 2 1

# Brief Contents

# Detailed Contents

# Preface

The authors of this book have taught research methods in several schools of social work. Before we became professors, we were passionate about research. Maybe our passion for research stems from having been taught by professors who presented the material in a manner that brought the content to life. With that being said, our intent is to present the contents of this book in an innovative and interactive way that will have *you* excited about learning how to conduct research. It has been demonstrated that interactive learning is associated with greater knowledge retention (Greene & Kirpalani, 2013) and mastery of content (Granić, Mifsud, & Ćukušić, 2009).

## Purpose of the Book

The purpose of this book is to expose you to the concepts of research that will allow you to be both knowledgeable consumers of research and skilled practitioners who can address the social service needs of your clients by using research. The former will be addressed by introducing you to the stages of the research process. The latter will be addressed by using a problem-based learning (PBL) approach. PBL is an instructional method that enhances student learning using problem scenarios as contexts for students to acquire skills, knowledge, and competencies (Albanese & Mitchell, 1993). PBL has been shown to enhance students' critical thinking and problem-solving skills (Karantzas et al., 2013) and is used in competency-driven curriculum (Leon, Winskell, McFarland, & del Rio, 2015). As a social worker, critical thinking and problem-solving skills are important skills to acquire. The Council on Social Work Education (CSWE), which accredits all baccalaureate and master's-level social work programs in the United States, using their Educational Policy and Accreditation Standards (EPAS), clearly indicates the importance of students being critical thinkers. Four out of the nine CSWE-prescribed competencies in the EPAS emphasize the need for social workers to be critical thinkers. Competence 1, *Demonstrate Ethical and Professional Behavior*, states that "social workers understand frameworks of ethical decision-making and how to apply principles of critical thinking to those frameworks in practice, research, and policy arenas" (CSWE, 2015, p. 7). Competence 4, *Engage in Practice-Informed Research and Research-Informed Practice*, emphasizes "critical thinking to engage in analysis of quantitative and qualitative research methods and research findings" (CSWE, 2015, p. 8). Competence 5, *Engage in Policy Practice*, emphasizes "critical thinking to analyze, formulate, and advocate for policies that advance human rights and social, economic, and environmental justice" (CSWE, 2015, p. 8). In Competence 7, *Assess Individuals, Families, Groups, Organizations, and Communities*, it states that social workers should "apply critical thinking to interpret information from clients and constituencies" (CSWE, 2015, p. 9).

In 2008, the Council on Social Work Education adopted a competency-based educational approach to curriculum design as part of its EPAS. A competency-based educational approach is a framework for designing a curriculum that focuses on outcome performance. For social work, the outcome performance is conceptualized as competencies. Social work competence "is the ability to integrate and apply social work knowledge, values, and skills to practice situations in a purposeful, intentional, and professional manner to promote human and community well- being" (CSWE, 2015, p. 6). All social work programs are mandated to assess students' attainment of the CSWE-prescribed competencies. Given that social work programs have a competency-driven curriculum, the PBL instructional approach used in this book is appropriate. Moreover, according to Kwan (2009), PBL "fits well with professional education since it was originally designed for nurturing students to be professionals" (p. 105). You have chosen to enroll in a school of social work to obtain your baccalaureate or master's degree because you are interested in becoming a professional social worker, who has the competencies, knowledge, and skills to practice effectively with diverse types of clients.

## Overview of the Topics Included in the Book

The material presented in this book will be similar to what you will find in most research books. What distinguishes this book from others is the pedagogical underpinning of the book. For example, in most research books where videos and cases are used, these materials are considered by the author to be supplemental materials. The authors of this book are using cases as part of the pedagogical instruction of the course content. These cases present problem-based scenarios. These problem-based scenarios will require you to come up with ways to address the problem identified in the case—thus enhancing your analytic problem-solving skills. The use of problem-based scenarios as part of the pedagogical instruction is consistent with PBL. Another difference between how the material is presented in this book and other research books is that the material is presented in an integrative manner—that is, information about sampling, ethics, and diversity are integrated into various chapters where appropriate. We believe that using an integrative approach will help you make a clearer connection between, for example, sampling and experimental research designs. This book unfolds as follows:

In Chapter 1, we will discuss how research informs practice and practice informs research, the importance of using evidence-based interventions with clients, and the need to evaluate these interventions. Furthermore, we will discuss the steps to effectively implement evidence-based interventions, which have been identified by implementation science. At the beginning of this chapter, you will be asked to read the case titled "Neighborhood House and Social Isolation."

Chapter 2 provides you with an overview of research ethics. You will learn about the principles of the *Belmont Report*. You will be introduced to the types of reviews that institutional review boards conduct to determine if you can conduct your study. At the beginning of this chapter, you will be asked to read the case titled "Can I Really Conduct This Research Study?"

In Chapter 3, we will provide an overview of the research process. You will learn about the various purposes and types of research. At the beginning of this chapter, you will be asked to read the case titled "Predictors of Bullying Behaviors."

Chapter 4 provides information on how to formulate researchable questions and how both ethics and diversity affect the problem formulation process. Additionally, you will learn the purpose for conducting a literature review, how to conduct a literature search, and how to write up a literature review. At the beginning of this chapter, you will be asked to reread the case titled "Can I Really Conduct This Research Study?"

Concepts related to measurement are introduced in Chapter 5. You will learn about the different types of reliability and validity and how to develop a measure. Additionally, you will learn how to develop culturally appropriate measures. You will learn about how to construct measurement instruments. At the beginning of this chapter, you will be asked to read the case titled "Should Maggie Really Be Using This Measure to Assess Kim's Concerns?"

Chapter 6 describes the different types of experimental research designs. You will learn when it is appropriate to use the various experimental research designs. Ethical and diversity issues associated with experimental designs will be discussed. At the beginning of this chapter, you will be asked to read the case titled "Is This Parenting Program Effective for Adolescent Fathers?"

The different types of quasi-experimental research designs will be presented in Chapter 7. You will learn when it is appropriate to use the various quasi-experimental research designs. Ethical and diversity issues associated with quasi-experimental research will be discussed. At the beginning of this chapter, you will be asked to read the case titled "What Are the Effects of a Diversion Program on Rearrest Rates, Re-Incarceration, and Mental Health Functioning?"

In Chapter 8, you will be introduced to qualitative research approaches. Ethical and diversity issues associated with qualitative research will be discussed. Sampling strategies that are used in qualitative research will be presented. At the beginning of this chapter, you will be asked to read the case titled "What Are the Perceptions of African American Adolescent Males About the Police?"

Chapter 9 presents information on mixed-methods research. This is a type of research where both quantitative and qualitative approaches are used. Appropriate sampling strategies to be used with mixed-methods research are described. At the beginning of this chapter, you will be asked to read the case titled "An Evaluation of an Intervention Designed to Increase Knowledge About Opioids."

In Chapter 10, you will be introduced to observational research. This approach is used when it is not ethical or feasible to conduct experimental or quasi-experimental research. Ethical and diversity issues associated with observational research will be discussed. At the beginning of this chapter, you will be asked to read the case titled "Prenatal Opioid Exposure: Implications for Children and Their Families."

Chapter 11 is devoted to discussing both probability and nonprobability sampling strategies. The various errors associated with sampling will be described. Ethical and diversity issues associated with sampling will be discussed. At the beginning of this chapter, you will be asked to read the case titled "Predictors of Bullying Behaviors: Variations Across Gender."

In Chapter 12, you will be introduced to the various methods of data collection for survey research. Information related to how one should sequence the questions on the survey will be provided. Ethical and diversity issues associated with survey research will be discussed. At the beginning of this chapter, you will be asked to read the case titled "Opioid Knowledge Among Older Adults."

In Chapter 13, you will learn how to analyze quantitative data and when it is appropriate to use a particular type of statistical analysis depending upon the type of data that has been collected. Furthermore, you will learn what is considered to be a significant finding and how to interpret the $p$ value. You will learn about the types of statistical packages available to analyze quantitative data. At the beginning of this chapter, you will be asked to reread the case titled "Is This Parenting Program Effective for Adolescent Fathers?"

Chapter 14 introduces you to the various methods to be used for analyzing qualitative data. You will learn about the types of statistical packages available to analyze qualitative data. At the beginning of this chapter, you will be asked to reread the case titled "What Are the Perceptions of African American Adolescent Males About Police Brutality?"

The use of single-case design methodology as a way to evaluate social work practice with individuals will be described in Chapter 15. Ethical and diversity issues associated with single-case design evaluation will be discussed. At the beginning of this chapter, you will be asked to read the case titled "Is Peer Mentoring Effective?"

Chapter 16 is devoted to describing the types of program evaluations: formative evaluation and summative evaluation. Ethical and diversity issues associated with program evaluation will be discussed. At the beginning of this chapter, you will be asked to reread the case titled "Is Peer Mentoring Effective?"

Because you may be asked to write a research paper as an assignment for your research course, we have included in the Appendix guidelines for writing a research proposal.

## Structure of the Chapters

At the beginning of each chapter, you will be instructed to read a case. In the case, there will be a problem that you will analyze. After reading the case, you will be asked to do the following: (1) identify the problem; (2) determine what you already know about the problem; (3) determine what information you need to solve the problem; and (4) list the questions needed to be answered related to the information you need to solve the problem. We ask you to read the case carefully before you read anything in the chapter because the PBL process starts with a problem, which starts the learning process (Kwan, 2009). By having you read the case before reading anything in the chapter, we have captured your interest and given you a glance of how it is to be a researcher. Researchers often start with a problem that they are interested in knowing more about, and they use the methods discussed in this book to study the problem. At the end of each chapter, we will list additional resources you need to be aware of and summarize the main points of the chapter, according to the learning objectives.

In 2015, CSWE's Commission on Educational Policy (COEP) developed nine new competencies that social work programs need to incorporate in their curricula and assess students' attainment of them. These competencies are multidimensional and are comprised of behavior, cognitive and affective reaction processes, knowledge, skills, and values at the general practice level. In each chapter, we will identify which of the competencies and their dimensions are associated with the learning objectives for that chapter.

Each chapter will have learning objectives, and the cases will have objectives as well. Bloom's Taxonomy is used to write the objectives. These learning objectives are written in such a way that they will help you become a critical thinker. Having you develop critical thinking skills is consistent with the use of PBL and CSWE's competencies 1, 4, 5, and 7.

## Applying Problem-Based Learning

### The PBL Approach

Several definitions have been used to describe PBL. For the purpose of this book, we are using the definition proposed by Albanese and Mitchell (1993), which states that PBL is an instructional method that enhances student learning using problem scenarios as contexts for students to acquire skills, knowledge, and competencies. PBL was first used in medical education at the McMasters University in Canada in the 1970s. Medical faculty developed this approach to enhance clinical problem-solving and life-learning skills, which the current instructional approach failed to do (Albanese & Mitchell, 1993; Barrows, 1996). For those of you who are interested in finding out more about how PBL has been used in elementary, secondary, and higher educational settings and disciplines, please refer to Barrows (1996) and Hung, Jonassen, and Liu (2008).

PBL is also widely used in social work. In South Wales and Australia, social work programs refer to PBL as "issue-based approach" learning (Kwan, 2009). The University of Hong Kong has used PBL in both their BSW and MSW programs (Pearson, Wong, Ho, & Wong, 2007; Wong & Lam, 2007). A number of schools of social work in the United States, such as Eastern Washington University and University of Missouri in Columbia, have experimented with PBL (Westhues, Barsen, Freymond, & Train, 2014). PBL is based on the following assumptions: (1) learning occurs when encountering authentic, ill-structured problems (Barrows, 1985; Hung, Jonassen, & Liu, 2008); (2) encountering problems acts as the stimulus for persons to acquire knowledge to solve the problem; and (3) learning is self-directed (Barrows, 1996; Hung et al., 2008). The first assumption takes into consideration that context is important for learning to occur. Students tend to find abstract ideas less useful if they cannot apply them to the context in which they are working. The authentic nature of the problem facilitates learning, as it enhances student engagement (Stinson & Milter, 1996). Therefore, in this text, the problems presented in the cases are ones that you are likely to encounter when doing micro- or macro-level social work practice. The authentic nature of the problem is also demonstrated by the problem being ill-structured, that is, not giving you all the information. In clinical practice, many times you will interview clients who cannot clearly articulate what brought them into treatment. In order to determine why your clients are coming into treatment, you need to have good listening, interviewing, and problem-solving skills. The questions you ask during the interview should lead you to think about what should be done to address a client's concerns.

## The PBL Learning Process

As mentioned earlier, one of the assumptions of PBL is learning occurs when encountering authentic, ill-structured problems. Therefore, at the beginning of each chapter, you will be presented with a case example related to micro- or macro-level social work practice. The case will provide you with some information about a situation (i.e., a problem) and you will be asked to make a recommendation on how to address the problem. Before you make a recommendation, you must think about what you already know about the problem, and what else needs to be learned—that is, what you do not know or what you need to know to solve the problem.

The learning process associated with PBL is facilitated by you engaging in the steps below. You will need to use all or some of these steps as you analyze the case presented to you at the beginning of each chapter.

1. Identify the problem.

2. Determine what you already know about the problem.

3. Determine what information you need to solve to the problem.

4. List the questions needed to be answered related to the information you need to solve the problem.

5. Read the textbook to help you solve the problem presented in the case.

6. Answer the Critical Thinking Questions.

7. Review the questions you have listed to determine if you have the answers for each.

8. Apply the information you have read in the textbook or learned elsewhere to solving the identified problem in the case.

Reflection is also an important part of the PBL process. As you read the chapters, you need to reflect on what you have read and think about how you could apply what you have learned to the case or other courses in the social work program. We encourage you to keep a journal and write each week how what you have learned in this course helped you in your field placement or other courses. At the end of the semester, you should reread what you have written. You will be amazed by how much you have learned.

## SAGE Edge

### Sage Edge for Instructors

A password-protected resource site available at edge.sagepub.com/farmer supports teaching, providing high-quality content to create a rich learning environment for students. The SAGE Edge site for this book includes the following instructor resources:

- **Test banks** built on Bloom's Taxonomy provide a diverse range of test items
- Editable, chapter-specific **PowerPoint slides** offer flexibility for creating a multimedia presentation for lectures
- **Sample course syllabi** for semester and quarter courses that provide suggested models for structuring your courses
- **Lecture notes** for each chapter align with the PowerPoint slides summarize key concepts to help with preparation for lectures and class discussion
- **Chapter-specific discussion questions** help launch engaging classroom interaction while reinforcing important content
- Engaging **class activities** reinforce concepts for students
- **Tables and figures** from the book are available for download

### SAGE Edge for Students

The open-access companion website helps students accomplish their coursework goals in an easy-to-use learning environment, featuring:

- An **open-access site** that makes it easy for students to maximize their study time, anywhere, anytime
- **eQuizzes** that encourage self-guided assessment and practice

# Acknowledgments

At the outset, we would like to thank Darlaine Manning, who recently retired from SAGE Publications, for encouraging us to write this book. I will never forget the day she came to my office stating that she was looking for faculty to write books for SAGE. Little did I know at that time that my husband and I would be writing a research methods book. Without you encouraging us to submit a book proposal to SAGE, we would never have done so.

I am especially grateful to Kassie Graves, who formerly worked for SAGE. After she read our book proposal, she told us that she liked it and thought it would be worth our effort to write the book. Along the way, we have worked with lots of great staff at SAGE who encouraged us to continue writing the book, at times when it was the most difficult thing to do. A special thanks goes to Joshua Perigo, who constantly checked in on us to see how the book was coming along. He was always responsive to our concerns and helped us develop the book into what you are reading today. Additionally, I am grateful for the efforts of Terri Lee Paulsen, who served as the copy editor for this book.

My colleagues at Rutgers, The State University of New Jersey, Drs. Allison Zippay, Jamey Lister, N. Andrew Peterson, and Felix Muchomba, were very gracious with their time and provided me with helpful feedback on numerous chapters. I thank you so much. I also want to extend words of gratitude to Dr. Jill Sinha. Her suggested revisions to the chapters were indeed helpful as well.

Finally, I would like to thank the reviewers who took time out of their busy schedules to read the chapters they were assigned, as they provided useful feedback to improve this work. Their feedback helped my husband and me think about adding more opportunities for students to evaluate their grasp of the material discussed in the chapters.

These reviewers were:

Mustapha Alhassan, Clark Atlanta University

Juan J. Barthelemy, Louisiana State University

Laurie Blackman, PhD, University of the District of Columbia

Yolanda Meade Byrd, Winston-Salem State University

Karen Chapman, Winston-Salem State University

Amanda Corbin, University of South Florida

Michael Fendrich, University of Connecticut

Sonja V. Harry, Winston-Salem State University

Daphne Henderson, The University of Tennessee at Martin

Pedro M. Hernandez, Jackson State University

Richard Hoefer, University of Texas at Arlington

Youngjo Im, Chicago State University

Elaine T. Jurkowski, Southern Illinois University Carbondale

Mansoor A. F. Kazi, PhD, University at Albany, State University of New York

John Lichtenwainer, Alvernia University

Michael J. Lyman, Shippensburg University of Pennsylvania

Jong Won Min, San Diego State University

Larry G. Morton II, Arkansas State University

Debra Mowery, University of South Florida

Duane R. Neff, Winthrop University

Julia Pryce, Loyola University, Chicago

Jaak Rakfeldt, Southern Connecticut State University

Patricia Saleeby, Southern Illinois University

Consoler Teboh, Florida Atlantic University

Kerry Fay Vandergrift, Radford University

Ohenewaa D. White-Ra, Alvernia University

# About the Authors

**Antoinette Y. Farmer**, PhD, is professor and former associate dean for academic affairs, and faculty affiliate, Center for Prevention Science, and Center for Violence Against Women and Children at Rutgers, The State University of New Jersey, School of Social Work. Dr. Farmer's research examines the social and interpersonal factors that affect parenting as well as how parenting practices influence adolescent high-risk behaviors, such as delinquency and substance use. Another strand of her research focuses on social work education, where she studies the effects of the implicit curriculum on students' outcomes and the use of research methods to study issues affecting diverse groups. She coedited a special issue of the *Journal of Social Service Research*, which was devoted to informing researchers of the methodological issues confronting them when conducting research with minority and oppressed populations. She is the coauthor of *Research with Diverse Groups: Research Designs and Multivariate Latent Modeling for Equivalence* (2014). She is a commissioner on the Council on Social Work Education (CSWE) Commission on Educational Policy and a Society for Social Work and Research (SSWR) Fellow. She previously served as a commissioner on CSWE Commission for Accreditation. She is currently on the editorial board for the *Journal of Religion and Spirituality in Social Work: Social Thought*.

**G. Lawrence Farmer**, MSW, PhD, is an associate professor and director of the doctoral program at Fordham University's Graduate School of Social Service. His scholarly interests focus on understanding those factors that promote the well-being of youth. His articles have been published in *Social Service Review*, *Children and Schools*, *Journal of Human Behavior in the Social Environment*, *Social Work in Health Care*, and *Journal of Social Service Research*. Two of the projects he is presently involved in, Resilient Scholars and Westchester Building the Future, seek to promote youths' well-being. Both projects aim to increase protective factors by transforming institutions that provide services to youth. The Resilient Scholars program promotes positive youth development by developing the social and emotional learning competencies of middle and high school students. The program also focuses on building schools' capability to implement youth-centered interventions that will be sustained over time. The Westchester Building the Future project is a collaboration between the Westchester County Department of Social Services, Westchester County Department of Community Mental Health, and Fordham University, with the aim of restructuring services to youth transitioning out of the foster care system. The intent of the program is to empower youth in their efforts to successfully navigate the transition and to achieve changes in the system of care for youth in the system.

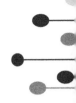

# CHAPTER

# 1

# Evidence-Based Practice

## Learning Objectives

1.1 Differentiate between the various ways of knowing.

1.2 Differentiate between evidence-based practices (EBPs) and evidence-based practice (EBP) as a decision-making framework.

| Competency Covered | Learning Objectives | Dimension |
|---|---|---|
| Competency 4<br>*Engage in Practice-Informed Research and Research-Informed Practice* | 1.1 Differentiate between the various ways of knowing.<br>1.2 Differentiate between evidence-based practices (EBPs) and evidence-based practice (EBP) as a decision-making framework. | Skills |

---

### PBL Case 1

### Neighborhood House and Social Isolation

As you consider what constitutes evidence-based practice (EBP) and how to infuse EBP into your decision-making as a social worker, the following case example will be used to illustrate the application of EBP as a decision-making framework. By answering the questions related to this case example, you will be able to apply the EBP decision-making framework.

During Neighborhood House's executive board meeting, one of the board members brought to the board's attention a story in the *New York Times* profiling a young man with autism who was participating in a peer mentoring program at his middle school. The program

Master the content at
**edge.sagepub.com/farmer**

1

attempts to address the problem of social isolation often experienced by those with autism. The board member asks, "Do peer mentoring programs work in reducing social isolation among youth with autism? Should we be developing one? Are there other programs we could offer to youth and their families to address social isolation that middle schoolers with autism sometime experience?"

At this point, take a few minutes to think about the case example and do the following:

1. Identify the problem.

2. Determine what you already know about the problem.

3. Determine what information you need to solve the problem.

4. List the questions needed to be answered related to the information you need to solve the problem.

Please write down your responses to each item. You will need to refer to them while reading this chapter.

**You are doing your field placement at Neighborhood House. Your field supervisor, Dr. Sage Hawthorne, has asked you and the other social work interns to help her find information to address the questions raised by the board member.**

## Introduction
· · · · · · · · · · · · · · · · · · · · · · · · · · · · · · · · · · · · · · · · · · · · · · · · · · · · · · · · · · · · · · · · ·

In this chapter, you will learn about the various ways persons acquire knowledge and about evidence-base practice as a decision-making process.

## Practice-Informed Research and Research-Informed Practice
· · · · · · · · · · · · · · · · · · · · · · · · · · · · · · · · · · · · · · · · · · · · · · · · · · · · · · · · · · · · · · · · ·

In order for the social work interns to address the questions raised by the board member, they need to demonstrate mastery of Competency 4, *Engage in Practice-Informed Research and Research-Informed Practice*. Competency 4 states that social work practice should both inform and be informed by cultural and ethical empirical research. Social workers must contribute to the identification of researchable practice questions and the generation of empirical knowledge. Additionally, they must develop the knowledge and skills needed to translate research findings into effective practice.

The practice of social work involves the identification, implementation, and evaluation of those actions or strategies that need to be undertaken in order to empower individuals, groups, and communities in their efforts to achieve well-being. Various conceptual and theoretical perspectives inform the social work profession; they include person-in-environment (PIE), scientific inquiry, global perspective, human rights, and social justice (Council on Social Work Education [CSWE] 2015; National Association of Social Workers [NASW], 2017). The importance of scientific inquiry to the profession is reflected in Competency 4, *Practice-Informed Research and Research-Informed Practice*. CSWE (2015) has identified social workers' ability to use knowledge from multiple sources to inform their practice and to use practice experience to inform attempts to generate new knowledge as competencies that all social workers must possess.

## The Search for Best Practices

*The search for best practices often involves the identification of what should go on during the therapeutic encounter, what are the best practices the organization should engage in, in order to support the implementation of interventions, and sustainability of the best practices that are implemented.*

Del Valle et al. (2014) used qualitative research strategies to study four high-performing and innovative vocational rehabilitation programs. EBP was an integral part of each of these programs. The authors identified the best practices associated with the implementation of state-wide vocational rehabilitation programs.

Research-informed practice begins with social workers attempting to identify those practices that are most likely to meet the needs of their clients. Social worker practice can be characterized as one involving a continual process of inquiry as to what are the *best practices* that can be undertaken to promote individuals' empowerment. The term *practice* is being used here to refer to all levels of social work practice (i.e., direct practice with individuals, groups or community, policy practice and research). **Best practices** are commonly known as those practices identified as most appropriate for use within a particular practice context, with particular groups to achieve particular outcomes (Mullen, Bellamy, & Bledsoe, 2008).

In the case example titled "Neighborhood House and Social Isolation," there is a need to identify those practices that the agency can engage in that will improve the social experiences of youth with special needs. That is, the staff in the agency need to determine if peer mentoring will reduce social isolation of youth with autism.

Identification of best practices begins with an understanding of strengths and weaknesses associated with the various ways in which individuals seek to acquire knowledge. Personal Experience, Tradition, Authority, Popular Media, and the Scientific Method represent ways social workers can acquire knowledge.

# Ways of Acquiring Knowledge

## Personal Experience

### Application Checkpoint 1.1

Think about the ways in which the agency staff's experience with children with special needs can influence their perceptions of what programs could address the social needs of children with autism.

Daniel Tammet, a linguist and educator who has linguistic, numerical, and visual synesthesia,[1] in his TED Talk titled "Different Ways of Knowing," illustrated how our experience of the world through our senses provides a powerful source of learning about the world. Tammet writes and speaks about how aesthetic judgment guides and shapes the way we learn about the world around us. His synesthesia, which he describes as a "cross talk" between the senses, is an extreme example of how senses shape knowledge development. For Tammet, learning about numbers involved learning about colors and shapes, because for him colors and shapes are properties of numbers. One's personal experience contributes to the development of a personal frame of reference that filters and organizes that individual's experience with the world. Our personal experiences provide a valuable method for the acquiring of new knowledge and skills. We learn vicariously by watching others and directly interacting with the environment (Bandura, 1986; Kolb & Fry, 1974). Not only does personal experience serve as a mechanism for acquiring new knowledge and skills, but it may be used to inform intervention development. For example, the knowledge derived from personal experience was used to inform the development of the successful implementation of a peer support intervention (Mendoza, Resko, Wohlert, & Baldwin, 2015) and mental and behavioral health interventions (Oates, Drey, & Jones, 2017). Personal experience as a social worker can contribute to the development of practice wisdom.

There are limits to the knowledge gathered via our personal experiences. Selectiveness of our perceptual system contributes to biases in reasoning such as

---

[1]Synesthesia is a neurologically based condition in which a person experiences "crossed" responses to stimuli. It occurs when stimulation of one sensory or cognitive pathway (e.g., hearing) leads to automatic, involuntary experiences in a second sensory or cognitive pathway (e.g., vision).

*observational selection* and *confirmation biases*. **Observational selection bias** is the effect of suddenly noticing things we did not notice before.

### Application Checkpoint 1.2

What can we learn from the experiences of those youth with autism, their family members, and friends about what might work to promote positive social experiences of those youth?

Along with noticing it more, your perception is that the numbers of that object in your environment have increased. For example, you buy a new red car, and you start to notice other red cars in your neighborhood like the one you own. It is a cognitive bias that could lead to attributing causality to events when coincidence or chance is the true explanation.

**Confirmation bias** focuses on our tendency to selectively attend to things that we agree with or that support our opinions. It is reflected in the tendency of those with liberal or conservative political opinions to favor talk show hosts with political opinions that mirror theirs. Confirmation bias also leads people to discount information that is inconsistent with their opinions. Information that is counter to a person's opinions can lead to an experience of cognitive dissonance. **Cognitive dissonance** is the discomfort one experiences when acting in a way that is incongruent with one's beliefs, norms, thoughts, or values (Festinger, 1957). People tend to want to avoid experiencing cognitive dissonance because of the mental stress associated with the experience. Additionally, an individual's beliefs, motivations, desires, expectations, and context all contribute both individually and collectively to biasing the accurateness and objectivity of one's perceptions (Pronin, 2007). Persons' lifetime of experiences with various groups based on age, ethnicity, social class, sexual orientation, and so on contribute to hidden biases in their perceptions.

## Practice Wisdom

**Practice wisdom** has been described as resulting from the accumulation of information, assumptions, and judgments that can be applied to practice. Personal experiences contribute to that accumulation of information and contribute to one's evaluation of that information (Chu & Tsui, 2008). Practice wisdom is included among the five areas of knowledge—theoretical, empirical, procedural, performance, and personal (Gambrill, 1999; Hudson, 1997). It is a source of knowledge that is not gained from a technical rational process of reasoning or the application of theory (Cheung, 2015). Practice wisdom is believed to have four features: agential, fluid, interactive, and moral reasoning and cognitive knowledge.

Consider the ways in which the director of Neighborhood House could use the practice wisdom of staff to develop new programs addressing the social isolation of youth with autism.

*Agential.* Practice wisdom involves the social worker actively reflecting on his or her experiences to give personal meaning to those experiences. The social worker is involved in developing a personal and practical knowledge that will guide his or her practice. The knowledge developed is not objective.

*Fluid.* Practice wisdom is part of an ongoing process of reflecting on actions. The knowledge that makes up practice wisdom is provisional and undergoes continuous revisions.

*Interactive.* Practice wisdom is part of a contextual, collaborative learning process. It emerges through the social worker's interaction with others in the practice setting. The active reflection of the social worker on his or her interactions with others in the practice environment contributes to the knowledge development.

*Moral Reasoning and Cognitive Knowledge.* Practice wisdom highlights the interplay between the values and ethics of social work practice and the social science cognitive knowledge base.

## Tradition

> Different ways of knowing differ in the extent to which they highlight uncertainty and are designed to weed out biases and distortions that may influence assumptions. (Gambrill, 2012, p. 206)

Looking to an organization's traditional or routine way of doing things can serve as a form of learning for social workers. It is comforting to those new to an organization to be able to look to those traditional practices for guidance as to what is expected. An organization's traditions sometimes represent the accumulated knowledge gained from the experiences of professionals at the organization. This accumulated experiential knowledge can represent the *organizational practice wisdom*. Those traditions can also be the product of *ingroup bias*. This represents confirmation bias at the group level. Over time, the reason for why an organization or groups established a tradition becomes lost to the group, yet the tradition continues without critical examination of its utility.

## Authority

Professionals often seek out knowledge and experience from those in position of authority to inform their actions. In those cases, where those in authority have come to their position because of their development of expertise in an area of practice, they become valuable problem solvers for the novice. Studies of novice and expert chess players have given us insight into differences in their approach to problems. Experts notice features and meaningful patterns of information in a problem that are missed by the novice. The experts have a deeper depth of content knowledge and have organized that information more efficiently than the novice. Individuals can use their position of authority to hinder innovation. When those in authority are not continuingly renewing their knowledge, outdated strategies for addressing a problem may be relied on. Having a position of authority in one's area may falsely give a person creditability to speak on issues outside his or her realm of expertise.

## Popular Media

The Internet age has created new sources of media to distribute information and support learning. Individuals are turning to Wikipedia, YouTube, Facebook, and Twitter to acquire news and information that just a generation ago was only available in bookstores, libraries, and classrooms (Sanger, 2010). The Pew Research Center's 2016 survey of Americans' Internet access determined that about four in 10 Americans often get news online (Mitchell, Gottfried, Barthel, & Shearer, 2016). In that same study, 62% of Americans got their news from social media (i.e., Facebook, Twitter, Reddit). A social worker can turn to YouTube or an MOOC[2] like edX[3] to learn about cognitive behavior therapy, comparative policy analysis, or any topic taught in a face-to-face classroom. The Internet has not only improved social workers' ability to access information, but it has also increased consumers' ability to engage in seeking health and wellness information. In 2019 there were nearly 14,000 open-access journals[4] giving anyone with Internet access free access to more than 2 million articles (see Directory of Open Access Journals, https://doaj.org/). Additionally, the digital divide has been closing with the increased smartphone ownership and use among young adults, minorities, and those with moderate incomes (Zickuhr & Smith, 2012). This point is illustrated as it relates to income in Figure 1.1. There is evidence that the amount of websites disseminating health information has increased. It has been documented that there are more than 70,000 websites disseminating health information and over 50 million individuals who accessed those sites (Cline & Haynes, 2001).

However, caution needs to be taken when consuming information from the Internet. The quality of information on the millions of sites varies. There is evidence that social media services such as Facebook and Twitter are susceptible to the *echo chamber effect*. The **echo chamber effect** is a phenomenon wherein information or beliefs are reinforced by repetitive transmission inside an enclosed virtual space (Vicarioa et al., 2016). Larry Sanger, the cofounder of Wikipedia, has expressed concern that there is no standard review process of the material on the site by experts (LarrySanger.org).

---

[2]Massive Open Online Courses

[3]edX was founded by Harvard University and MIT in 2012.

[4]Open-access journals are scholarly journals that are available online without individuals having to have a subscription or pay to view the articles published in the journal.

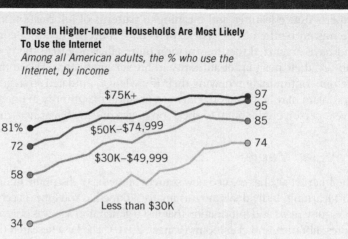

**Figure 1.1   Closing the Digital Divide**

**Those In Higher-Income Households Are Most Likely To Use the Internet**
*Among all American adults, the % who use the Internet, by income*

$75K+ — 97
95
81% — $50K–$74,999
72 — 85
$30K–$49,999
58 — 74
Less than $30K
34

2000    2005    2010    2015

While those with higher income continue to have higher rates of access to the Internet, the gap among the various income groups has decreased between 2000 and 2014.

*Source:* "Those In Higher-Income Households Are Most Likely To Use Internet." Pew Research Center, Washington, DC (2015) https://www.pewinternet.org/chart/those-in-higher-income-households-are-most-likely-to-use-internet/

Personal experience, tradition, authority, and popular media represent ways social workers can acquire knowledge that are often contrasted to the scientific method.

---

**Critical Thinking Question 1.1**

How would you hypothesize the ways in which the staff's experiences with youth who have special needs, the agency's typical approaches to program design, the perspective of board members, and recent TV shows with characters with autism might shape the agency's effort to develop new programming to address problem social isolation? Justify your response.

---

## Scientific Method

### Top Down or Bottom Up

Stereotypical portrayals of the scientific process have a researcher sitting in his or her office or lab, reviewing previous research, and from that review generating a new study. In this picture, the researcher guides the study process. He or she is responsible for the identification of the research questions, data collection, data analysis, and the reporting of findings. However, based on Competency 4 (*Engage in Practice-Informed Research and Research-Informed Practice*) and the evidence-based movement in social work, there is recognition that social work practice must inform social work research and social work research must inform social work practice—that is, the research generated in the university is used by practitioners and practitioners generate practice knowledge that inform research conducted by researchers. The data mining work conducted by social work researchers has demonstrated how the practice-to-research process contributes to the development of evidence-based practices in social work (Bradt, Roose, Bouverne-De Bie, & De Schryver, 2011; Epstein, 2011; Plath & Gibbons, 2010).

While the procedures carried out when the scientific method is being implemented differs across scientific disciplines, there are spheres of activities common to the process (see Figure 1.2). These spheres are: *Observation, Question Identification, Literature Review, Theory Formulation, Empirical Research Question, Research Design,*

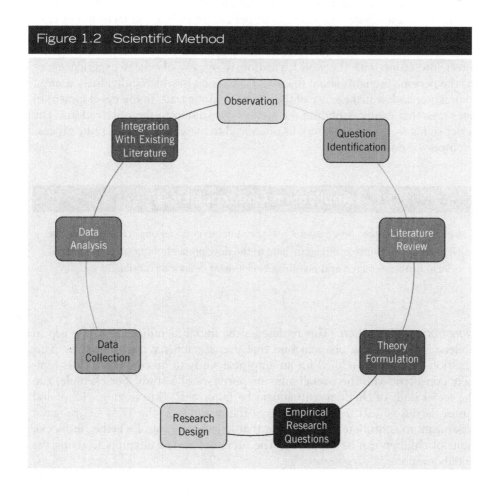

Figure 1.2  Scientific Method

*Data Collection, Data Analysis,* and *Integration With Existing Literature.* For those disciplines using the scientific method, knowledge is established by the use of rigorous and systematic testing (Jaccard & Jacoby, 2012). These activities attempt to address the limitations associated with other methods used to acquire knowledge. It is assumed that all knowledge is provisional and subject to refutation. The scientific method makes the knowledge development process both transparent and subject to replication. The ability for others to independently replicate findings provides a safeguard against bias.

*Observation.* The process often begins with a set of observations an individual has about a phenomena or experience. The scientific method attempts to provide structure to an individual's observations that will address inherent biases. For social workers, the process often begins with observations about our clients or the client's systems. For example, we can observe those characteristics of the social networks of children with a learning disability. Or we could observe what we think are the effects that changes in policies regarding the inclusion of children with learning disabilities in general education classrooms has on incidences of bullying at the school. Those observations can be grounded in the individual's direct interaction with the world, vicariously by way of others' experiences, or via the person's thoughts about the world. The ways in which individuals attempt to organize and/or make sense of those observations leads to the development of questions that can possibly impose some organization to the observations. The selective nature of our observations often lead to biases that the scientific process attempts to address.

## Application Checkpoint 1.4

Consider how the observations of the interactions among children at the Neighborhood House could contribute to the development of questions that could inform further research and possible development of an intervention.

*Question Identification.* This represents the initial identification of the gap in understanding about a phenomenon that the researcher wants to address. This question needs to be refined for an empirical study to be conducted. It is typically consistent with the overall aims or purposes of a study. For example, can the social skills of children with autism be improved? Virues-Ortega, Julio, and Pastor-Barriuso's (2013) meta-analysis of the research on the TEACCH program was meant to contribute to addressing that larger question of whether the social skills of children can be improved. The literature review attempts to refine the initial question.

Without the use of professional jargon, what are two questions that staff at the Neighborhood House should formulate that would support their efforts to develop an intervention?

*Literature Review.* The formulation of a question grounded in one's experience of the world leads to an examination of the existing literature. The literature review process attempts to place these initial observations and questions within a larger body of observations and potential theory and/or conceptual framework. The literature review can take on various forms, from the concise and targeted reviews found in journal articles to the lengthier reviews found in systematic reviews. For example, consider a social worker providing services to older adults living in an assisted-living center who has a question about the type of lifestyle activities most beneficial to his or her clients. The social worker might find a brief review of the literature on the topic in Akbaraly and colleagues' (2009) study of leisure activities and risk of dementia or take a look at a comprehensive systematic review conducted by Anderson et al. (2014). The literature review provided by Akbaraly et al. (2009) has the purpose of placing the study within an empirical and theoretical context that will provide the reader with a concise and clear rationale for the study; the systematic review conducted by Anderson et al. (2014) has the larger purpose of synthesizing the findings of the larger body of empirical studies on the topic, with the goal of drawing conclusions about the status of knowledge in the area. The brief literature review found in the typical research article represents a narrative analysis of the findings from others' research and typically does not report on new or original research findings. On the other hand, the systematic literature review can incorporate the secondary analysis of data from studies that were previously conducted and can generate new research findings. Systematic literature reviews that involved the secondary analysis of quantitative data found in previously conducted research studies are called meta-analyses. For example, Scherder et al. (2014) conducted a systematic review that incorporated a meta-analysis of the research on moderate physical activity on cognitive functioning of older adults.

Both our personal experiences and engaging in a review of literature can each contribute to the formulation of a theory. A **theory** is used to explain why a phenomenon or the relationships among variables exists. The interrelationship among the variables contributes to our understanding of a phenomenon.

*Theory Formulation.* As staff at the Neighborhood House seek to develop an intervention to address social isolation that children with autism experience, they might want to consider Bauminger, Shulman, and Agam's (2003) use of social development theory to understand social initiation behavior of children with autism. Theory is used to develop hypotheses. Hypotheses are testable predictions about the relationships among variables. They can take on an "If–then" format—for example, "If typically developing children serve as role models for children with autism, then children with autism will be more motivated to engage in schoolwork than those students who do not have these role models." Hypotheses can also be statements about associations among variables—for example, "Group-based discrimination is related to hopeful thinking." The predictions made by the hypotheses must have the potential to be testable. A hypothesis is testable when it is possible to observe information that could provide support or disconfirm that hypothesis.

There may be times when technology has not advanced enough to provide a direct observation of variables identified in the hypothesis. In 1546, Girolamo Fracastoro proposed the germ theory of disease. The theory proposed that microorganisms caused diseases, but the development of the microscope that would make it possible to see germs was not invented until the 1620s (Porter, 1997). The observation of microorganisms was not to occur until the 1670s (Porter, 1997).

Within the scientific method, there is a complex interplay between research activities and the development or refinement of theories. Theories play a role in shaping the questions individuals may ask about their observations. For example, theories of human behaviors, such as attachment theory or systems theory, could be used to provide guidance on what questions to ask to gain understanding of the observations. Theory can also play a role in the development of hypotheses. The research process often, but not always, involves the development of specific hypotheses or testable predictions about the nature of the relationships among variables associated with the phenomenon. During early stages of our understanding of some phenomena, we may not have enough information or have identified a theory to guide in the development of testable hypotheses. In the absence of theory, researchers may use a conceptual framework to guide the exploratory analysis of the phenomena. For example, when studying the changing phenomena of bullying among teenage girls, Jamal, Bonell, Harden, and Lorenc (2015) used the social-ecology framework to guide their study in determining the role the school structure, policies, and practices may have in maintaining stable "bully" and "victim" roles, which contribute to unhealthy interpersonal relationships in the school.

*Empirical Research Questions.* Researchable questions can come from many sources: findings from previous research, observations, theory, and merely thinking about the world can all be sources. Many times, findings from previous research and challenges faced in practice are the source of research questions. For example, Mazzola's (2016) research questions were sparked by her desire to learn more about how students' connection to their school community affected the amount of time and attention they invest into their school work. Larsson, Pettersson, Eriksson, and Skoog (2016) formulated their research questions that focused on exploring mentors' motivation from research on mentoring programs. They identified the recruitment of mentors as a problem. Observations can lead to the development of specific hypotheses or predictions about relationships among variables associated with the phenomenon or how to best describe the phenomenon. Zhang, Cui, Iyer,

Jetten, and Hao (2014) developed hypotheses regarding the barriers to the development of hopeful thinking when individuals face discrimination based on their group membership. Their study provided support for how individuals' position in a socio-cultural group plays a role in their life satisfaction.

Competency 4, *Engage in Practice-Informed Research and Research-Informed Practice*, states that social workers "use practice experiences to inform scientific inquiry and research and use and translate research evidence to inform and improve practice, policy, and service delivery" (CSWE, 2105, p. 8). In other words, social workers' practice experiences contribute to the creation of researchable questions, and the engaging in the research process can lead to development of research questions relevant to practice. The illustration of this process can be seen in Figure 1.3.

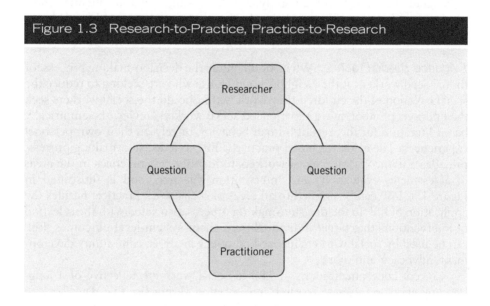

Figure 1.3 Research-to-Practice, Practice-to-Research

*Research Design, Data Collection, and Analysis.* Research design refers to the procedures that will be undertaken to gather and analyze the information needed to evaluate the accuracy of the study's hypotheses or research questions. Chapters 6, 7, and 10 provide a detailed discussion of three classes of research designs: experimental, quasi-experimental, and observational that can be used to gather data to answer research questions and test hypotheses. Research designs provide an alignment among the research questions, when appropriate hypotheses, analysis, and interpretation of the results. Research questions and hypothesis tend to lend themselves to specific study designs, for example, questions about causal relationship lend themselves to the use of experimental and quasi-experimental designs, while questions about associations among a series of variables lend themselves to observational designs. Chapter 13 covers the aspects of quantitative data analysis, and Chapter 14 covers the aspects of qualitative data analysis.

*Integration With Existing Literature.* The scientific method is grounded in the assumption that knowledge is cumulative in nature. The ability to develop knowledge by integrating across the multiple observations of study participants and across independently conducted research studies is essential to the scientific process. One of the tasks of the researcher when developing the discussion section of a journal article is to demonstrate to the reader how the findings contribute to the existing body of empirical literature. For example, Feldman and Crandall (2007) in their discussion section focused on how their finding linking social distance ratings with various characteristics associated with different psychiatric diagnoses contributed to an understanding of specific aspects of a mental illness, which contributed to the stigma experienced by those with the illness. As researchers attempt to integrate the findings of their study into the existing literature, attention must be given to what research is needed to further the development of knowledge in the study area.

*Evidence-Based Practice.* What should guide the decision-making process for those social workers at the Neighborhood House who are seeking to reduce the social isolation of the children they work with? Should the social workers seek the opinions of other, more experienced social workers, review the empirically based literature for theories of human behavior, or rely on their own personal experiences? The evidence-based practice (EBP), as a decision-making process, provides a framework for social workers to identify best practices in the areas of assessment, evaluation, and intervention selection, and is illustrated in Figure 1.4. EBP can be applied to all areas of social work practice. Besides the application of EBP to the decision-making process associated with the selection of interventions that target individual- and client system-level outcomes, EBP can be used by social workers focused on policy analysis, community development, advocacy, and more.

Current conceptualizations of EBP in social work are reflective of a long-standing effort to integrate research into social work practice that dates back to the work of Mary Richmond (Fisher, 2012) along with the current evidence-based medicine (EBM) movement (Mullen & Shuluk, 2011). EBP has spread beyond medicine and social work into other disciplines, for example, education (Simons, Kushner, Jones, & James, 2003), public policy (Parsons, 2002), and conservation (Sutherland, Pullin, Dolman, & Knight, 2004). The EBP model focuses on practice decision-making being the intersection among the best available empirical knowledge, a client's values and preferences, and the professional expertise of the social worker (see Figure 1.4). The EBP decision-making process occurs within the context of the larger practice environment. The practice environment includes such things as the legal and ethical constraints, and the organizational and community resources present in the practice setting.

EBP is a proactive and reflective decision-making process used to identify best practices for a given practice situation. The process is multidimensional and value conscious (Petr & Walter, 2005). The process should be guided by an awareness of

Figure 1.4   EBP Decision-Making Framework

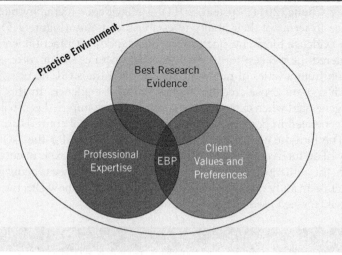

the multidimensional nature of knowledge—knowledge that can be acquired from the existing research, individuals and client systems, and the experiences of professionals (Petr & Walter, 2005). EBP should be differentiated from evidence-based practices (EBPs)—the interventions strategies that have a body of empirical evidence to support their efficacy are considered evidence-based practices (EBPs). Program registries have been established by various nonprofit organizations and governmental agencies to review the nature and quality of the empirical evidence available on interventions to determine their status as EBPs. Examples of EBP registries are presented below.

## Example EBP Registries

The California Department of Social Service established the California Evidence-Based Clearinghouse for Child Welfare (CEBC). The CEBC (http://www.cebc4cw.org/) maintains an online database of evidence-based practices relevant to child welfare.

The Substance Abuse and Mental Health Service Administration (SAMHSA) established the National Registry of Evidence-Based Programs and Practices (NREPP; http://www.samhsa.gov/nrepp) in the area of behavioral health interventions.

Coalition for Evidence-Based Policy http://toptierevidence.org/ provides information about research-supported social programs in such areas as health, education, and community development.

A critical and controversial element of EBP is the establishment of a hierarchical system of classifying evidence and the classification of interventions (Burns, Rohrich, & Chung, 2011; Epstein, 2011). The evidence hierarchy rates sources of evidence in terms of their ability to establish causality (Figure 1.5). In looking at the evidence hierarchy, one can see that experts' or practitioners' opinions are considered the weakest form of evidence and studies that involve combining information from a series of randomized controlled trials (RCTs) or experiments (meta-analyses) are considered the highest form of evidence. In this hierarchy, evidence generated when experimental controls can be imposed is privileged over evidence generated in practice settings where experimental controls are often not present. The introduction of experimental controls allows for the establishment of efficacy of an intervention. Typically, the introduction of experimental controls will reduce the authenticity of the setting in which the evidence is being generated. This reduction in authenticity reduces an understanding of how effective the intervention will be when used in real-world practice settings.

## Figure 1.5  The Evidence Hierarchy

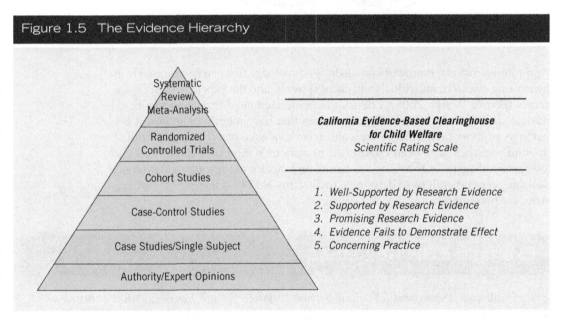

**California Evidence-Based Clearinghouse for Child Welfare**
*Scientific Rating Scale*

1. *Well-Supported by Research Evidence*
2. *Supported by Research Evidence*
3. *Promising Research Evidence*
4. *Evidence Fails to Demonstrate Effect*
5. *Concerning Practice*

(Pyramid levels from top to bottom: Systematic Review/Meta-Analysis; Randomized Controlled Trials; Cohort Studies; Case-Control Studies; Case Studies/Single Subject; Authority/Expert Opinions)

There are several classifications systems for the identification of EBPs. They all attempt to look at the quality of research evidence supporting the effectiveness of the practice. The California Evidence-Based Clearinghouse for Child Welfare has a rating classification system for interventions used in child welfare and is an example of an EBPs classification system. The categories in this classification system are: *Concerning Practice, Evidence Fails to Demonstrate Effect, Promising Research Evidence, Supported by Research Evidence,* and *Well Supported by Research Evidence.*

*Concerning Practice.* A practice that receives a Concerning Practice classification is one where there exists research evidence that the practice may be harmful or that the practice places individuals at risk for harm above what would be the case if other practices were used.

*Evidence Fails to Demonstrate Effect.* This classification is for an intervention that has been subjected to two or more RCTs that failed to demonstrate positive outcomes. There is no evidence of the intervention having harmful effects.

*Promising Research Evidence.* There is evidence from at least one study with a control group that had positive results. There is no evidence of the intervention having harmful effects.

*Supported by Research Evidence.* In this category, at least one RCT was carried out in the usual care or practice settings that provided evidence of positive outcomes. The positive effects have been sustained for at least six months.

*Well Supported by Research Evidence.* A practice that receives a Well Supported by Research Evidence classification is one where at least two RCTs were carried out in the usual care or practice settings. The RCTs provided evidence of the effectiveness of the intervention. The evaluation studies of the intervention provided evidence of sustained effects for at least one year.

Engaging in EBP as a decision-making activity involves moving through five steps: *Question Identification, Evidence Search, Critical Appraisal, Integrate Professional Expertise and Consumer's Values and Preferences, and Implementation and Evaluation* (Figure 1.6).

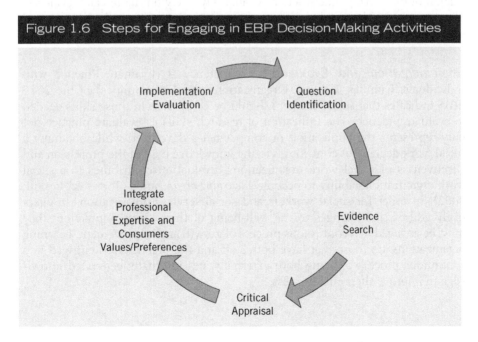

Figure 1.6  Steps for Engaging in EBP Decision-Making Activities

Implementation/
Evaluation

Question
Identification

Integrate
Professional
Expertise and
Consumers
Values/Preferences

Evidence
Search

Critical
Appraisal

*Question Identification.* The process begins with the development of a practice-centered question that is focused on achieving some practice goal. Sometimes referred to as a COPES question (client-oriented practical evidence search; Gibbs, 2005), these are questions generated to guide the decision-making of the social worker. They can take on many forms—questions about the best intervention to use, the best assessment strategies to engage in, or the best theoretical framework to use to understand the situation the social worker is facing. They are questions that will be used to search the existing published empirical literature.

*Evidence Search.* The COPES question is used to search the existing published literature and literature found outside of mainstream research journals (i.e., government reports, dissertations, and conference proceedings)—for example, searching Social Work Abstracts, PsychINFO, Cochrane Library, Google Scholar, and so on. Additionally, evidence from agency records obtained by mining administrative records can also be included in the search process (Epstein, 2015).

*Critical Appraisal.* Critical appraisal involves using knowledge of strengths and weaknesses of various methods used to generate evidence; the quality of the evidence needs to be evaluated. Questions about the reliability, validity, and generalizability of the evidence should be evaluated.

*Integrate Professional Expertise and Consumer Values/Preferences.* Justification of the social worker's actions cannot rely solely on the research evidence. The consumer's values and preferences along with the social worker's values and expertise need to be integrated into the decision-making process.

*Implementation and Evaluation.* Competency 9 (Evaluate Practice with Individuals, Families, Groups, Organizations and Communities) of the 2015 EPAS indicates that social workers should be competent in those skills needed to evaluate practice. The utilization of research skills to evaluate practice not only represents the application of competencies developed while obtaining a social work degree but contributes to the knowledge base of the profession and effectiveness of social work organizations. Evaluation contributes to a social work organization's ability to become a *learning organization* (Torres & Preskill, 2002). In order for social workers and social services organizations to effectively address the changes to the well-being of their client population, they must be engaged in a continuous process of growth and improvement. Learning organizations are those that have both staff and the organization engaged in a continuous process of using both externally and internally generated knowledge to improve their effectiveness.

# SUMMARY, REVIEW, AND ASSIGNMENTS

## CHAPTER SUMMARY ORGANIZED BY LEARNING OBJECTIVES

LO 1.1 Differentiate between the various ways of knowing.

Personal experience contributes to the development of a personal frame of reference that filters and organizes an individual's experience with the world. It provides a valuable method for the acquiring of new knowledge and skills.

Practice wisdom comes from the accumulation of information, assumptions, and judgments that can be applied to practice. It is a source of knowledge that is not gained from a technical rational process of reasoning or the application of theory. Practice wisdom is believed to have four features: agential, fluid, interactive, and moral reasoning and cognitive knowledge.

An organization's traditions sometimes represent the accumulated knowledge gained from the experiences of professionals at the organization.

Professionals often seek out knowledge and experience from those in a position of authority to inform their actions.

The Internet age has created new sources of media to distribute information and support learning.

LO 1.2 Differentiate between evidence-based practices (EBPs) and evidence-based practice (EBP) as a decision-making framework.

EBPs—the interventions strategies that have a body of empirical evidence to support their efficacy are considered evidence-based practices.

EBP—a proactive and reflective decision-making process used to identify best practices for a given practice situation.

## KEY TERMS

Best practices   3
Observational selection
  bias   5

Confirmation bias   5
Cognitive dissonance   5
Practice wisdom   5

Echo chamber effect   7
Theory   11

## COMPETENCY NOTE

In this chapter, you were introduced to the competency below:

Competency 4, *Engage in Practice-Informed Research and Research-Informed Practice.*

Social workers engage in the EBP decision-making in working with clients.

## ASSESSMENT QUESTIONS

1. How did the information in this chapter enhance your knowledge about evidence-based practice?

2. How did the information in this chapter enhance your knowledge about the ways of knowing?

3. What specific content discussed in this chapter is still unclear to you? If there is still content that is unclear, schedule an appointment with your instructor to gain more clarity.

## END-OF-CHAPTER EXERCISES

1. Interview the field instructor at your field placement to determine why the staff use particular treatments.

2. Select one of the treatments your field supervisor told you about and find an article discussing its effectiveness. What information did the author use to support the treatment effectiveness?

3. Using the same article you found for Question #2, identify an expert on the treatment that was discussed. Indicate why you identified this person as an expert. Find the expert's curriculum vitae (CV) on the Internet. Is there information from the CV that can be used to justify your deeming this person as an expert? What information is there, and how does this compare with the original information you used to classify this person as an expert?

# $SAGE edge™

Get the tools you need to sharpen your study skills. SAGE Edge offers a robust online environment featuring an impressive array of free tools and resources.

Access practice quizzes at **edge.sagepub.com/farmer**

# CHAPTER 2

# Research Ethics

## *Learning Objectives*

2.1 Define research ethics.

2.2 Differentiate between the three ethical principles outlined in the *Belmont Report* and apply these principles in conducting research.

2.3 Develop and implement ethical research studies.

2.4 Differentiate between the different types of institutional review board (IRB) reviews.

2.5 Take the Collaborative Institution Training Initiative (CITI) test.

| Competency Covered | Learning Objectives | Dimension |
|---|---|---|
| Competency 1 *Demonstrate Ethical and Professional Behavior* | 2.2 Differentiate between the three ethical principles outlined in the *Belmont Report* and apply these principles in conducting research. | Skills |
| | 2.3 Develop and implement ethical research studies. | |

## PBL Case 2

### Can I Really Conduct This Research Study?

By responding to the questions related to this case, you will be able to determine what ethical issues you must consider before conducting a research project.

Master the content at
edge.sagepub.com/farmer

You are doing your internship at Pine Valley Community Mental Health Center. The center is dedicated to providing comprehensive mental health services including, but not limited to, individual, family, and group treatment; substance use treatment; treatment for anxiety and depression; and crisis management to those who reside in Bucks County and surrounding communities. Staff are trained in a variety of treatment modalities and use evidence-based treatments to alleviate the distress of their clients. Services are provided to children, adolescents, and adults regardless of their socioeconomic status, race/ethnicity, religious backgrounds, sexual orientation, and so on.

You have been co-leading a group for pregnant and parenting adolescent girls. You notice that many of them have mentioned that they were abused during their pregnancy by the father of their child or other relatives. Based on what you have learned from the girls, you think you should conduct a study on the effects of abuse during pregnancy on maternal attachment.

In thinking about your study, you recall hearing on the news that a parent was suing a school district because researchers administered a survey to her child, who was an adolescent, without her knowledge. You begin to wonder if the study you are proposing may raise concerns from the parents of these adolescents.

At this point, take a few minutes to think about the case example and do the following:

1. Identify the problem.

2. Determine what you already know about the problem.

3. Determine what information you need to solve the problem.

4. List the questions needed to be answered related to the information you need to solve the problem.

Please write down your responses to each item. You will need to refer to them while reading this chapter.

During your weekly supervision with your field supervisor, Ms. Porter, you mention that you are interested in conducting a research study with the adolescents in your group and possibly with the adolescents in the other groups. You further state that your study will focus on understanding the effects of abuse during pregnancy on maternal attachment. Ms. Porter tells you that she believes that this study would be interesting, and perhaps the findings could lead to modifying what is done in the groups. She goes on to say that prior to conducting the study you need to provide her with a research proposal, as she needs to submit it to the board of directors of the agency, as they need to approve any research that will be conducted at Pine Valley Community Mental Health Center.

# Introduction

In this chapter, you will learn about ethical practices that should be followed while conducting research, including the guidelines specified in the Council on Social Work Education (CSWE) Educational Policy and Accreditation Standards (EPAS) and National Association of Social Workers (NASW) standards that apply to research ethics. A brief history of research ethics is provided. The *Belmont Report*, an important document that provides the framework to guide the resolution of ethical problems arising from research involving human participants, is described. You will also learn how Institutional Review Boards (IRBs) ensure that the rights and welfare of individuals are protected when they are involved in research.

## A Brief History of Ethical Practices in Research

The need to consider ethics in research is the result of several experiments that occurred and were egregiously unethical. One of the most infamous cases of unethical research occurred during Nazi rule of Germany in World War II. In December 1946, 23 Nazi medical professionals went on trial in Nuremberg, Germany, because of the atrocities performed—in guise of medical treatment, on Jewish persons in concentration camps. As a result of the Nuremberg Trial, the Nuremberg Code developed in 1949 was the first internationally recognized guideline for conducting research in an ethical manner. The code focused on ensuring the rights and welfare of human subjects. The Nuremberg Code established that participation in research is voluntary, informed consent must be obtained, participants have the right to withdraw from treatment at any time, and it is the responsibility of the researcher to obtain informed consent. Codes related to the conducting of research have continued to be developed over the years. For example, the Declaration of Helsinki (1964) provided guidelines for physicians involved in clinical research, established the need for researchers to assess the risk and benefits of participation, and emphasized participants' privacy. This declaration has been revised several times since its adoption, with the last time being in 2013.

In 1974, the U.S. Congress passed the National Research Act that established the National Commission for the Protection of Human Subjects of Biomedical and Behavioral Research. This commission was created after the public outrage over the Tuskegee Experiment conducted by the U.S. Public Health Service (PHS). This study began in 1932, when there was no known treatment for syphilis, and continued through the time period when it became known that penicillin was effective in treating syphilis, which was in 1947. A total of 600 African American males, mostly sharecroppers, were told that they would receive free treatment for their "bad blood," a term used at the time for a variety of ailments. Doctors from the U.S. PHS diagnosed these men as having syphilis and never provided them with treatment for their disease; they merely documented the progression of the disease. Initially this study was to last six months, but it actually lasted 40 years. For more information about the Tuskegee Experiment, go to https://www.history .com/news/the-infamous-40-year-tuskegee-study. This commission was charged with developing guidelines to be followed when conducting biomedical and behavioral research on human participants. Moreover, this commission wrote the *Belmont Report* (1979), which you will read about later in this chapter.

## What Is Research Ethics?

**Research ethics** is a set of guidelines developed by one's profession that state the standards for conducting research with human participants. For social work, both CSWE and NASW have developed standards related to the ethical conduct of research by social workers. CSWE's Competency 1, *Demonstrate Ethical and Professional Behavior*, states that "social workers make ethical decisions by applying the standards of the NASW Code of Ethics, relevant laws and regulations, models for ethical decision-making, ethical conduct of research, and additional codes of ethics as appropriate to context" (CSWE, 2015, p. 7). In other words, social workers must engage in the ethical conduct of research in all stages of the research process. The *NASW Code of Ethics: Evaluation and Research Standards* (Section 5.0.2) outlines the guidelines for conducting program and practice evaluation and research. These ethical standards can be viewed by going to https://www.socialworkers.org/about/ethics/ code-of-ethics.

### Application Checkpoint 2.1

Take a moment to review the NASW *Code of Ethics: Evaluation and Research Standards* (Section 5.0.2) and think about how it applies to the research study that is being proposed to be conducted at Pine Valley Community Mental Health Center.

## The *Belmont Report*

It has been 40 years since the National Commission for the Protection of Human Subjects of Biomedical and Behavioral Research issued the *Belmont Report: Ethical Principles and Guidelines for the Protection of Human Subjects of Research*. The report provides a federal framework that guides the resolution of ethical problems arising from research involving human participants (Department of Health, Education, and Welfare [DHEW], 1979, now referred to as the Department of Health and Human Services [HHS]). In the report, there is a distinction made between biomedical and social research and practice, three ethical principles that are used to guide research were outlined, and discussion about how these three general principles should be applied. **Practice** refers to "interventions that are designed solely to enhance the well-being of an individual patient or client and that have a reasonable expectation of success" (DHEW, 1979, p. 2). Meanwhile "research designates an activity designed to test a hypothesis, permit conclusions to be drawn, and thereby to develop or contribute to generalizable knowledge (expressed, for example, in theories, principles, and statements of relationships" (DHEW, 1979, p. 3).

In thinking about the distinction between practice and research and what is being proposed in the case example, would you consider this to be research? Yes, it is research because the study you are proposing would permit conclusions to be drawn. Let us say, for example, you find that adolescent females who were psychologically abused during their pregnancy are less attached to their infants than adolescent females who were never abused. Based on this finding, you can could conclude that being psychologically abused during pregnancy has an effect on maternal attachment. Your finding also allows you to make a statement about the relationship between psychological abuse and maternal attachment. The statement would be that psychological abuse is associated with less maternal attachment.

The three ethical principles are respect for persons, beneficence, and justice. The first principle, **respect for persons**, asserts that individuals are autonomous and have the right to make decisions for themselves whether or not they are willing to participate in a research study. It is the responsibility of the researcher to ensure that persons who cannot make their own decisions to participate in a research study are protected. The respect for persons principle directly leads to the practice of informed consent. **Informed consent** requires that individuals are provided information that will allow them to understand the potential risks and benefits associated with participation in the study. Additionally, this principle requires that information regarding the study's purpose and procedures should be presented in a manner that all individuals can comprehend, especially individuals whose ability to make a decision in their own best interest may be compromised, such as persons with special needs and persons who are institutionalized. The informed consent also ensures that individuals know that at no time should they be compelled in any manner to participate in the study.

The second ethical principle is beneficence. **Beneficence** refers to the researcher not conducting research that would be harmful to the participants. This includes research that would cause physical or psychological harm to the participants. Not only is the researcher responsible for not harming the participants, but he or she needs to maximize the possible benefits of the research. In other words, the research needs to be of benefit to the participants, society, and the scientific community, and yet, cause no harm to the participants. The principle highlights that any study conducted should, at a minimum, promote the *common good*. In other words, while a study's participants may not themselves receive any direct benefits for participation, others in society may benefit from the study's findings. The potential benefits should be explained to the participants. For example, while a cancer patient may not directly benefit from participation in a study, what is learned from their data may benefit future cancer patients.

Thinking about the ethical principle of beneficence, how would the proposed research to be conducted at Pine Valley Community Mental Health Center be of benefit to the potential participants, society, and the scientific community, and yet, cause no harm to the participants?

The third ethical principle is justice. **Justice** requires that the benefits and burdens of research be distributed equitably through the selection of participants. In other words, some group of individuals, such as persons from disadvantage backgrounds or prisoners, should not bear the *cost* of research while a different group of individuals, such as persons from upper-middle-class backgrounds, *gain the most benefit* from the study. That would be unjust. The principle of justice directly applies to how researchers select their participants for their research. This principle also calls attention to the fact that individuals from marginalized groups should not have their issues ignored by researchers. For example, there is as much of a need for research to be conducted on access to health care for transgender individuals as other gender groups.

## Applying the Three Ethical Principles

As mentioned earlier, the *Belmont Report* discussed how to apply each principle. The principle of respect for persons can be applied via the informed consent process. Informed consent is the process of acquiring the research participants' consent prior to their participating in any research. The informed consent process involves (1) providing potential participants with information needed to make an informed decision about their participation in the study; (2) presenting the information about the research in a manner that the individual can understand what the research entails, what they may be asked to do, and how the research may affect them; and (3) making sure the participant is aware that participation is voluntary and that they have the right to withdraw from participating at any time, without penalty. Informed consent must be obtained and documented using an informed consent form, which each participant signs. A copy of the consent form will be given to the participant. Samples of informed consent forms should be available through your university's **institutional review board (IRB)** website or via an office for sponsored research. IRBs, which you will read more about in this chapter, are responsible for protecting the rights and welfare of individuals participating in research.

Listed below are the basic elements included in an informed consent.

1.  Statement of the purpose of the research. The purpose of the study, and that it is research, must be made explicit, along with the duration of the

research should also be noted. A description of the procedures to be followed should be provided.

2. Description of risks to the participants, including physical and psychological risks.

3. Description of benefits to the participants and others.

4. A disclosure of appropriate alternative procedures, if you are conducting research on an intervention.

5. Statement about available medical treatment if research-related injury or other harm occurs.

6. Description of how confidentiality will be maintained.

7. Contact information for whom the participants should direct further questions about the research and whom to contact in the event of a research-related injury.

8. Statement that participation is voluntary and the participant has a right to withdraw from the research anytime without penalty.

There are instances where research can be conducted without documentation of informed consent. An IRB may waive the requirement for the investigator to obtain a signed informed consent form when it is culturally inappropriate to have the participants sign forms. In such an instance, an alternative method of getting informed consent must be used, such as verbal consent. When verbal consent is obtained, there must be documentation of this.

Special guidelines have been developed for the participation of **minors**, or persons under the age of 18, in research. Minors, or children, are legally unable to provide their own informed consent to participate in research; however, they might be able to give assent. **Assent** means a child's affirmative agreement to participate in research. A child's failure to object should not be considered as assent. Although a child has provided his or her assent to participate in the research, his or her parent or guardian must provide written permission. Federal regulations (§45 CFR 46.4.02 (a)) define children as individuals who have not attained the legal age for consent to be involved in treatment or research. Only the IRB can determine if parental permission can be waived.

In thinking about the case presented at the beginning of the chapter, several steps would be required in order to apply the principle of respect for others. A first step would be to look at the information on each client to determine their age. If they are of legal age for consent to be involved in treatment or research, then you would obtain their informed consent. The informed consent process typically requires meeting with potential participants to tell them about the study, the risks and benefits of their participation, and letting them know that there participation is voluntary and they can withdraw from the study at any time without penalty. Signing of the consent form is also done at this meeting.

Similarly, in an informed assent process the same information that is shared at the informed consent process is provided. Along with participants' assent, their parents or a guardian must provide written permission for the minor to participate in the study.

Again, thinking about the case example, how will the principle of beneficence be applied? Before conducting a study, researchers must take into the consideration the risks and benefits of conducting the research. A researcher should ask himself or herself the following questions: "Do the risks outweigh the benefits of the research, or do the benefits outweigh the risks to participants?"; "Is there any way to gain the knowledge about the topic or effectiveness of the intervention but with a lower risk to the participants?"; and "Does the study need to be conducted to achieve the goals and objectives of the research?" Researchers must use their best judgment to ensure the research does not harm the participants.

During the informed consent process, researchers must clearly indicate the amount of risk, as well as the type of risk. For example, an informed consent form might state, "by participating in this study, you may experience a minimal amount of distress." Contact information for whom the participants should reach in case of a research-related injury and where services can be obtained to deal with the stress associated with the research should be described on the informed consent form. Additionally, it should be noted if the participant or the researcher will be responsible for paying for these services.

## Critical Thinking Question 2.1

Consider the case example. Identify at least two potential risks and benefits of conducting this study.

In your estimation, would the risks outweigh the benefits or would the benefits outweigh the risks to participants? Would there be another way to gain the knowledge about the topic of interest? In your opinion, does this study need to be conducted to achieve the goals and objectives of the research?

Finally, in thinking about the case, how will the principle of justice be applied? This principle is implemented through the procedures and processes for selecting the study's participants. Researchers should not be biased in the way they select their participants. That is, researchers should not select participants from vulnerable groups (e.g., pregnant women and prisoners) just because they have access to them or they perceive them to be easily manipulated. Do you see that it would be equally unethical if researchers were to select participants from advantaged groups in order to make the study results appear to be more effective? Researchers need to make sure that they are selecting their participants based on the inclusion criteria for their study and excluding individuals based on the exclusion criteria for their study. **Inclusion criteria** "are a set of predefined characteristics used to identify (participants) to be included in a research study" (Velasco, 2010b, p. 589). On the other hand, **exclusion criteria** "are a set of predefined definitions that is used to identify subjects who will not be included or who will have to withdraw from a research study after being included" (Velasco, 2010a, p. 438). Both inclusion and exclusion criteria are used to establish who is or is not eligible to participate in the research study.

The principle of justice clearly states that researchers should not select participants from vulnerable groups merely because they have access to this population. Think about the case example again. Because you are working with and therefore have access to pregnant adolescents should not be the primary reason for conducting the proposed study. It is important that an inclusion criteria and exclusion criteria be developed. For example, the inclusion criteria for the study proposed in the case example could be as follows: Only those adolescent females who have experienced psychological abuse during pregnancy by the father of their baby will be included in this study. The exclusion criteria would be as follows: Adolescent females who have experienced psychological abuse during pregnancy by persons other than the father of their baby are not eligible to participate in this study. Additionally, adolescent females who have experienced any other type of abuse besides psychological abuse by the father of their baby will not be eligible to participate in this study.

## Other Considerations for Conducting Ethical Research

Ethical research is dependent on implementing the three ethical principles set forth in the *Belmont Report*; however, there are other considerations for a researcher when conducting research that is ethical. In particular, the safety of participants is of paramount importance. The researcher is responsible for identifying all the potential risks associated with the study and weighing these risks against the benefits of the study. Once the study is underway, as a researcher, you must continue to monitor the ongoing research to determine if any participants experience an unanticipated **adverse event**. An adverse event is any behavioral, medical, physiological, psychological, or social event that is undesirable or unintended. Prior to the study being implemented, you need to have a plan to address the possibility of the participants being exposed to an adverse event or experiencing distress. In devising the plan to respond to an adverse event, the researcher must decide whether participants will pay for the services needed to address such distress. Moreover, you need to be prepared to stop the research if your participants have been put at risk.

Along with safety, researchers are responsible to protect participants' privacy and confidentiality. Researchers must think through such decisions as who will have access to the data, how and where the data will be stored, the process for destroying the data, and how to prevent disclosure of the participants' personal information.

# Institutional Review Board

Federal regulations require that all universities and other entities that receive federal funding must have an IRB. IRBs register with the federal government's Office of Human Research Protection. All research studies are required to be vetted by the IRB, which is responsible for ensuring that the rights and welfare of participants are protected. An IRB has a number of responsibilities. The IRB reviews, approves, disapproves, and requests modifications to all research (whether funded or not) involving human participants, prior to it being conducted. Once the research has been approved, the IRB is responsible for conducting continuous review of the research, suspending approved research in the case of adverse events, and enforcing the informed consent and research procedures.

An IRB committee is made up of at least five members; of these five, it is federally mandated that one of the committee members should not be affiliated with the university, one whose primary concerns are in a scientific area, and one whose primary concerns are not in a scientific area. Both men and women must be members of the IRB. When members of the IRB review research, they take into consideration the three ethical principles outlined in the *Belmont Report* and make a determination if the research fits the U.S. Department of Health and Human Services (HHS) Federal Policy for Human Subjects regulations at 45 CFR part 46, also known as the "Revised Common Rule," definition of research involving human participants. The Revised Common Rule defines research as follows: (1) a systematic investigation designed to develop or contribute to knowledge (45CFR 46.102 (d)), (2) involves obtaining information from living individuals (45 CFR 46.102 (f)), and (3) involves an intervention or interaction with individuals (45 CFR 46.102 (f)). If the IRB determines that the research meets the Revised Common Rule definition, then it considers if the research involving human participants is covered by the regulations. If the research is covered by the regulations, the IRB will determine if the research can be approved for an **exemption** (also referred to as an **exempt review**). In other words, the IRB is determining if your research can be exempt from a full review by the IRB. Studies that may qualify for an exempt review are described in Table 2.1.

Research that is not exempted from review may be considered for expedited or full review. An **expedited review** applies to proposed research that presents no more than minimal risk to the participants, meets the criteria for research being reviewed through the expedited procedure, and has measures in place to ensure the participants experience no more than minimal risk. Minimal risk, as defined in 45 CFR, §46.104 is "the probability and magnitude of harm or discomfort anticipated in the research are not greater in and of themselves than those ordinarily encountered in daily life or during the performance of routine physical or psychological examinations or tests" (DHEW, 1979, p. 132). Expedited review may also be used when minor changes are proposed to an approved research project. Expedited review may be done by a subset of the IRB, which may include the chairperson or one or two members of the IRB designated by the chairperson.

## Table 2.1 Studies That May Qualify for an Exempt Review

1. Research, conducted in established or commonly accepted educational settings, that specifically involves normal educational practices that are not likely to adversely impact students' opportunity to learn required educational content or the assessment of educators who provide instruction. This includes most research on regular and special education instructional strategies and research on the effectiveness of or the comparison among instructional techniques, curricula, or classroom management methods.

2. Research that only includes interactions involving educational tests (cognitive, diagnostic, aptitude, achievement), survey procedures, interview procedures, or observation of public behavior (including visual or auditory recording) if at least one of the following criteria is met: (a) the information obtained is recorded by the investigator in such a manner that the identity of the participants cannot readily be ascertained, directly or through identifiers linked to the participants; (b) any disclosure of the participants' responses outside the research would not reasonably place the subjects at risk of criminal or civil liability or be damaging to the participants' financial standing, employability, educational advancement, or reputation; or (c) the information obtained is recorded by the investigator in such a manner that the identity of the participants can readily be ascertained, directly or through identifiers linked to the participants, and an IRB conducts a limited IRB review to make the determination required by §46.111(a)(7).

3. Research involving benign behavioral interventions (are brief in duration, harmless, painless, not physically abusive, not likely to have a significant adverse lasting impact on the participant) in conjunction with the collection of information from an adult participant through verbal or written responses (including data entry) or audiovisual recording if the participant prospectively agrees to the intervention and information collection and at least one of the following criteria is met: (a) the information obtained is recorded by the investigator in such a manner that the identity of the participant cannot readily be ascertained, directly or through identifiers linked to the participant; (b) any disclosure of the participants' responses outside the research would not reasonably place the participants at risk of criminal or civil liability or be damaging to the participants' financial standing, employability, educational advancement, or reputation; or (c) the information obtained is recorded by the investigator in such a manner that the identity of the participants can readily be ascertained, directly or through identifiers linked to the participants, and an IRB conducts a limited IRB review to make the determination required by §46.111(a)(7).

4. Secondary research for which consent is not required; secondary research uses of identifiable private information or identifiable biospecimens, if at least one of the following criteria is met: (a) the identifiable private information or identifiable biospecimens are publicly available; (b) the identifiable private information about biospecimens is recorded by the investigator in such a manner that the identity of the participant cannot readily be ascertained directly or through identifiers linked to the participants, the investigator does not contact the participants, and the investigator will not re-identify participants; (c) the research involves only information collection and analysis involving the investigator's use of identifiable health information when that use is regulated under C45 CFR parts 160 and 164, subparts A and E, for purposes of "health care operations" or "research" as those terms are defined at 45 CFR 164.501 or for "public health activities and purposes" as described under 45 CFR; or (d) The research is conducted by, or on behalf of, a Federal department or agency using government-generated or government-collected information obtained for nonresearch activities, if the research generates identifiable private information that is or will be maintained on information technology that is subject to and in compliance with section 208(b) of the E-Government Act of 2002, 44 U.S.C. 3501 note, if all of the identifiable private information collected, used, or generated as part of the activity will be maintained in systems of records subject to the Privacy Act of 1974, 5 U.S.C. 552a, and, if applicable, the information used in the research was collected subject to the Paperwork Reduction Act of 1995, 44 U.S.C. 3501 *et seq.*

*(Continued)*

Table 2.1   (Continued)

5. Research and demonstration projects that are conducted or supported by a Federal department or agency, or otherwise subject to the approval of department or agency heads (or the approval of the heads of bureaus or other subordinate agencies that have been delegated authority to conduct the research and demonstration projects), and that are designed to study, evaluate, improve, or otherwise examine public benefit or service programs, including procedures for obtaining benefits or services under those programs, possible changes in or alternatives to those programs or procedures, or possible changes in methods or levels of payment for benefits or services under those programs. Such projects include, but are not limited to, internal studies by Federal employees, and studies under contracts or consulting arrangements, cooperative agreements, or grants. Exempt projects also include waivers of otherwise mandatory requirements using authorities such as sections 1115 and 1115A of the Social Security Act, as amended. Each Federal department or agency conducting or supporting the research and demonstration projects must establish, on a publicly accessible Federal Web site or in such other manner as the department or agency head may determine, a list of the research and demonstration projects that the Federal department or agency conducts or supports under this provision. The research or demonstration project must be published on this list prior to commencing the research involving participants.

6. Research involving taste and food quality or consumer acceptance studies (a) if wholesome foods without additives consumed that contains a food ingredient, agricultural chemical, or environmental contaminant at or below the level found to be safe by the Environmental Protection Agency of the Food Safety and Inspection Service by the U.S. Department of Agriculture.

7. Storage or maintenance for secondary research for which broad consent is required: Storage or maintenance of identifiable private information or identifiable biospecimens for potential secondary research use if an IRB conducts a limited IRB review and makes the determinations required by §46.111(a)(8).

8. Secondary research for which broad consent is required: Research involving the use of identifiable private information or identifiable biospecimens for secondary research use, if the following criteria are met:(a) broad consent for the storage, maintenance, and secondary research use of the identifiable private information or identifiable biospecimens was obtained in accordance with §46.116(a)(1) through (4), (a)(6), and (d);(b) documentation of informed consent or waiver of documentation of consent was obtained in accordance with §46.117; or (c) an IRB conducts a limited IRB review and makes the determination required by §46.111(a)(7) and makes the determination that the research to be conducted is within the scope of the broad consent referenced in paragraph (d)(8)(i) of this section; and (iv) The investigator does not include returning individual research results to participants as part of the study plan. This provision does not prevent an investigator from abiding by any legal requirements to return individual research results.

*Source:* U.S. Department of Health and Human Services (HHS).

*Note:* The word *participants* was substituted for *subjects* and *human subjects*.

Any research that did not qualify for the exempt status or expedited review requires a **full review** by all the members of the IRB. A full review is warranted because such research has more than minimal risk and may not adequately have safeguards in place to reduce such risk. Typically, if a researcher proposed to include vulnerable groups as participants, the study will need to undergo a full review by the IRB. Groups that are defined as **vulnerable populations** are pregnant women, minors (children), prisoners, persons with developmental disabilities, or economically or educationally disadvantaged persons. These groups are categorized as such because they may be more vulnerable to coercion or undue influence because of their status or situation.

The IRB uses the following criteria when it determines whether proposed research will be approved:

1. Minimal risk to participants

2. Risks are adequate in comparison to anticipated benefits

3. Selection of participants is equitable

4. Informed consent will be obtained

5. Informed consent will be documented appropriately

6. Adequate provisions for data collection to ensure safety to participants

7. Adequate provisions to protect privacy

8. Safeguards in place to protect participants from vulnerable populations, if included in the research

Once a research project has been approved by the IRB, it is the researcher's responsibility to inform the IRB of any modifications that need to be made to the research and of any research-related injury a participant has experienced. Failure to do so can result in the researcher's research being suspended along with other already approved research, inability to publish the results, and termination of employment.

## Critical Thinking Question 2.2

Pretend that you are a member of the IRB at your university. You and the other members have been assigned to review the proposed study mentioned in the case example. Would this study be exempted from review? Why or why not? If not, what type of review would be required? Justify your response.

## CITI Certification

Federal regulations require that all persons conducting research with human participants, including students and other research staff, must undergo training to ensure the protection of participants. This training must be successfully completed prior to conducting any research with human participants. An online course about the Protection of Human Subjects is offered by the Collaborative Institution Training Initiative (CITI). This training provides an overview of the

Belmont Report, the role and functions of IRBs, the types of research that qualify for the exempted, expedited, or full review, and the Revised Common Rule. After reviewing the materials, you take the CITI Certification Test. Persons who successfully complete the training, as indicated by your passing score on the test are awarded a copy of the CITI Certificate. The certificate serves as proof that the online training was successfully completed, and it must be submitted to the IRB along with the research protocol for all persons who will work with research participants during the course of the study.

---

### Critical Thinking Question 2.3

During weekly supervision, Ms. Porter mentions that she has informed her staff and board of directors that an intern will be conducting a research study to understand the effects of abuse during pregnancy on maternal attachment. The board members asked about possible ethical concerns. Ms. Porter asked the intern to give a presentation to the board about these concerns.

Given your understanding of ethical research practices, identify the potential ethical issues. How would your presentation address these concerns? Be sure to refer to the ethical principles in the Belmont Report. Develop a short outline of what would be included in the presentation.

---

# SUMMARY, REVIEW, AND ASSIGNMENTS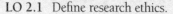

## CHAPTER SUMMARY ORGANIZED BY LEARNING OBJECTIVES

LO 2.1 Define research ethics.

Research ethics is a set of guidelines developed by one's profession that state the standards for conducting research with human participants.

LO 2.2 Differentiate between the three ethical principles outlined in the *Belmont Report* and apply these principles in conducting research.

The principle of respect for persons asserts that individuals are autonomous and have the right to make decisions for themselves, if they are willing or not willing to participate in a research study.

The principle of beneficence refers to the researcher not conducting research that would be harmful to the participants.

The principle of justice requires that the benefits and burdens of research be distributed equitably through the selection of participants.

**LO 2.3** Develop and implement ethical research studies.

Developing and implementing ethical research studies requires obtaining informed consent or assent, identifying the risks and benefits associated with the research studies, devising a plan to address the possibility of participants being exposed to an adverse event, and protecting participants' privacy and confidentiality.

**LO 2.4** Differentiate between the different types of institutional review board (IRB) reviews.

Research that meets the qualifications specified by federal regulations may be eligible for exempt status.

Research that meets the qualifications specified by the federal regulations and involves no more than minimal risk and approved research where minor changes are being made are eligible for expedited review.

Research that has more than minimal risk and may not adequately have safeguards in place to reduce such risk are required to be reviewed by the full IRB.

**LO 2.5** Take the Collaborative Institution Training Initiative (CITI) test.

Federal regulations require that all persons conducting research with human participants must undergo training to ensure protection of human participants.

## KEY TERMS

Research ethics   24
Practice   24
Respect for persons   25
Informed consent   25
Beneficence   25
Justice   26

Institutional review board (IRB)   26
Minors   27
Assent   27
Inclusion criteria   29
Exclusion criteria   29

Adverse event   29
Exemption   30
Exempt review   30
Expedited review   30
Full review   32
Vulnerable populations   33

## COMPETENCY NOTE

In this chapter, you were introduced to the competency below:

Competence 1: *Demonstrate Ethical and Professional Behavior*. Social workers engage in the ethical conduct of research in all stages of the research process. Social workers apply the NASW Code of Ethics and other relevant codes when conducting research.

## ASSESSMENT QUESTIONS

1. How did the information in this chapter enhance your knowledge about research ethics?

2. How did the information in the chapter enhance your knowledge about the IRB process?

3. What specific content discussed in this chapter is still unclear to you? If there is still content that is unclear, schedule an appointment with your instructor to gain more clarity.

# END-OF-CHAPTER EXERCISES

1. Go to your university's IRB website and download the template for the assent form and develop the assent form for the study proposed in the case example.

2. Develop a consent form for the study proposed in the case example. Give this consent form to one of your classmates and have him or her provide you with feedback.

3. Read about the "Tuskegee Experiment: The Infamous Syphilis Study" at https://www.history.com/news/the-infamous-40-year-tuskegee-study. After reading this study, indicate if any of the ethical principles described in the *Belmont Report* were violated or not.

4. Visit the CITI (Collaborative Institution Training Initiative) online course for training on the Protection of Human Subjects. Skim the topics and take one section of the certificate test.

# ADDITIONAL READINGS

Hooke, S., Hackworth, N. J., Quin, N., Bennetts, S. K., Win, H. Y., Nicholson, J. M., et al. (2018). Ethical issues in using the internet to engage participants in family and child research: A scoping review. *PLoS, 13*(9), 1–30. doi:10.1371/journal.pone.0204572

Landau, R. (2008). Social work research ethics: Dual roles and boundary issues. *Families in Society: Journal of Contemporary Social Services, 89*(4), 571–577. doi:10.1606/1044-3826

McInroy, L. B. (2016). Pitfalls, potentials, and the ethics of online survey research: LGBTQ and other marginalized and hard-to- access youth. *Social Work Research, 40*(2), 83–93. doi:10.1093/swr/svw005

# $SAGE edge™

Get the tools you need to sharpen your study skills. SAGE Edge offers a robust online environment featuring an impressive array of free tools and resources.

Access practice quizzes at **edge.sagepub.com/farmer**

## Learning Objectives

3.1   Recognize the importance of learning about research for professional development.

3.2   Differentiate between the various forms of research.

3.3   Differentiate between the various purposes of research.

3.4   Differentiate between the various research designs.

3.5   Differentiate between the various phases of the research process.

| Competencies Covered | Learning Objectives | Dimension |
|---|---|---|
| Competency 4<br><br>*Engage in Practice-Informed Research and Research-Informed Practice* | 3.2  Differentiate between the various forms of research.<br>3.3  Differentiate between the various purposes of research.<br>3.4  Differentiate between the various research designs.<br>3.5  Differentiate between the various phases of the research process. | Skills |
| Competency 9<br><br>*Evaluate Practice With Individuals, Families, Groups, Organizations, and Communities* | 3.2  Differentiate between the various forms of research.<br>3.3  Differentiate between the various purposes of research.<br>3.4  Differentiate between the various research designs.<br>3.5  Differentiate between the various phases of the research process. | Skills |

Master the content at
**edge.sagepub.com/farmer**

## Predictors of Bullying Behaviors

By responding to the questions related to this case, you will be able to recommend whether a descriptive, exploratory, explanatory, or evaluative research study should be conducted.

The principal of Eastside Elementary School called a meeting with all the teachers, school social workers, and student interns at the beginning of the school year. At the meeting, the principal spoke about a national conference she attended on bullying and victimization in schools. She learned that in order to address this issue, schools first needed to collect data on the factors that contribute to bullying and other forms of victimization. These factors include characteristics of the individuals who are being bullied; the persons who are doing the bullying; the school, including school policies and the quality of instruction; and the community in which the school is located. Eastside Elementary School is located in a suburban area; currently there are 750 students enrolled, with 20% receiving free lunch and 30% having an individualized educational plan (IEP). The population of the school is 56% male. The children who attend this school are from diverse backgrounds.

At the end of the meeting, the principal asked attendees to volunteer to be part of a work group to help determine the contributing factors to bullying and other forms of victimization at her school. Ms. Pauline Patterson, a school social worker, tells the principal that she and her interns are volunteering to be a part of the work group. You are doing your field placement at the Eastside Elementary School.

At this point, take a few minutes to think about the case example and do the following:

1. Identify the problem.

2. Determine what you already know about the problem.

3. Determine what information you need to solve the problem.

4. List the questions needed to be answered related to the information you need to solve the problem.

Please write down your responses to each item. You will need to refer to them while reading this chapter.

Your field supervisor, Ms. Pauline Patterson, calls a meeting with you and the other social work interns. She wants to discuss how to assist the principal in gathering information about the characteristics of the individuals who are being bullied; the persons who are doing the bullying; the school, including school policies and the quality of instruction; and the community in which the school is located.

You tell Ms. Patterson that you are taking a research course and this week you are discussing the research process, and you may be able to let the work group know what type of research study should be conducted to determine the contributing factors to bullying and other forms of victimization in the school.

---

## Introduction
................................................................................

In this chapter, you will learn about the importance of learning about research for professional development. The various types of research and purposes of research are described. A brief overview of the research process is provided.

## Why Is Learning About Research Important for Your Professional Development?
................................................................................

Many of you might be wondering why you are taking a research course. You are probably saying to yourself, "I could be taking a more interesting course where I will be learning the knowledge and skills I will be using with the clients I will be working with in my field placements or in the future." A commitment to conduct research is at the heart of the social work profession. Jane Addams, a pioneer in development of the social work profession and the founder of the U.S. Settlement House Movement, was also a leading scholar at the University of Chicago, Department of Sociology (1892–1918). The development of evidence-based practices, such as cognitive behavioral therapy (CBT), would not be possible without research-practitioners like Aaron Beck, conducting research on the effectiveness of cognitive behavioral therapy (CBT) for treating depression.

Research has also been instrumental in informing and changing policies. Schmidt's (2019) study, "An Overview and Critique of U.S. Immigration and Asylum Policies in the Trump Era," is an example of a study that has implications for informing policy.

### Competency Connection

Why should you learn about conducting research? We can tell you that every student taking this course probably has asked this question. Well, it is quite clear that the social work profession expects social workers to know how to conduct research and not merely be consumers of research. More specifically, three out of the nine CSWE-prescribed competencies emphasize the need for social workers to learn about research.

**Competency 1**, *Demonstrate Ethical and Professional Behavior*, states, "Social workers understand frameworks of ethical decision-making and how to apply principles of critical thinking to those frameworks in practice, research, and policy arenas. . . . Social workers make ethical decisions by applying the standards of the NASW Code of Ethics relevant laws and regulations, models for ethical decision-making, ethical conduct of research, and additional codes of ethics as appropriate to context" (CSWE, 2015, p. 7).

In other words, this competency implies that social workers engage in the ethical conduct of research in all stages of the research process.

**Competency 4**, *Engage in Practice-Informed Research and Research-Informed Practice*, "Social workers understand quantitative and qualitative research methods and their respective roles in advancing a science of social work and in evaluating their practice. Social workers know the principles of logic, scientific inquiry, and culturally informed and ethical approaches to building knowledge. Social workers understand that evidence that informs practice derives from multi-disciplinary sources and multiple ways of knowing. They also understand the processes for translating research findings into effective practice. Social workers use practice experience and theory to inform scientific inquiry and research; apply critical thinking to engage in analysis of quantitative and qualitative research methods and research findings; and use and translate research evidence to inform and improve practice, policy, and service delivery" (CSWE, 2018, p. 8).

**Competency 9**, *Evaluate Practice with Individuals, Families, Groups, Organizations, and Communities*, states, "Social workers understand that evaluation is an ongoing component of the dynamic and interactive process of social work practice with, and on behalf of, diverse individuals, families, groups, organizations and communities. Social workers recognize the importance of evaluating processes and outcomes to advance practice, policy, and service delivery effectiveness. Social workers understand theories of human behavior and the social environment, and critically evaluate and apply this knowledge in evaluating outcomes. Social workers understand qualitative and quantitative methods for evaluating outcomes and practice effectiveness. Social workers select and use appropriate methods for evaluation of outcomes; apply knowledge of human behavior and the social environment, person-in-environment, and other multidisciplinary theoretical frameworks in the evaluation of outcomes; critically analyze, monitor, and evaluate intervention and program processes and outcomes; and apply evaluation findings to improve practice effectiveness at the micro, mezzo, and macro levels" (CSWE, 2018, p. 9).

Research has been essential in the evolution of social work practice with those with serious mental illnesses (i.e., schizophrenia, severe bipolar disorder, and severe depression). Moreover, research has informed the development of the ecological approach, which is central to social work as a profession (Pardeck, 1988). The framework is used by social workers, for example, to study the complex interplay of the economic, social, geographical, and structural causes of poverty.

To continue addressing the complex issues faced in providing treatment that is ethical and effective, schools of social work are obligated to equip the next generation of social workers with the knowledge and skills to not only consume research but also be able to conduct it.

Will you ever engage in conducting a research study during your career as a social worker? We cannot say that you will conduct research in the future; however, we can say that you will always be using research to inform your practice and policies. For example, the interventions you learn about and use with your clients today may not be the ones you will use in the future. As knowledge changes, you will need to ensure that you are using effective interventions with your clients. And to do so, you must be competent in your ability to critically evaluate the empirically based literature. For example, how will you know if the studies you have read were designed appropriately? This requires that you have knowledge about the purposes of research and the various research designs. If the studies are not designed appropriately, then you may be using flawed studies to inform your practice. The use of methodologically flawed studies to inform your practice has the potential to harm your clients. We know that you do not want to harm your clients, therefore, you are open to learning what will be discussed in this course.

This research book has been written to give you the knowledge and skills pertaining to the research process, such as testing hypotheses, confirming theories, describing phenomenon, exploring relationships between variables, designing studies, analyzing data, and interpreting the findings from these analyses. Additionally, in reading this book you will learn knowledge and skills to help you be effective in your work with clients and be able to evaluate the programs in the agency where you are employed. This type of research is referred to as program or practice evaluation.

The knowledge and skills you learn in this research course have life-learning implications. We as authors of this book can attest that what you learn in this course can be used for the rest of your life. By applying what you learned through using this book, you will be equipped to ensure you are working effectively with your clients based on the most up-to-date literature.

## What Is Research?

**Research** is a systematic process of inquiry designed to collect, analyze, and interpret data. It is based on the scientific method. The research process is often guided by the interplay between deductive and inductive reasoning. **Deductive reasoning** involves using a theory to inform the development of a hypothesis (see Figure 3.1).

Figure 3.1   Deduction and Induction

**DEDUCTION**

Theory → Hypothesis → Observation → Confirmation

**INDUCTION**

Observation → Pattern → Hypotheses → Theory

The goal of deductive reasoning is to determine the extent to which observations, or data, confirm a theory, based on whether the data confirm the hypothesis or fail to confirm the hypothesis. A **hypothesis** is a testable prediction about the relationships among variables. A hypothesis is testable when it is possible to observe information that could provide support or disconfirm that hypothesis. Observations or data are collected to evaluate the hypothesis. The purpose of a hypothesis is to determine if one variable results in a change in the other variable. In other words, a hypothesis is used to determine a relationship between the variables. A **variable** is any factor, trait, quality, or condition that can be measured. Most importantly, in order for a factor, trait, quality, or condition to be a variable it must vary. In other words, it must have different quantitative values. For example, height is a variable, because we could meet someone who is 4 feet 11 inches tall, someone who is 5 feet tall, and someone who is 5 feet 1 inch tall. A variable that results in a change in the other variable is known as the **independent variable**. In other words, the independent variable explains or causes the change in the other variable. Conversely, the variable being explained or caused is the **dependent variable**. A dependent variable can also be described as the variable affected by the independent variable or the outcome of the independent variable.

Thinking about the case example, let us say, for example, that the principal hypothesized that children who have a disability are more likely to be bullied than children who do not have a disability. In this hypothesis, the independent variable is having a disability, as this variable can be used to explain why the bullying occurs. Being bullied is the outcome of having a disability. The theory the principal used to formulate her hypothesis is social capital. Evans and Smokowski (2016) suggest students who are bullied lack social capital. That is, they lack friends who will stop them from being bullied.

## Application Checkpoint 3.1

Given that the principal is interested in knowing what characteristics of the school are associated with bullying and other forms of victimization, think about some hypotheses she could test.

Rather than start with a hypothesis, **inductive reasoning** begins with a set of observations (see Figure 3.1). Through continued observation, the researcher tries to determine if there is a pattern that can be used to inform a hypothesis that describes the pattern. For example, while riding the subway train, you may observe on multiple occasions, as additional people get on the train, where they choose to sit. Over time, you see patterns—that women tend to sit near other women or that people always choose to sit by themselves until no empty seats remain. If you develop a hypothesis, like "People always choose to sit by themselves first" or "When entering a train, people tend to sit with others who are like themselves," then you are engaging in inductive reasoning.

A researcher may begin the research process using either deductive (starting with theory) or inductive reasoning (starting with an observation). Often, in reality, a researcher may shift between the two given what has been gleaned from the data. For example, in the case of bullying at a school, a review of teachers' referrals of students because of their bullying behavior may result in an attempt to determine if there is a pattern to the referrals. Are there particular students, settings, or situations that are frequently present in the referrals for bullying? Do these observed patterns in the referrals suggest hypotheses about what factors (such as particular students), or in which situations or settings that bullying is likely to occur? Is there a theory of human or organizational behavior that would help in understanding the referral patterns that emerged? Inductive reasoning is used to examine whether there is a pattern in the bullying behavior. And if one uses a theory of organizational or human behavior to understand or explain the pattern, then deductive reasoning is being used. Inductive reasoning informs the development of a theory that could be used to select an intervention that could be used to address the bullying problems. One might develop a hypothesis, such as, "Bullying is more likely to occur during portions of the school day when students are not supervised by adults." This hypothesis could be tested by observing bullying incidents to determine if they occur in the presence of an adult or in the absence of an adult. Testing the hypothesis in this way reflects deductive reasoning.

As mentioned earlier, research is a systematic process of inquiry designed to collect, analyze, and interpret data. It typically involves a series of steps (scientific method), which you were introduced to in Chapter 2. The steps are as follows: *observation, question identification, literature review, theory formulation, empirical research question, research design, data collection, data analysis, and integration with the literature* (see Figure 3.2).

## Categories of Research

Research can be categorized into two functions: applied and basic research. **Applied research** is conducted to address or solve problems. An example of an applied research study is one where a researcher is interested in determining the effectiveness of an intervention to reduce substance use. On the other hand, **basic research** is conducted to increase scientific knowledge and the application of the research for the development and refinement of theory is typically the focus. Whereas in disciplines, such as theoretical condensed matter physics, which are not focused on solving social and individual problems, basic research is the dominate type of research.

Figure 3.2  Scientific Method

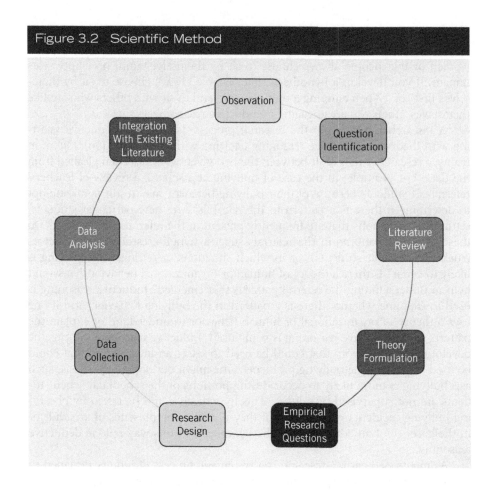

Considering that social work is an applied profession, results from basic research should have implications for practice and policy. An example of a basic research study is one by Rhodes and Jason (1990), where they evaluated a social stress model of substance abuse. Their study can be considered an example of basic research, because the focus of the study was to provide empirical confirmation of a theory. Additionally, implications of their findings for the development of prevention programs were discussed. Each type of research has made and will continue to make valuable contributions to the social work empirically based literature.

In thinking about the case example, given that the principal is interested in finding out more about individual, school, and community factors that contribute to bullying and other forms of victimization in her school, you would say that she is doing basic research. She is conducting basic research because she is interested in gaining more knowledge about the factors that contribute to bullying and other forms of victimization. Let us say, for example, that the principal is interested in conducting research to determine if a social skills program would reduce the amount of bullying in her school. Undertaking a study to determine if the social skills program is effective in reducing bullying is applied research. The principal is conducting applied research because she is addressing a problem in her school.

Another way research is categorized is by the methods used and the research paradigms associated with the research approach. **Quantitative research** is a method of inquiry where the researcher engages in gathering data in such a way that the data can be counted or described in a quantifiable way. Because the data can be quantified enables the use of statistical procedures (e.g., $t$-test, analysis of variance [ANOVA], or multiple regression analysis) to analyze the data collected and to determine whether there is a statistical relationship between variables. Quantitative research is often guided by deductive reasoning. The researcher is gathering the data to test a specific hypothesis or is looking for an explanation for the phenomenon being studied. Hypotheses are developed prior to the collection of the data, derived from the literature the researcher has reviewed. Quantitative research is aligned with the **positivism research paradigm**, which is a belief system that assumes objective universal truth can be derived via observation and experience with the phenomena. Using this paradigm, researchers provide support for theories based on hypothesis testing. Variables are operationalized to assess the constructs of interest. Using a positivism research paradigm, the researcher uses prescribed methods to ensure that the results of the study can be replicated. Experimental research designs, including pre-experimental, experimental, or quasi-experimental, are often used in quantitative research. With quantitative methods, the data collected via questionnaires, surveys, and standardized measures can be described using numbers. Data collection is conducted prior to the analysis and the results are presented in quantifiable forms.

**Qualitative research**, on the other hand, is a method of inquiry where the researcher is interested in understanding the lived experiences of the participants from their own perspective. Common types of studies that rely on a qualitative approach are ethnographic research, grounded theory, and phenomenological studies. These studies are based on inductive reasoning, where data about the phenomenon are observed and gathered without the researcher specifying a specific hypothesis or theory explaining the occurs of the phenomenon being studied. Therefore, hypotheses and theories are derived from patterns observed in the data instead of the researcher developing a hypothesis or theory first. Qualitative research is aligned with the **social constructivism research paradigm**, which is a "belief that assumes that 'universal truth' cannot exist because there are multiple contextual perspectives and subjective voices that can label truth in scientific pursuit" (Hays & Singh, 2012, p. 41). Qualitative methods for data collection include interviews, focus groups, documents, archival data, and observations, including video recordings, and the goal is to capture data in a narrative and detailed way. In qualitative research, both the collection and analysis of the data are conducted simultaneously, as opposed to quantitative research where the data are collected first and then analyzed. The findings from qualitative research are more likely to be presented in a narrative form, such as quotes and vignettes, as opposed to quantifiable forms, such as numbers. An example of a qualitative study is one by Jamal, Bonell, Harden, and Lorenc (2015). The researchers conducted interviews and focus groups and reviewed a school's policies on bullying as a means of exploring students' accounts of bullying practices and how the school environment enabled and constrained bullying in two secondary schools in East London.

Quantitative and qualitative research designs should not be confused with quantitative and qualitative data. Quantitative and qualitative data refer to different ways in which variables are operationalized. Quantitative data involves reducing observations to numerical data (e.g., scores on a measure). On the other hand, qualitative data involves characterizing observations in a non-numerical manner. For example, describing the interaction that your instructor has with students during a class session as "respectful and engaging" might represent an attempt to use qualitative labels to characterize interactions you observed during the class session. Quantitative and qualitative research designs refer to the procedures and the research approaches carried out when conducting a study.

Some studies rely on purely quantitative or qualitative methods, but another approach to research combines the use of quantitative and qualitative methods for data collection and these studies are referred to as **mixed methods**. Mixed-methods research is an approach where the researchers use both quantitative and qualitative data collection methods to understand the phenomenon under investigation.

## Critical Thinking Question 3.1

The principal meets with you, your field instructor, and the other social work interns to tell everyone her thoughts about gathering information on the characteristics of individuals who are bullied, the persons who are doing the bullying, the school—including school policies and the quality of instruction—and the community in which the school is located. She tells you that she is interested in surveying the students to determine if they have been bullied or not, the reason(s) why they were bullied, how many times they were bullied, and where they were bullied. Furthermore, she states that she hypothesizes that children who have a disability, wear glasses, or are homeless are bullied more than their counterparts.

Based on what you heard, is the principal using deductive or inductive reasoning at this point? Justify your response.

Given what the principal stated as her hypothesis, what type of research approach (e.g., qualitative, quantitative, or mixed methods) would you recommend? Justify your response.

Given what the principal stated as her hypothesis, identify the independent and dependent variable.

A research approach can also be categorized based on a time dimension. The time dimension refers to how often the data will be collected. If the data are collected at only one point in time, this is referred to as **cross-sectional research**. If the data are collected at multiple points in time, this is referred to as **longitudinal research**. Longitudinal research is conducted to assess change over time in the variable of interest. An example of longitudinal research would be a study where a social work researcher would collect data from the participants prior to their participation in the intervention, after their participation in the intervention, and 6 months after their participation in the intervention.

There are three types of longitudinal research studies, and they differ in design according to how the participants are selected. In a **trend study**, the participants are selected from a pool of potential participants. Different participants are selected at different points in time from the pool, and the pool of participants changes over time. An example of a trend study is one where an instructor is interested in assessing how satisfied students are with a family therapy course. The instructor assessed student satisfaction with the course every semester since 1996. In the above example, the pool consists of students in the program, and each year there are different students taking the course.

In a **cohort study**, "the pool of potential participants does not change, but the specific cases selected for the study differ during the stages of data collection" (Yegidis, Weinbach, & Myers, 2006, p.123). Additionally, persons in the cohort are similar in some way or experienced the same event, such as being born during the same time period. An example of a longitudinal cohort study is the National Child Development Study (NCDS), which is also referred to as the 1958 Birth Cohort Study. Participants were born in 1958 in England, Scotland, or Wales. Data have been collected from these individuals when they were aged 7, 11, 16, 23, 33, 42, 46, 50, and 55. In the analysis from the data collected at these different times, the exact same individuals may not have participated each time, but the researcher describes all the participants as a cohort.

In a **panel study**, the exact same participants are studied over time. Changes in the group composition would be due to attrition. **Attrition** refers to participants dropping out of the study. An example of a longitudinal panel study is the Panel Study of Income Dynamics (PSID), which is conducted by the Survey Research Center at the University of Michigan. Data have been collected from the same families and their descendants over time for the last 51 years, with the first data collection starting in 1968.

In reading the case example, you should have noticed that there is no mention of how often the data would be collected. If the principal only wants to collect the data once, say, in the fall of the school year, she would be conducting a cross-sectional study. On the other hand, if the principal would like to collect the data in the fall and the spring every year to determine if the rate of bullying is decreasing or increasing over the years, then she would be conducting a longitudinal research study.

# What Is the Purpose of Research?

The previous section discussed approaches to different categories of research. But in order to know what type of approach, you need to know the purpose or intent of your study. Speaking broadly, research is conducted for four purposes, and these are to *describe*, *explore*, *explain*, and *evaluate*.

**Descriptive research** is conducted to describe the phenomenon under investigation. When researchers conduct descriptive research, they are not interested or prepared to test hypotheses or manipulate variables to see their effect on another variable. Descriptive research studies are conducted to answer the question, "What is going on?" Both quantitative and qualitative research methods can be used to conduct a descriptive study. Often, descriptive research lays the groundwork for future research. An example of a descriptive research study is one where the researcher describes the needs of adolescents transitioning out of foster care. In thinking about the case example, if the principal is interested in describing the school factors that contribute to bullying, then this would be a descriptive study.

**Exploratory research** is conducted when we do not know much about the phenomenon or when you want to gain new insight about the phenomenon. This type of research aims to determine if there is a relationship between the variables of interest. Often, based on the results of an exploratory study, one can develop an explanatory study. Both quantitative and qualitative research methods can be used to conduct an exploratory study. An example of an exploratory research study is one where the researcher is interested in studying the influence of the Internet on friendship formation.

## Example of an Exploratory Research Study

Meyers (2017) conducted an exploratory research study to understand the experiences of those who had been abused by their siblings during childhood through adolescence. She conducted her study because there is limited research on the topic, despite the prevalence of sibling abuse.

Qualitative research methods were employed, both grounded theory and phenomenological. In-depth interviews were conducted with 19 participants.

Both phenomenological and grounded theory approaches were used to analyze the data. Phenomenological analysis was used to understand the experiences of those who had been abused by their siblings, and grounded theory analysis was used to determine how the abuse affected the individual. Themes that emerged from the data were (1) the unpredictable nature of the abuse, (2) sense of powerlessness, (3) abuse amnesia, and (4) resounding emotional impact.

**Explanatory research** is conducted to examine the causal relationships among variables. When researchers conduct explanatory research, they are interested in testing hypotheses. Quantitative methods are used to conduct explanatory research. Explanatory research is conducted to answer the question, "Why is this going on?" An explanatory research study is one where a researcher is interested in examining the effectiveness of an intervention on a specific outcome. Another example is a study where the researcher has hypothesized that social support is associated with well-being.

**Evaluation research**, also referred to as *program evaluation* or *practice evaluation*, is conducted to determine if a new program is needed (formative evaluation), the effectiveness of an existing program (summative evaluation), and to determine if the program resulted in the participants attaining certain outcomes (summative evaluation). This type of research is often conducted in social service agencies, such as hospitals, clinics, or other community-based agencies. An example of a formative evaluation is one conducted by Madiba and Mokgatle (2015). They conducted a formative evaluation to determine the acceptability of HIV testing and counseling in schools in South Africa.

---

### Critical Thinking Question 3.2

Referring back to the case example, the principal meets with you, your field supervisor, and the other social work interns. She says that after the data have been collected on the characteristics of the children who have experienced bullying in her school, she plans to develop a program to reduce the amount of bullying in the school. Furthermore, she mentioned that she would like to conduct a study to determine if the program reduces the incidents of bullying.

Based on what you heard, would you say the purpose of her research study is descriptive, exploratory, explanatory, or evaluation? Justify your response.

---

## What Is Research Design?

**Research design** refers to the "plan that provides the logical structure that guides the investigator to address the research problems and answer research questions" (DeForge, 2010, p. 1253). It sometimes is referred to as the *blueprint* of the steps undertaking to achieve the objective of the research (Sahu, 2013). Many decisions need to be made to carry out research, ranging from "What are the specific research questions?" to "Who should the participants be, and how will they be selected?" to "What variables will need to be measured, and how?" The research design will help you answer all these questions. It consists of the processes and procedures detailing when and how the data will be collected, analyzed and disseminated, which variables will be measured and how, and who will make up the sample and how they will be selected.

The research question(s) and hypothesis dictate the type of research design that will be employed. In other words, there is an alignment between the research question, hypothesis, and research design. Research questions and hypotheses tend to lend themselves to specific study designs. For example, questions about causal relationships lend themselves to the use of experimental and quasi-experimental designs, while questions about the associations or correlations among a series of variables lend themselves to observational or nonexperimental designs. Broadly speaking, there are three categories of research designs: *experimental*, *nonexperimental*, and *observational*.

**Experimental research designs** are ones in which there is manipulation of the independent variable by the researcher and the focus of the study is on examining causality. In this case, the researcher wants to provide evidence that the independent variable(s) affected or influenced the dependent variable in the way that was hypothesized. In order to control the presence of the independent variable, the researcher manipulates participants' exposure to the independent variable by randomly assigning persons to the various treatment conditions. Let us say a social work researcher is interested in answering the following research question: "Is cognitive behavioral therapy effective in enhancing the self-esteem of Mexican adolescent females as compared to problem-solving therapy?" The social work researcher would choose an experimental research design because he or she plans to randomly assign each participant to the two treatment conditions (cognitive behavioral therapy or problem-solving therapy). Research designs where there is manipulation of the independent variable by the researcher are pre-experimental, experimental, and quasi-experimental.

**Nonexperimental research designs** are also referred to as *correlational research designs*. In these studies, the researcher may be interested in providing evidence that two or more variables are associated or correlated with one another, but the researcher does not or cannot control or manipulate the independent variable and therefore one cannot prove that the independent variable causes the change in dependent variable. In correlational research, the focus of the study is on examining the association among variables and not demonstrating causality. There are many types of nonexperimental research designs that will be further discussed in later chapters.

**Observational research designs** are used to examine the effects of exposure to a variable of interest that is not under the control of the researcher. This variable could potentially serve as the independent variable in a study examining a causal relationship. This type of research design is employed when it is unethical to conduct an experimental research design. An example of an unethical study would be one where the researcher exposed the participants to a toxic gas to determine the effects on their lungs. As a researcher, doing so would be considered unethical. However, in an ethical observational study, you may study persons who have already been exposed to such gas. Two observational research designs that will be discussed in later chapters, case control and cohort studies, are commonly used by public health researchers to explore possible causes of diseases. For example,

Dantchev, Zammit, and Wolke (2018) conducted a prospective cohort study looking at the relationship between sibling bullying reported at age 12 and psychotic symptomology experiences at age 18. The researchers did not induce bullying but used retrospective evidence to look at later symptoms. Bejerot, Edgar, and Humble (2011) conducted a case-control study to examine the association between having poor motor skills in childhood and bullying victimization.

---

### Critical Thinking Question 3.3

The principal convenes a meeting with the work group and reiterates that she wants to gather information about the characteristics of the individuals who are being bullied, the persons who are doing the bullying, the school—including school policies and the quality of instruction—and the community in which the school is located.

Given your knowledge about the purpose of research (descriptive, exploratory, explanatory, and evaluative), what is the purpose of the study that would be conducted? Justify your response.

What type of research design (experimental, nonexperimental, or observational) would be appropriate and ethical given the purpose of the proposed research? Justify your response.

---

## The Research Process

Research studies are designed via the following phases: problem formulation, research design, sampling, measurement selection, data collection, data analysis, and dissemination. In the problem formulation phase, you are concerned with identifying the research problem to be examined and the research question to be asked. Referring to the case example, there are several research questions to be asked. They are, for example, "What are the characteristics of the students who are bullied?," "What other forms of victimization have the students experienced besides bullying?," and "What are the characteristics of the students who never have been bullied?" After you have selected your research problem and identified the research question, you are now ready to select the research design (experimental, nonexperimental, or observational). In thinking about your sample, you are concerned about the type of sampling strategy you will use to select the participants for your study. The measure you select to collect the data to answer your research question must be reliable and valid. As for data collection, you are concerned about the methods to be used to collect the data, such as focus groups, interviews, observations, and standardized measures. Once the data have been collected, you are faced with the task of analysis. The type of analysis you will use is dependent upon the way the variables were measured or operationalized. For quantitative methods, how you analyze the data depends on the level of measurement of the variables. Qualitatively gathered data are often analyzed for patterns and themes. Finally, after the data have been analyzed and interpreted, you are now ready to disseminate or share the findings through various outlets. Findings may be disseminated via a peer-reviewed/scholarly journal, as a poster presentation or oral presentation at a conference, through infographics, via a podcast, or with colleagues during a staff meeting. A **peer-reviewed/scholarly journal** is one where the articles have been reviewed by peer evaluators who are deemed to be experts in their fields. The peer evaluators are referred to as **referees**. These referees determine the worthiness of the article to be published, quality and originality of the research, and make recommendation about changes, if any, that should be made to the research paper before it is published. A **poster presentation** allows a researcher to disseminate his or her research in a form of a poster or electronic poster presentation. **Infographics** are "visual media that present data and concepts using visual imagery, and aim to convey information in a clear, rapid, and aesthetic manner" (Gallagher et al., 2017, pp. 129–130). A **podcast** is an audio recording of one's research that can be accessed via a computer, smartphone, or other media device.

## Application Checkpoint 3.2

The principal would like to share the results of the study with her staff after it has been conducted. Think about the best way for her to do this.

Throughout the following chapters, where we discuss the phases of the research process, we will present information on ethical considerations and the role of diversity. Unlike most research method books that have one chapter on diversity and one chapter on ethics, we wanted you to see how ethics and diversity should be considered at each stage of the research process.

# SUMMARY, REVIEW, AND ASSIGNMENTS

## CHAPTER SUMMARY ORGANIZED BY LEARNING OBJECTIVES

LO 3.1 Recognize the importance of learning about research for professional development.

The social work profession expects social workers to know how to conduct research and not merely be consumers of research.

In order to ensure that you are providing your clients with effective interventions, you must be competent in your ability to critically evaluate the empirically based literature.

LO 3.2 Differentiate between the various forms of research.

*Applied research* is conducted to address or solve problems.

*Basic research* is conducted to increase scientific knowledge and the application of the research for the development and refinement of theory is typically the focus.

*Quantitative research* is a method of inquiry where the researcher engages in gathering quantifiable data about the phenomenon under investigation and uses statistical procedures (e.g., *t*-test, analysis of variance [ANOVA], or multiple regression analysis) to analyze the data collected.

*Qualitative research* is a method of inquiry where the researcher is interested in understanding the lived experiences of the participants from their perspectives using a variety of qualitative approaches (e.g., case study, ethnographic research, grounded theory, and phenomenological).

*Observational research designs* are used to examine the effects of exposure to a variable of interest that is not under the control of the researcher. This variable could potentially serve as the independent variable in a study examining a causal relationship.

*Mixed-methods research* is a research approach where the researcher uses both quantitative and qualitative research methods to understand the phenomenon under investigation.

*Cross-sectional research* is where the data are collected at one point in time.

*Longitudinal research* is where the data are collected at multiple points in time.

LO 3.3 Differentiate between the various purposes of research.

*Descriptive research* is conducted to describe the phenomenon under investigation.

*Exploratory research* is conducted when we do not know much about the phenomenon or when you want to gain insight about the phenomenon.

*Explanatory research* is conducted to examine the causal relationships among variables and when researchers are interested in testing an hypothesis.

*Evaluation research* is conducted to determine if a new program is needed (formative evaluation), the effectiveness of an existing program (summative evaluation), and to determine if the program resulted in the participants attaining certain outcomes (summative evaluation).

LO 3.4 Differentiate between the various research designs.

*Nonexperimental research designs* are ones in which there is no manipulation of the independent variable by the researcher and the focus of the study is on examining the association among variables.

*Experimental research designs* are ones in which there is manipulation of the independent variable by the researcher and the focus of the study is on examining causality.

*Observational research designs* are used to examine the effects of exposure to a variable of interest that is not under the control of the researcher.

**LO 3.5** Differentiate between the various phases of the research process.

The phases of the research process are problem formulation, research design, sampling, measurement selection, data collection, data analysis, and dissemination.

## KEY TERMS

Research   41
Deductive reasoning   41
Hypothesis   42
Variable   42
Independent variable   42
Dependent variable   42
Inductive reasoning   42
Applied research   43
Basic research   43
Quantitative research   45
Positivism research paradigm   45
Qualitative research   45

Social constructivism research paradigm   45
Mixed methods   46
Cross-sectional research   47
Longitudinal research   47
Trend study   47
Cohort study   47
Panel study   47
Attrition   47
Descriptive research   48
Exploratory research   48
Explanatory research   49
Evaluation research   49

Research design   49
Experimental research designs   50
Nonexperimental research designs   50
Observational research designs   50
Peer-reviewed/scholarly journal   52
Referees   52
Poster presentation   52
Infographics   52
Podcast   52

## COMPETENCY NOTES

In this chapter, you were introduced to the competencies below:

Competency 4, *Engage in Practice-Informed Research and Research-Informed Practice.* Social workers can apply the various research designs, methods, and purposes to engage in practice-informed research and research-informed practice.

Competency 9, *Evaluate Practice With Individuals, Families, Groups, Organizations, and Communities.* Social workers can apply the various research designs, methods, and purposes to evaluate practice with individuals, families, groups, organizations, and communities.

## ASSESSMENT QUESTIONS

1. How did the information in this chapter enhance your knowledge about the research process?

2. How did the information in this chapter enhance your knowledge about when one should conduct a descriptive research study as opposed to an explanatory research study?

3. What specific content discussed in this chapter is still unclear to you? If there is still content that is unclear, schedule an appointment with your instructor to gain more clarity.

# END-OF-CHAPTER EXERCISES

1. Find an article that describes a research study. Identify whether the study is descriptive, exploratory, explanatory, or evaluative. Describe why you think the study is descriptive, exploratory, explanatory, or evaluative.

2. Develop a research question and identify if it is appropriate for descriptive, exploratory, or explanatory research.

3. Read the article "Lifting the Veil: The Lived Experience of Sibling Abuse," by Amy Meyers (2017). Using the article, identify the following:

   - 3a. The study approach (deductive or inductive; applied or basic; quantitative, qualitative, or mixed methods)

   - 3b. The study purpose (descriptive, exploratory, explanatory, or evaluation)

   - 3c. The study design (experimental, nonexperimental, or observational)

4. Again referring to the "Lifting the Veil" article by Meyers, identify the parts of the article that describe the research process steps:

   - Problem formulation
   - Sampling strategy
   - Which variables were selected and how they were measured?
   - How were data collected, through what methods?
   - How were data analyzed?
   - How were study findings disseminated?

5. What suggestions would you have for Meyers if she were to make her study an explanatory study?

---

**$SAGE edge™**

Get the tools you need to sharpen your study skills. SAGE Edge offers a robust online environment featuring an impressive array of free tools and resources.

Access practice quizzes at **edge.sagepub.com/farmer**

# Problem Formulation

## Learning Objectives

4.1   Develop a good research question.

4.2   Explain the purpose of a literature review.

4.3   Conduct a literature search.

4.4   Write up a literature review.

4.5   Identify the ethical issues associated with designing a research study.

4.6   Identify the diversity issues associated with developing a research question.

| Competencies Covered | Learning Objectives | Dimension |
|---|---|---|
| Competency 1 *Demonstrate Ethical and Professional Behavior* | 4.5  Identify the ethical issues associated with designing a research study. | Skills |
| Competency 2 *Engage Diversity and Difference in Practice* | 4.5  Identify the diversity issues associated with developing a research question. | Skills |
| Competency 4 *Engage in Practice-Informed Research and Research-Informed Practice* | 4.4  Write up a literature review. | Skills |

Master the content at
**edge.sagepub.com/farmer**

## Can I Really Conduct This Research Study?

By responding to the questions related to this case example, you will be able to determine if the topic of interest is researchable.

You are doing your internship at Pine Valley Community Mental Health Center. The center is dedicated to providing comprehensive mental health services including, but not limited to, individual, family, and group treatment; substance use treatment; treatment for anxiety and depression; and crisis management to those who reside in Bucks County and surrounding communities. Staff are trained in a variety of treatment modalities and use evidence-based treatments to alleviate the distress of their clients. Services are provided to children, adolescents, and adults regardless of their socioeconomic status, race/ethnicity, religious backgrounds, sexual orientation, and so on.

You have been co-leading a group for pregnant and parenting adolescent girls. You notice that many of them have mentioned that they were abused during their pregnancy by the father of their child or other relatives. Based on what you have learned from the girls, you think you should conduct a study on the effects of abuse during pregnancy on maternal attachment.

At this point, take a few minutes to think about the case example and do the following:

1. Identify the problem.

2. Determine what you already know about the problem.

3. Determine what information you need to solve the problem.

4. List the questions needed to be answered related to the information you need to solve the problem.

Please write down your responses to each item. You will need to refer to them while reading this chapter.

During your weekly supervision with your field supervisor, Ms. Porter, you mention that you are interested in conducting a study to understand the effects of abuse during pregnancy on maternal attachment. Ms. Porter tells you that she believes this study would be interesting, and perhaps the findings could lead to modifying what is done in the groups. She goes on to say that prior to conducting the study you need to provide her with a research proposal, as she needs to submit it to the board of directors of the agency, as they need to approve any research that will be conducted at Pine Valley Community Mental Health Center.

# Introduction

In this chapter, you will learn about the problem formulation phase of the research process, focusing on how to develop a research question. The chapter also describes the purposes of the literature review, explains how to search for relevant literature, and offers tips on writing a literature review.

# Problem Formulation Defined

The formulation of the research problem is the initial phase of the research process. It begins with the researcher identifying a central question or sets of questions that will guide the design of the research study. Typically, the researcher's questions are derived from the identification of a gap in one's existing knowledge base. Oftentimes, for social workers the problems that occur in practice are the impetus for identifying a gap in their knowledge. Usually the gaps are related to how to best intervene with individuals, families, groups, communities, or organizations. Here are three examples of such gaps:

1. A social worker working in a homeless shelter might think, "If only I would have been better prepared to work with homeless individuals who have co-occurring disorders."

2. A social work student working with a faculty member on a research project might think, "If only I knew what recruitment strategies can be used to increase the number of African Americans in the sample."

3. A school social worker has noticed an increase in the number of students who are experiencing behavioral problems. Most of these students have parents who have recently returned home from Afghanistan. He or she might think, "If only I knew what these children are experiencing and how to best work with them."

The gaps identified can be used as the foundation for developing a research problem to be studied. A **research problem** refers to some difficulty one encounters in the context of practice or other situations which one wants to obtain a solution to address this difficulty.

In thinking about the above examples, the research problem for Example 1 would be: "lack of knowledge about working with homeless persons who have co-occurring disorders." The research problem for Example 2 is "lack of knowledge about the appropriate strategies for recruiting African Americans into a research study." As for Example 3, the research problems are "lack of knowledge about the experiences of children whose parents have been deployed and lack of knowledge of how to best intervene with children whose parents have been deployed."

A **research question** is used to address a research problem. Research questions challenge the assumptions we make about the world, or about practice, and this can lead to beneficial changes in the way we think about or address an identified "problem" (Alvesson & Sandberg, 2013). The research question(s) narrows the focus of the research problem. Thus, the research question drives the development of a research study (Alvesson & Sandberg, 2013) as it has implications for what research methods and designs should be used, and what statistical procedures should be conducted to analyze the data to answer the research question. For example, the research question, "What is the association between trauma and depression?" is best answered using a nonexperimental research design.

Good research questions are researchable and feasible. How do you know if a research question is a good one? A researchable question is one for which observable evidence can be gathered to answer the proposed research question. A feasible question is one that will allow you to carry out the research you would like to conduct. An example of a poor research question would be one that requires a simple yes or no answer, one that is vague or unclear, or one that contains terms that are likely to elicit a biased response. Poor research questions may also be too broad and unfocused, or too narrowly focused. In Table 4.1, we present examples of well-conceptualized research questions and poorly conceptualized research questions.

## Table 4.1 Examples of Well- and Poorly Conceptualized Research Questions

Well-Conceptualized Research Questions

1. How does shift work affect the social and emotional well-being of persons who do such work?

2. How does discrimination in the workplace affect a worker's productivity?

3. How effective is cognitive behavioral therapy in increasing self-esteem in Egyptian women ages 18–25?

4. What are the characteristics of males and females who graduate early from high school?

Poorly Conceptualized Research Questions

1. Does social media affect friendship formation? (This question can be answered with a yes/no response. The use of the term *social media* is vague. What type of social media is being referred to?)

2. What affects self-image of Hispanics? (This question is too vague, and the population is not defined.)

3. How do first-year doctoral students in social work at University X, who entered the class of 2019, find, understand, and use online instructions to develop their dissertation proposals? (We must consider what we are losing when we focus on a particular group of students, during a specific year, at a specific school.)

### Critical Thinking Question 4.2

During your weekly supervision with Ms. Porter, she tells you that she is still very excited about the research study you proposed doing at the center. She asks you to tell her your research question(s). Thinking about what you have learned thus far, write two possible research questions that are researchable and feasible.

## The Importance of Conducting a Literature Review

Every researcher, regardless if they conduct a qualitative or quantitative research study, all start their study by conducting a literature review. They conduct a literature review to determine the following:

1. What is already known about the topic?

2. What are gaps in knowledge about the topic?

3. What research has been done that is similar to what the researcher is thinking about conducting?

4. How have other researchers defined and measured key concepts in the research question?

5. What data sources have researchers used?

6. Who are existing experts on the topic?

7. Are there research questions about the topic that need further research?

8. What methods have been used to study the topic?

9. What is the best way to frame a rationale for the study? In other words, it enables the researcher to answer the question, "Why conduct this research in this way, at this time?"

Upon completion of the literature review, a researcher should have a better understanding of the topic and a good sense of what his or her research will add to the understanding of the topic and research problem that was identified.

For this class, and for other classes, searching the literature, and then writing up the literature review, is the process to gather the background information that will be used in the research paper. In this way, a literature review is both the process that one engages in prior to conducting one's research and also an outcome—that is, the section of the research study or paper that you write. In summary, according to Boote and Beile (2005), the literature review (the written product)

> sets the broad context of the study, clearly demarcates what is and what is not within the scope of the investigation, and justifies those decisions. It also situates an existing literature in a broader scholarly and historical context. It should not only report the claims made in the existing literature but also examine critically the research methods used to better understand whether the claims are warranted. Such an examination of the literature enables the author to distinguish what has been learned and accomplished. Moreover, this type of review allows the author not only to summarize the existing literature but also to synthesize it in a way that permits a new perspective. Thus a good literature review is the basis of both theoretical and methodological sophistication, thereby improving the quality and usefulness of subsequent research. (p. 4)

In fact, even while formulating a research question, it is important that you become aware of the existing literature in order to see what is already known about the topic and research problem. You may find out that there are well-developed theories and conceptual frameworks that have been used to study the research problem and topic. Or you may not find much has been published about the problem you identified. Conducting a literature review will provide you with the information that will help you further develop a research question.

Social workers are often motivated to conduct a literature review by a need to find solutions to practice problems. In thinking about the case example, when engaged in group work with pregnant and parenting adolescent girls, the social work intern needs to find information on the challenges experienced by these adolescent girls as they transition into motherhood. As we think about what literature should be included in a review, the areas associated with Client Oriented Practical Evidence Search (COPES) may be useful. These five areas are:

(1) effectiveness, (2) prevention, (3) assessment, (4) description, and (5) risk (Sackett, Richardson, Rosenberg, & Haynes, 1997). Effectiveness focuses on the identification of an evidence-based intervention or evidence for an intervention. Prevention focuses on the identification of actions that could serve to prevent a problem from occurring. Assessment focuses on identification of evidence-based assessment tools and/or strategies (Youngstrom et al., 2017). Description questions focus on gathering information that would allow one to describe a phenomenon. Risk assessments focus on the identification of factors—characteristics of individuals and/or circumstances in which individuals find themselves in—that are associated with eliminating the risk of the individuals experiencing some unwanted outcome (Cohen et al., 2019; Williams, Ayele, Shimasaki, Tung, & Olds, 2019).

It is important to conduct a literature review when you are interested in learning more about a topic. Selection of topics that have relevance for social work should be given priority.

## Application Checkpoint 4.1

Thinking about the case example, is the proposed study of relevance for social work?

In conducting a literature review on a topic you are interested in learning more about, you need to consider finding answers to the following questions: "What is currently the state of knowledge about the topic?," "What questions have been investigated?," "What questions have researchers stated need to be addressed in future research?," and "What have researchers identified as limitations of the research on the topic?" Finding answers to these questions will help you decide if this topic is one you should select for your research study.

## How to Conduct a Literature Review

When starting to review the literature on an identified research problem or topic, it can feel a little overwhelming. "Where to start?," you may ask yourself. We suggest four sources that you should use to find information on your research problem or topic: *literature reviews*, *systematic reviews*, *electronic databases*, and the *grey literature*. First, according to Mertens (2015), a good place to start is to search for a literature review on your topic. A **literature review** will give you a good overview of the current knowledge on the topic, the theories used to explain the topic, the methods used to study the topic, and suggestions for future research. An example of a literature review is one conducted by Bellieni and Buonocore (2013). They reviewed the empirically based literature published between 1995 and 2011 on the psychological effects of having an abortion. The researchers used inclusion and exclusion criteria to determine which studies would be reviewed within that time frame. For instance, one of the inclusion criteria was the studies had to have examined a correlation between mental health and abortion, and one of the exclusion criteria was studies that were case studies or commentaries about abortion. Using these criteria, the researchers identified and reviewed 30 studies. Of the 30 studies, 13 showed an association between having an abortion and subsequent mental health issues.

Besides looking for a literature review on your topic, we also recommend that you search for a systematic review. A **systematic review**, according to Denyer and Tranfield (2009), "is a specific methodology that locates existing studies, selects and evaluates contributions, analyses, and synthesizes data, and reports the evidence in such a way that allows reasonably clear conclusions to be reached about what is and not known" (p. 671) about the topic of interest. Systematic reviews do not generate new knowledge per se but synthesize existing literature, and this may lead to the production of new knowledge. Huang, Zhao, Qiang, and Fan (2018) reviewed the empirically based literature published from 1993 to 2011 to determine the effectiveness of cognitive behavioral therapy (CBT) in reducing postnatal depression. Using inclusion and exclusion criteria to determine which studies would be reviewed, they identified and reviewed 20 studies. Of these 20 studies, 13 demonstrated that cognitive behavioral therapy was effective in reducing postnatal depression. Systematic reviews can be easily retrieved by going to Cochrane Library (https://www.cochranelibrary.com/cdsr/about-cdsr). In order to review these systematic reviews, you need to select from the menu "Cochrane Reviews," then select "Search Reviews," and then type the name of your topic in the search field.

## Sources of Information for a Literature Review

The most common way of searching for literature on one's topic is using electronic databases. Many libraries have instructional materials that will help students learn about which electronic databases the library subscribes to and how to access them. Students should take advantage of the training provided by the library on how to access these electronic databases and how to conduct a literature review. The librarian, who usually conducts these trainings, is an expert in conducting database searches and is a valuable resource who can help you develop an effective search strategy.

Here, we briefly describe three examples of databases that include studies that are relevant for social work. These databases are as follows: (1) *Academic Search Premier* contains abstracts to books, conference proceedings, magazines, newspapers, peer-reviewed journals, and government proceedings. Full-text articles can be retrieved. These abstracts and full-text articles are relevant for persons in any discipline. Additional features include the help link, which you can click on to get help on how to find an article on your topic; the ability to save your searches and citations using RefWorks; and the ability to receive alerts when a new issue of a particular journal has been entered into the database.

(2) *PsychINFO* contains abstracts to books, book chapters, dissertations, peer-reviewed journal articles, and technical reports. Full-text articles can be retrieved. These abstracts and full-text articles focus on topics relevant for business, psychology, psychiatry, and behavioral and social science. A thesaurus of psychological terms, which can be used to help you refine your topic, is also provided. Additional features are the ability to receive alerts when a new issue of a particular journal has been entered into the database. These abstracts are from 1974 to the present. (3) *Social Work Abstracts* contains abstracts to journals dealing with issues related to social work. These abstracts are from 1965 to the present. These electronic databases can be accessed free of charge by students via their college libraries.

Once a researcher has selected a database, he or she then enters the keyword(s) related to the topic to begin the search. Selecting keywords can significantly affect how effective your search is in identifying studies that are relevant to your topic. Let us think about the case example, for which you are interested in studying the effects of abuse during pregnancy on maternal attachment. The following example illustrates the use of Academic Search Premier to search for literature on the topic of interest. Once we have entered the database, a screen will appear. On the top left-hand side of the screen, there will be three boxes (see Figure 4.1). You enter your keyword or keywords in these boxes and then hit the green search button. For this example, we entered the keyword "abuse" in Box #1, and the keyword "pregnancy or pregnant" in Box #2. The use of these keywords resulted in us being able to retrieve 15,440 abstracts. That is a large number of abstracts, and far too many to read. This large number of abstracts indicates that we need to more narrowly define the type of abuse we are interested in examining. For the purpose of the case example, we are interested in abuse as intimate partner violence. In a new search, we entered the keyword "intimate partner violence" (IPV) in Box #1 and "pregnancy or pregnant" in Box #2. Now the search resulted in 1,363 abstracts (see Figure 4.2).

We can further limit the number of articles retrieved, for example, by requesting the search option for only search for scholarly/peer-reviewed articles that have been published in the last five years. The large number of publications on this topic is a reason to narrow the initial search to the most recent peer-reviewed sources. Peer-reviewed articles are credible sources of information on a particular topic as these articles have been reviewed by experts who reviewed the quality of the article before it is published based on the validity of the research methods and procedures. When we limited our search in this way, we retrieved 951 abstracts. This is still too many to read to determine the current state of knowledge on the topic. We might want to look at the first 10 articles to see how well they provide the information needed. Information on those articles we found most useful could be used to further limit the search. For example, each article will have additional keywords used to index the article.

For example, in Figure 4.3, you see the keywords associated with the article by Willie et al. (2019) are "*Adolescents, *Domestic Violence, *Intimate

**Figure 4.1    Depiction of the Initial Step in Conducting a Literature Search**

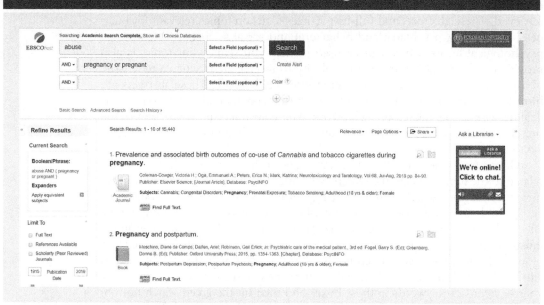

**Figure 4.2    Depiction of the Revision to the Initial Literature Search**

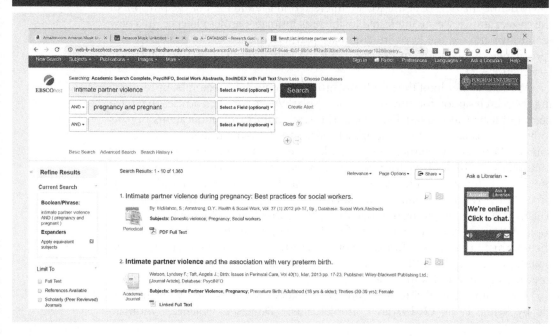

Partner Violence Victimization, *Reproductive Coercion, and *Actor-Partner Interdependence Model." We would use different combinations of keywords from this list in our next search for abstracts. Additionally, we could consider whether we want to limit the search to a population, for example, adolescent pregnant girls. When the search was limited to "Intimate Partner Violence" and "Adolescent Pregnancy" for peer-review publications between 2014 and 2019, the number of abstracts retrieved was 43. Forty-three is a good number for the initial review of the literature.

Another way to limit your search is to focus on journals that might specifically focus on your topic. For example, two peer-review journals, *Journal of Interpersonal Violence* and *Violence and Victims*, specifically focus on articles on the topics in this case example. Looking over the publications in these two journals would be a valuable step in the literature search process. The electronic databases used to do your search also will allow you to search for journals that published articles on your topic.

Once you have identified a smaller set of abstracts or articles based on your keywords, it is time to review the abstracts to see if they are indeed relevant to your research topic. When reading an abstract, how do you know it is relevant? This is done by thinking carefully about your research problem/research topic.

Figure 4.3 Example of Article With Keywords That Were Used for Indexing

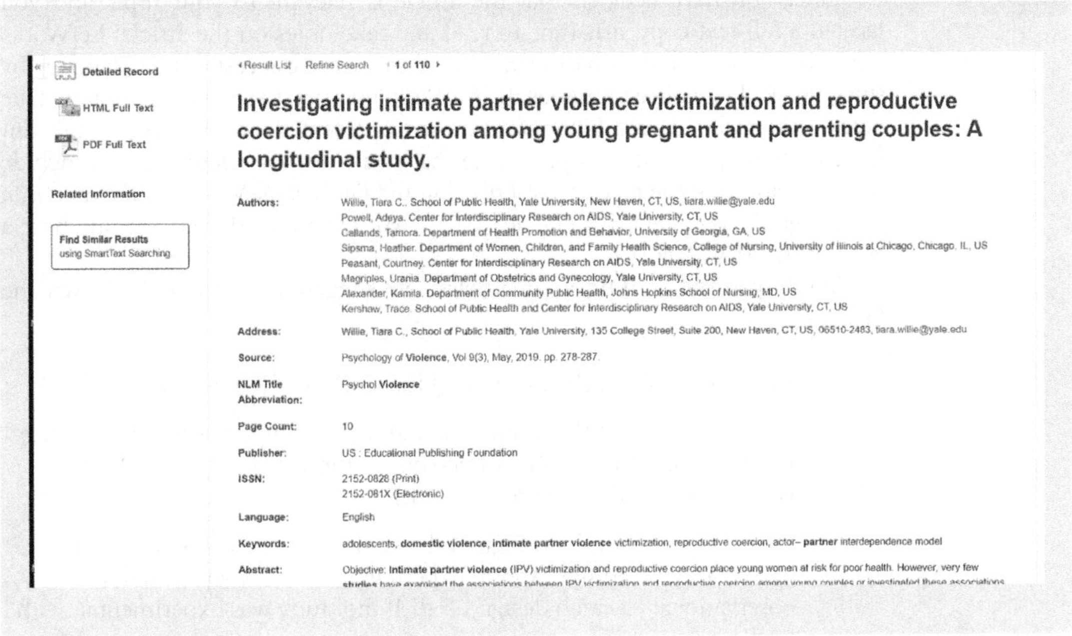

Now consider what type of study is being described in the abstract. Is the study empirical or conceptual? An **empirical study** is one where the research is based on quantitative or qualitative methods. An empirical study based on quantitative methods would be one where the researcher included participants in an experiment, used surveys or questionnaires to collect the data from the participants, or used statistical procedures (e.g., *t*-test, *z*-test, Pearson product-moment correlations) to analyze the data. On the other hand, an empirical study based on qualitative methods would be one where the researcher used focus groups or interviews to collect the data or used content or thematic analysis to analyze the data. Some studies are theoretical or conceptual. **Conceptual/theoretical studies** describe the concepts or theories that explain or describe the phenomenon under investigation. Additionally, you need to consider how many participants were in the study. Some studies have very small sample sizes, and often the results of these studies cannot be generalizable to a much wider population. You may also think about where the study took place. A study that took place in Japan, for example, although interesting, may not have findings that apply to the practice questions that you are interested in, since culturally the practice interventions may be different.

Once you have identified a certain number of abstracts where the studies are relevant to your topic, the next step is to read the full-text article. To obtain the full-text article, if included in the electronic database, all you need to do is click on "Linked Full-Text." If the full text is not included in the electronic database, you will need to go through your library's website and enter the name of the journal in the search field to see if the library owns the journal. If the library does not own the journal, you will need to request it through interlibrary loan.

Once you have decided that the article is relevant to your topic and you located a full-text copy, it is time to read and take notes on the article. RefWorks is a web-based citation management system that can be accessed free of charge by students via their college libraries. RefWorks allows you to save and annotate (take notes on) articles, create bibliographies, and present your citations in different formats. In social work, it is preferable that you cite your references and include in-text citations in the format prescribed in the *Publication Manual of the American Psychological Association, 7th Edition* (2020). We recommend that you purchase a copy of the *APA Manual*.

While you are reading your articles, we suggest that you write down the following:

1. Information about the purpose of the study and hypotheses.

2. Information about the sample, including what type of sampling strategy was used, and the number of persons in the sample along with their gender and ethnic/racial backgrounds.

3. Information about the design of the study: Was it a cross-sectional or longitudinal study? Was an experimental, nonexperimental, or observational research design used? If the study was experimental, with

a comparison or control group, was random assignment used to assign persons to the group(s)? Finally, describe the interventions and outcome measure that were used.

4. Information about the statistical procedures used to analyze the data.

5. Information about the independent and dependent variables, including how they were conceptualized and/or operationalized.

6. Information about the limitations of the study.

7. Information about recommendations for future studies.

8. The research question(s).

9. Any methodological flaws you see in the study, including ethical violations.

10. Recommendations for how the study can be improved.

11. Research question(s) that come to your mind as a result of reading the study.

12. Inconsistencies in the findings between different studies; document what these differences are and why they may exist.

13. The reason(s) why you believe an article is and is not relevant to your topic.

It can take a fair amount of time to carefully read an article and note the information suggested here. However, the notes you have taken on the articles will allow you to more quickly synthesize the literature and have it available to you as you are writing and want to refer back to a specific article with an in-text citation.

Synthesizing the literature is more than just describing what you have read. **Synthesizing** means that you examined each article so that you can identify how the literature described the significance of the research problem, the theories used to explain the problem, the research approaches used to study the research problem, and data analytic strategies used to analyze the data. This will require you to look for themes or patterns across the articles, develop categories for the information obtained, and critique the information. Additionally, you can compare the findings from the different articles and how they differ. Based on your synthesis of the literature, you will be able to identify your research questions, hypotheses, sampling strategy, data analysis strategy, and research design.

Your search of the literature should not be limited to just the literature found in published journals and books, which does not represent all the empirical literature that needs to be incorporated in a literature review; one needs to search the grey literature as well. The **grey literature** represents research produced by governments, academics, business, and industry in printed or electronic formats that are not found in journals or books published by commercial publishers (Aloia, 2016).

GreyNet International Services is an organization that seeks to facilitate research and communication among organizations seeking to make grey literature more accessible. Grey Literature Network Service provides an online guide to searching the grey literature (http://greyguide.isti.cnr.it/). They publish a quarterly newsletter and hold an annual international conference (http://greyguide.isti.cnr .it/index.php/homepage/42-greynet-quarterly-newsletter).

## Writing Up the Literature Review

According to Pyrczak (2014), the literature review should "(1) introduce the problem area, (2) establish its importance, (3) provide an overview of the relevant literature, (4) show how the current study will advance knowledge in the area, and (5) describe the researcher's specific research questions, purposes, or hypothesis, which usually are stated in the last paragraph of the introduction" (p. 33). Introducing the problem should be done in the opening paragraph of the literature review: The problem should be succinctly stated in one sentence and the specific problem area should be mentioned.

Next, it is crucial to describe why this problem is important to be researched. You may establish the importance of the problem by citing statistics about its prevalence or how many individuals have been affected by the problem. These statistics give a sense of how widespread the problem is. It is important that you cite the most recent statistics, as this provides information about the current status of the problem area. Another way to establish the importance of the problem is by citing legislation or policies that have been passed to address the problem. Relevant literature to cite includes literature that defines the variables, describes the theories used to explain how the problem developed, and identifies the methods used to collect the data and the statistical methods used to analyze the data. Finally, showing how your study will advance knowledge about the problem area is done by critiquing what has previously been done and demonstrating how what you are proposing will build upon what has already been done or differs than what has previously been done. Your study could differ because you are using a different theory than what was previously used, or you are using a different statistical approach to analyze the data. Merely using a different population than what has participated in the previous studies may not be a strong rationale for conducting your study, unless you can demonstrate that studying this particular population will advance our understanding of the problem area.

## Tips for Writing Up the Literature Review

It is important that the readers of your literature review clearly see how your research question(s) and hypothesis were derived from the existing scholarly literature. Your literature review should not be just a collection of direct quotes. Rather, your literature review must demonstrate to the reader that you are a critical thinker who carefully read and thought about the existing knowledge on the topic and are able to synthesize it in your own words. Competence 4, *Engage in Practice-Informed Research and Research-Informed Practice*, emphasizes that social workers use critical thinking to engage in the analysis of research findings. Use direct quotes sparingly, and make sure the information is enclosed within quotation marks. Patten (2004) recommends that direct quotes be used when "(1) presenting definitions, (2) presenting important points made by notable individuals, and (3) clarifying differences of opinion in the literature when seeing the differences in wording (such as the wording of theories) might help readers understand the issue involved" (p. 37). When you paraphrase information, make sure you cite the information correctly. It is important that subheadings be used to introduce the sections of the literature review.

# Ethics and the Study Design

Not all research studies are ethical! An ethical research study does not violate any of the NASW Code of Ethics standards related to research and evaluation or other professional codes of conduct, or require you or the participants to engage in unethical behaviors or practices (Competency 1, *Demonstrate Ethical and Professional Behavior*). Additionally, an ethical research study does not require the researcher to engage in behavior or practices that would put participants in harm or danger. Let us say a researcher is interested in examining the effects of cocaine on one's driving ability. The research question would be, "What are the effects of cocaine on one's driving ability?" This is an ethical research question, however, the ways in which a researcher goes about obtaining information to get the answer to this question could be unethical. It would be unethical for the researcher to give the participants cocaine and then ask them to get in their cars and see how they drive to find out the answer to the proposed research question. An ethical way to examine the effects of cocaine on one's driving would be to ask on a questionnaire the following questions: "Have you used cocaine?," "If so, have you ever driven a vehicle while under the influence of cocaine?," and "Thinking about your driving when you were under the influence of cocaine compared to when you were not driving under the influence, did you observe any differences in your driving. If so, what were these differences?" Because cocaine is a controlled and illegal substance, participants' identities would need to be protected and kept either confidential or anonymous. Otherwise, participants would be at risk for being reported for criminal activity.

## Diversity and the Research Question

In formulating a research question, it is increasingly important that researchers think carefully about diversity (Competency 2, *Engage Diversity and Difference in Practice*). It has been argued by Rodgers-Farmer and Potocky-Tripodi (2001) that the problem formulation phase by its very use of the term *problem*, implies that researchers operate from a "deficit perspective" when it comes to conducting research with diverse groups or populations who are considered as a minority. That is, researchers develop research questions that focus on the problems of the diverse groups instead of focusing on strengths and resiliencies. An excellent strategy to avoid this issue is to include members of the diverse group in defining the research question. Hughes, Seidman, and Williams (1993) state that researchers may formulate the "wrong problem" or have errors in their "conceptualization of the problem" when conducting research with diverse groups because of selecting a research problem to investigate based on their own experiences with the group or the findings of previous research.

In conceptualizing the research problem, it is important to consider the role gender may play. If a researcher is interested in studying binge drinking among college students, it is important that binge drinking be defined as having five or more alcoholic drinks for males or four or more alcoholic drinks for females on the same occasion. Otherwise, using the binge drinking definition for males when studying females may underestimate the prevalence of binge drinking. On the other hand, using the binge drinking definition for females when studying males may overestimate the prevalence of binge drinking.

# SUMMARY, REVIEW, AND ASSIGNMENTS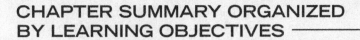

## CHAPTER SUMMARY ORGANIZED BY LEARNING OBJECTIVES

**LO 4.1** Develop a good research question.

A good research question is one that is feasible and researchable.

**LO 4.2** Explain the purpose of a literature review.

A literature review will give you a good overview of the current knowledge on the topic, the theories used to explain the topic, the methods used to study the topic, and suggestions for future research.

**LO 4.3** Conduct a literature search.

There are four sources that you should use to find information on your research problem or topic—literature reviews, systematic reviews, electronic databases and the grey literature.

**LO 4.4** Write up a literature review.

In writing up a literature review, use direct quotes sparingly and make sure the information is enclosed within quotation marks. Writing up a literature review requires you to be a critical thinker. When you paraphrase

information, make sure you cite the information correctly. It is important that subheadings be used to introduce the sections of the literature review.

**LO 4.5** Identify the ethical issues associated with designing a research study.

Ethical research studies do not violate any of the NASW Code of Ethics standards related to research and evaluation or other professional codes of conduct or requires you or the participants to engage in unethical behavior or practices. Additionally, they do not require the researcher to engage in behavior or practices that would put the participants in harm or danger.

**LO 4.6** Identify the diversity issues associated with developing a research study question.

In developing a research question when conducting research with diverse groups, it is important to get input from members of the particular group. In conceptualizing the research problem, it is important to consider the role gender may play.

## KEY TERMS

Research problem 59
Research question 60
Literature
  review 63

Systematic review 64
Empirical study 68
Conceptual/theoretical
  studies 68

Synthesizing 69
Grey literature 69

## COMPETENCY NOTES

In this chapter, you were introduced to the competencies below:

Competency 1, *Demonstrate Ethical and Professional Behavior.* Social workers should develop research questions that are ethical in nature.

Competency 2, *Engage Diversity and Difference in Practice.* Social workers, when formulating their research questions, should consider the role of diversity and gender.

Competence 4, *Engage in Practice-Informed Research and Research-Informed Practice.* Social workers should use critical thinking to engage in the analysis of research findings.

## ASSESSMENT QUESTIONS

1. How did the information in this chapter enhance your knowledge about the problem formulation phase of the research process?

2. How did the information in this chapter enhance your knowledge about how to conduct a literature review?

3. What specific content discussed in this chapter is still unclear to you? If there is still content that is unclear, schedule an appointment with your instructor to gain more clarity.

## END-OF-CHAPTER EXERCISES

1. Use a different electronic database than Academic Search Premier to look up articles on abuse and pregnancy. Write down how many articles you retrieved. Redo the search using different terms for abuse. If the electronic database has a thesaurus, you should use it to help you refine your topic.

2. Find an empirical study and read it. Critique the literature review to determine if it includes the five elements suggested by Pyrczak.

3. Using the same article, look for how the authors used direct quotes to see if any fall into the categories Patten described.

4. Use three articles from Exercise #1. Identify whether the studies are empirical or conceptual/theoretical. How do you know this?

## ADDITIONAL READINGS

Pyrczak, F. (2014). *Evaluating research in academic journals: A practical guide to realistic evaluation* (6th ed.). Glendale, CA: Pyrczak Publishing.

Ridley, D. (2012). *The literature review: A step-by-step guide for students* (2nd ed.). London, England: Sage.

# $SAGE edge™

Get the tools you need to sharpen your study skills. SAGE Edge offers a robust online environment featuring an impressive array of free tools and resources.

Access practice quizzes at **edge.sagepub.com/farmer**

# Measurement

## Learning Objectives

5.1  Distinguish between the conceptual and operational definition of a variable.

5.2  Differentiate between the various levels of measurement.

5.3  Distinguish between the different sources of measurement error.

5.4  Distinguish between the various types of reliability and validity.

5.5  Select a standardized measure to assess a client's presenting problem.

5.6  Develop a measure.

5.7  Identify the ethical and diversity issues associated with measurement.

| Competencies Covered | Learning Objectives | Dimension |
|---|---|---|
| Competency 1<br>*Demonstrate Ethical and Professional Behavior* | 5.7  Identify the ethical issues associated with measurement. | Skills |
| Competency 3<br>*Advance Human Rights and Social, Economic, and Environmental Justice* | 5.7  Identify the diversity issues associated with measurement. | Skills |
| Competency 4<br>*Engage in Diversity and Difference* | 5.7  Identify the diversity issues associated with measurement. | Skills |

(Continued)

Master the content at
**edge.sagepub.com/farmer**

(Continued)

| Competencies Covered | Learning Objectives | Dimension |
|---|---|---|
| Competency 7<br>*Assess Individuals, Families, Groups, Organizations, and Communities* | 5.5 Select a standardized measure to assess a client's presenting problem. | Skills |
| Competency 9<br>*Evaluate Practice With Individuals, Families, Groups, Organizations, and Communities* | 5.5 Select a standardized measure to assess a client's presenting problem. | Skills |

## PBL Case 5

### Should Maggie Really Be Using This Measure to Assess Kim's Concerns?

By responding to the questions related to this case, you will be able to determine what level of measurement is appropriate for assessing the client's presenting concerns and be able to determine if the use of a standardized measure to assess the presenting concern is appropriate or not.

Kim is a 25-year-old African American female who is seeking services because she has not been feeling like herself lately. She called the Bedford Community Counseling Center (BCCC) to see if she can come in to speak to someone about what has been happening to her. She tells the person who answered the phone that she thinks she is depressed. She is scheduled to come in for her appointment the day after she called the BCCC.

You are doing your field placement at this agency. Maggie, your field supervisor, asks you to sit in on an intake with her. She tells you that after the intake is over, she will meet with you to discuss the information that was collected and Kim's diagnosis. Moreover, she tells you that she would like for you to review the intake form so that you can familiarize yourself with the questions. She casually mentions that some of the newly hired staff have questioned the usefulness of the form as a way of collecting the data they need and have asked her to think about revising it.

At this point, take a few minutes to think about the case example and do the following:

1. Identify the problem.

2. Determine what you already know about the problem.

3. Determine what information you need to solve the problem.

4. List the questions needed to be answered related to the information you need to solve the problem.

Please write down your responses to each item. You will need to refer to them while reading this chapter.

During the intake, Kim stated that she has not been feeling well for the past two months but has been afraid to tell anyone or seek treatment. She stated that she really wanted to tell her friends how she has been feeling but was hesitant to do so because they would tell her that nothing was wrong with her. She did state that she told her mother and sister about how she was feeling, and they both told her to pray and that she would feel better. She stated that she did follow their suggestions but seems to have gotten worse. She reported that she has had some suicidal ideations. Maggie asked her to describe what other symptoms she has been experiencing. Kim stated that she has been extremely tired but has been going to work. She further reported that she does not seem to be motivated to work or try new things. She stated she cries easily, feels depressed, and has had trouble concentrating and sleeping. It usually takes her three hours to go to sleep after she has gone to bed. When asked about how often the above symptoms occur, she stated that they occur almost every day. She further stated that she has gained 10 pounds in the two-month period as well. Although Kim goes to work every day, she stated she does not always take a shower and the last time she cleaned her house was a month ago. When Maggie asked Kim why she had not done these things, she stated that she has been too depressed to do so. When Maggie inquired about symptoms of mania and psychosis, Kim stated that she had not experienced any of these symptoms.

In your meeting with your field supervisor, Maggie, she goes over all the information that Kim provided during the intake. Maggie tells you that she is diagnosing Kim as having major depressive disorder, single episode, severe without psychotic features. She further explains that she diagnosed Kim with this because she has had the following symptoms for a two-month period: suicidal ideations, insomnia, lack of motivation to work or try new things, cries easily (depressed mood), weight gain, extreme tiredness, and difficulty concentrating. Maggie further elaborates that Kim has more than the required five of the nine symptoms to meet a *Diagnostic and Statistical Manual of Mental Disorders* (*DSM-5*)* diagnosis of major depressive disorder, single episode, severe without psychotic features. Additionally, Maggie states that Kim also warrants a diagnosis of major depressive disorder, according the *DSM-5* criteria, because her symptoms caused distressed in her social functioning; her symptoms are not due to substance use, another medical condition, or other mental disorders, such as schizoaffective disorder, schizophrenia, schizophreniform disorder, or delusional disorder;

*The *Diagnostic and Statistical Manual of Mental Disorders* (5th ed.; DSM-5), authored by the American Psychological Association, is a handbook used by mental health care professionals to guide their diagnosing of mental disorders.

and she never experienced a manic or hypomanic episode. She explains that she gave Kim the diagnosis of single episode because she has never had a prior major depressive episode. She goes on to state that she gave Kim the diagnosis of severe because of the number of symptoms and a marked decrease in her ability to keep up with household tasks and her hygiene. Moreover, Maggie states that she gave Kim the diagnosis of without psychotic features because she had not experienced any symptoms of psychosis during this time period.

---

# Introduction

In this chapter, you will learn about the levels of measurement—nominal, ordinal, interval, and ratio. An overview of each type of reliability and validity is provided. A brief discussion of the criteria used to select a standardized measure to assess a client's presenting problem is presented. Ethical and diversity issues related to measurement are discussed.

# Measurement Defined

**Measurement** is the process of quantifying a set of observations of a phenomenon. Measurement involves developing a set of procedures that can be systematically preformed reliably. It may involve having individuals respond to a series of questions to determine their well-being or having someone rate the cooperativeness of a work colleague. An important phase of the measurement process is to define what it is we want to measure.

# Conceptual Versus Operational Definition

## Defining a Variable: Conceptual Versus Operational Definition

How would you define diversity, multiculturalism, and cultural competence? Write down your responses. Ask some of your friends to define these concepts. Compare your responses with your friends, and I bet you will be surprised to see their definitions vary from yours. The reason why there is variability among the definitions is because these terms are abstract concepts, and they may mean different things to different people. Because these terms are abstract concepts, it is hard to determine what one means when using them. Not knowing what one means when using these terms makes it hard to study the effects of diversity, multiculturalism, or cultural competence on student engagement, for example. To address this concern, researchers need to provide a conceptual definition of the abstract concepts they are interested in studying. The **conceptual definition** "is the working definition a researcher uses for a concept" (Wolfer, 2007, p. 127). Let us say, for example, you are interested in examining the effects of cultural competence on Chinese parents' engagement in parent management training. In reviewing the literature, you decide to base your conceptual definition on the work of Lin, Lee, and Huang (2017), who defined cultural competence as "the ability to acknowledge, appreciate, and respect the values, preferences, and expressed needs of the client" (p. 174). This conceptual definition rules out other possible definitions of cultural competence that do not focus on skills, such as awareness. Having a conceptual definition helps researchers hone in on what they will research and allows the readers of their research to understand what phenomenon was studied.

In thinking about the case example, when Kim called the BCCC she stated that she thought she was depressed. Depression is an abstract concept. To determine if Kim is depressed, Maggie used the conceptual definition of depression as specified in the *DSM-5* (American Psychological Association, 2013; see Table 5.1).

| Table 5.1   Major Depressive Disorder Diagnostic Criteria |
| --- |

A. Five (or more) of the following symptoms have been present during the same 2-week period and represent a change from previous functioning; at least one of the symptoms is either (1) depressed mood or (2) loss of interest or pleasure.

- **Note:** Do not include symptoms that are clearly attributable to another medical condition.

1. Depressed mood most of the day, nearly every day, as indicated by either subjective report (e.g., feels sad, empty, hopeless) or observation made by others (e.g., appears tearful). (**Note:** In children and adolescents, can be irritable mood.)

2. Markedly diminished interest or pleasure in all, or almost all, activities most of the day, nearly every day (as indicated by either subjective account or observation).

3. Significant weight loss when not dieting or weight gain (e.g., a change of more than 5% of body weight in a month), or decrease or increase in appetite nearly every day. (**Note:** In children, consider failure to make expected weight gain.)

4. Insomnia or hypersomnia nearly every day.

5. Psychomotor agitation or retardation nearly every day (observable by others, not merely subjective feelings of restlessness or being slowed down).

6. Fatigue or loss of energy nearly every day.

7. Feelings of worthlessness or excessive or inappropriate guilt (which may be delusional) nearly every day (not merely self-reproach or guilt about being sick).

8. Diminished ability to think or concentrate, or indecisiveness, nearly every day (either by subjective account or as observed by others).

9. Recurrent thoughts of death (not just fear of dying), recurrent suicidal ideation without a specific plan, or a suicide attempt or a specific plan for committing suicide.

*(Continued)*

Table 5.1 (Continued)

B. The symptoms cause clinically significant distress or impairment in social, occupational, or other important areas of functioning.

C. The episode is not attributable to the physiological effects of a substance or another medical condition.

**Note:** Criteria A–C represent a major depressive episode.

**Note:** Responses to a significant loss (e.g., bereavement, financial ruin, losses from a natural disaster, a serious medical illness or disability) may include the feelings of intense sadness, rumination about the loss, insomnia, poor appetite, and weight loss noted in Criterion A, which may resemble a depressive episode. Although such symptoms may be understandable or considered appropriate to the loss, the presence of a major depressive episode in addition to the normal response to a significant loss should also be carefully considered. This decision inevitably requires the exercise of clinical judgment based on the individual's history and the cultural norms for the expression of distress in the context of loss.

In distinguishing grief from a major depressive episode (MDE), it is useful to consider that in grief the predominant affect is feelings of emptiness and loss, while in an MDE it is persistent depressed mood and the inability to anticipate happiness or pleasure. The dysphoria in grief is likely to decrease in intensity over days to weeks and occurs in waves, the so-called pangs of grief. These waves tend to be associated with thoughts or reminders of the deceased. The depressed mood of an MDE is more persistent and not tied to specific thoughts or preoccupations. The pain of grief may be accompanied by positive emotions and humor that are uncharacteristic of the pervasive unhappiness and misery characteristic of an MDE. The thought content associated with grief generally features a preoccupation with thoughts and memories of the deceased, rather than the self-critical or pessimistic ruminations seen in an MDE. In grief, self-esteem is generally preserved, whereas in an MDE feelings of worthlessness and self-loathing are common. If self-derogatory ideation is present in grief, it typically involves perceived failings vis-à-vis the deceased (e.g., not visiting frequently enough, not telling the deceased how much he or she was loved). If a bereaved individual thinks about death and dying, such thoughts are generally focused on the deceased and possibly about "joining" the deceased, whereas in an MDE such thoughts are focused on ending one's own life because of feeling worthless, undeserving of life, or unable to cope with the pain of depression.

D. The occurrence of the major depressive episode is not better explained by schizoaffective disorder, schizophrenia, schizophreniform disorder, delusional disorder, or other specified and unspecified schizophrenia spectrum and other psychotic disorders.

E. There has never been a manic episode or a hypomanic episode.

- **Note:** This exclusion does not apply if all of the manic-like or hypomanic-like episodes are substance-induced or are attributable to the physiological effects of another medical condition.

*Source:* Reprinted with permission from the Diagnostic and Statistical Manual of Mental Disorders, Fifth Edition, (Copyright 2013). American Psychiatric Association.

This conceptual definition rules out the possibility of Maggie diagnosing Kim with any other mental disorder.

Once you have decided on your conceptual definition, you are now ready to operationalize the concept you have just defined. **Operationalization** is the process of defining the exact way you plan to measure the concept. In other words, this is the **operational definition** of the concept. For example, you are interested in looking at the effects of stigma on the mental health services utilization. Based on the work of Corrigan (2004), you may want to operationalize stigma as the public perceptions, beliefs, or stereotypes when internalized that affects one's help-seeking ability. As for mental health services utilization, you may want to operationalize this variable as utilizing the services of a mental health professional to address alcohol use, anxiety, stress, or emotional problems. To measure the effects of stigma on mental health services utilization, you would ask persons to fill out a survey or questionnaire. The diagram below (see Figure 5.1) illustrates the operationalization of mental health services utilization. The concept we want to operationalize is mental health utilization, which is enclosed in the circle. The items on the survey are displayed in the squares. The survey question, for example, would be "Have you ever seen a mental health professional in the last year for any of the following: alcohol use, anxiety, stress, or emotional problems? Please place a checkmark in the box next to your response." Respondents' answers to the question will help you determine if they have used mental services in the last year.

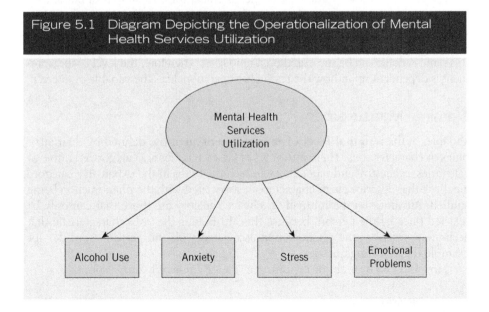

Figure 5.1   Diagram Depicting the Operationalization of Mental Health Services Utilization

In thinking about the case example, Maggie may want to operationalize depression by asking Kim to fill out a questionnaire that asks her to indicate how often she is depressed, cries, has difficulty sleeping and concentrating, lacks motivation, and has suicidal ideations. By having Kim answer these questions, Maggie can determine if she is depressed or not.

For researchers, the concept that was operationalized is referred to as a variable. A **variable** is any factor, trait, quality, or condition that can be measured. Most importantly, in order for a factor, trait, quality, or condition to be a variable it must vary. That is, the factor, trait, quality, or condition can take on different values. The ways in which a variable can be measured will be discussed in the next section.

## Levels of Measurement

Measuring the variable involves assigning the variable a numeric value. The numeric value is used to operationalize a qualitative experience someone has had. In thinking about the case example, Maggie would be interested in quantifying Kim's qualitative experiences of feeling depressed.

Based on how a researcher wants to conceptualize the variable of interest, one of four levels of measurement will be used to operationalize the variable. These four levels are *nominal*, *ordinal*, *interval*, or *ratio*, depending upon their nature or attributes. The nominal level is the lowest level of measurement, while ratio is the highest level of measurement. Knowing the level of measurement for a variable is important for determining what type of statistical procedures researchers will use to analyze their data. At the outset, it is important for you to know that in one study, for example, a variable, such as income, can be measured on a nominal level and in another study this same variable can be measured on a ratio level. Therefore, the level of measurement is dependent upon how the researcher operationalizes the variable of interest.

### Nominal Measurement

Variables at the **nominal level of measurement** are those defined by their attributes or characteristics. These attributes or characteristics are categorized into two categories: *exhaustive* and *mutually exclusive*. Attributes in the exhaustive category are those that describe every characteristic associated with the phenomenon being studied. Attributes in the mutually exclusive category are those that can only be selected once by the person, because this attribute is the only characteristic that accurately describes the phenomenon associated with the person. Consider for example the following question:

How did you hear about my practice? Please circle only one response.

1. Television
2. Newspaper

3. Word-of-Mouth

4. Internet

5. Radio

6. Other: Please specify_____

Does the above question fit the criteria of being exhaustive and mutually exclusive? Yes. The criteria of being exhaustive is met because there is an answer choice for everyone. Persons who may have heard about my practice another way besides items 1–5 are given the opportunity to identify how they heard. Does the above question fit the criteria of being mutually exclusive? Yes. The criteria of mutually exclusive is met because there is only one category that can be selected per individual respondent. If the instructions were for persons to select all that apply, then the mutually exclusive criteria would not have been met.

In order to measure a variable at the nominal level, the researcher needs to assign the variable a numeric value. The process of assigning a variable measured at the nominal level a numeric value is known as **coding**. For instance, when coding the response to the question, "How did you hear about my practice?," the researcher might assign the response as television = 1, newspaper = 2, word-of-mouth = 3, Internet = 4, radio = 5, and other: please specify = 6. The numeric value does not suggest that the responses are qualitatively or quantitatively different from one another. The numeric value is used so the researcher can perform the appropriate statistical procedure. The appropriate statistical procedure to be performed when one has a variable at the nominal level of measurement will be discussed in Chapter 13. Examples of variables measured at the nominal level are gender, race/ethnicity, and colors.

## Critical Thinking Question 5.1

During your weekly supervision with Maggie, she again mentions that her staff does not think the intake form is useful. She tells you that she has decided to revise the portion of the form used to determine if persons meet a specific diagnosis. She further states that she will be meeting with Kim tonight and plans to assess Kim's depression using a nominal level measurement. What question or questions would she ask? Is measuring Kim's depression on a nominal level the best way of assessing if Kim is depressed or not? Justify your response.

## Ordinal Measurement

Variables at the **ordinal level of measurement** are those defined by their attributes or characteristics that are categorized into two categories: exhaustive and mutually exclusive; however, the numeric value assigned to them by the researcher can be logically ranked, but the intervals between categories may not be equal. Going back to the case example, if the social worker seeing Kim asked her to rate how satisfied she was with the services received, using a 6-point Likert scale—0 = not satisfied, 1 = a little satisfied, 2 = neither satisfied or dissatisfied, 3 = somewhat satisfied, 4 = satisfied, and 5 = very satisfied—this would be an example of a variable measured on an ordinal level. The above meets the criteria of being measured as an ordinal level variable because the responses are exhaustive because everyone can select a response. There is a neutral category for Kim to indicate that she was neither satisfied or dissatisfied with the services received; thus, she is not forced to respond in a positive or negative manner about the services received. The criteria for being mutually exclusive is met because she cannot simultaneously select being satisfied and not satisfied. The responses can be rank ordered. One can say that if Kim chose the response "very satisfied" that would be better than selecting the other responses; however, one cannot say if Kim selected the response "a little satisfied," how quantitatively different this choice is from the other responses. The intervals between the ranked categories may not be equal. In other words, one cannot assume that the difference between Kim's rating of 2 is different from a rating of 0 and that the difference between her rating of 2 is different from a rating of 3. The appropriate statistical procedure to be performed when one has a variable at the ordinal level of measurement will be discussed in Chapter 13. Examples of variables measured at the ordinal level of measurement are income, social economic status, and degrees earned. Let us say, for example, a researcher asked the respondents to respond to the following question about their income: Please indicate your yearly salary. Circle your response.

1. Less than $10,000

2. $10,000–$19,999

3. $20,000–$49,999

4. $50,000 or greater

The respondents are reporting their salary based on selecting a category and not the actual salary based in dollars. Because the intervals between each person's salary is unknown and cannot be assumed to be equal, income is considered to be measured on an ordinal level.

## Critical Thinking Question 5.2

Thinking about the case example, should Maggie use an ordinal level of measurement to assess Kim's depression? Is the ordinal level of measurement preferable to the nominal level of measurement? Justify your response. What question(s) should she ask?

## Interval Measurement

Similar to variables measured on the nominal or ordinal level of measurement, variables measured on the **interval level of measurement** also have to meet the criteria of being exhaustive and mutually exclusive. The numeric value assigned to the categories by the researcher can be logically ranked, which is similar to variables measured on the ordinal level of measurement. Variables measured on the interval level, unlike variables measured on the ordinal level, have intervals between the categories that are equal. Let us say, for example, that your child complains to you about not feeling well and you decide to take his or her temperature. In looking at the thermometer, you noticed that your child's temperature is 103.6° F. Compared to 98.6° F, which is considered a normal temperature, you can say that your child's temperature is five degrees above normal. You take your child's temperature two hours later. This time his or her temperature is 93.6° F, which is five degrees below normal. In the above example, you can see that the interval between normal temperature and 103.6° F and the interval between normal temperature and 93.6° F are equal. The interval level measurement has a zero value; however, this zero value is not absolute. In other words, the zero does not mean absence of the construct. The appropriate statistical procedure to be performed when one has a variable at the interval level of measurement will be discussed in Chapter 13. An example of a variable measured at the interval level of measurement is income. Income is measured on an interval level if you ask your respondents to report their income in dollars. Let us say you have five respondents who responded to the question and their responses are as follows: Respondent #1: $10,000, Respondent #2: $20,000, Respondent #3: $30,000, Respondent #4: $40,000, and Respondent #5: $50,000. You can see that the interval between $20,000 and $30,000 is the same as the interval between $40,000 and $50,000 ($10,000).

---

### Critical Thinking Question 5.3

Maggie is seriously considering using an interval level measurement to assess Kim's depression. What are some issues she needs to consider before selecting this type of measurement? Justify your response. What questions should she ask?

---

## Ratio Measurement

Variables at the **ratio level of measurement** have all the characteristics of variables measured at the interval level, in addition to a true zero value. In other words, the zero does mean the absence of the construct or whatever is being measured; the zero value has real meaning. For example, let us say that the social worker who is treating Kim in the case example for depression asked Kim to rate how often she felt depressed during the last two weeks, using a 3-point Likert scale, where 0 = never, 1 = sometimes, and 2 = always. Let us say Kim selected never, which is coded as zero. Her response would indicate that she did not experience depression during this two-week time period. The appropriate statistical procedure to be performed when one has a variable at the ratio level of measurement will be discussed in Chapter 13. An example of a variable measured at the ratio level of measurement is income if the question is asked, "How much money did you make in the last year?" Income is considered to be measured on an interval level because a respondent could report making zero dollars last year.

## Sources of Measurement Error

Measurement is never perfect. Researchers are unable to measure variables accurately because of measurement error. **Measurement error** occurs when the data collected do not accurately reflect the construct we are attempting to measure. There are two types of measurement error researchers need to be concerned about: systematic error and random error. We will begin by discussing systematic error.

### Systematic Error

**Systematic error** occurs when there is a pattern to the error. There are several ways in which systematic error is introduced into the research process. The wording of the items may inadvertently lead the respondents toward or away from a particular response. The question, "Do you think the government should force all U.S. citizens to have health insurance?," because of the word *force* may make it hard for the respondents to respond affirmatively to the question, even if the respondents favor universal health care. In studies where data are collected via individual interviews or focus groups, systematic error may be introduced by the interviewer. Depending on the topics for the individual interviews or focus groups and/or the participants in the study, the characteristics of the interviewer could result in the participants not being candid about their responses. For example, women survivors of intimate partner violence might feel more comfortable being interviewed by a woman about their experiences with intimate partner violence than a man. The clothes worn by the interviewer may result in more or less candid responses from the participants. It seems that depending on the population, an interviewer who is casually dressed or dressed in business attire may elicit more candid responses from participants, compare to an interviewer not dressed in such attire. Interviewers who express their opinions or express a verbal or nonverbal disapproval to the participants' responses may result in them changing their responses. The interviewer should avoid expressing approval of the participants' responses, because this may lead the participants to tailor their answers in order to receive the interviewer's approval. The best response from an interviewer is complete neutrality. The only exception is when a neutral response from the interviewer would be inappropriate. For example, if when responding to the question the participant states that her husband died two months ago, it would be appropriate for the interviewer to express sympathy. Systematic error can be caused by the participant providing the same response to all or most of the items on a measure. This is referred to as **response set**. An **acquiescent response set** is the tendency of a person to respond in a positive manner to a question regardless of the question being asked. **Social desirability bias** occurs when the participants respond in a way that conveys a favorable impression of themselves or in a manner they believe will be more consistent with the researcher's views. **Recall bias** occurs when one group of study participants is more likely to recall the information requested than other groups of participants. For example, in conducting a study to learn whether taking a particular prescription medication during pregnancy resulted in a birth defect, mothers of children with that birth defect may be more likely to recall taking the medication than mothers of healthy children because they are more motivated to recall this information. It is possible that the medication did not cause the birth defect, but it could appear that it does if the mothers of children with the birth defect are more likely to remember taking the medication than mothers of healthy children. Another type of bias that results in systematic error is the **Hawthorne effect**. This may occur when study participants improve or change their behavior simply because they know they are being studied. The term *Hawthorne effect* comes from experiments that were conducted from 1924 to 1932 at the Hawthorne Works, a Western Electric factory outside Chicago. The intent of the study was to test which working conditions led to increased production. One of the conditions they tested was installing brighter lights in the factory. After installing the brighter lights, it was noticed that production increased. When they tested dimmer lights, production also increased. In fact, no matter what type of lighting was installed, production increased. The study at the Western Electric Production Facility, as well as subsequent studies, demonstrated that merely observing people can change their behavior.

## Random Error

**Random error** occurs when there is no consistent pattern of measurement error. Random error does not result in bias toward accepting a hypothesis. Instead, it weakens our ability to find a relationship between the variables specified in our hypothesis. Random error diminishes the ability to reject the null hypothesis. This is called **bias toward the null**. Random error may occur when the participants do not understand an item on the survey they are asked to complete, for example, or they are tired, bored, distracted, or in a hurry to complete the survey. An example of a question that may produce random error is one that is ambiguous—"Do you think access to health care is a right of all U.S citizens?" It is not clear if the question is referring to government-funded health care or private health care. In a study where a researcher is conducting interviews, random error may occur if the interviewer is not sure how to interpret or record the participant's answers. Another source of random error may be due to difficulty recalling the information requested. If the question asks about something that happened too long ago or was not important enough to remember, the participant may not be able to provide accurate information. The less salient or more distant an event that the researcher is asking about, the more difficult it will be for the participant to remember or recall the event. For example, asking your participants if they have ever been hospitalized due to injuries from a car accident is something that most people will remember for their entire lives. Few people accurately remember what they had for lunch a week ago.

## Reliability and Validity

### Types of Reliability

Two concepts that describe the quality of a measurement process or measurement instrument are reliability and validity. **Reliability** is the degree to which a measure is consistent or dependable. It is the degree to which a measure gives the same result over and over again, assuming the underlying phenomenon that you are measuring is not changing. Reliability is assessed by looking at the correlation between measures or items comprising a measure.

There are different types of reliability. One type is consistency among multiple observers. This is referred to as inter-rater reliability, which is also referred to as inter-observer reliability. **Inter-rater reliability** is defined as the degree of agreement between the raters and **inter-observer reliability** is the degree of agreement between the observers. An example of inter-rater reliability would be as follows: Kim in the case study is interviewed by Maggie about her concerns and is then later interviewed by Tina, another social worker at the agency about her concerns. Maggie and Tina meet to discuss their diagnosis of Kim to determine if they are in agreement about the diagnosis.

**Cohen's kappa** is a statistic that is used to quantify the degree to which two raters or observers are in agreement. It indicates the level of inter-rater reliability. Cohen's kappa is based on the extent to which the agreement between the two raters or observers is due to chance or actual consistency between the raters. Cohen's kappa ranges from 0, which indicates no agreement between the raters, to 1, which indicates perfect agreement between the raters.

When one is determining agreement between more than two raters, Fleiss' kappa is used, rather than Cohen's kappa. **Fleiss' kappa** ranges from 0, which indicates no agreement between the raters, to 1, which indicates perfect agreement between the raters.

**Test-retest reliability** assesses the stability or consistency of a measure over time. If a measure is reliable, the participant should get the same response each time the question is asked, assuming that the question is about something that does not change over time. Assessing a measure's reliability by test-retest reliability may not be appropriate for all measures. For example, assessing the test-retest reliability of a measure to assess depression is not appropriate because one's scores on the scale may change a month later because depression levels fluctuate.

The **Pearson product-moment correlation** coefficient can be used to assess the test-retest reliability of two administrations of a measure. One disadvantage of the Pearson product-moment correlation coefficient is that it overestimates the true relationship between the administrations when the sample size is small.

The **intraclass correlation coefficient** is used to assess the test-retest reliability in those situations involving more than two administrations of a measure. Unlike the Pearson product-moment correlation, it does not overestimate the true relationship among the administrations when the sample size is small.

**Split-half reliability** is used to determine the consistency of items on a scale. First, the entire scale is administered to study participants, and then the items from the scale are randomly divided across two new constructed measures. Each of these has half of the items of the original scale. It is assumed that both of these new measures are assessing the underlying construct that was measured by the original measure. These two measures are administered to one group of participants at the same time. The scores on each of the halves are compared statistically to determine the degree of similarity. If all of the items on the scales are consistent with each other, the two halves should yield very similar scores.

Another indicator of the reliability of a scale is internal consistency. **Internal consistency** is achieved when the items on a scale are consistent with each other. **Cronbach's alpha** is used to assess the degree of internal consistency of the scale's items. It is assessed by calculating the degree of similarity each item has with each of the other items. This is done by correlating each item on the scale with each other. The average of all of these correlations is referred to as Cronbach's alpha. A higher Cronbach's alpha represents stronger evidence that all of the scale items are measuring the same construct. Cronbach's alpha should be at least .70, and preferably .80 or higher.

## Types of Validity

**Validity** is the degree to which the measure actually measures what it was designed to measure. There are several types of validity that one can assess. **Face validity** is based simply on whether the measure appears to be valid "on its face" (Babbie, 2010). The face validity of a measure is determined by making a subjective judgment about whether the items on a scale appear to be measuring depression. Face validity is the least rigorous form of validity of a measure. In the case example, Maggie mentioned that newly hired staff already have questioned the usefulness of the intake form as a way of collecting the data they need. In order to assess the face validity of the form, one needs to review it to determine, for example, if it has items that assess depression. It would be important to see such items as depressed mood, cries easily, difficulty sleeping and concentrating, suicidal ideation, and weight gain or weigh lost, as these are indicators of depression based on the *DSM-5* (APA, 2013) criteria for major depressive disorder. If the form had the above-mentioned items, then one could say that the measure has face validity.

Unlike face validity, the evaluation of content validity is not based merely on subjective opinion but is based on theory and/or empirical research findings.

**Content validity** is assessed by asking experts on the topic to evaluate whether the items on the measure cover the full range of the concept (Babbie, 2010).

**Criterion validity** is based on how the measure compares to a criterion. The criterion is another measure that assesses the same variable your measure intends to assess. The criterion validity of a depression scale could be assessed by determining how well it identifies depression in individuals who have been diagnosed with depression. The clinical diagnosis is the criterion used to assess the measure. There are two types of criterion validity: concurrent validity and predictive validity. **Concurrent validity** indicates how well the measure corresponds with a criterion that is measured at the same time. To determine the concurrent validity of a depression scale, for example, the measure would be administered to the study participants. An experienced clinician would diagnose the study participants using the *DSM-5* criteria for depression, preferably the same day as they completed the depression scale. The depression scale scores would be examined by the researcher and would be compared to the clinician's diagnosis to see if both provided evidence to indicate the participants met the diagnostic criteria for depression. The degree to which the depression scale and the clinician's diagnosis agree indicates the concurrent criterion validity of the depression scale. There is one obvious weakness to this method. It presumes that the gold standard is itself valid. However, so-called gold standards are often imperfect. Clinicians often disagree about diagnosis. One way to improve the gold standard might be to have several clinicians diagnose the participants and use a diagnosis that is a consensus of the three clinicians.

**Known groups validity** is a type of concurrent validity that assesses whether a measure can differentiate between groups known to differ on the variable being measured. Known groups validity can be used to determine whether the social work licensing exam, which is a measure of practice knowledge and skills, differentiates between MSW social workers and lay helpers.

**Predictive validity** assesses the ability of the measure to predict a criterion that occurs in the future. Evidence of predictive validity is found when a measure accurately predicts future performance. To determine whether the SAT is a valid measure of ability to perform well in college, the researcher compares SAT scores in high school with college GPA.

**Construct validity** is an assessment of how well the concept of the variable was translated into a measure. It is the most stringent type of validity and also the most difficult type of validity to demonstrate. The two types of construct validity are divergent validity and convergent validity. A measure has **convergent validity** when it is correlated with measures that it should be related to, based on theory or empirical evidence. For example, previous research and clinical knowledge indicates that depression is related to life satisfaction. Therefore, a measure of depression should be correlated with a measure of life satisfaction. If a measure of depression is not correlated with a life satisfaction measure, it calls into question whether the depression measure is valid. A measure has **divergent validity** when it is not correlated with other measures to which it should not be related. For example, if a depression scale is not correlated with a measure of math ability, this strengthens our confidence that the depression measure is valid.

Maggie, your field supervisor, decides that she wants to use the Weinstein Depression Scale to assess if her clients are depressed. She cannot find any information in the literature about the reliability or validity of this scale. What can she do to assess the reliability and validity of this measure? Justify your response.

## The Relationship Between Reliability and Validity

Reliability and validity are related to each other. A measure may be reliable, but that does not mean it is measuring what we believe it to be measuring. For example, consider a situation where the researcher wants to measure a person's level of depression. The researcher decides to do so by weighing the person before and after each therapy session. The scale used to measure weight was determined to be reliable. It provides a consistently accurate measure of the person's weight. Unfortunately, the scale would not be a valid assessment of the level of depression. In this case, we have a reliable measure that lacks validity as a measure of depression. Just because a measure is reliable does not mean it is valid. A measure that is reliable has consistent responses; however, they may not be the true, valid responses. You want to use measures that are both reliable and valid.

The use of more than one measure or method, or using multiple sources, to measure a variable can strengthen the validity of measurement. Reliability and validity are not fixed properties of a measure. They are specific to the population and the particular circumstances under which the measure is used. A measure that is reliable and valid for one population may not be reliable or valid for another. These properties may vary based on gender, age, culture, and other characteristics of the population. It is important to choose measures that have been validated in a sample as similar as possible to the target population of your study (Competency 2, *Engage Diversity and Difference*). The researcher should also check that the measures are performing as expected in a new study. In social work research, selecting measures that are reliable and valid can be challenging because many of the concepts in which we are interested in measuring are complex, ambiguous, and have multiple dimensions. Additionally, there is not always adequate evidence of the reliability and validity of these measures. This should not prevent us from conducting the research necessary to answer questions that are important to social workers. Instead, researchers should choose the best measures possible for their study and remain aware of the limitations.

## Selecting Standardized Measures

It is important that social workers use standardized measures when conducting assessments with individuals, families, groups, organizations, and communities (Competency 7, *Assess Individuals, Families, Groups, Organizations, and Communities*).

The appropriate use of standardized measures may enhance the quality of the services by providing reliable indicators of the clients' concerns (Beattie, 2001). **Standardized measures** are ones that have established reliability and validity. These measures should have a Cronbach's alpha of .80 or higher and should be able to discriminate between high and low levels of the construct of interest. Standardized measures may have cut-off scores. **Cut-off scores** are established scores that are used to determine if someone meets or does not meet a specific criterion. For example, the cut-off scores for the Beck Depression Inventory-II (BDI-II; Beck, Steer, & Brown, 1996) to determine if someone is minimally or severely depressed are as follows: scores between 0 and 13 (minimal depression) scores between 14 and 19 (mild depression), scores between 20 and 28 (moderate depression), and scores between 29 and 60 (severe depression). The use of standardized measures that have cut-off scores can provide helpful information to determine the effectiveness of interventions used with individuals, families, groups, organizations, and communities (Competency 9, *Evaluate Practice With Individuals, Families, Groups, Organizations, and Communities*).

When using a standardized measure in a language other than the one in which it was created, you should proceed carefully. It is not a simple matter of translating the words into another language. First, check whether there is an official translated version. Even if a translated version exists, one should not assume that the translation is correct. You may need to make revisions to the measure. Just as there are regional and national variations in the meaning of certain words in English, this is also true for other languages. The translation of the items on the measure must be appropriate for the population you are studying. The question "Are you blue?" may have one meaning for English-speakers but if translated literally, would have a different meaning in other languages. If a translated measure does not exist, you will need to translate the measure for your study. The goal of translating a measure into another language is to create a culturally equivalent version in the new language (Competency 2, *Engage Diversity and Difference*). You must not only capture the denotative meaning of the word, but also the connotative meaning. The **denotative meaning** is the literal translation of the words. The **connotative meaning** also captures the weight or intensity of the words. There are different methods that can be used for translating a measure into a second language. Regardless of which method is used, translation should always be done by individuals who are not only bilingual, but also bicultural.

In **one-way translation**, one person translates from the original language to the second language. This type of translation is prone to a lot of errors because it relies on an individual's knowledge, experience, and interpretation. The translation of "How old are you?" is correct, but it may not be culturally appropriate for all Spanish-speaking study participants. The translation of the question "How old are you?" as ¿Cuántos años tiene?, which is an informal form of the question, may be off-putting for some study participants. While translating this same question as ¿Cuántos años tienes?, which is the formal form of the question, may be more appropriate. Translation by a committee may be better, because there is more input into the translation process. If all the translators on the committee are similar to each other and different from the population to be studied, the translation may still not be appropriate.

In **back translation**, one person translates from the original language into the second language and another person then translates back into the original language. Back translation is not perfect. When there are discrepancies found in the back translation, seeking a consensus translation between the two translators, or getting a third opinion, can be helpful.

**Decentering** is a process in which the original items are translated. After comparing the original and translated items, the original items may be revised and then another translation is produced. This process continues until equivalent items are obtained in both languages. Decentering allows the wording in the original language to be modified when the grammatical structures produce an awkward version in the target language or when the concepts in the original are inappropriate, unknown, or lack an equivalence in the second language. Decentering is the optimal method for producing linguistically equivalent and culturally appropriate measures because one assumption of this approach is that the original language of the measure does not need to be the language that is used for the final version of the measure. The final version of the measure may have words in both languages. Decentering should not be used when translating a standardized measure because the wording of the items in the original language should not be changed. When translating standardized measures, use back translation and consensus to achieve the best translation.

Samples of standardized measures can be obtained by looking up the measure when doing a literature review or by obtaining these two books—*Measures for Clinical Practice and Research: A Sourcebook, Fifth Edition, Volume I and II* (2013) by Kevin Corcoran and Joel Fischer. Volume I describes standardized measures that can be used with couples, families and children and Volume II describes standardized measures that can be used with adults. The measures in these books can be used to evaluate social work interventions.

## Constructing Measurement Instruments

Even when there are standardized measures available, there are many reasons why social work researchers might want to develop a new measure. The reasons include wanting a measure that has fewer items or takes less time to administer, or a measure that can be completed by the respondents rather than requiring an interviewer to read the questions to them. Below are some guidelines that should be taken into consideration when developing a measure.

### Determine the Type of Measure You Want to Develop

If you decide to develop your own measure, you must first determine what type of measure you are developing. You need to ask yourself if your measure will be one where the respondents complete the questions themselves or will an interviewer read the questions to the respondents. A measure where the respondents complete the question is referred to as a **self-administered measure/questionnaire**. On the other hand, a measure where an interviewer reads the questions to the respondents is referred to as an **interview schedule**.

## Determine the Type of Questions That Will Be Asked

You need to think about the type of questions that you will ask. There are two types of questions that you need to take into consideration: open-ended and closed-ended. **Open-ended questions** are ones in which the respondents are asked to provide their own answers to the question. An example of an open-ended question is, "When is the last time you took your medication?" **Closed-ended questions** are ones in which the respondent is asked to select an option provided by the researcher. An example of a closed-ended question is, "How satisfied are you with the services received?" Please respond to this question using the following responses: 0= not satisfied, 1 = a little satisfied, 2 = neither satisfied or dissatisfied, 3 = somewhat satisfied, 4 = satisfied, and 5 = very satisfied.

The response option has a numeric value assigned to it. The response categories should be both exhaustive and mutually exclusive. That is, everyone can select a response (exhaustive) and there is only one response option that can be selected (mutually exclusive).

## Determine the Wording of the Questions

Whether you choose open-ended or closed-ended questions, the respondents must be able to understand the questions that are being asked. In other words, the questions must be clear, concise, and unambiguous. Your questions need to be clear, as you should not take for granted that the persons responding to your questions know what you are asking them. Questions that are ambiguous may affect the person's ability to answer the question—therefore, producing random error. An example of an ambiguous question is, "How many times did you visit the doctor?" This question is ambiguous because there are different types of doctors. Therefore, someone responding to this question may be thinking about a podiatrist, while someone else could be thinking about a dermatologist. This question is also ambiguous because no time period has been specified. Some persons responding to the questions could be thinking about the past week, while others may be thinking about the past year. A better way to write the question is, "In the past 30 days, how many times did you visit the podiatrist?"

The careful wording of the questions increases the reliability of your measure and reduces random error. The use of negatively worded items should be avoided. **Negatively worded items** usually contain the word *no* or *not*. Negatively worded items can reduce the reliability of the measure (Barnette, 2000). You should avoid the use of double-barreled, loaded, and biased questions, to name a few, as such questions increase random error. **Double-barreled questions** are ones that contain more than one issue or topic yet allows for only one response. An example of a double-barreled question is as follows: "How satisfied are you with your living conditions and your landlord's ability to address your concerns?" **Loaded questions** are ones that contain an assumption. This is an example of a loaded question: "Have you quit smoking?" The assumption is that you are still smoking. **Biased questions** are ones that encourage the respondents to respond in a particular way. An example of a biased question is as follows: "Should the voting age be lowered to 16, as today's youth are more politically engaged compared to youth in the past?" In this question, there is an assumption stated to make the respondent say *yes*, as it was stated that today's youth are more politically engaged compared to youth of the past.

## Determine the Scaling Format for the Response Options

You need to decide how the response options will be rated. Your choice of how the response option will be rated is dependent upon the type of question being asked. For example, you want to use a dichotomous rating when you have a question that requires a *yes* or *no* or a *true* or *false* response. You may want to code "yes" as 1 and "no" as 0. For questions where you want to inquire about a person's attitudes, feelings, or opinions, you should use a Likert scale format (Burns & Groves, 2009). A **Likert scale format** is the presentation of items on a survey where the respondents are asked to rate their responses using a specified scale. The items on the survey are referred to as **Likert items**, and the **Likert scale** is the sum of responses of the Likert items. Likert items are normally formatted as follows:

1 = Strongly disagree

2 = Disagree

3 = Neither agree nor disagree

4 = Agree

5 = Strongly Agree

The response options for the Likert items vary. Researchers have used three-point, five-point, and seven-point response options; however, the five-point response option is the most common. In referring to the case example, let us say that Maggie plans to ask Kim to fill out a questionnaire after she has been terminated from treatment. An example of a Likert item that Maggie should include on the questionnaire is as follows: Please rate the extent to which you agree/disagree with this statement: The treatment I received was effective. 1 = strongly disagree, 2 = disagree, 3 = neither agree or disagree, 4 = agree, 5 = strongly agree.

## Ethics and Measurement

Neither the CSWE-prescribed competencies nor the NASW Code of Ethics (2017) explicitly mention the role of ethics and measurement. Although the above-mentioned entities do not explicitly mention the role of ethics and measurement, the NASW Code of Ethics states that social workers are ethically responsible to their clients and the first CSWE competency (*Demonstrate Ethical and Professional Behavior*) states that social workers demonstrate ethical and professional behavior. Therefore, the role of ethics and measurement are implicit in the NASW Code and the first CSWE competency.

The American Psychological Association (APA)'s *Ethical Principles of Psychologists and Conduct of Code* has an ethical standard on assessment. This standard covers 11 areas: (9.01) the bases for assessments, (9.02) use of assessments, (9.03) informed consent in assessments, (9.04) release of test data, (9.05) test construction, (9.06) interpreting assessment results, (9.07) assessment by unqualified persons, (9.08) obsolete tests and outdated test results, (9.09) test scoring and interpretation services, (9.10) explaining assessment results, and (9.11) maintaining security (APA, 2002). The APA's ethical standard on assessment and the areas covered can also apply to social work. We will select the following areas to demonstrate how they apply to social work: (9.02) use of assessments, (9.03) informed consent in assessment, and (9.08) obsolete tests and outdated test results. As it relates to the use of assessments, to be ethically responsible to their clients, social workers must, whenever possible, use measures that are reliable and valid for the populations they serve. Prior to conducting any type of assessment, it is important for social workers to obtain informed consent (9.03). The consent form must be in the language that your client can understand. It is imperative that social workers ensure they use the most up-to-date version of the assessment tool when working with their clients (9.08). Using obsolete and outdated measures could result in potential harm to your clients.

## Diversity and Measurement

Competency 4, *Engage in Practice-Informed Research and Research-Informed Practice*, states that social workers know the principles of culturally informed approaches to building knowledge (CSWE, 2015). In order to build such knowledge, it is important that measurement issues be considered when working with diverse groups (Competency 2, *Engage Diversity and Difference in Practice*). Researchers who are culturally competent use measurements that have been shown to be reliable and valid for the population they are studying.

To ensure that the interpretation of the measure is the same across different ethnocultural populations, social workers need to be concerned about establishing measurement equivalence. **Measurement equivalence** focuses on establishing equivalence by examining how items function across groups. There are three types of measurement equivalence that must be assessed in order to interpret the meaning of a measure across groups: linguistic, conceptual, and metric.

In 2008, Unger et al., researchers from five continents, met to discuss how to measure community resilience. Some of the questions they wanted to answer were: "How do different cultures around the world define successful, healthy communities?" and "Can we develop a single measure of community resilience?" The first challenge the group had was how this very basic question—"What makes a community resilient?"—could be asked in a way that has the same meaning in different languages. These are translations of the English sentence (see Box 5.1). The question is whether these literal translations have the same meaning across the three cultural groups. In other words, the researchers were concerned with ensuring that the question has linguistic equivalence. **Linguistic equivalence** is the extent to which a measure is compatible with the language and culture to which it will be adapted.

## Linguistic Equivalence

What makes a community resilient?

¿Qué hace que un elástico de la comunidad? (Spanish)

Hvad gør et samfund Elastisk? (Danish)

Mit tesz egy rugalmas közösség? (Hungarian)

**Conceptual equivalence** is the extent to which the concepts represented by the items making up the measure are understood to have the same meaning across cultural groups. This assumes that equivalent terms have been used. Does "community" mean the same thing conceptually across the groups? For example, in cultures that have high use of social network sites such as Facebook, community is not conceptualized merely as a physical space but as a virtual space as well. This would not be true in cultures with limited Internet access.

Once there is both linguistic and conceptual equivalence of the question, the next step is to make sure that the response categories have the same meaning across groups. **Metric equivalence** refers to equivalence in item or question difficulty across groups. A measure has metric equivalence, for example, when individuals from different communities, with the same perception of support, select the same response category. One should not assume that a measure developed for one cultural group can be used with a different cultural group. When using a measure outside of the cultural group that participated in the original development and validation of the measure, the researcher should check whether studies of measurement equivalence have been conducted using members of the particular group under investigation (Competency 2, *Engage in Diversity and Difference*). Without measurement equivalence, interpretation of the measure may not be reliable or valid for the group. This could lead to inaccurate conclusions of the study's findings. The use of culturally appropriate measures is a human right. It is also a way of promoting social justice (Competency 3, *Advance Human Rights and Social, Economic, and Environmental Justice*). Research is often used to inform and evaluate social policies. When the findings of research are biased due to measures that are not valid or reliable for a particular group, that group could be adversely affected. The need for measurement equivalence applies not only across cultural groups but also for other demographics of the population, such as age, gender, sexual orientation, and so on. Prior to conducting studies with diverse groups, one should seek consultation about the how to measure the concept of interest and what measure would be appropriate to use. By doing this, social work researchers demonstrate their "understanding of methods of assessment with diverse groups and constituents to advance practice effectiveness" (CSWE, 2015, p. 9; Competency 7, *Assess, Individuals, Families, Groups, Organizations, and Communities*) and demonstrate ethical and professional behavior (Competency 1, *Demonstrate Ethical and Professional Behavior*).

---

### Critical Thinking Question 5.5

During your weekly supervision, Maggie informs you that she has seen an increase in the number of African American clients. She states that she is thinking about using the Beck Depression Inventory-II, which has excellent internal reliability and predictive validity, to determine if they are depressed. Do you have any concerns about her use of this measure with this population? Justify your response. (Hint: Before you answer this question, we suggest you consult the literature.)

# SUMMARY, REVIEW, AND ASSIGNMENTS

## CHAPTER SUMMARY ORGANIZED BY LEARNING OBJECTIVES

**LO 5.1** Distinguish between the conceptual and operational definition of a variable.

*Conceptual definition* "is the working definition a researcher uses for a concept" (Wolfer, 2007, p. 127).

*Operational definition* is the process of defining the exact way you plan to measure the concept.

**LO 5.2** Differentiate between the various levels of measurement.

There are four levels of measurement: *nominal* (categorical variable), *ordinal* (numeric value assigned to the response categories can be logically ranked but the intervals between the categories may not be equal), *interval* (numeric value assigned to the response categories can be logically ranked, intervals between the categories are equal, and zero-value is not absolute), and *ratio* (numeric value assigned to the response categories can be logically ranked, intervals between the categories are equal, and zero-value is absolute).

**LO 5.3** Distinguish between the different sources of measurement error.

There are two sources of measurement error one needs to be concern about: *systematic* (occurs when there is a pattern to the error) and *random* (occurs when there is no consistent pattern of measurement error).

**LO 5.4** Distinguish between the various types of reliability and validity.

*Reliability* is the degree to which a measure is consistent or dependable. There are several types of reliability— inter-rater, inter-observer, test-retest, split-half, and internal consistency.

*Validity* is the degree to which the measure actually measures what it was designed to measure. There are several types of validity—face, criterion, concurrent, known groups, predictive, construct, convergent, and divergent.

**LO 5.5** Select a standardized measure to assess a client's presenting problem.

Both reliability and validity are the criteria for selecting standardized measures.

**LO 5.6** Develop a measure.

When developing a measure, you need to determine (1) the type of measure you want to develop, (2) the types of questions that will be asked, (3) the wording of the questions, and (4) the scaling format for the response options.

**LO 5.7** Identify the ethical and diversity issues associated with measurement.

To be ethically responsive to their clients, social workers must (1) whenever possible, use measures that are reliable and valid for the population they serve; (2) obtain informed consent prior to conducting an assessment; and

(3) use the most up-to-date version of the assessment tool.

Researchers who are culturally competent use measurements that are reliable and valid for the population they are studying.

There are three types of measurement equivalence that must be assessed in order to interpret the meaning of a measure across groups: *linguistic* (the extent to which a measure is compatible with the language and culture to which it will be adapted), *conceptual* (the extent to which the concepts represented in the items making up the measure are understood to have the same meaning across cultural groups), and *metric* (equivalence in item or question difficulty across groups).

## KEY TERMS

## COMPETENCY NOTES

In this chapter, you were introduced to the competencies below:

> Competency 1, *Demonstrate Ethical and Professional Behavior*. Social workers are

ethically responsible to their clients as it relates to assessment. Social workers demonstrate ethical and professional behavior when they seek consultation about how to measure concepts of interest and what measure would be appropriate to use when working with diverse groups.

Competency 2, *Engage in Diversity and Difference.* Social workers should consider issues of measurement when selecting measures to assess the concerns of clients from diverse groups. Social workers must select measures that are reliable and valid for the populations they serve.

Competency 3, *Advance Human Rights and Social, Economic, and Environmental Justice.* Social workers should use culturally appropriate measures as this is a human right and is a way of promoting social justice.

Competency 4, *Engage in Practice-Informed Research and Research-Informed Practice.* Social workers know the principles of culturally informed approaches to building knowledge.

Competency 7, *Assess Individuals, Families, Groups, Organizations, and Communities.* Social workers understand the methods of assessment and the criteria used to select measures to do such assessment. Social workers demonstrate their understanding of the methods of assessment when they seek consultation about how to measure concepts of interest and what measure would be appropriate to use when working with diverse groups.

Competency 9, *Evaluate Practice With Individuals, Families, Groups, Organizations, and Communities.* Social workers recognize that selecting measurement tools for the purpose of assessment has implications for the improvement of practice effectiveness at the micro, mezzo, and macro levels.

## ASSESSMENT QUESTIONS

1. How did the information in this chapter enhance your knowledge about the various types of reliability and validity?

2. In what ways did the information in this chapter enhance your knowledge about developing a measure?

3. What specific content discussed in this chapter is still unclear to you? If there is still content that is unclear, schedule an appointment with your instructor to gain more clarity.

## END-OF-CHAPTER EXERCISES

1. Find a peer-reviewed journal article and answer the following questions: (a) Does the author provide information related to the reliability and validity of the measure?; (b) If so, what type of reliability and validity were established?; (c) Was the reliability and validity established for the population under study?; and (d) If not, what are some of your concerns about the use of this measure in this particular study?

2. Using the same article as you did for Question #1, please identify how all the variables were operationalized.

3. Using the same article as you did for Questions #1 and #2, please identify the level of measurement for each variable.

# ADDITIONAL READINGS

Casado, B. L., Negi, N. J., & Hong, M. (2012). Culturally competent social work research: Methodological considerations for research with language minorities. *Social Work*, 57(1), 1–10. doi:10.1093/sw/swr002

Evans, S., Greenhalgh, J., & Connelly, J. (2000). Selecting a mental health needs assessment scale: Guidance on the critical appraisal of standardized measures. *Journal of Evaluation in Clinical Practice, 6*(4) 379–393.

Harford, T. C. (1993). The measurement of alcohol-related accidents. *Addiction, 88*(7), 907–912.

Niederhauser, V. P., & Mattheus, D. (2010). The anatomy of survey questions. *Journal of Pediatric Health Care, 24*(5) 351–354. doi:10.1016/j.pedhc.2010.04.013

Prakash, S., Pratap, S., & Sood, M. (2016). A study on phenomenology of Dhat syndrome in men in a general medical setting. *Indian Journal of Psychiatry, 58*(2) 129–141. doi:10.4103/0019-5545.183776

Tran, T. V., Dung, N., & Conway, K. (2003). A cross-cultural measure of depressive/symptoms among Vietnamese. *Social Work Research, 27*(1), 56–64. 10.1093/swr/27.1.56

## ⑤SAGE edge™

Get the tools you need to sharpen your study skills. SAGE Edge offers a robust online environment featuring an impressive array of free tools and resources.

Access practice quizzes at **edge.sagepub.com/farmer**

# Learning Objectives

**6.1** Identify the ways in which experimental designs can be used.

**6.2** Differentiate between the various types of pre-experimental and experimental designs.

**6.3** Identify the ethical and diversity issues associated with experimental designs.

| Competencies Covered | Learning Objectives | Dimension |
|---|---|---|
| Competency 1<br>*Demonstrate Ethical and Professional Behavior* | 6.3 Identify the ethical issues associated with experimental designs. | Skills |
| Competency 2<br>*Engage Diversity and Difference in Practice* | 6.3 Identify the diversity issues associated with experimental designs. | Skills |
| Competency 4<br>*Engage in Practice-Informed Research and Research-Informed Practice* | 6.1 Identify the ways in which experimental designs can be used.<br>6.2 Differentiate between the various types of pre-experimental and experimental designs. | Skills |
| Competency 9<br>*Evaluate Practice With Individuals, Families, Groups, Organizations, and Communities* | 6.1 Identify the ways in which experimental designs can be used.<br>6.2 Differentiate between the various types of pre-experimental and experimental designs. | Skills |

Master the content at
**edge.sagepub.com/farmer**

## Is This Parenting Program Effective for Adolescent Fathers?

By responding to the questions related to this case example, you will be able to identify what type of pre-experimental or experimental design is appropriate for evaluative research purposes, and you will be able to support your choice by critically analyzing the strengths and weaknesses of the pre-experimental and experimental designs described in this chapter.

Mary, Chris, Tamela, and Juan work in a community-based agency. The agency's mission is to provide services to all persons regardless of their ethnic/racial background, socioeconomic status, sexual orientation, or religious beliefs. Such services are age and culturally appropriate and are delivered by competent social service providers.

In recent months, the social service providers and clients have been asking about providing services for adolescent fathers. Mary, the director of the agency, has noticed an increase in the number of families being served at her agency where there is an adolescent father in the household.

Mary convened a meeting with Chris, Tamela, and Juan and told them she is interested in developing a parenting program for these adolescent fathers and she wants to evaluate its effectiveness.

You are doing your field placement at this agency. Mary has asked you along with Chris, Tamela, and Juan to develop the parenting program and evaluate its effectiveness.

At this point, take a few minutes to think about the case example and do the following:

1. Identify the problem.

2. Determine what you already know about the problem.

3. Determine what information you need to solve the problem.

4. List the questions needed to be answered related to the information you need to solve the problem.

Please write down your responses to each item. You will need to refer to them while reading this chapter.

Mary is interested in developing a parenting program for these adolescent fathers and she wants to evaluate its effectiveness. Many of these fathers have less than a high school education, and if they are employed, they are working at jobs that only pay them minimum wage. Many have children 2 to 5 years of age. Although these children do not live with their fathers, many have the children in their care two or three times a week.

At the close of Mary's initial meeting with her staff, she provided them with articles to read to determine what preexisting parenting programs have been used with this population. She told her staff that no matter what program they choose to implement, it is important that they think about how to demonstrate its effectiveness. Furthermore, she stated, according to the mothers and fathers of these adolescent fathers, the young fathers do not know what their children should be doing at specific developmental time periods of their lives, they do not spend quality time with their children, and they do not engage in appropriate play with their children. Mary states that given the concerns of their parents, it is important to find a parenting intervention that will enhance the fathers' knowledge of child development, their quality time with their children, and their ability to engage in appropriate play.

## Introduction

In this chapter, you will learn about the different types of experimental designs. Ethical and diversity issues are discussed. The threats to internal and external validity are covered.

## Experimental Research Designs Defined

An **experimental design** is a research design where the researcher manipulates an independent (causal) variable and observes changes in the dependent (outcome) variable, as a result of the manipulation of the independent variable. In other words, the **independent variable** explains or causes the change in the dependent variable. The notation used to represent the independent variable is an X. Conversely, the variable being explained or caused is the **dependent variable**. The notation used to represent the dependent variable is a Y. As for experimental designs, the independent variable is the intervention and the dependent variable is the variable the intervention is targeting. In referring to the case example, the independent variable would be the parenting program and the dependent variables are fathers' knowledge of child development, quality time with their children, and ability to engage in appropriate play. Manipulation is accomplished via randomly assigning the participants to the experimental or control group. **Random assignment** is a way of assigning persons to different groups in an experimental study, ensuring that persons have an equal chance of being in the experimental or control group. It is done, for example, by flipping a coin and assigning persons to be in the experimental or control group. Random assignment ensures that the groups are the same at the outset of the experiment; therefore, any changes in the groups can be attributed to the intervention received. Referring to the case example, Mary indicated that she was interested in determining the effectiveness of the parenting program for the adolescent fathers. To determine if the parenting program is more effective than the standard intervention the agency offers its clients, Mary would randomly assign fathers to the parenting program and the standard intervention.

Experimental designs are useful for evaluating the effectiveness of social work interventions with individuals, families, groups, organizations, communities, and policies. Competency 9, *Evaluate Practice With Individuals, Families, Groups, Organizations, and Communities*, emphasizes the importance of social workers "evaluating process and outcomes to advance practice, policy, and service delivery effectiveness" (CSWE, 2015, p. 9). Moreover, experimental designs are useful for advancing a science of social work. Competency 4, *Engage in Practice-Informed Research and Research-Informed Practice*, states that "social workers understand quantitative . . . research methods and their respective roles in advancing a science of social work" (CSWE, 2015, p. 8). Additionally, experimental designs are useful for informing practice because they establish causality (Competency 4, *Engage in Practice-Informed Research and Research-Informed Practice*). **Causality** is the relationship between cause and effect. Causality is established by ensuring that three conditions have been met. The first condition needed to establish causality is *the cause must precede the outcome in time*. This condition makes both logical and conceptual sense. Take, for example, a social worker who is interested in developing an intervention that will alleviate depression symptoms in African American males who have been exposed to gang violence. She researches the literature to determine what intervention is the most effective to treat depression. She finds out that cognitive behavioral interventions have been identified to be the most effective intervention to treat depression. She solicits African American males between 15 and 18 years of age to participate in her study. Prior to the intervention, she has the participants sign a consent form and administers the Beck Depression Inventory-II (BDI-II; Beck, Steer, & Brown, 1996) to assess the adolescents' depression. Once they completed the consent form and the BDI-II, she tells them that she will see them in two weeks, as this is when the intervention will start. The day of the intervention she again asked them to complete the BDI-II. In comparing the results of this administration of the BDI-II with the ones obtained two weeks earlier, she notices that all the adolescents experienced a 5-point decrease in their depression scores. Knowing that each of the adolescents experienced a 5-point decrease in their depression scores prior to receiving the intervention, it should be quite obvious that the social worker cannot claim that the changes in their depression scores can be attributed to the intervention, because the adolescents never received the intervention. Therefore, the first condition to establish causality has not been met, as the cause (in this case, the intervention) did not precede the outcome (in this case, the decrease in depression scores), because the adolescents never received the intervention. Given that the adolescents never received the intervention, the social worker must attribute the decrease in their depression scores to some other variable, which is oftentimes referred to as an extraneous variable. **Extraneous variables** are ones in which the researcher did not include in the study that have an effect on the relationship between the independent and dependent variable. The notation for representing an extraneous variable is a Z. Extraneous variables are sometimes referred to as confounding variables (or spurious or lurking variables). In thinking about the case example, Mary is interested in evaluating the effectiveness of a parenting program on fathers' knowledge of child development, quality time with their children, and ability to engage in appropriate play. One possible extraneous variable that might affect her ability to say that the intervention resulted in changes in the fathers' knowledge and behavior is the fathers' concurrent involvement in another parenting program. Because of this, Mary cannot determine if her program resulted in the changes.

The second condition needed to the establish causality is that the *independent variable and the dependent variable must be empirically correlated*. To determine if the independent variable (the intervention) is associated with the dependent variable (the outcome), one must collect data on the outcome variable prior to the intervention being implemented and after the intervention has been implemented. Collecting the data prior to the intervention is often considered as conducting a **pretest**, and collecting the data after the intervention has been implemented is often considered as conducting a **posttest**. Comparing the pretest data with the posttest data and seeing a change in the data from pretest to posttest is indicative of there being an empirical correlation between the two variables. The change in the data from pretest to posttest is attributed to the intervention. In the example, the second condition would have been met if the intervention would have been implemented and then the social worker saw a 5-point decrease in each adolescent's depression score.

The third condition needed to establish causality is *the relationship between the independent variable and the dependent variable cannot be attributed to another variable that explains away the relationship between these two variables*. Let us say the social worker, in the example, was able to deliver the intervention and in comparing the pretest data with the posttest data, she noticed that all of the adolescents' depression scores have decreased after receiving the intervention. During the exit interview, 10 adolescents admitted that besides seeing her for treatment, they were also seeing another therapist for their depression symptoms. Upon hearing this, the social worker no longer believes that she can attribute the decrease in these adolescents' depression scores to the intervention that she provided. Hence, the third condition to establish causality has not been met, as the decrease in the 10 adolescents' depression scores could have been due to having two interventions and not merely the intervention delivered by the social worker in the example. Because the social worker cannot conclude that her intervention resulted in the decrease in the depression scores for these 10 adolescents, the decrease in the depression scores must be attributed to an extraneous (spurious or lurking) variable. In this case, it was the treatment for depression by another therapist.

To summarize, in order to establish causality these are the only criteria that need to be satisfied: (1) *the cause must precede the outcome in time*, (2) *independent variable and the dependent variable must be empirically correlated*, and

(3) *the relationship between the independent variable and the dependent variable cannot be attributed to another variable that explains away the relationship between these two variables.*

## Types of Experimental Research Designs

There are three types of experimental designs: pre-experimental designs, true experimental designs, and quasi-experimental designs. Quasi-experimental designs will be discussed in the next chapter; single-case designs, which is type of quasi-experimental design, will be discussed in Chapter 15. The reason for this is that social workers are often encouraged to use single-case designs to evaluate their practice.

### Pre-Experimental Designs

A **pre-experimental design** is a research design where the researcher manipulates an independent (causal) variable and observes changes in the dependent (outcome) variable, as a result of the manipulation of the independent variable; however, the researcher does not randomly assign persons to an experimental group and there is not a control group. It should be noted there are times that the researcher will not be the one manipulating the independent variable (causal) variable, but someone else will be responsible for doing this. Take, for example, a school teacher uses a specialized reading program with one group of students to enhance their reading skills, but for another group of students the teacher does not use the specialized reading program. The teacher wants you to determine if the reading skills of the students who received the specialized reading program improved. In the above example, the teacher manipulated the independent variable, but she did not randomly assign the students to the groups; therefore, she is using a pre-experimental design. There are three types of pre-experimental designs: one-shot case study (one-group posttest-only design), one-group pretest-posttest design, and the posttest-only design with nonequivalent groups (static-group comparison design). A pretest is a measurement of the dependent variable prior to the manipulation of the independent variable, while a posttest is a measurement of the dependent variable after the manipulation of the independent variable. Each of these pre-experimental designs will be described later in this section.

*Purpose.* Pre-experimental designs are well-suited for exploratory research. You may recall that in Chapter 3 we stated that the aim of an exploratory study is to provide the researcher with insight about the phenomenon under investigation. Pre-experimental designs are well-suited for exploratory studies, as they allow the researcher to examine the relationship between the independent variable and the dependent variable, a necessary condition for establishing causality. These designs allow persons to merely infer causality but not establish causality because they do not meet all three conditions to establish causality, which were described earlier in this chapter. As mentioned earlier, these designs lack randomization of the participants to either the experimental or control group. Randomization is one of the three conditions used to establish causality. The results of an exploratory study can be used to lay the groundwork for an explanatory study. As you may recall, explanatory studies are used to determine the causal relationships between variables.

*Research Questions.* Pre-experimental designs can be used when researchers propose research questions that examine the association between the independent and dependent variables. These questions allow you to establish temporal order because you as the researcher can ensure that the independent (causal) variable comes before the dependent (outcome) variable, due to your control over the timing of the intervention or timing of observation of the dependent variable. Appropriate questions for a study using a pre-experimental design would be as follows: Is there an association between being exposed to an intervention for posttraumatic stress disorder and a decrease in posttraumatic stress symptoms? Will persons who receive a mindfulness intervention report a decrease in their symptoms?

*Hypothesis.* Given that the research question for pre-experimental designs focuses on the association between the independent (causal) variable and dependent (outcome) variable, the hypothesis must do the same. An example of a hypothesis that states the association between the independent and dependent variable would be as follows: Persons who received a mindfulness intervention will report a decrease in their symptoms.

A hypothesis that states that there is no relationship (a non-directional hypothesis) between receiving the intervention and depression scores would not be appropriate for a pre-experimental design, as a pre-experimental design helps researchers see if there is association between the independent (causal) variable and the dependent (outcome) variable. A hypothesis that indicates there is no relationship between the variables means there is not an association between the independent (causal) variable and the dependent (outcome) variable. An example of a non-directional hypothesis would be as follows: Persons who receive a mindfulness intervention will report symptoms of depression that are different from those who did not receive the intervention. In reading the above hypothesis, one cannot tell if the persons who received the mindfulness intervention are expected to have higher or lower depression than those who did not receive the intervention.

There will be some instances where one will not have a hypothesis when using a pre-experimental design. One will not need to have a hypothesis when one is using a pre-experimental design for exploratory research purposes.

*Sampling Strategy.* The research participants in a study using a pre-experimental design are usually selected via a purposeful sampling or convenience sampling strategy. A purposeful sampling strategy is used to select persons to participate in the study based on one's knowledge of the population. Let us say you are interested in knowing if a particular intervention will help children who are experiencing depression as a result of one of their parents being deployed. There does not exist a list that has the names of every child in the United States whose parent is deployed; therefore, you may need to select the children to participate in the study by posting fliers in social service agencies. Convenience sampling entails selecting participants who you readily have access to, such as students in a classroom or clients in an agency where you are employed.

*Data Analysis Strategy.* Data from pre-experimental designs are analyzed using descriptive statistics, such as frequencies, as well as inferential statistics such as z-tests or t-tests. The type of z-test or t-test one employs is dependent upon the design of the study and the level of measurement of the independent and dependent variables. The z-test is appropriate when the independent variable is nominal (e.g., group, experimental, control) and the dependent variable is nominal (e.g., success, failure, or reduction in depression scores or no reduction in depression score). The z-test focuses on assessing the difference between the proportion for the groups. For example, the z-test would be appropriate for assessing the difference between those participants who received a reduction in their depression score by 3 points in the experimental group versus those in the control group. The z-test is preferable if the sample size is greater than 30. The t-test is appropriate when the independent variable is nominal (e.g., group, experimental, control) and the dependent variable is interval or ratio (or a scale). The t-test focuses on assessing the difference between the means for the groups. The t-test is preferable if the sample size is less than 30. The appropriate z-test or t-test for each pre-experimental design will be discussed later in this chapter.

## Critical Thinking Question 6.1

Mary, the director of the agency, convenes a meeting with you, Chris, Tamela, and Juan to discuss the purpose of the study, the research question(s), and the hypothesis. During the meeting, Tamela suggests that a pre-experimental research design be used. What do you think is the purpose of the study Mary is proposing? What should be the research question(s) and hypothesis? Will a pre-experimental design, as Tamela suggested, allow Mary to determine the effectiveness of the parenting program? Justify your response.

## Types of Pre-Experimental Designs

### One-Shot Case Study (One-Group Posttest-Only Design)

A **one-shot case study (one-group posttest-only design)** is a research design where there is only one group, one intervention, and no pretest (only a posttest). In other words, in this research design, the researcher manipulates an independent (causal) variable and observes changes in the dependent (outcome) variable, as a result of the manipulation of the independent variable only for one group. The researcher measures the dependent (outcome) variable after the intervention has been implemented (posttest-only). This type of design does not allow one to study the association between the independent and dependent variables because there is no variation in the independent variable. This is the weakest type of pre-experimental design. The standard notation for this design, based on the work of Campbell and Stanley (1963), is as follows:

$$X \quad O_1$$

The X stands for the intervention and O stands for measures of the observation. The observation refers to the measurement of the dependent variable.

Without there being an assessment of the dependent variable prior to the implementation of the intervention, there is no pretest data for comparison with the posttest data. Therefore, one cannot conclude that the intervention led to changes in the outcome. Although one cannot conclude that the intervention led to changes in the outcome, one can compare the scores on the outcome variable with the cut-off score for the measure used to assess the outcome variable as a way of determining where the participants are in comparison. A **cut-off score** is a score that is used to indicate if someone's score puts them in a certain category. Let us say you are interested in seeing if persons who received treatment for depression responded to the treatment received. You used the Beck Depression Inventory-II (BDI-II) to assess their depression. To determine if the participants responded to the treatment, you would compare their scores to the BDI-II cut-off scores, which are as follows: 0–13 minimal depression, 14–19 mild depression, 20–28 moderate depression, and 29–63 severe depression. If, for example, one of the participants had a score of 40, you would infer that he or she did not respond to the treatment, because he or she is still severely depressed according to the cut-off scores. In a one-shot case study (one-group posttest-only design) persons are not randomly assigned to the group; therefore, extraneous variables are not controlled. Because this design does not control for extraneous variables, which are those variables, other than the intervention, that could have contributed to the outcome, this design is considered to have weak internal validity. **Internal validity** refers to a researcher's ability to conclude that the change in the dependent variable is definitely attributed to the manipulation of the independent variable. This design fails to control for many of the threats to internal validity.

1. **History:** History refers to an extraneous event coinciding with the time the participants receive the intervention, which results in the outcome.

2. **Maturation:** Maturation refers to the biological or psychological processes associated with the individual that changes with the passage of time. Unlike history, maturation is reflective of events that are internal to the participants. If there is a long lapse in time between the participants receiving the intervention and the assessment of the dependent variable in which changes to the participants, such as they got older, become less or more depressed, or bored, then maturation might account for the outcome score.

3. **Mortality:** Mortality refers to attrition. This threat occurs if there is a lapse in time between the intervention and assessment of the dependent variable. In other words, participants may have dropped out of the group prior to the assessment of the outcome.

According to Campbell and Stanley (1963), this design is of no scientific value. Despite this design not meeting two out of the three conditions to establish causality and having weak internal validity, this design helps researchers explore if the intervention is having or not having the intended effect.

Let us say you are a director of a social service agency delivering an online intervention to women suffering from depression. You believe that this intervention is helping these women. The women have been involved with the program for seven weeks. You decide to assess their depression level using the Center for Epidemiologic Studies Depression Scale (CES-D; Radloff, 1977). You administer the scale and you find out some of the women's depression scores fall within the normal range and some of the women's depression scores fall within the clinical depression range. You determine that these women's depression scores fell into the above ranges because you compared their scores to the cut-off scores for the CES-D. You conclude that you cannot determine if the intervention is effective or not because you did not assess the women's depression level prior to them receiving the intervention. You can, however, infer that some of the women are responding to the treatment, as their depression scores fall within the normal range.

**External validity** refers to the researcher's ability to generalize the study's results beyond those persons included in the study. This design is affected by **Interaction of selection and X**; a characteristic of the participant, such as motivation to change, may have resulted in the participant responding differently to the intervention. Hence, the results may not be generalizable beyond persons who were motivated.

The data from the one-shot case study (one-group posttest-only design) could be analyzed using the z-test or one-sample t-test. Either of these statistical procedures are appropriate because the dependent variable was only assessed once, and the independent variable is measured on a nominal level and the dependent variable is measured on an interval level.

> ### Critical Thinking Question 6.2
>
> Would using a one-shot case study (one-group posttest-only design) provide Mary and her staff with the information they need to determine the effectiveness of their proposed intervention? Justify your response.

## One-Group Pretest-Posttest Design

This design is referred to as a **one-group pretest-posttest design** because there is only one group, one intervention, and there is a pretest and posttest. This design allows one to examine the association between the independent variable and the dependent variable because the assessment of the dependent variable before and after the intervention has been done. The pretest and posttest scores are compared to determine if there is a change in the scores after the intervention. With this design, time order is also established. Time order is established by manipulating the independent (causal) variable and assessing the dependent (outcome) variable prior to the implementation of the intervention and again after the intervention has been implemented. The standard notation for this design, based on the work of Campbell and Stanley (1963), is as follows:

$$O_1 \ X \ O_2$$

The $O_1$ stands for assessment (pretest) of the dependent variable prior to the intervention and $O_2$ stands for assessment (posttest) of the dependent variable after the implementation of the intervention. Typically, in this type of design persons are not randomly assigned to the group; therefore, extraneous variables are not controlled. Moreover, this design is affected by the following threats to internal validity:

1. **History:** History is a threat to this design if a change between the pretesting and the posttesting can be attributed to some event that occurred at the same time the participant received the intervention.

2. **Maturation:** If there is a long lapse in time between the pretest and posttest in which changes to the participants, such as they got older, become less or more depressed, or bored, then maturation might account for the differences between the pretest and posttest.

3. **Testing:** Persons do well on the posttest because of taking the pretest.

4. **Instrumentation:** A change in the measure used to assess the dependent variable. For example, a researcher uses the BDI-II to assess depression at pretest but uses the CES-D to assess depression at posttest. The change in the depression scores cannot be attributed to the intervention but to the change in the measure used to assess depression.

5. **Statistical Regression to the Mean:** If participants were selected to receive the intervention based on having extreme low or high scores on the pretest, when comparing the pretest scores with the posttest scores, you find the participants perform better on average on the posttest than the pretest. These participants do better on average on the posttest "as an artifact of the elliptical shape of the scatter diagram for a positive relationship between the pretest and posttest scores" (Knapp, 2016, p. 469).

Furthermore, this design is affected by the following threats to external validity:

1. **Interaction of testing and X:** As a result of the pretesting, the participants may become sensitized to the treatment. Therefore, the results of the study are only generalizable to the pretested population.

2. **Interaction of selection and X:** This threat was defined under the section titled "One-shot case study (One-group posttest-only design)."

Given the limitation of this design, researchers, such as Glass (1965), Johnson (1986), and Marin, Marin, Perez-Stable, Otero-Sabogal, and Sabogal (1990), have suggested ways to improve it. Johnson suggests that persons be randomly assigned to the various times the dependent variable is measured. Marin et al. suggest that you collect the pretest data twice before the intervention is implemented. According to Marin and his colleagues, if the difference between the pretest and posttest is greater than the difference between the two pretests then one can conclude the intervention accounts for the findings. Marin and his colleagues are suggesting that a time series design will enhance one's ability to infer causality. The strengths and weaknesses of a time series design will be discussed in the next chapter. Although the above suggested strategies improve upon this design, they are not substitutes for having a control group and randomly assigning persons to the experimental or control groups.

The data from the one-group pretest-posttest design could be analyzed using a paired $z$-test or dependent samples $t$-test (sometimes referred to as a paired $t$-test), to account for correlation of measures from the same individuals. Either of these statistical procedures are appropriate because the dependent variable was assessed twice using the same research participants, and the independent variable is measured on a nominal level and the dependent variable is measured on an interval level.

Celik et al. (2014) examined how sending short text messages enhanced the knowledge and skills related to insulin injection of 221 patients. They used a single group pretest-posttest study design. Patients were asked to fill out the "Demographic and diabetes-related form" and the "Insulin injection technique and knowledge form," and their AC-1 level was assessed prior to the intervention being implemented. Over a six-month period, patients received 12 different text messages instructing them on the proper administration of insulin. Their insulin injection technique and AC-1 levels were assessed at 3 months, 6 months, and 12 months. The results indicated that the patients had increased knowledge and skills related to insulin injection technique, comparing baseline scores with scores at 3, 6, and 12 months. On the other hand, the scores at 12 months were not statistically significantly different from the 3 months and 6 months scores. As for the AC-1 levels, it was lower at 3, 6, and 12 months compared to the baseline score. Surprisingly, the AC-1 level at 12 months was higher than at 6 months, which was when the study ended. The researchers noted that they were not able to evaluate the efficacy of using text messages to enhance patients' knowledge and skills related to insulin injection because they did not have a control group in their study.

### Critical Thinking Question 6.3

Mary and her staff have decided that they would prefer to use a one-group pretest-posttest design for their study. Is this research design preferable to the one-group posttest they chose earlier? Justify your response.

## Posttest-Only Design With Nonequivalent Groups (Static-Group Comparison Design)

A **posttest-only design with nonequivalent groups (static-group comparison design)** is a research design where there are two groups (i.e., experimental and comparison), one intervention, and no pretest (only a posttest). In other words, in this research design, the researcher manipulates an independent (causal) variable and observes changes in the dependent (outcome) variable, as a result of the manipulation of the independent variable only for one group. The researcher measures the dependent (outcome) variable after the intervention has been implemented (posttest-only) for both groups. Furthermore, with this design, randomization is not used to determine who will be assigned to the comparison group and who will be assigned to the experimental group. This design is referred to as a static-group comparison because there is only one observation point. This design allows you to determine if there is an association between the independent (causal) variable and the dependent variable, by comparing the means of the two groups. If there is a difference in the means between the groups, one can say there is an association between the causal variable and the dependent variable. Moreover, this design does not allow one to conclude that the intervention was effective because there is not any pretest data collected from the experimental group or comparison group. Without any pretest data from any of the groups, you do not know if the groups are similar or different at the outset. In other words, any differences found may be due to the groups being different. Because the groups are different, they are referred to as nonequivalent groups. The standard notation for this design, based on the work of Campbell and Stanley (1963), is as follows:

$$X \qquad O_1$$

$$O_1$$

Typically, in this type of design, persons are not randomly assigned to the groups; therefore, extraneous variables are not controlled. Moreover, this design is affected by the following threats to internal validity:

1. **Selection Bias:** Selection bias occurs because you are comparing groups that are nonequivalent at the outset. In other words, the experimental and comparison groups could have been different on the dependent variable prior to the experimental group getting the intervention. Without pretest scores for both groups, one cannot determine if the groups were the same or different on the dependent variable prior to the experimental group receiving the intervention.

2. **Mortality:** Differences between the groups maybe due to the differential drop out of participants across the groups.

3. **Interaction of Selection and Maturation:** Changes in the experimental and comparison groups are occurring as a function of maturation and selection. The groups differ because of the developmental changes in the individuals within the groups.

Furthermore, this design is affected by the following threat to external validity: interaction of selection and X. This threat was defined under the section titled "One shot-case study (One-group posttest-only design)."

The data from the posttest-only design with nonequivalent groups (static-group comparison design) should be analyzed using the two-sample $z$-test or independent samples $t$-test. Either of these statistical procedures is appropriate because the dependent variable was assessed once using two different samples, and the independent variable was measured on a nominal level and the dependent variable was measured on an interval level.

---

### Critical Thinking Question 6.4

Paul and Mary disagree about the appropriateness of the use of a posttest-only design with nonequivalent groups to assess the effectiveness of the parenting program. Paul believes strongly that this design is appropriate while Mary believes strongly that this design is not appropriate. What would you tell Paul to convince him that the use of his design is not appropriate? Justify your response.

---

In summary, pre-experimental designs cannot be used to establish causality and they lack internal validity. Because of this, pre-experimental designs are considered the weakest type of experimental designs. Pre-experimental designs are useful for pilot studies and when one does not have adequate resources to conduct an experimental design study. It should be noted that results from the pilot studies should be interpreted with caution. The results of the pre-experimental designs cannot be generalized to other samples or settings, due to the lack of randomization in research participants' selection or assignment. Pre-experimental designs can be used for exploratory research purposes, which allows you as a social worker to make use of the available data in your agency to engage in practice-based research (Epstein, 1996). Despite the limitations of pre-experimental designs, within the context of social work practice, these designs may be the only designs that you can use because you may not have access to clients who can be in a control group. Table 6.1 provides an overview of the purpose of each pre-experimental design, the research question that can be addressed using each design, and the analysis that can be used to analyze the data from each design.

## Types of Experimental Designs

An **experimental design** is a research design where the researcher manipulates an independent (causal) variable and observes changes in the dependent (outcome) variable, as a result of the manipulation of the independent variable. Manipulation is accomplished via randomly assigning the participants to the experimental or control group. There are four types of experimental designs: pretest-posttest control group design, posttest-only control group design, Solomon four-group design, and alternative treatment design with pretest. Please note that we will not discuss the Solomon four-group design or the alternative treatment design with pretest in this chapter, as

Table 6.1 Pre-Experimental and Experimental Designs

| Designs | | Purpose | Research Question/Hypothesis | Analysis Strategies |
|---|---|---|---|---|
| **Pre-Experimental Designs** | | | | |
| One-shot case study (One-group posttest-only design) | Intervention   posttest<br>   X         $O_1$ | Pilot studies exploration of the association between the intervention and outcome | Is there an association between being exposed to an intervention for posttraumatic stress disorder and a decrease in posttraumatic stress symptoms? | One-sample $t$-test<br>$z$-test |
| One-group pretest-posttest design | Pretest intervention posttest<br>$O_1$        X          $O_2$ | To establish the temporary relationship between the intervention and outcome | Is exposure to an intervention associated with a *change* in the level of stress? | Paired sample $t$-test<br>Paired-sample $z$-test |
| Posttest-only design with nonequivalent groups (static-group comparison design) | Intervention   posttest<br>   X          $O_1$<br>              $O_2$ | To establish whether the manipulation of an individual's exposure to an intervention is related to an outcome | As a result of exposure to an intervention, is there a difference in the outcome? | Two-sample $z$-test<br>Independent samples $t$-test |
| **Experimental Designs** | | | | |
| Pretest-posttest control group design (random assignment) | Pretest intervention posttest<br>R  $O_1$     X     $O_2$<br>R  $O_1$           $O_2$ | To establish whether the manipulation of an individual's exposure to an intervention is related to an outcome when levels of the outcome variables before exposure to the intervention are controlled | As a result of exposure to an intervention, are there differences in the outcome when levels of the outcome prior to the intervention are controlled? | $2 \times 2$ repeated measures analysis of variance ($2 \times 2$ repeated ANOVA) |
| Posttest-only design with equivalent groups (random assignment) | Intervention posttest<br>R    X     $O_1$<br>R          $O_1$ | To establish whether the manipulation of an individual's exposure to an intervention is related to an outcome | As a result of exposure to an intervention, is there a difference in the outcome? | Two-sample $z$-test<br>Independent samples $t$-test |

they are rarely used in social work research. If you would like to read more about these designs, refer to Campbell and Stanley, 1963. These four designs are called experimental designs because randomization is used to assign participants to the experimental or control group. These designs allow one to determine causality.

*Purpose.* Experimental designs are well-suited for explanatory and evaluation research. Explanatory studies are used to determine the causal relationships between variables. In developing an experimental design study for the purposes of explanatory research, the researcher would have an independent variable that is manipulated. Manipulation is accomplished via randomly assigning the participants to the experimental or control group. Additionally, the researcher would collect both pretest and posttest data from both groups.

Experimental designs are also useful for evaluation research, especially when you are trying to determine the effectiveness of an intervention or policy. An example of an experimental design study for evaluation research would be where a social worker is interested in developing a study to determine the effectiveness of a cognitive behavioral intervention to alleviate the depressive symptoms of African American males exposed to gang violence. In order to determine the effectiveness of the proposed intervention, the social worker would randomly assign the men to the cognitive behavioral intervention or the standard intervention used in the agency. Additionally, the social worker would collect both pretest and posttest data from both groups.

*Research Question.* Experimental designs require that researchers propose research questions that will determine causality; therefore, the independent variable (the cause of the outcome) must be manipulated. Take, for example, a social worker is interested in determining if a mindfulness intervention can reduce the posttraumatic symptoms of veterans. His or her research question could be, "Does a mindfulness intervention reduce the posttraumatic symptoms of veterans?"; "Can mindfulness reduce posttraumatic symptoms of veterans?"; or "Is mindfulness effective in reducing posttraumatic symptoms of veterans?" To answer each of these questions would require that the social worker design a study where one group of the veterans receive the mindfulness intervention and the other group receive the standard treatment provided by the agency. Because the researcher has control over who does or does not receive the mindfulness intervention, the above questions are appropriate for an experimental design.

When you have a research question where the independent variable cannot be manipulated, then it is not one that can be answered by using an experimental design. Such questions would include "Are boys more likely to engage in violent behaviors than girls?," "Does having a college degree result in more opportunities to enhance one's buying power?," and "Is a permissive parenting style associated with more delinquent behavior?" You cannot decide a person's gender, if someone obtains a college degree or not, or if someone is raised by parents who use or do not use a permissive parenting style. Therefore, the above questions are not appropriate for an experimental design. Research questions that examine how a person's attributes contribute to an outcome are not good research questions to use with experimental designs.

*Hypothesis.* By their very nature, experimental designs require that a hypothesis be directional. A directional hypothesis predicts the direction of the relationship between the independent and dependent variables. An example of a directional hypothesis would be "African American males who received the cognitive behavioral intervention plus peer support will have lower anxiety and depression scores than those who received the cognitive behavioral intervention without peer support." A hypothesis that states there is no relationship (a nondirectional hypothesis) between receiving the intervention and depression scores would not be appropriate for an experimental design, because it is not congruent with the second condition to establish causality, which is the independent variable and the dependent variable must be empirically correlated. A hypothesis that indicates there is no relationship between the variables means that a causation cannot exist nor an association between the variables or correlation.

*Sampling Strategy.* Both purposeful and convenience sampling strategies are employed to select research participants. These sampling strategies were described earlier in the chapter.

*Data Analysis Strategy.* Data from experimental designs are analyzed using descriptive statistics, such as frequencies, as well as inferential statistics such as $z$-tests or $t$-tests. The type of $z$-test or $t$-test one employs is the two-sample $z$-test or independent samples $t$-test. Analysis of variance (ANOVA), or Analysis of covariance (ANCOVA) to statistically control for extraneous variables is also appropriate to use for analyzing data from experimental designs. The appropriate statistical procedure to analyze data for each experimental design will be discussed later in the chapter.

## Pretest-Posttest Control Group Design

This design is referred to as a **pretest-posttest control group design** because there are two groups (i.e., experimental and control), one intervention, and a pretest and a posttest. Individuals are randomly assigned to either the experimental or control group. The pretest and posttest scores for both groups are compared, and any differences between the groups can be attributed to the intervention. There should not be a change in the posttest scores for individuals in the control group, because they did not receive the intervention. The pretest-posttest control group design is also referred to as a classical experimental design, as it has all the elements necessary to establish causality. As stated earlier in this chapter, causality is established by ensuring that three conditions have been met. These three conditions are: *the cause must precede the outcome in time; the independent variable and the dependent variable must be empirically correlated (associated with); and the relationship between the independent variable and the dependent variable cannot be attributed to* *another variable that explains away the relationship between these two variables.* The pretest-posttest control group design satisfies the above criteria by using randomization and having an experimental and control group and pretest and posttest. According to Chambliss and Schutt (2006), this experimental design meets the three conditions by having the following:

1. Two comparison groups (in the simplest case, an experimental group and a control group), to establish association;

2. Variation in the independent variable before assessment of change in the dependent variable, to establish time order; and

3. Random assignment to the two (or more) comparison groups, to establish nonspuriousness (pp. 111–112).

To determine if the independent variable is associated with the dependent variable, the researcher needs to collect data from both the experimental and control groups after the experimental group has received the intervention. This data collection is normally referred to as the posttest. The data from both groups are compared, and any differences between the groups can be attributed to the intervention.

The time order is established by the manipulation of the independent variable. The researcher determines who gets the intervention and who does not. This determination is done prior to assessing the outcome of the experimental and control group.

Random assignment is done to assure that the relationship between the independent variable and the dependent variable cannot be attributed to another variable that explains away the relationship between these two variables. It is a way of assigning persons to different groups in an experimental study and ensures that persons have an equal chance of being in the experimental or control group. Random assignment ensures that the groups are the same at the outset of the experiment; therefore, any changes in the groups can be attributed to the intervention received. In other words, random assignment rules out that the explanation of the outcome was due to some personal characteristic of the participants in the experimental or control group.

The standard notation for this design, based on the work of Campbell and Stanley (1963), is as follows:

R $\quad\quad\quad\quad$ $O_1$ $\quad\quad\quad\quad$ X $\quad\quad\quad\quad$ $O_2$

R $\quad\quad\quad\quad$ $O_1$ $\quad\quad\quad\quad\quad\quad\quad\quad\quad\quad$ $O_2$

The R stands for random assignment of the research participants to the experimental or control group. The $O_1$ stands for the pretest and $O_2$ stands for posttest, while X represents the intervention.

The pretest-posttest control group design is one of the strongest designs to establish causality and is not affected by many of the threats to internal validity.

It potentially could be affected by testing. As stated earlier, testing is a result of persons doing well on the posttest because of taking the pretest.

A possible external validity threat to this design is interaction of testing and X. As a result of the pretesting, the participants may become sensitized to the treatment. Therefore, the results of the study are only generalizable to the pretested population.

Data from the pretest-posttest control group design could be analyzed using a 2 × 2 repeated measures ANOVA testing the pre-post difference as the within-group factor, and the group difference as the between-group factor, and the interaction effect of both factors.

---

### Critical Thinking Question 6.5

Would using an experimental pretest-posttest control group design provide Mary and her staff with the information they need to determine the effectiveness of their proposed intervention? Justify your response. Select one of the pre-experimental designs and identify why the experimental pretest-posttest control group design would be preferable than the design you selected. Justify your response.

---

## Posttest-Only Control Group

$$R \qquad\qquad X \qquad\qquad O_1$$
$$R \qquad\qquad\qquad\qquad O_1$$

This design is referred to as a **posttest control group design** because there are two groups (i.e., experimental and control), one intervention, and only a posttest. Individuals are randomly assigned to either the experimental or control group. The posttest control group design is appropriate to use if you think the pretesting may affect the posttest in some manner or if the pretesting cannot be done. The standard notation for this design, based on the work of Campbell and Stanley (1963), is as follows:

$$R \qquad\qquad X \qquad\qquad O$$
$$R \qquad\qquad\qquad\qquad O$$

Random assignment ensures that the groups are the same at the outset of the experiment; however, without a pretest, you cannot conclude that differences in the posttest scores are a result of the experimental group receiving the intervention, nor can you determine the amount of change in the dependent variable for both groups (Wolfer, 2007). One can only infer the differences in the posttest scores are due to the intervention.

The data from the posttest-only control group design could be analyzed using the two-sample $z$-test or independent samples $t$-test. Either of these statistical procedures are appropriate because the dependent variable was only assessed once, and the independent variable was measured on a nominal level and the dependent variable was measured on an interval level.

## Example of a Study With a Posttest-Only Control Group Design

Heyman and Gutheil (2010) used a posttest-only control group design to assess the effects of two educational interventions delivered in Spanish. These interventions were designed to influence attitudes toward end-of-life planning. Latino elders receiving in-home services were randomly assigned to one of three groups: Conversación A, Conversación B, and control group. Those in the Conversación A group received the standard information as those who received services from the agency, which was the New York State Health Care Proxy form and instructions in Spanish and English. Additionally, they engaged in a discussion in Spanish about end-of-life planning. The participants in the Conversación B group received the same information as those in Conversación A, and additionally received information about end-of-life-planning based on themes that emerged from focus groups conducted with Latino elders who were not part of this current study. The discussion of these themes was in Spanish. The participants in the control group received the standard information as those who received services from the agency, which was the proxy form and instructions in Spanish and English. The results indicated that participants who received either intervention had higher attitudes than those who were in the control group. On the other hand, participants in the Conversación A group had higher comfort scores than those in the control group. The researchers noted that their study was not a true experimental design and lacked pretest data. Hence, they can only infer that their results are attributed to the interventions.

In summary, experimental designs are used to establish causality. Causality is established by manipulating the independent (causal) variable; having a control group and an experimental group; and randomly assigning the participants to the control group or experimental group. Experimental designs are used for both explanatory and evaluative research purposes. Table 6.1 provides an overview of the purpose of each experimental design, the research question that can be addressed using each design, and the analysis that can be used to analyze the data from each design.

## Ethics and Experimental Designs

Competency 1, *Demonstrate Ethical and Professional Behavior*, emphasizes that "social workers understand frameworks of ethical decision-making and how to apply principles of critical thinking to those frameworks in practice, research and policy arenas" (CSWE, 2015, p. 7). Given the type of research social workers conduct typically involves human participants, it necessitates engaging in ethical decision-making at every stage of the research process. One ethical decision that needs to be made when conducting experimental research is related to determining if the participants in the comparison or control group will receive treatment. Having research participants in a comparison or control group where they are not receiving treatment is unethical. One way to ensure that individuals in the comparison or control group receive treatment would be for these individuals to receive the standard treatment normally provided to persons seeking treatment at the agency. Another way is to have persons in the comparison or control group be placed on a waiting list until the study is over and then offer these individuals the same treatment as those in the experimental group. This type of design is known as a **wait-list control design** or **wait-list comparison design**. Persons in the comparison or control group will receive treatment, but the treatment is delayed. A wait-list control design addresses the issue of not having individuals in the comparison or control group not receiving treatment; however, employing this design could cause harm because the treatment is delayed.

<hr>

## Application Checkpoint 6.2

How can Mary and her staff demonstrate ethical and professional behavior as it relates to evaluating the effectiveness of the parenting program for adolescent fathers?

<hr>

The principle of respect for persons, which was discussed in Chapter 2, asserts that individuals have a right to determine if they will or will not participate in research and when they will stop participating. Individuals may feel undue pressure to participate in research because of their status in society or the status of the researcher. For example, immigrants or refugees may feel undue pressure to participate in research because they fear if they do not participate, they may be deported. Being in a dual-role relationship, especially if you are both the researcher and therapist for the individuals, could put undue pressure on the individuals to participate. If you are in a dual role as both researcher and therapist, you must ensure that your clients know they have the right to refuse to participate in your research and their refusal will not result in the termination of the services provided by the agency. They should also have the right to seek treatment from another therapist in the agency if they feel that the dual relationship is causing them harm or distress. One safeguard that you may want to put in place as it relates to obtaining informed consent is to have someone else besides you ask the client for his or her consent to participate in the research (Hohmann-Marriott, 2001).

# Diversity and Experimental Designs

The practices of obtaining informed consent may need to be modified depending upon the cultural background of the research participant (Olsen, Wang, & Pang, 2010). In some cultures, individual decision-making is not the norm but family decision-making is common. Within this cultural context, it is important that the family members be involved in the informed consent process (Competency 2, *Engage Diversity and Difference in Practice*).

Competency 2, *Engage Diversity and Difference in Practice*, underscores the importance of social workers needing to "understand the forms and mechanisms of oppression and discrimination and recognize the extent to which a culture's structures and values, including social, economic, political, and cultural exclusions, may oppress, marginalize, alienate, or create privilege and power" (CSWE, 2015, p. 7). The conducting of experimental research can lead to oppression, abuse of power, marginalization, and alienation if safeguards are not put into place in order to keep the above-mentioned things from occurring. Obtaining informed consent is the way we prevent oppression, abuse of power, marginalization, and alienation from occurring when we conduct experimental research. Therefore, as social workers we need to understand if we conduct research without getting informed consent from the study's participants or if we do not keep the data collected confidential we may cause the research participants to experience oppression or discrimination.

If the participant's primary language is not English, one may need to translate the consent forms into the language spoken by the participant. Many researchers use the Brislin method of forward and back translation to translate the consent form (Hanrahan et al., 2015). On the surface, translating the consent form into the language spoken by the participants seems easy; however, as a researcher you need to take into consideration if you are going to do a word-for-word translation or use colloquial speech. You also need to keep in mind that there may be some words in the English language that may not be in the participant's language.

Getting a participant's written consent may be inappropriate in a culture when there are low levels of education and literacy (Hanrahan et al., 2015). Therefore, the researcher may want to obtain oral consent from the participant or employ a third party. The third party may serve as a witness to the reading of the consent form to the participant and verifies that the participant understood what was read to him or her or the third party may actually read the consent form to the participant, given that he or she speaks the language of the participant.

Empirical evidence indicates that culturally adapted interventions are effective in improving health and mental health outcomes (Barrera, Castro, Strycker, & Toobert, 2013). Culturally adapted interventions are those evidence-based interventions that have been systematically modified to fit the needs of a cultural group (Hall, 2001). Modifications to the interventions are based on the cultural group's values, beliefs, and behaviors (Bernal, Jimenez-Chafey, & Domenech Rodriguez, 2009). Culturally adapted interventions have positive effects on a client's engagement and retention (Smith, Domenech Rodriguez, & Bernal, 2010). When working with a particular cultural group, you may want to use a culturally adapted intervention as the independent variable when conducting experimental research.

---

**Critical Thinking Question 6.6**

Mary, the director of the agency, convenes a meeting with you, Chris, Tamela, and Juan to discuss the research design. What type of research design would you recommend Mary and her staff use to assess the effectiveness of the parenting program for adolescent fathers? What threats to internal or external validity are associated with the research design selected? What ethical issues should Mary and her staff consider? Justify your response.

---

# SUMMARY, REVIEW, AND ASSIGNMENTS

# CHAPTER SUMMARY ORGANIZED BY LEARNING OBJECTIVES

**LO 6.1** Identify the ways in which experimental designs can be used.

Experimental designs are useful for informing practice because they establish causality.

Experimental designs are useful for advancing a science of social work.

Experimental designs are useful because they allow social workers to evaluate practice with individuals, families, groups, organizations, communities, and policies.

**LO 6.2** Differentiate between the various types of pre-experimental and experimental designs.

Pre-Experimental Designs

A *one-shot case study (one-group posttest-only design)* is a research design where there is only one group, one

intervention, and no pretest (only a posttest).

A *one-group pretest-posttest design* is a research design where there is only one group, one intervention, and a pretest and posttest.

A *posttest-only design with nonequivalent groups (static-group comparison design)* is a research design where there are two groups (i.e., experimental and comparison), one intervention, and no pretest (only a posttest). This design is referred to as a static-group comparison because there is only one observation point.

Experimental Designs

A *pretest-posttest control group design* is a research design where there are two groups (i.e., experimental and control), one intervention, and a pretest and a posttest. Individuals are randomly assigned to either the experimental or control group.

A *posttest control group design* is a research design where there are two groups (i.e., experimental and control), one intervention, and only a posttest. Individuals are randomly assigned to either the experimental or control group.

LO 6.3 Identify the ethical and diversity issues associated with experimental designs.

One ethical decision that needs to be made when conducting experimental research is related to determining if the participants in the comparison or control group will receive treatment. Having research participants in a comparison or control group where they are not receiving treatment is unethical.

Obtaining informed consent is the way we prevent oppression, abuse of power, marginalization, and alienation from occurring when we conduct experimental research.

Individuals have a right to determine if they will or will not participate in research and when they will stop participating.

If you are in a dual role as both researcher and therapist, you must ensure that your clients know they have the right to refuse to participate in your research and their refusal will not result in the termination of the services provided by your agency.

If you are in a dual role as both researcher and therapist, you may want to get someone besides yourself to obtain the client's consent to participate in your research.

The practices of obtaining informed consent may need to be modified depending upon the cultural background of the research participant.

Getting a participant's written consent may be inappropriate in a culture when there are low levels of education and literacy. Therefore, the researcher may want to obtain oral consent from the participant or employ a third party.

Whenever possible, select culturally adapted interventions.

## KEY TERMS

## COMPETENCY NOTES

In this chapter, you were introduced to the competencies below:

Competency 1, *Demonstrate Ethical and Professional Behavior.* Social workers will be involved in ethical decision-making at every stage of the research process.

Competency 2, *Engage Diversity and Difference in Practice.* Social workers must take into consideration culture when selecting an intervention. Moreover, social workers should be aware of how a participant's culture may play a role in the obtaining of informed consent.

Competency 4, *Engage in Practice-Informed Research and Research-Informed Practice.* Social workers can advance a science of social work by using experimental designs, which will inform practice.

Competency 9, *Evaluate Practice With Individuals, Families, Groups, Organizations, and Communities.* Social workers should use pre-experimental and experimental designs to evaluate practice with individuals, families, groups, organizations, and communities.

## ASSESSMENT QUESTIONS

1. How did the information in this chapter enhance your knowledge about when one should use a pre-experimental design?

2. How did the information in this chapter enhance your knowledge about when one should use an experimental design?

3. In what ways did the case enhance your ability to determine what type of research design is appropriate for determining if an intervention is effective?

4. What specific content discussed in this chapter is still unclear to you? If there is still content that is unclear, schedule an appointment with your instructor to gain more clarity.

## END-OF-CHAPTER EXERCISES

1. Come to class prepared to discuss how you would advise Celik and her colleagues on how they could improve their study to enhance their ability to demonstrate causality.

2. This semester you are doing your field placement where more than half of the clients are caring for their terminally ill parent. You told your supervisor about the article by Heyman and Gutheil. Your supervisor has asked you to develop an intervention similar to the one described in the article by Heyman and Gutheil and evaluate its effectiveness. What type of research design would you recommend? What threats to internal and external validity are associated with the research design you selected? Justify your response.

## ADDITIONAL READINGS

Mazza, C. (2002). Young dads: The effects of a parenting program on urban African-American adolescent fathers. *Adolescence, 37*(148), 681–693.

Mishara, B. L., & Weisstub, D. (2005). Ethical and legal issues in suicide research. *International Journal of Law and Psychiatry, 28*(1), 23–41.

Parra-Cardona, J. R., Bybee, D., Sullivan, C. M., Dates, B., Domenech Rodríguez, M. M., Tams, L., & Bernal, G. (2017). Examining the impact of differential cultural adaption with Latina/o immigrants exposed to adapted parenting training interventions. *Journal of Consulting and Clinical Psychiatry, 85*(1), 58–71.

Stahlschmidt, M. J., Threlfall, J., Seay, K. D., Lewis, E. M., & Kohl, P. L. (2003). Recruiting fathers to parenting programs: Advice from dads and fatherhood providers. *Children and Youth Services Review, 35*(10), 1734–1741. doi:10.1016/j.childyouth.2013.07.004

## ⑤SAGE edge™

Get the tools you need to sharpen your study skills. SAGE Edge offers a robust online environment featuring an impressive array of free tools and resources.

Access practice quizzes at **edge.sagepub.com/farmer**

# Quasi-Experimental Designs

## Learning Objectives

7.1 Identify the ways in which quasi-experimental designs can be used.

7.2 Differentiate between the various types of quasi-experimental designs.

7.3 Identify the ethical and diversity issues associated with quasi-experimental designs.

| Competencies Covered | Learning Objectives | Dimension |
|---|---|---|
| Competency 1 <br> *Demonstrate Ethical and Professional Behavior* | 7.3 Identify the ethical issues associated with quasi-experimental designs. | Skills |
| Competency 2 <br> *Engage Diversity and Difference in Practice* | 7.3 Identify the diversity issues associated with quasi-experimental designs. | Skills |
| Competency 4 <br> *Engage in Practice-Informed Research and Research-Informed Practice* | 7.1 Identify the ways in which quasi-experimental designs can be used. <br><br> 7.2 Differentiate between the various types of quasi-experimental designs. | Skills |
| Competency 5 <br> *Engage in Policy Practice* | 7.1 Identify the ways in which quasi-experimental designs can be used. <br><br> 7.2 Differentiate between the various types of quasi-experimental designs. | Skills |
| Competency 9 <br> *Evaluate Practice With Individuals, Families, Groups, Organizations, and Communities* | 7.1 Identify the ways in which quasi-experimental designs can be used. <br><br> 7.2 Differentiate between the various types of quasi-experimental designs. | Skills |

Master the content at
**edge.sagepub.com/farmer**

## What Are the Effects of a Diversion Program on Rearrest Rates, Re-Incarceration, and Mental Health Functioning?

By responding to the questions related to this case, you will be able to identify what type of quasi-experimental design is appropriate for evaluative research purposes.

Dr. Janice Grossman works for the Department of Mental Health and Addiction Services (DMHAS) as the director of the Office of Prevention and Administration. She recently read an article about Connecticut's specialized mental health jail diversion program called the Advanced Supervision and Intervention Support Team (ASIST), which offers criminal justice supervision in conjunction with mental health and support services. Evaluation studies have shown that this program is effective in enhancing mental health and reducing rearrest and re-incarceration rates. Several days after reading this article, she received an e-mail stating that the National Institute of Justice (NIJ) is accepting grant proposals to evaluate the effectiveness of diversion programs for juveniles.

You are doing your field placement at DMHAS along with other social work interns who are attending other schools of social work in the area. Dr. Grossman has asked you and the other interns to assist her with the grant proposal.

At this point, take a few minutes to think about the case example and do the following:

1. Identify the problem.

2. Determine what you already know about the problem.

3. Determine what information you need to solve the problem.

4. List the questions needed to be answered related to the information you need to solve the problem.

Please write down your responses to each item. You will need to refer to them while reading this chapter.

Dr. Grossman convenes a meeting with you and the other social work interns to discuss the article and her ideas for the grant proposal. She states that in 2007, Connecticut's Criminal Justice Policy Advisory Commission's Behavioral Health Subcommittee developed the ASIST program to provide criminal justice supervision in conjunction with mental health treatment to address behaviors related to criminality risk. Individuals involved in the program received mental health services from local mental health facilities. ASIST aimed to reduce rearrest and re-incarceration by focusing on supervision, treatment engagement, and case management. Additionally, individuals were involved in a skill development program.

The ASIST program was six weeks in duration. Upon completion of the program, charges against the participants were dropped. Individuals could opt to continue in the program if they wanted. Prior to entering and after program completion, the participants filled out questionnaires on mental health functioning, substance use, medication adherence, and trauma symptoms. Arrest and incarceration history was also collected during the above-mentioned time periods.

As for the grant proposal she plans to submit to NIJ, Dr. Grossman states that she is interested in evaluating the effectiveness of ASIST with juveniles. She would like to examine the effects of the program on rearrest rates, mental health functioning, and re-incarceration. Dr. Grossman states the criteria for participating in the program is as follows: the participants need to be African American, Hispanic, and Asian adolescents ages 13 to 19 who have been arrested or were on probation supervision during the 2018 calendar year, engage in substance use, or have been diagnosed with a mental health disorder. Moreover, they cannot currently be involved in another diversion program or in treatment for their mental health issues.

During the meeting, she asked you and Monique to work on the sampling strategy and the research design, while Marcus and Kara were asked to work on the literature review.

## Introduction

In this chapter, you will learn about the different types of quasi-experiment designs, except for single-case designs, which will be in Chapter 15. The reason for that is social workers are often encouraged to use single-case designs to evaluate their practice. Ethical and diversity issues are discussed. The threats to internal and external validity are covered.

## Quasi-Experimental Designs Defined

A **quasi-experimental design** is one where the researcher manipulates the independent variable without the random assignment of participants to an experimental or control group. In this design, the group not receiving the intervention is referred to as the **comparison group** and not as the control group, because there is no random assignment to this group. Because there is no random assignment, quasi-experimental designs cannot be used to establish causality. Given that random assignment to the groups is not used, researchers generally try to ensure that the participants in the comparison group are similar as much as possible to the participants in the experimental group. This is done by matching. **Matching** refers to the selection of persons to include in the comparison group who are similar—for example, on demographics—to those who are in the experimental group. Referring to the case example, Dr. Grossman's comparison group should include African American, Hispanic, and Asian males ages 13 to 19 who have been arrested or on probation supervision and received mental health services during the same time period as those in the ASIST program. Quasi-experimental designs are used when it is not feasible or ethical to assign participants to an experimental or control group. Random assignment is unethical when one is interested in studying the effects of a new medication on attention deficit disorder (ADD) symptoms. The best way to study the effects of this new medication is to use a quasi-experimental design. Those who are taking the medication would be considered the experimental group and those who did not receive any medication for their ADD symptoms would be the comparison group. Similar to experimental designs, quasi-experimental designs allow social workers to address questions where research can inform practice and practice can inform research. According to Thyer (2012), the use of quasi-experimental designs to evaluate the effectiveness of a particular intervention where the studies reach the same conclusions can be used to inform social work practice. Results from quasi-experimental design studies can lay the groundwork for developing an experimental study. Moreover, these designs are useful for evaluating the effectiveness of social work interventions with individuals, families, groups, organizations, and communities (Competency 9, *Evaluate Practice With Individuals, Families, Groups, Organizations, and Communities*). For example, Azeez (2015) used a pretest-posttest quasi-experimental design to assess the effectiveness of life skill education on the psychological well-being and self-esteem of adolescents ages 15–19. The results of the study revealed there was a significant difference between the pretest and posttest scores of the outcome variables. Overall, there was an improvement in both the psychological well-being and self-esteem of the adolescents. Quasi-experimental designs are also appropriate for evaluating the effects of policy (Competency 5, *Engage in Policy Practice*). For example, Meda, Dumont, Kouanda, and Ridde (2018) used a quasi-experimental design to study the effects of a national subsidy policy that off-set the cost of deliveries, emergency obstetric, and neonatal care in Burkina Faso, West Africa. The national policy covered 60% to 80% of the medical cost associated with having a baby, with the remaining 20% to 40% of the expenses being covered by the parent. The purpose of their study was to determine if the implementation of the policy resulted in more women delivering their babies in hospitals and other medical settings and a decrease in neonatal deaths. The data were derived from the Demographic and Health Survey conducted in Burkina Faso in 2010. The researchers compared the number of deliveries in hospitals and medical settings and live births before the implementation of the policy and after the implementation of the policy. The results revealed a significant increase in deliveries in hospitals and medical settings. There was a decrease in the number of neonatal deaths; however, it was not a significant finding.

*Purpose.* Quasi-experimental designs are well-suited for exploratory research, as they allow the researcher to examine the relationship between the independent variable and the dependent variable, thus establishing at least an association between the intervention and outcome. The results of quasi-experimental designs can be used to provide insight about the effectiveness of the intervention.

*Research Questions.* Quasi-experimental designs require researchers to propose research questions that examine the association between the independent and dependent variables. Appropriate questions for a study using a quasi-experimental design would be as follows: Will students taking an online psychopathology course have higher knowledge scores about diagnosing than students who are taking this course in person? Is there an association between receiving job training and obtaining a job?

*Sampling Strategy.* The research participants in a study using a quasi-experimental design are usually selected via a purposeful sampling strategy or a convenience sampling strategy. A purposeful sampling strategy involves selecting persons from the target population because of their fit with the purpose of the study and inclusion criteria. On the other hand, a convenience sampling strategy involves selecting persons from the target population because they are accessible to the researcher. Usually the participants in a quasi-experimental design study come from naturally occurring groups (as in a classroom, group home, or community). Thinking about the case example, Dr. Grossman should employ a purposeful sampling strategy, as she specified who should be in her study based her inclusion criteria. Recall that Dr. Grossman stated the criteria for participating in the program is as follows: the participants need to be African American, Hispanic, and Asian adolescents ages 13 to 19 who have been arrested or were on probation supervision during the 2018 calendar year, engage in substance use, or have been diagnosed with a mental health disorder. Moreover, they cannot currently be involved in another diversion program or in treatment for their mental health issues.

*Data Analysis Strategy.* Data from quasi-experimental designs are analyzed using the same statistical methods discussed in Chapters 6 and 13. The appropriate statistical methods for the type of quasi-experimental designs described in this chapter will be discussed later.

## Critical Thinking Question 7.1

Dr. Grossman convenes a meeting with the social work interns to discuss the purpose of the study, research question(s), and hypothesis. During the meeting, Monique suggests that a quasi-experimental design should be used for the proposed study. What is the purpose of the study, research question(s), and hypothesis? Will a quasi-experimental design, as Monique suggested, allow Dr. Grossman to determine the effectiveness of the ASIST program? Justify your response.

# Types of Quasi-Experimental Designs

In this chapter, we will discuss three quasi-experimental designs: *non-equivalent comparison group design, time series design,* and *natural experiments.*

## Non-Equivalent Comparison Group Design

This design is referred to as a **non-equivalent comparison group design** because there are two groups (i.e., experimental and comparison), one intervention, and a pretest and a posttest. Individuals are not randomly assigned to either the experimental or comparison groups. The pretest and posttest scores for both groups are compared, and any differences between the groups can be attributed to the intervention. There should not be a change in the posttest scores for individuals in the comparison group, because they did not receive the intervention. The standard notation for this design, based on the work of Campbell and Stanley (1963), is as follows:

$$O_1 \qquad\qquad X \qquad\qquad O_2$$
$$O_1 \qquad\qquad\qquad\qquad\quad O_2$$

The $O_1$ stands for the pretest and $O_2$ stands for posttest, while X represents the intervention. This notation is similar to the Pretest-Posttest Control Group Design, which you learned about in Chapter 6, except the R, which stands for randomization, is not noted. This design is affected by the following threats to internal validity:

1. **Selection bias**: The changes you see in the outcome may be due to the groups not being equivalent at the outset because randomization was not used to form the groups.

2. **Interaction of selection and maturation**: Changes in the experimental and comparison groups are occurring as a function of maturation and selection. The groups differ because of the developmental changes in the individuals within the groups.

3. **Statistical regression to the mean**: If participants were selected to receive the intervention based on having extreme low or high scores on the pretest, when comparing the pretest with the posttest scores, you find the participants perform better on average on the posttest than the pretest.

4. **Contamination effect**: This occurs when participants in the intervention group have an influence on participants in the comparison group. It should be noted that this threat is hard to detect.

A contamination effect can occur if you are doing a social skills training program with Mr. Scott's class, but the training is not given to the students in Ms. Bryce's class. During lunchtime several of the students in Mr. Scott's class teach several of the students in Ms. Bryce's class the social skills they learned. Although the students in Ms. Bryce's class did not receive the social skill training, you notice that their posttest social skills scores are the same or higher than the children in Mr. Scott's class. The above is an example of diffusion of treatment, which is a type of contamination effect.

5. **Resentful demoralization:** Resentful demoralization, which is another type of contamination effect, occurs when participants in the comparison group become aware of the intervention and feel they are being denied the benefits of such intervention, and therefore do less well on the dependent variable than they would have outside of the experiment.

### Application Checkpoint 7.1

Given what you have learned about diffusion of treatment and resentful demoralization, how might both occur in the study proposed by Dr. Grossman? What can be done to prevent these two contamination effects from occurring?

Furthermore, this design is affected by the following threats to external validity:

1. **Interaction of testing and X:** As a result of the pretesting, the participants may become sensitized to the treatment. Therefore, the results of the study are only generalizable to the pretested population.

2. **Interaction of selection and X:** A characteristic of the participant, such as motivation to change, may have resulted in the participant responding differently to the intervention. Hence, the results may not be generalizable beyond persons who were motivated.

3. **Multiple treatment inference:** Participants were exposed to interventions prior to receiving the current intervention. Think about Dr. Grossman's inclusion criteria for her study. One criterion was that persons could not currently be involved in another diversion program or in treatment for their mental health issues. She used this criterion as a way to control for the threat of multiple treatment inference.

Data from the non-equivalent comparison group design can be analyzed using a 2 × 2 repeated measures ANOVA, testing the pretest-posttest difference as the within-group factor, and the group difference as the between-group factor, and the interaction effect of both factors. Additionally, a 2 × 2 analysis of covariance (ANCOVA) is also appropriate, especially if you have collected data on confounding variables that you did not use to match the samples.

For further understanding, here is an example of a study using a non-comparison control group design.

## Example of a Study Using a Non-Comparison Group Design

Bender, Altschul, Yoder, Parrish, and Nickels (2014) used a non-equivalent quasi-experimental comparison design to examine the effects of integrating evidence-based practice (EBP) process into the master of social work (MSW) research curriculum.

Participants were 180 MSW students in 12 sections of the research course. Students in the sections (N = 7) where the EBP process was integrated were designated as being in the intervention group, and the students in the remaining sections (N = 5) who had the traditional curriculum were designated as the comparison group.

To assess change on the five outcomes—familiarity with the EBP process, attitudes toward

the EBP process, feasibility to engage in the EBP process, intention to engage in the EBP process, and current engagement in the EPB process—a paired *t*-test was performed. An independent *t*-test was conducted to assess for differences among the intervention and comparison group.

At posttest, the intervention group had significantly higher ratings on familiarity with the EBP process than the comparison group. There were no differences between the groups on the other four outcome measures. Both groups had significant increases in their scores on intention to engage in the EBP process, familiarity with the EBP process, and attitudes toward the EBP process from pretest to posttest.

## Time-Series Design

A **time-series design** is one where there is repeated measurement (observation) of the dependent variable prior to the implementation of the intervention (independent variable) and after the intervention has been implemented. The standard notation for the time-series design below, also known as the **interrupted time-series design** (because the observations are interrupted by the intervention), based on the work of Campbell and Stanley (1963), is as follows:

OOOOOO X OOOOOO

The X stands for the intervention and O stands for observation. The observation refers to the measurement of the dependent variable. In the above example, you will see that there were six observations of the dependent variable made before the intervention was implemented and there were six observations of the dependent variable made after the intervention was implemented. This design can establish association between the intervention and the outcome variable. The association is determined by looking at the observations of the dependent variable prior to the implementation of the intervention and comparing them with the observations of the dependent variable after the implementation of the intervention. If, for example, the comparison indicates that the participants got better after receiving the intervention, one can conclude there is an association between the intervention and the dependent variable. The measurements prior to the implementation of the intervention and after the intervention are graphed, and by looking at the graphed data (see Figure 7.1), you will see that after the intervention was introduced there was improvement in the client's behavior. This design is affected by the following threats to internal validity:

1. **History:** History is a threat to this design if some event occurred at the same time the client received the intervention, which resulted in the outcome.

2. **Reactivity:** Changes in the target behavior are due to the client recording his or her behavior.

3. **Instrumentation:** This is a change in the measure used to assess the dependent variable. For example, a researcher uses the Beck Depression Inventory-II (BDI-II) to assess depression at pretest but uses the Center for Epidemiologic Studies Depression Scale (CES-D) to assess depression at posttest. The change in the depression scores cannot be attributed to the intervention but to the change in the measure used to assess depression.

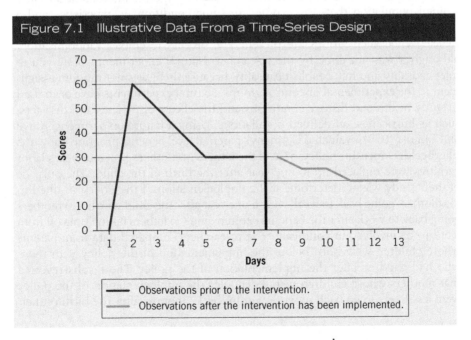

Figure 7.1  Illustrative Data From a Time-Series Design

Observations prior to the intervention.
Observations after the intervention has been implemented.

Furthermore, this design is affected by the following threats to external validity: Interaction of Selection and X, Interaction of History and X, and Reactivity. The threats of interaction of selection and X and interaction of history were discussed in Chapter 6.

Data from the time-series design can be analyzed by looking at the trend line. A **trend line** is a line on the graph that indicates the general pattern or direction of time-series data. The slope of the trend line prior to the implementation of the intervention is compared to the slope of the trend line after the implementation of the intervention. If the change in the slope is significant, one can infer that the intervention led to the outcome.

---

### Critical Thinking Question 7.2

Thinking about the purpose of Dr. Grossman's proposed study, would the time-series design be preferable to the non-equivalent comparison group design? Justify your response.

---

## Natural Experiments

**Natural experiments** are ones in which the researcher did not determine who would or would not get the intervention or exposure to the independent variable, but the intervention or exposure was determined by nature or other factors outside of the researcher's control. In natural experiments there is a clearly defined population that was exposed to some condition or experience and a clearly defined population that was not exposed to some condition or experience. When such groups are present, the process resembles randomization, although it was not done by the researcher. Natural experiments allow you to infer causality and not establish causality, because there was not random assignment to the experimental or control groups. Natural experiments have been used to study health and disease conditions and the effects of policies and disasters, such as hurricanes, on defined populations. Using a natural experiment, Kluve and Tamm (2013), evaluated Germany's parental level benefits program known as Elterngeld. Under this policy, 67% of the father's or mother's previous year's labor earnings were replaced up to one year after the birth of the child. The purpose of their study was to determine if the implementation of the policy resulted in (1) mothers going back to work within one year after the child's birth, (2) mothers going back to work after the benefits expired, and (3) fathers taking time off from work to be involved in child care. The researchers compared data from parents whose children were born before the implementation of the policy with those who had children after the implementation of the policy. The results revealed that mothers whose children were born after the implementation of the policy were less likely to go back to work within the 12 months after the birth of their child than mothers whose children were born before the implementation of the policy. Re-entry back into the labor market was dependent upon the availability of public child care for a subgroup of the women. The policy had no effect on fathers' participation in child care.

Craig et al. (2012) recommend that "quantitative natural experimental studies should only be attempted when exposed and unexposed populations (or groups subject to varying levels of exposure) can be compared, using samples large enough to detect the expected effects, and when accurate data can be obtained on exposures, outcomes and potential confounders" (p. 1184). One of the strengths of natural experiments is that they are useful for evaluating policy effectiveness (Leatherdale, 2019). This design is affected by the following threats to internal validity:

1. **History:** History is a threat to this design if some event occurred at the same time as the natural event, which resulted in the outcome.

2. **Confounding:** A situation in which the outcome is produced by something other than the intervention. A confounder variable is one that is associated with both the intervention and the outcome of interest.

Although this design is not affected by any of the threats to external validity you have already learned, establishing the external validity of natural experiments is still of concern. As you know, the more representative the sample is of the population, the more confident you can be in generalizing your results to the population.

Data from natural experiments can be analyzed using a variety of inferential statistics, depending on the level of measurement of the variables, the number of independent and dependent variables, and the research question being asked.

## Ethics and Quasi-Experimental Designs

The ethical considerations discussed in Chapters 3 and 6 are applicable to conducting quasi-experimental designs as well. Because many times quasi-experimental designs are conducted using preexisting or self-selected groups of individuals who are already participating in a program (i.e., already receiving an intervention), ethical concerns about the withholding or delaying of treatment are not applicable. We ask that you re-read the above-named chapters to refamiliarize yourself with these ethical considerations.

## Diversity and Quasi-Experimental Designs

The same issues related to diversity in Chapter 6 are applicable to conducting quasi-experimental designs as well. We ask that you re-read the above-named chapter to refamiliarize yourself with the issues related to diversity.

# SUMMARY, REVIEW, AND ASSIGNMENTS

# CHAPTER SUMMARY ORGANIZED BY LEARNING OBJECTIVES

LO 7.1  Identify the usefulness of quasi-experimental designs for engaging in practice-informed research and research-informed practice.

Quasi-experimental designs are used when it is not feasible or ethical to assign participants to an experimental or control group.

Quasi-experimental designs are useful because they allow social workers to evaluate practice with individuals, families, groups, organizations, communities, and policies.

LO 7.2  Differentiate between the various types of quasi-experimental designs.

Non-Equivalent Comparison Group Design

A *non-equivalent comparison group design* is where there are two groups (i.e., experimental and comparison), one intervention, and a pretest and posttest. Individuals are not randomly assigned to either the experimental or comparison group.

Time-Series Design

A *time-series design*, also referred to as an interrupted time-series

design, is one where there is repeated measurement (observation) of the dependent variable prior to the implementation of the intervention (independent variable) and after the intervention has been implemented.

Natural Experiments

*Natural experiments* are ones in which the researcher did not determine who would or would not get the intervention or exposure to the independent variable, but the intervention or exposure was determined by nature or other factors outside of the researcher's control.

LO 7.3  Identify the ethical and diversity issues associated with quasi-experimental designs.

Obtaining informed consent is the way we prevent oppression, abuse of power, marginalization, and alienation from occurring when we conduct quasi-experimental research.

Individuals have a right to determine if they will or will not participate in research and when they will stop participating.

If you are in a dual role as both researcher and therapist, you must ensure that your clients know they have the right to refuse to participate in your research and their refusal will not result in the termination of the services provided by your agency.

If you are in a dual role as both researcher and therapist, you may want to get someone besides yourself to obtain the client's consent to participate in your research.

The practices of obtaining informed consent may need to be modified depending upon the cultural background of the research participant.

Getting a participant's written consent may be inappropriate in a culture where there are low levels of education and literacy. Therefore, the researcher may want to obtain oral consent from the participant or employ a third party.

Whenever possible, select interventions to be evaluated that are culturally appropriate.

## KEY TERMS

## COMPETENCY NOTES

In this chapter, you were introduced to the competencies below:

Competency 1, *Demonstrate Ethical and Professional Behavior*. Social workers will be involved in ethical decision-making at every stage of the research process.

Competency 2, *Engage Diversity and Difference in Practice*. Social workers must be aware of how a participant's culture may play a role in the obtaining of informed consent.

Competency 4, *Engage in Practice-Informed Research and Research-Informed Practice*.

Social workers can advance the science of social work by using quasi- experimental designs, which will inform practice.

Competency 5, *Engage in Policy Practice*. Social workers can use quasi-experimental designs to engage in policy practice.

Competency 9, *Evaluate Practice With Individuals, Families, Groups, Organizations, and Communities*. Social workers can use quasi-experimental designs to evaluate practice with individuals, families, groups, organizations, and communities.

## ASSESSMENT QUESTIONS

1. How did the information in this chapter enhance your knowledge about when one should use a quasi-experimental design?

2. In what ways did the case example enhance your ability to determine what type of quasi-experimental research design is appropriate for determining if an intervention is effective?

3. What specific content discussed in this chapter is still unclear to you? If there is still content that is unclear, schedule an appointment with your instructor to gain more clarity.

## END-OF-CHAPTER EXERCISES

1. Your research instructor asked you and two other students to examine the effects of the Temporary Assistance to Needy Families (TANF) program on child and family health outcomes. What type of design will you used to assess the effects and why? What are the threats to internal and external validity associated with your design?

2. Read the following study:

   Lee, E. O., Brown, M., & Bertera, E. M. (2010). The use of an online diversity forum to facilitate social work students' dialogue on sensitive issues: A quasi-experimental design. *Journal of Teaching in Social Work, 30,* 272–287.

   What could the researchers do to ensure that their groups were similar? Identify the threats to internal and external validity of the study that the researchers did not mention. Do you have less confidence in their study after you have identified these additional threats? Why or why not?

## ADDITIONAL READINGS

Dunning, T. (2012). *Natural experiments in the social sciences: A design based approach.* New York, NY: Cambridge University Press.

Law, M., Anaby, D., Imms, C., Teplicky, R., & Turner, L. (2015). Improving the participation of youth with physical disabilities in community activities: An interrupted time series design. *Australian Occupational Therapy Journal, 62*(2), 105–115, doi:10.1111/1440-1630.12177

## $SAGE edge™

Get the tools you need to sharpen your study skills. SAGE Edge offers a robust online environment featuring an impressive array of free tools and resources.

Access practice quizzes at **edge.sagepub.com/farmer**

# Qualitative Research

## Learning Objectives

**8.1**   Identify the ways in which qualitative research can be used.

**8.2**   Differentiate between the various sampling strategies employed in qualitative research.

**8.3**   Differentiate between the various types of qualitative research methods.

**8.4**   Establish the trustworthiness of the data collected for qualitative research.

**8.5**   Identify the ethical and diversity issues associated with qualitative research methods.

| Competencies Covered | Learning Objectives | Dimension |
|---|---|---|
| Competency 1<br>*Demonstrate Ethical and Professional Behavior* | 8.5  Identify the ethical issues associated with qualitative research methods. | Skills |
| Competency 2<br>*Engage Diversity and Difference in Practice* | 8.5  Identify the diversity issues associated with qualitative research methods. | Skills |
| Competency 4<br>*Engage in Practice-Informed Research and Research-Informed Practice* | 8.3  Differentiate between the various types of qualitative research methods. | Skills |
| Competency 5<br>*Engage in Policy Practice* | 8.3  Differentiate between the various types of qualitative research methods. | Skills |

Master the content at
**edge.sagepub.com/farmer**

## What Are the Perceptions of African American Adolescent Males About the Police?

By responding to the questions related to this case, you will be able to identify what type of qualitative research method is appropriate and support your choice by critically analyzing the strengths and limitations of the qualitative research methods described in this chapter.

You are employed as a graduate research assistant for Dr. Booker, whose research focuses on juvenile justice and community policing and organizing. Dr. Booker is working on a grant proposal he plans to submit to the Department of Juvenile Justice to conduct a study examining the perceptions of African American adolescent males about the police.

Dr. Booker meets with you, two graduate research assistants, and two doctoral students to tell you what he plans to work on this semester. He thanks each of you for wanting to work with him and tells you that the next time he meets with you he will provide you with more details about the grant proposal.

At this point, take a few minutes to think about the case example and do the following:

1. Identify the problem.

2. Determine what you already know about the problem.

3. Determine what information you need to solve the problem.

4. List the questions needed to be answered related to the information you need to solve the problem.

Please write down your responses to each item. You will need to refer to them while reading this chapter.

Dr. Booker convenes another meeting with you, two graduate research assistants, and two doctoral students. He explains that the impetus for his study was the high-profile cases in several states where there was police brutality involved. He states that he has observed that after such cases are discussed in the media, the police are perceived in a negative light and they are not respected by persons in the communities they serve. He goes on to say that previous research has demonstrated that a person's perceptions of the police are shaped by that person's age, race/ethnicity, social class, personal experience, and type of community in which he/she resides.

## Introduction

In this chapter, you will learn about the different types of qualitative research methods. Ethical and diversity issues when conducting qualitative studies are discussed. Sampling strategies used in conducting qualitative research are described. Analytic procedures to use with qualitative data are discussed in Chapter 14.

## Qualitative Research Defined

According to Denzin and Lincoln (2011),

> Qualitative research is a situated activity that locates the observer in the world. It consists of a set of interpretive, material practices that make the world visible. These practices transform the world. They turn the world into a series of representations, including field notes, interviews, conversations, photographs, recordings, and memos to the self. At this level, qualitative research involves an interpretive, naturalistic approach to the world. This means that qualitative researchers study things in their natural settings, attempting to make sense of or to interpret phenomena in terms of the meanings people bring to them.
>
> Qualitative research involves the studied use and collection of a variety of empirical materials—case study, personal experience, introspective, life story, interview, observational, historical, interactional, and visual texts—that describe routine and problematic moments and meaning in individuals' lives. (pp. 3–4)

Qualitative research is based on an **inductive philosophy**—that is, where data about the phenomenon are observed and gathered without the researcher specifying a specific hypothesis or theory explaining the occurrence of the phenomenon being studied. Qualitative researchers may use a theoretical framework to guide their research; however, they do not use the theoretical framework to derive a hypothesis about the phenomenon. They want the data to generate their hypothesis.

The focus of qualitative research is to discover the meaning individuals give to their interactions with others and the events that happen in their lives. Focusing on the participants providing meaning to what is occurring instead of the researcher is a key part of qualitative research. Qualitative researchers demonstrate Competency 2, *Engage Diversity and Difference in Practice*, because they see the participants in their research as experts when it comes to their own experiences. In qualitative research, the researcher is the instrument for data collection and analysis. Hence, researchers need to reflect on their assumptions, beliefs, biases, and values they bring to the research throughout the entire research process. Reflecting on the above is known as **researcher's reflexivity**. Researcher's reflexivity is central for establishing the trustworthiness of the qualitative research. In addition to addressing reflexivity, qualitative researchers need to address their subjectivity. **Subjectivity** is the researcher's understanding of the phenomenon (Schneider, 1999). Additionally, the researcher needs to reflect on the position of self as an insider- or outsider-researcher. **Insider-researchers** choose to study a group they belong to, while **outsider-researchers** choose to study a group to which they do not belong. Referring to the case example, let us say that during the second meeting Dr. Booker held with the persons assisting with the grant proposal, he selected Sean, a 19-year-old African American male, and Tyler, an 18-year-old Asian American male, to conduct the interviews for the project. Considering Sean's age, gender, and racial background he would be an insider-researcher, while Tyler would be an outsider-researcher, because he does not belong to the group being studied. One advantage of being an insider-researcher is that you may understand the feelings and experiences of the group. A drawback of being an insider-researcher is that because you understand the feelings and experiences of the group, you may lose your objectivity. Some scholars have argued that objectivity does not exist. **Objectivity** is also referred to as empathic neutrality (Patton, 2015), which could bias your research. One advantage of being an outsider-researcher is that it may result in the participants sharing information without feeling that they are being judged (Tinker & Armstron, 2008). A drawback of being an outsider-researcher is that it may take a long time to build rapport with your participants—therefore, increasing one's time in the field.

In conducting qualitative research, the researcher needs to determine if he or she will be an observer, observer as participant, participant as observer, or full participant. As an **observer**, the researcher has no or minimal interactions with the participant. The role as **observer as participant** involves being an observer with some interaction with the participants. As a **participant-observer**, one is interacting more with the participants than observing them. **Full participant** refers to being both a member of the setting in which the research is being conducted and being the one conducting the research. Qualitative research is used (1) to study phenomenon that has not been studied or need to be examined to gain additional insight; (2) when you want to learn from the participants about their perceptions about beliefs, behaviors, events, or social interactions; and (3) when you want to understand phenomena more in-depth. Qualitative research methods are also used in mixed-methods research. Mixed-methods research employs both quantitative and qualitative methods to answer the research question(s).

## Application Checkpoint 8.1

Suppose you are conducting the research study instead of Dr. Booker. What are some assumptions, beliefs, biases, and values you need to keep track of throughout the research process?

There are several examples in the social work literature demonstrating how qualitative research has informed practice, policy, and service. For example, Haight, Kayama, and Korang-Okrah (2014) used the results of their ethnographic research study to design a culturally sensitive, evidence-informed intervention for rural substance-involved families. Meanwhile, Jobling (2014) used qualitative research to evaluate policy. Jobling (2014) conducted an ethnographic research study to examine the implementation of Community Treatment Orders (CTOs) in England. CTOs were established as part of the 2007 Mental Health Act.

## Sampling Strategies Used in Qualitative Research

In conducting qualitative research, a purposive sampling method (also referred to as purposeful sampling) is normally employed. A purposive sampling strategy involves selecting persons from the target population because of their fit with the purpose of the study and inclusion criteria. Miles and Huberman (1994) identified the sampling strategies researchers can employ when conducting qualitative research. Table 8.1 lists these sampling strategies along with the characteristics of the sample that emerges from their use.

| Table 8.1   Sampling Strategies | |
| --- | --- |
| **Types of Sampling Strategies** | **Characteristics of the Sample** |
| Convenience | Participants are easily accessible to the researcher |
| Homogeneous | Participants share many similarities to one another |
| Maximum variation | Participants share many differences from one another |
| Random purposeful sampling | Participants are randomly selected from a purposeful sample |
| Stratified purposeful sampling | Participants are selected based on a specific characteristic (e.g., race/ethnic background, gender) the researcher is interested in making a comparison on |
| Comprehensive sampling | The entire group of participants are selected based on a set of criteria established by the researcher (e.g., researcher selects entire group of students because they had a specific course) |
| Typical case sampling | A case that is selected to demonstrate the average example of the focus of the study |

*(Continued)*

| Types of Sampling Strategies | Characteristics of the Sample |
|---|---|
| Intensity sampling | Cases selected to intensely demonstrate the phenomenon of investigation |
| Critical case sampling | A case that serves as a "benchmark" with which to compare other cases |
| Politically important sampling | Cases that draw political attention to the phenomenon; cases that will draw the attention of the media |
| Extreme or deviant case sampling | Participants are selected based on having the most positive or most negative experiences |
| Snowball sampling | Participants are referred to participate by someone they know |
| Opportunistic sampling | Participants are selected based on how the research evolves |
| Criterion sampling | Participants are selected based on a criterion established by the researcher |
| Theoretical sampling | Theory derived from your data collection guides the sampling strategy |
| Confirming and disconfirming sampling | During the theoretical sampling, the researcher searches for cases to support or refute findings |

**Table 8.1 (Continued)**

*Source:* Adapted from Hays, D. G. & Sigh, A. A. (2012). Qualitative inquiry in clinical and educational settings. New York, New York, Guilford Press.

Given the number of sampling strategies you can choose from, we recommend that you select the sampling strategy that best fits your study. In order to do this, you need to keep in mind the following:

1. What are the goals of the study? You need to determine the focus of your study.

2. Do you want a homogenous or heterogenous sample? A homogenous sample is one where individuals share similarities on some characteristics (e.g., age, gender, racial/ethnic background). Meanwhile, a heterogenous sample is one where individuals differ on some characteristics (e.g., age, gender, racial/ethnic background).

3. Do you want to make a comparison between the different subgroups? If so, you need to use a stratified purposive sample. For example, if a researcher is interested in studying the quality of social work practice in health care settings, he or she would need to stratify the sample by health care setting size (small, medium, large). Referring to the case example, let us say that Dr. Booker is interesting in comparing the perceptions about the police based on the communities in which the African American

males reside. To do this, Dr. Booker would use a stratified sampling strategy, with the strata being type of community (i.e., urban, suburban, rural).

4. Do you have a specific criterion that the participants need to meet to be eligible for your study? Referring to the case example, let us say that Dr. Booker wants to interview African American males ages 13 to 19. To do this, he would use a criterion sampling strategy. **Criterion sampling strategy** involves selecting persons from the target population based on a criterion established by the researcher.

5. Do you want to highlight a specific case? Referring to the case example, let us say that Dr. Booker wants to interview African American males ages 13 to 19 who had the most negative and the most positive experiences with the police. To do this, he would use extreme or deviant case sampling. **Extreme or deviant case sampling** involves selecting participants based on having the most positive or most negative experiences.

A common question for those conducting qualitative research is "What should be my sample size?" The answer to this question is the subject of much debate. Some suggest that your sample size should be based on the number of participants you need to understand the phenomenon under investigation. Still others such as Creswell (2006) and Morse (1995) have suggested specific guidelines, according to the type of qualitative method being used. Creswell suggests using three to five participants for case study research, for phenomenological research up to 10 participants, and for grounded theory research between 20 and 30 participants. Meanwhile, for grounded theory research, Patton (2015) suggests that one continues interviewing persons to the point of theoretical saturation. **Theoretical saturation** is the process of collecting and analyzing data until all relevant information has been collected that is needed to gain complete insights into the topic. In other words, it is the point at which the researcher does not gain anymore insights, identify any new themes, and develop any more coding categories (Strauss & Corbin, 1990). As for ethnographic research, Morse suggests 30 to 50 participants should be interviewed.

---

### Critical Thinking Question 8.1

Thinking about the case example, propose two research questions. What type of sampling strategy would you recommend Dr. Booker use to answer the research questions you proposed? Justify your response.

---

# Types of Qualitative Research

There are several types of qualitative research methods; however, we decided to limit our discussion in this chapter to four types:

1. Case study

2. Ethnographic research

3. Grounded theory

4. Phenomenological research

## Case Study

**Case study** research involves examining a phenomenon by studying in-depth a single case. The case can be an individual, an event, a group, a family, an institution, a community, or any entity that can be readily defined. Yin (2018) defines a case study "as an empirical inquiry that investigates a contemporary phenomenon (the "case") in depth and within its real-world context, especially when the boundaries between the phenomenon and context may not be clearly evident" (p. 18). According to him, a case study design should be considered when (1) the focus of the study is to answer "how" and "why" questions, (2) you cannot manipulate the event, and (3) your focus is on contemporary events. A strength of a case study is that it provides the researcher with a detailed description of the phenomenon under study. A limitation of a case study is that its results are not generalizable due to only having a single case. There are instances where researchers use more than one single case in their case study. In this instance, generalizability would not be an issue. An example of a case study where more than one case is being studied is one where the researcher studies five Head Start programs, data from each are analyzed, and then there is a cross-case comparison to see if there are themes that are common across the cases.

Typically, researchers use a constructivist perspective to conduct a case study. From a **constructivist perspective**, the development of knowledge is derived from persons' experiences and their reflecting on those experiences. In other words, the meaning of these experiences is constructed by individuals; in essence, individuals are responsible for constructing their realities (Charmaz, 2006). Constructivists believe that truth is relative and that it is dependent on one's perspective. Constructivism is built upon the premise of a social construction of reality. Using a constructivist approach, the aim of the research is to understand how participants construct their meaning about the phenomenon under investigation. With this approach, there is close collaboration between the researcher and participants.

According to Yin (2018), the case study design must have five components: the research question(s), its propositions, its unit(s) of analysis, a determination of how the data are linked to the propositions, and criteria to interpret the findings.

1. *Determine the research question(s).* The first step in any research process is determining what will be your research question. Given that a case study design should be considered when the focus of the study is to answer "how" and "why" questions, then your research question should start with "how" or "why." Let us say, for example, a social worker is working in an adoption agency and she has reviewed the agency's records for the past five years. She notices that during this time period that none of the teenage children who were eligible to be adopted were adopted. She wonders why this happened. Therefore, she developed the following research question: "Why were these children not adopted?"

2. *Identify the proposition (if any) for the study.* A proposition is a statement that states why you think a certain relationship or behavior exists. Going back to the example in Step 1, the proposition, for example, would be, "The teenage children who were eligible for adoption were not adopted because the potential adoptees wanted to adopt infants and believed that these teens would be too difficult to parent." A proposition can be based on the literature or personal or professional experiences (Baxter & Jack, 2008). Exploratory case studies will not have a proposition statement. For these types of cases, Yin (2018) recommends that you state the purpose of the case study. Going back to the example in Step 1, the purpose of the case study would be as follows: "To determine why teenage children who were eligible for adoption were not adopted."

3. *Specify the unit of analysis.* While you are developing your research question, you should simultaneously be thinking about what the case is—that is, the unit of analysis. Baxter and Jack (2008), suggest one ask the following questions to determine the unit of analysis: "Do I want to 'analyze' the individual? Do I want to 'analyze' a program? Do I want to 'analyze' the process? Do I want to 'analyze the difference between organizations?" (pp. 545–546). Referring to the example in Step 1, the case would be the individual.

   When one is determining what is the case, one is also determining what the case is not. In order to determine what the case is, you need to place boundaries on a case. This is referred to as **binding a case**. You can bind a case by time and place (Creswell, 2003), time and activity (Stake, 1995), and definition and context (Miles & Huberman, 1994). Binding ensures that the topic is not too broad. Referring to the example in Step 1, the social worker will bind the case by time and place. For time, she is only looking at why teenage children who were eligible for adoption were not adopted in the past five years. As for place, she is only looking at what happened in her agency.

In determining the case, one must also decide if the case will consist of a single case or multiple cases. A single case is one where you limit your case to one organization, whereas a multiple-case study would involve conducting one's study in more than one organization. The use of multiple cases allows one to compare the phenomenon being studied across settings.

Additionally, you need to decide the purpose of the case study. A descriptive case study describes the phenomenon. An exploratory case study seeks to understand what the phenomenon means. An explanatory case study seeks to explain how or why a phenomenon occurs.

4. *Determination of how the data are linked to the propositions.* Examine the pattern in the data to see how it provides evidence related to the propositions. This is known as **pattern-matching** and is an interpretational analysis. **Interpretational analysis** involves examining the data for constructs, themes, or patterns. By doing this, one focuses on data related to the proposition while ignoring data that does not. Additionally, one should examine the data to see if there is information to indicate an alternative explanation for the findings.

5. *Criteria to interpret the findings.* One cannot use statistical methods to interpret the findings because of the qualitative nature of the data. Therefore, you need to use your judgment in interpreting the findings.

Yin (2018) recommends six types of data sources that can be used by researchers when conducting a case study. Five of the sources Yin suggests will be discussed below, as one of the sources, physical artifacts, is perhaps not relevant for social work research.

Documentations—Documents one may consider using include emails, letters, newspaper articles, diaries, agendas from meetings, progress reports, and other personal documents.

Archival records—Data such as U.S. census data, statistical data, records indicating how many clients were seen, and publicly available data are considered archival records.

Interviews—**Unstructured interviews** are conversational in nature, and **semi-structured interviews** are more focused in nature. The researcher asks questions during the interview, using an interview guide. The **interview guide** has a list of questions and prompts to facilitate a more focused discussion.

Direct observations—Data are collected via observations. Examples of things one may observe include, but are not limited to, behaviors, interactions with others, the events persons engage in, and conversations. Generally, these observations are unstructured. **Unstructured observations** are ones where the researcher records the observations without a structured instrument. Unstructured observations are recorded in the form of detailed notes or narratives.

Participant-observation—Data are collected via observations done by the researcher in which the researcher participates to some extent with the people being studied.

## Ethnographic Research

**Ethnographic research** involves studying people or communities within their natural environment in order to understand their lived experiences from their perspective (Buch & Staller, 2007). Gaining an understanding of the people or community from their perspective is known as the **emic perspective**, while gaining understanding of the people or community from the researcher's perspective is known as the **etic perspective**. Ethnographic research is used for both descriptive and exploratory research. The ethnographer provides descriptions about events, behaviors, interactions, and the insights about the meaning into what is happening. Ethnographic research is appropriate for studying phenomenon that we do not know much about and typically involves the researcher as being the participant, observer, or both. A strength of ethnographic research is that it allows one to gain information about phenomenon that we do not know much about. Ethnographic research takes a long time to conduct, as it is dependent upon how long it takes to build rapport with those the researcher plans to observe or interview. This is one of its limitations and strengths—time in the field is a mark of the rigor and trustworthiness of the ethnography.

Typically, researchers use an epistemological or ontology perspective when conducting ethnographic research. **Epistemology** is the theory of understanding. It focuses on the "relationship between the known and what can be known" (Guba & Lincoln, 1994, p. 108). **Ontology**, on the other hand, focuses on the nature of the reality (Guba & Lincoln, 1994). Some examples of questions appropriate for ethnographic research are: "How effective is an opioid treatment center in Baltimore, Maryland, for older adults?"; "What are the substance use histories of youth transitioning out of foster care?"; and "What are the processes and procedures that make case management effective or ineffective for traumatized youth?"

Singleton and Straits (2005) have outlined five steps for conducting ethnographic research:

1. *Problem formulation:* A statement focused on understanding certain human experiences or a way of living, a particular community. The statement should mention why it is important to understand the experiences of those being studied.

2. *Selecting a research setting:* The place where you will carry out your study.

3. *Gaining access:* How will you gain access to the individuals, groups, organizations, or communities you plan to study? Will you ask a member of the group to introduce you to members of the group as a way of gaining access?

4. *Presenting oneself:* How do you plan to introduce yourself to the members of the group or community you plan to study? Will you be an observer, participant-observer, observer as participant, or full participant?

5. *Gathering and recording information:* What type of data gathering will you be doing? Will you be doing observations or interviews? What type of documents will you be reviewing? Will you record the observations while you are conducting your observations or immediately after the observations have been completed? Will you carry a notebook or computer to the site to record your observations or interviews?

Typically, there are three types of data sources that are used by researchers when conducting ethnographic research: documentations, interviews, and observations. Social media, such as Twitter feeds, online communities, Facebook and Snapchat posts are also sources of data for ethnographic research. Ethnographic research based on these sources is referred to as a virtual ethnography, *netnography*, *digital ethnographic*, *online ethnographic*, or *cyber ethnography*. According to Kozinets (2006), a **virtual ethnography** is "an ethnography conducted on the Internet; a qualitative, interpretive research methodology that adapts the traditional, in-person ethnographic research techniques of anthropology to the study of online cultures and communities formed through computer-mediated communications" (p. 135).

---

### Critical Thinking Question 8.2

Given what you have learned thus far, what qualitative research method (i.e., case study, ethnographic research) would you recommend that Dr. Booker use for his proposed study? Justify your response. For the qualitative research method you selected, write your response to the relevant steps used to carry out this approach.

---

## Grounded Theory

**Grounded theory**, developed by Glaser and Strauss (1967), is used to understand the meaning individuals give to the events that occur in their lives. Understanding the meaning individuals give to these events provides the researcher with insights about how these individuals react to these events and cope after the events have occurred. Grounded theory can be used for both descriptive and exploratory research. It is appropriate to use when there is little known about the phenomenon under investigation. The aim of grounded theory is to generate theory derived from the data collected and not to test theories described in the empirically based literature. Researchers generate theory from the data by constantly being engaged with the data. They are constantly asking questions of the data. This process allows the researcher to think about hypotheses and theories derived from the data. Another strategy that researchers use is theoretical sampling. **Theoretical sampling** is a process of collecting and analyzing the data simultaneously to generate a theory. Asking questions of the data is also involved, but this time the researcher asks questions of the data that will lead to collecting additional data that will help fill in the gaps in his or her theoretical formulation. Grounded theory is based on **interpretivism**, which focuses on the way people make sense of their reality. More specifically, grounded theory is based on the theories of **symbolic interaction**, which indicates that persons derived meanings of events that occur in their lives due, in part, to their interactions with others. A strength of grounded theory is that it can be used for theory development. Another strength is it promotes the researcher to look deeply at the data without being constricted to looking at the patterns in the data to support a theoretical framework. A disadvantage of grounded theory is that the coding of data can become so cumbersome that the researcher loses sight of discovering the themes that emerge from the data (Hussein, Hirst, Salyers, & Osuji, 2014). Some examples of questions appropriate for grounded theory research are: "How does training for leadership in child welfare occur in schools of social work?"; "What are the facilitators and barriers of the adoption process when it comes to the adoption of adolescents?"; and "What do you think university administrators can do to prevent sexual assault on college campuses?" For further understanding, the box below contains an example of a study using grounded theory.

## Example of a Study Using Grounded Theory

McLendon (2014) conducted a grounded theory study to explore social workers' experiences using the *Diagnostic and Statistical Manual of Mental Disorders (DSM)* with children and how the use of the DSM influence their practice with children.

Twenty social workers were interviewed, using an interview guide. Interviews were audiotaped.

A thematic analysis was used to code the data. Both initial (open) and axial coding were used prior to the development of the themes. Codes were constantly compared to see what themes emerged.

The criteria proposed by Lincoln and Guba (1985) was used to establish the trustworthiness of the data.

Four themes emerged: (1) DSM education specific to children, (2) experience of diagnosing when first in the field, (3) experience of diagnosing after some time in the field, and (4) lack of knowledge of long-term implications of diagnoses.

There are five stages for conducting grounded theory research. They are outlined below:

1. *Formulate the problem:* A statement about the focus of your study or problem you plan to study. The statement should mention why it is important to understand the problem.

2. *Make a decision about whom you will interview:* You need to make a decision about the specific individuals or groups of people you will interview. They should be knowledgeable about the topic under investigation.

3. *Collect the data and start analyzing it:* Data will be collected via semi-structured interviews. Data derived from these interviews will be analyzed immediately, with a focus on developing emerging theories and concepts (theoretical sampling).

4. *Conduct further interviews:* The focus of these interviews is to specifically inquire about the theories and concepts that emerged in Step 4.

5. *Continue engaging in Steps 3 and 4.* Interviews and data analysis should continue until theoretical saturation is reached.

Typically, semi-structured interviews are used by researchers conducting grounded theory research. The researcher asks the participants a set of predetermined open-ended questions. Although the researcher plans to ask these questions, questions need not be asked in the order written and additional questions can be included to ensure that data are gathered to fully understand the phenomenon under investigation.

## Phenomenological Research

**Phenomenological research** focuses on understanding the lived experience about a phenomenon from the participant's perspective. Researchers are interested in four aspects of the lived experience: lived space, lived body, lived time, and lived human interactions. Phenomenological research is conducted for descriptive purposes. Therefore, the researcher is not conducting this type of research to test hypotheses or is using a theory to guide the research. Typically, researchers use in-depth interviews to collect the data. These interviews are based on open-ended questions. Examples of appropriate questions for phenomenological research are: "What is it like to be a Hispanic faculty member in a department where you are the only one?" "How do you cope with having a terminal illness?" and "What is it like to be caring for a husband who has a traumatic brain injury?" A strength of phenomenological research is that it may result in the generation of new theory about the phenomenon. A limitation of phenomenological research is that it is time-consuming as it relates to data collection and analysis.

Four steps are usually followed when conducting phenomenological research, and they are outlined below.

1. Bracketing—The researcher identifies any preconceived beliefs or notions about the phenomenon.

2. Intuition—The researcher becomes totally immersed in the study and the phenomenon. During the process, the researcher remains open to discovering the meaning of the phenomenon based on the participant's perspective. This openness may lead to more questions and additional methods of data collection.

3. Analysis—The researcher looks thoroughly at the data to code, group coding categories, and develop themes that describe the phenomenon from the participant's perspective.

4. Description—Based on the analysis of the data, the researcher describes the phenomenon from the participant's perspective.

## Criteria for Ensuring the Trustworthiness of the Data

Lincoln and Guba (1985) identified four criteria that researchers should use for ensuring the trustworthiness of data derived from qualitative research—creditability, transferability, dependability, and confirmability. These criteria are the gold standard in judging the trustworthiness of qualitative research. In 1994, Guba and Lincoln added the criteria of authenticity. **Creditability** refers to the "believ-ability" of the study. The believability of the study is enhanced by the researcher accurately describing and interpreting the participants' understanding of the phe-nomenon. Creditability can be established using several methods. One way to establish creditability is to ensure that the audio-recordings are transcribed ver-batim and the transcripts are checked for accuracy. Another way is to do member checking. **Member checking** involves the researcher asking the participants to review the findings of the study to determine if they accurately reflect what was said and confirm the researcher's interpretation of the data. There are drawbacks to member checking. One such drawback is that the participants may disagree with the researcher's interpretation, thus calling into question the interpretations of the findings. **Negative case analysis** refers to examining the data to determine if there are cases that disconfirm the researcher's findings. When such a case is found, this is an opportunity for the researcher to ask him- or herself the question, "What else could be going on?" and revise his or her hypothesis, if necessary. Creating an **audit trail** by writing a memo or journaling one's thoughts and feelings throughout the research process is another way to establish creditability. **Triangulation** is done by looking for consistency of the information across the various sources used to collect the data. Another method that can be used is prolonged engagement. **Prolonged engagement** involves spending extensive time "in the field" to build a trusting relationship with the participants so that an accurate description of the phenomenon can be obtained. A drawback to this approach is that spending too much time could lead to bias, if the researcher loses his or her objectivity. **Peer debriefing** is another strategy that can be employed. The person doing the debriefing should not be a member of your research team and should challenge your findings, the methods you employed in the study, and the strategies used to analyze the data.

**Transferability** refers to the researcher providing enough detailed description of the research process, the participants, and the setting so that the readers of the findings can make decisions about whether the findings are applicable to the individuals who they work with or the setting in which they work. There are two strategies used to established transferability. The first one is thick description. **Thick description** refers to the detailed account of the research process, context, and the participants. Multiple cases can be used as well, as they demonstrate to the reader that the findings have occurred across individuals and settings.

**Dependability** is used when the phenomenon is likely to change depending on the research method, time, or environment, calling into question the stability of the research (Lincoln & Guba, 1985). Thus, dependability focuses on demonstrating the consistency of the research process, where both research and phenomenon appear to be unstable. Dependability can be established by creating a dependability audit, in which a third-party auditor is employed to check the researcher's work by reviewing the audit trail. Dependability can also be established by using a reflexive journal. The journal is used to document why certain methodological decisions were made, such as how codes were created and research questions were developed, and why specific sampling decisions were made.

**Confirmability** establishes that the findings are derived from the data collected. Establishing confirmability can be done by creating a confirmability audit trail, which documents the decisions made throughout the research process. The rationale for how (1) the data were coded and analyzed, (2) the themes were developed, and (3) the interpretations of the findings were made should be noted. Another way to establish conformability is the use of a reflexive journal. In the journal, the researcher should document his or her biases, thoughts, feelings, and challenges throughout the research process.

**Authenticity** is the degree to which the researcher fairly and completely shows a range of the lived experiences or realities of the participants (Polit & Beck, 2014). This criterion can be established by providing thick descriptions.

## Ethics and Qualitative Research

Ethical issues associated with qualitative research are not fundamentally different than those associated with quantitative research; however, there are some specific to qualitative research (Competency 1, *Demonstrate Ethical and Professional*

*Behavior*). Given that the data reported for qualitative studies is in the form of text, it is important that quotes used to illustrate the findings be verbatim. It is unethical to use quotes that have been modified to change the original intent of the participants. Demonstrating the trustworthiness of the data derived from qualitative research is of great importance. Given this, Hays and Singh (2012) have stated that researchers are engaging in unethical behavior when they fail to document their research process via an audit trail. Failure to demonstrate the trustworthiness of one's findings could potentially be harmful to others, especially if these findings are used to develop interventions and policies.

To ensure anonymity, you should use pseudonyms instead of the participant's real name when reporting the findings or if you are linking a specific quote with a participant. Information that might reveal the identification of the participants needs to be disguised.

The mention of third parties in the quotes to illustrate a finding could potentially raise some ethical concerns (Hadjistavropoulos & Smythe, 2001). The ethical concerns stem from the fact that the third parties did not give their consent for you to use their information for research purposes. To address this issue, Hadjistavropoulos and Smythe recommend altering information associated with the third parties and noting how this may have affected your research. Altering the information is a way of ensuring the third parties' anonymity.

## Diversity and Qualitative Research
.................................................................

Green, Creswell, Shope, and Clark (2007) stated that the lack of focus on diversity in conducting grounded theory research has stifled the development of new theories to address issues facing diverse populations. The lack of focus on diversity in other types of qualitative research might have affected the advancement of our understanding of the phenomenon under investigation (Lyons, Bike, Johnson, & Bethea, 2012). Therefore, it is important for those persons who conduct qualitative research to think about how to focus on diversity at all stages of the research process (Competency 2, *Engage Diversity and Difference in Practice*). The first stage of the research process where diversity can be addressed is when the researcher formulates the research question. The researcher needs to make it explicit in the research question that diversity is of importance. For example, a research question could be, "How do Filipino mothers cope with having to care for children with special needs?" This question clearly indicates that in order to understand the phenomenon under investigation, it is important to view it through the lens of Filipino mothers, and that it is necessary to conduct research on this group for theory development. Moreover, the researcher needs to make it explicit in stating the purpose of the research that diversity is being considered. Referring to the above example, the statement of the purpose of the research would be as follows: "The current research focuses on the lived experiences of Filipino mothers caring for their children with special needs."

Researchers conducting qualitative research may want to think about how the sampling strategy employed restricted the diversity of the sample. As mentioned earlier, qualitative researchers typically employ a purposive sampling strategy, with the most common one being snowball sampling. One criticism of snowball sampling is that it tends to yield a homogenous sample, because persons tend to associate with persons similar to oneself. To make the sample more diverse, the researcher may want to employ a stratified purposive sampling strategy, where the sample is stratified on racial/ethnic background. Moreover, the researcher could employ researchers from diverse backgrounds to assist with the project, as this may result in obtaining a diverse sample. These individuals may have access to communities that may be more diverse.

---

### Critical Thinking Question 8.3

Dr. Booker convenes a meeting with you, the two graduate assistants, and the two doctoral students to discuss what type of qualitative research method he should use for his study. What type of qualitative research method (i.e., case study, ethnographic research, grounded theory, or phenomenological research) and sampling strategy would you recommend he use? Justify your response. Identify two criteria that Dr. Booker should consider to ensure the trustworthiness of his data and the strategies he should use to do so.

---

# SUMMARY, REVIEW, AND ASSIGNMENTS

# CHAPTER SUMMARY ORGANIZED BY LEARNING OBJECTIVES

LO 8.1 Identify the ways in which qualitative research methods can be used.

Qualitative research methods are useful for informing research and practice.

Qualitative research methods are useful because they allow social workers to evaluate practice with individuals, families, groups, organizations, communities, and policies.

LO 8.2 Differentiate between the various sampling strategies employed in qualitative research.

If you want to highlight specific cases, consider using any of the following sampling strategies: extreme deviant, intensity, critical case, politically important, or typical case.

If you want a homogeneous sample, consider using any of the following sampling strategies: convenience, homogenous, or snowball.

If you want a heterogeneous sample, consider using either of the following sampling strategies: maximum variant or stratified purposeful.

If you have established criteria for selecting who will participate in your study, consider using either of the following sampling strategies: random purposeful or comprehensive.

If you want the data collection to guide who should be in the sample, you need to consider the theoretical sampling strategy.

If you used the theoretical sampling strategy, you then need to consider using the confirming and disconfirming sampling strategy.

**LO 8.3** Differentiate between the various types of qualitative research methods.

*Case study* research involves examining a phenomenon by studying in-depth a single case.

*Ethnographic research* involves studying people or communities within their natural environment in order to understand their lived experiences from their perspective.

*Grounded theory*, developed by Glaser and Strauss (1967), is used to understand the meaning individuals give to the events that occur in their lives and to develop theory.

*Phenomenological research* focuses on understanding the lived experience about a phenomenon from the participant's perspective.

**LO 8.4** Establish the trustworthiness of the data collected for qualitative research.

*Authenticity* is the degree to which the researcher fairly and completely shows a range of the lived experiences or realities of the participants.

*Confirmability* establishes that the findings are derived from the data collected.

*Creditability* refers to the "believability" of the study.

*Dependability* focuses on demonstrating the consistency of the research process, where both research and phenomenon appear to be unstable.

*Transferability* refers to the researcher providing enough detailed description of the research process, the participants, and the setting so that the readers of the findings can make decisions about whether the findings are applicable to the individuals who they work with or the setting in which they work.

**LO 8.5** Identify the ethical and diversity issues associated with qualitative research methods.

It is unethical to (1) modify quotes so it changes the original intent of the participants, (2) not document the research process via an audit trail, and (3) violate the participant's and the third parties' anonymity.

Researchers should make it explicit in their research question and statement of the purpose of the research that diversity is the focus.

Stratified purposive sampling should be used to yield a diverse sample.

Having persons on your research team who are from diverse backgrounds may be instrumental in obtaining a diverse sample.

# KEY TERMS

Inductive philosophy    149
Researcher's reflexivity    150
Subjectivity    150
Insider-researchers    150
Outsider-researchers    150
Objectivity    150
Observer    150
Observer as
    participant    150
Participant-observer    150
Full participant    150
Criterion sampling
    strategy    153
Extreme or deviant case
    sampling    153
Theoretical saturation    153
Case study    154

Constructivist perspective    154
Binding a case    155
Pattern-matching    156
Interpretational analysis    156
Unstructured interviews    156
Semi-structured
    interviews    156
Interview guide    156
Unstructured
    observations    156
Ethnographic research    157
Emic perspective    157
Etic perspective    157
Epistemology    157
Ontology    157
Virtual ethnography    158
Grounded theory    158

Theoretical sampling    159
Interpretivism    159
Symbolic interaction    159
Phenomenological
    research    160
Creditability    161
Member checking    161
Negative case analysis    161
Audit trail    161
Triangulation    161
Prolonged engagement    162
Peer debriefing    162
Transferability    162
Thick description    162
Dependability    162
Confirmability    162
Authenticity    162

# COMPETENCY NOTES

In this chapter, you were introduced to the competencies below:

Competency 1, *Demonstrate Ethical and Professional Behavior.* Social workers conducting qualitative research should document their research process via an audit trail and use pseudonyms to ensure participants' and third parties' anonymity.

Competency 2, *Engage Diversity and Difference in Practice.* Social workers see participants in their research as experts when it comes to their own experiences. Social workers recognize that focusing on

diversity in qualitative research will advance our understanding of the phenomenon under investigation.

Competency 4, *Engage in Practice-Informed Research and Research-Informed Practice.* Social workers use qualitative research to inform and improve practice, policy, and service delivery and advance the science of social work.

Competency 5, *Engage in Policy Practice.* Social workers use qualitative research to assess how policies affect the delivery of and access to social services.

# ASSESSMENT QUESTIONS

1. How did the information in this chapter enhance your knowledge about qualitative research?

2. In what ways did the information in this chapter enhance your knowledge about how to establish the trustworthiness of qualitative research?

3. What specific content discussed in this chapter is still unclear to you? If there is still content that is unclear, schedule an appointment with your instructor to gain more clarity.

## END-OF-CHAPTER EXERCISES

1. Read Chapter 6 from the book, *Gangleader for a Day: A Rogue Sociologists Takes to the Streets* by Sudhir Venkatesh (2008), and identify the ethical dilemmas. What should the author have done to address these issues prior to conducting the research?

2. Design an ethnographic study. Be sure to address all five steps recommended by Singleton and Straits (2005) for conducting ethnographic research.

Additionally, identify some potential pitfalls you may encounter if you were to actually carry out your study.

3. Propose a study using one of the research methods discussed in this chapter. Discuss why you chose the specific method. Write two research questions and a purpose statement. Share this with a student in your class and have him or her provide you with feedback on what you wrote.

## ADDITIONAL READINGS

Corden, A. (2007). *Using verbatim quotations in reporting qualitative social research: A review of selected publications.* Social Policy Research Unit, University of York.

Eysenbach, G., & Till, J. E. (2001). Ethical issues in qualitative research on Internet communities. *British Medical Journal, 323*(7321),1103–1105. doi.org/10.1136/bmj.323.7321.1103

Houghton, C., Casey, D., Shaw, D., & Murphy, K. (2013). Rigour in qualitative case-study research. *Nursing Researcher, 20*(4), 12–17.

Lyons, H. Z., Bike, D. H., Johnson, A., & Bethea, A. (2012). Culturally competent research with people of African descent. *Journal of Black Psychology, 38*(2), 153–171. doi:10.1177/0095798411414019

Padgett, D. K. (2016). *Qualitative methods in social work research* (3rd ed.). Thousand Oaks, CA: Sage.

Sanjari, M., Bahramnezhad, F., Fomani, F. K., Shoghi, M., & Cheraghi, M. A. (2014). Ethical challenges of researchers in qualitative studies: The necessity to develop a specific guideline. *Journal of Medical Ethics and History of Medicine, 7*(14), 7–14.

Windsong, E. A. (2016). Incorporating intersectionality into research design: An example using qualitative interviews. *International Journal of Social Research Methodology, 21*(2), 1–13. doi:10.1080/13645579.2016.1268361

## $SAGE edge™

Get the tools you need to sharpen your study skills. SAGE Edge offers a robust online environment featuring an impressive array of free tools and resources.

Access practice quizzes at **edge.sagepub.com/farmer**

# Learning Objectives

9.1    Identify the ways in which mixed-methods research can be used.

9.2    Differentiate between the various types of mixed-methods strategies.

9.3    Differentiate between the various sampling strategies used in mixed-methods research.

9.4    Identify the ethical and diversity issues associated with mixed-methods research.

| Competencies Covered | Learning Objectives | Dimension |
|---|---|---|
| Competency 1<br>*Demonstrate Ethical and Professional Behavior* | 9.4   Identify the ethical issues associated with mixed-methods research. | Skills |
| Competency 2<br>*Engage Diversity and Difference in Practice* | 9.4   Identify the diversity issues associated with mixed-methods research. | Skills |
| Competency 4<br>*Engage in Practice-Informed Research and Research-Informed Practice* | 9.1   Identify the ways in which mixed-methods research can be used. | Skills |
| Competency 5<br>*Engage in Policy Practice* | 9.1   Identify the ways in which mixed-methods research can be used. | Skills |
| Competency 9<br>*Evaluative Practice With Individuals, Families, Groups, Organizations and Communities* | 9.1   Identify the ways in which mixed-methods research can be used. | Skills |

Master the content at
**edge.sagepub.com/farmer**

## An Evaluation of an Intervention
## Designed to Increase Knowledge about Opioids

By responding to the questions related to this case, you will be able to identify if a mixed-methods research design is appropriate for determining the effectiveness of the proposed intervention.

Dr. Michelle Avery works for Parkside Senior Wellness Center. She recently read an article that said older adults (i.e., adults age 50 and above) were often overlooked when discussing the opioid epidemic. She was surprised to learn that between 2000 and 2013, the misuse of prescription opioid use more than doubled for older adults. Opioid misuse in older adults is associated with heart attacks, fall-related injuries, and suicide ideations. The article also mentioned the risk factors for opioid use, including previous illicit drug use in the past year, being bothered by pain, and posttraumatic stress disorder.

Dr. Avery convened a meeting with her staff, telling them about her plans to develop an intervention to increase the knowledge of adults ages 50 and above about the consequences of and risk factors for opioid use. Not only does she want to develop the intervention, but she wants to evaluate its effectiveness.

You are doing your field placement in this agency. Dr. Avery has asked you and her staff to develop the program and evaluate its effectiveness. In addition, she wants to know what facilitated or hindered the implementation of the program.

At this point, take a few minutes to think about the case example and do the following:

1. Identify the problem.

2. Determine what you already know about the problem.

3. Determine what information you need to solve the problem.

4. List the questions needed to be answered related to the information you need to solve the problem.

Please write down your responses to each item. You will need to refer to them while reading this chapter.

Dr. Avery convenes a meeting with you and her staff. You inform her that it has been decided that a pretest-posttest experimental design should be used to evaluate the effectiveness of the proposed program. Persons will be randomly assigned to two groups. Those in the experimental group will receive information that will increase their knowledge about the consequences of and risk factors for opioid use. Individuals in this group will also learn about alternative ways to manage pain. For those persons in the control group, they will receive information that will increase their knowledge about the consequences of and risk factors for opioid use. They, however, will not learn about alternative ways to manage pain. All participants prior to and after the intervention will fill out a questionnaire assessing their knowledge about the consequences of and risk factors for opioid use and the ways they manage pain and if these management techniques are effective.

Prior to ending the meeting, Dr. Avery asked, "How do you plan to gather information on the facilitators and barriers to the implementation of the intervention?" She requests that you and her staff meet with her in two weeks to discuss what strategies will be used to address her question.

# Introduction

In this chapter, you will learn about the different types of mixed-methods. The appropriate sampling strategies to use with mixed-methods research are described. Ethical and diversity issues are discussed.

# Mixed-Methods Research Defined

**Mixed-methods research** is defined as research that includes the aspects of both qualitative and quantitative methods in the design, data collection, and analysis (Teddlie & Tashakkori, 2009). Mixed-methods research also refers to

> the use of both qualitative and quantitative methods to answer research questions in a single study, as well as those studies that are part of a larger research program and are designed as complementary to provide information related to several research questions, each answered with a different methodological approach. (Mertens, 2015, p. 304)

In order to effectively conduct a mixed-methods research study, it is important that the researcher is competent in both qualitative and quantitative methods or consult with persons who have these skill sets.

There are several examples in the social work literature demonstrating how mixed-methods research has informed practice (Competency 4, *Engage in Practice-Informed Research and Research-Informed Practice*), policy (Competency 5, *Engage in Policy Practice*), and service delivery. For example, Teasley, Canifield, Archuleta, Crutchfield, and Chavis (2012) used a concurrent nested mixed-methods research design to examine the barriers and facilitators of school social work practice. This research design allowed them to gather both qualitative and quantitative data to describe the phenomenon. Analyses performed on the quantitative data were descriptive statistics (means and percentages), Pearson's correlation, and analysis of variances. The qualitative data were analyzed using content analysis. To assess the agreement between the two persons conducting the content analysis, a Cohen's kappa was computed. The findings indicated that school environments that facilitate multidisciplinary practice can reduce the effects of barriers on the implementation of school interventions. An example of a study demonstrating how mixed-methods research can be used to engage in policy practice is one conducted by Brophy and McDermott (2013). The purpose of their study was to explore what represents good practice with people on Community Treatment Orders (CTOs). The CTOs are mandated as part of the mental health legislation passed in Australia. It requires individuals to adhere to community-based treatment or risk being involuntarily committed for psychiatric treatment. The qualitative data were derived from four case studies and semi-structured interviews. These data were triangulated to establish the creditability of the data. Demographic data from 164 individuals on CTOs were analyzed via cluster analysis. The results yielded five principles of good practice with persons on CTOs: "(1) use and develop direct practice skills, (2) take a human rights perspectives, (3) focus on goals and desired outcomes, (4) aim for quality of service delivery, and (5) enhance and enable the role of key stakeholders" (Brophy & McDermott, p. 78).

Mixed-methods research is appropriate to use in conjunction with experimental designs, for example, when one is interested in knowing the barriers and facilitators of implementing a specific intervention. The results of the qualitative data can be used to develop a new intervention, addressing the identified barriers and enhancing the facilitators. Moreover, mixed-methods research allows social workers to evaluate practice with individuals, families, groups, organizations, and communities (Competency 9, *Evaluative Practice With Individuals, Families, Groups, Organizations, and Communities*). Mixed-methods research designs can be used for survey development. Referring to the case example, let us say that the staff member Dr. Avery asked to do a literature search did not find a survey to assess one's knowledge of the consequences of and risks factors for opioid use. The staff member informs Dr. Avery and she suggests that focus groups and interviews be conducted with 30 persons who attend the center to determine what items should be included on the survey. The focus groups and interviews are used to collect the qualitative data and the survey is used to collect the quantitative data. Another example of when a mixed-methods research design would be appropriate is when a researcher wants to corroborate or validate the findings from different methods. In order to do this, the researcher would simultaneously use the qualitative and quantitative methods to collect the data related to the same research question.

Researchers planning to use a mixed-methods research design must consider when they plan to introduce the qualitative or quantitative method into the design. Creswell, Plano Clark, Gutmann, and Hanson (2003) proposed four questions researchers must consider. They are outlined as follows.

1. When will the qualitative or quantitative method be used? If they are both used simultaneously, then one has a **concurrent design**. Both the qualitative and quantitative data are used to answer the same research question. If the researcher introduces the qualitative or quantitative method first depending upon the research purpose, then one has a **sequential design**. In this design, the type of data collected (e. g., quantitative) lays the foundation for another type of data collection (e.g., qualitative). If the researcher uses the qualitative method first, then the design is referred to as an **exploratory design**. If the researcher uses the quantitative method first, then the design is referred to as an **explanatory design**.

2. Which method will be given more priority? If a concurrent design is used, then both methods are of equal value. If a sequential design is used, then the method that is used first is the one that is valued.

3. When will each method be integrated within a study? If a concurrent design is used, qualitative and quantitative methods are integrated after a single data collection. If a sequential design is used, data from each method is analyzed independently. The order in which the data from each method will be analyzed is dependent upon the order the method was introduced into the design. The results from each method are then integrated.

4. What theoretical perspective will be used to guide the study?

Creswell and colleagues (2003) identified six mixed-methods research designs based on when the qualitative and quantitative methods are introduced into the research design (see Table 9.1).

| Table 9.1 Mixed-Methods Strategies | |
| --- | --- |
| **Strategy** | **Description and Purpose** |
| **Sequential Explanatory** | Collection and analysis of quantitative data followed by collection and analysis of qualitative data |
| | Purpose: Qualitative data are used to assist in interpreting the results of a quantitative study |
| **Sequential Exploratory** | Collection and analysis of qualitative data followed by collection and analysis of quantitative data |
| | Purpose: To explore a phenomenon |

*(Continued)*

Table 9.1   (Continued)

| Strategy | Description and Purpose |
| --- | --- |
| Sequential Transformative | Either the qualitative or quantitative data are collected and analyzed first |
| | Purpose: Use the best strategy that aligns with the theoretical perspective |
| Concurrent Triangulation | Both methods are introduced simultaneously |
| | Purpose: To corroborate the study's findings |
| Concurrent Nested | Priority is given to one method over another, while the other one is embedded or nested |
| | Purpose: To address a different question than the main research question |
| Concurrent Transformative | Both methods are introduced simultaneously |
| | Purpose: To evaluate the theoretical perspective used |

*Source:* Adapted from Hays, D. G. & Sigh, A. A. (2012). Qualitative inquiry in clinical and educational settings. New York, New York, Guilford Press.

In conducting mixed-methods research, one still needs to be concerned about internal and external validity, and trustworthiness of the data. In mixed-methods research, issues related to internal validity (quantitative data) or trustworthiness (qualitative data) are referred to as **inference quality**.

## Example of a Study Using a Mixed-Methods Research Design

Austin, Craig, & McInroy (2016) used a mixed-method research design to explore the perceptions of transgender issues in social work education. The sample included 97 transgender social work students. Students responded to 11 closed-ended questions and 9 open-ended questions.

Analysis performed on the quantitative data were descriptive statistics (percentages) and chi-square analysis. Qualitative data were analyzed using grounded theory procedures and thematic analysis.

Based on the results of the data, four recommendations were made: "(1) making the T visible, (2) comprehensively integrating LGBQT issues throughout the curriculum, (3) improving faculty trans competency, and (4) emphasizing an antioppressive and socially just practice" (p. 305).

# Sampling Strategies
# Used in Mixed-Methods Research

Collins, Onwuegbuzie, and Jiao (2007) recommend that researchers conducting mixed-methods studies use the following sample strategies:

**Identical sampling** produces a sample where the same individuals are included in both the qualitative and quantitative samples. An example of the use of the identical sampling strategy is as follows: Referring to the case example, let us say the staff suggest that the same persons who completed the pretest and posttest questionnaires (quantitative data) be interviewed (qualitative data) about the facilitators and barriers to the implementation of the intervention.

**Parallel sampling** produces a sample where different individuals are included in both the qualitative and quantitative samples, but these individuals have been chosen from the same population (e.g., students attending social work program A are included in the quantitative sample, and students attending social work program B are included in the qualitative sample).

---

### Application Checkpoint 9.1

Think about how Dr. Avery could use a parallel sampling strategy in her proposed mixed-methods research study.

---

**Nested sampling** involves selecting a subset of individuals, for example, who participated in the quantitative data collection, and including them in the qualitative sample. An example of the use of the nested sampling strategy is as follows: Referring to the case example, let us say there were 100 persons ages 50 and above who participated in the intervention aimed at increasing their knowledge about the consequences of and risk factors for opioid use. All of the participants completed the pretest and the posttest (quantitative data). Of these, only 40 were interviewed (qualitative data) about the facilitators and barriers to implementation of the intervention.

**Multilevel sampling** involves selecting individuals from different populations for the qualitative and quantitative samples. An example of the use of the multilevel sampling strategy is as follows: Referring to the case example, Dr. Avery is interested in knowing about the facilitators and barriers to the implementation of the intervention to increase older adults' knowledge about the consequences of and risk factors of opioid use. Upon completion of the intervention, each participant is asked to fill out the posttest (quantitative data) asking them to identify the facilitators or barriers. Following that data collection, staff are then interviewed (qualitative data) to determine the facilitators and barriers to implementation of the intervention.

# Ethics and Mixed-Methods Research

Ethical issues associated with mixed-methods are not fundamentally different than those associated with experimental and quasi-experimental designs (Competency 1, *Demonstrate Ethical and Professional Behavior*). Please re-read Chapters 6 and 7 to re-familiarize yourself with these ethical issues.

---

### Application Checkpoint 9.2

What are some ethical issues related to experimental research designs and qualitative research that Dr. Avery needs to consider before conducting the proposed mixed-methods research study?

---

# Diversity and Mixed-Methods Research

Diversity issues associated with mixed-methods are not fundamentally different than those associated with experimental and quasi-experimental designs (Competency 2, *Engage in Diversity and Differences*). Please re-read Chapters 6 and 7 to re-familiarize yourself with the role of diversity associated with quantitative and qualitative research.

---

### Critical Thinking Question 9.1

Several weeks have passed since your last meeting with Dr. Avery and her staff. She asked you to meet with her to discuss your plan to address the question she raised (How do you plan to gather information on the facilitators and barriers to the implementation of the intervention?) during your initial meeting. Given what you have learned in this chapter, would a mixed-methods research design be preferable to a pretest-posttest experimental design? Justify your response. If you prefer a mixed-methods research design, which type of mixed-methods and sampling strategy would you recommend? Justify your response.

---

# SUMMARY, REVIEW, AND ASSIGNMENTS

## CHAPTER SUMMARY ORGANIZED BY LEARNING OBJECTIVES

**LO 9.1** Identify the ways in which mixed-methods research can be used.

Mixed-methods research designs can be used to evaluate practice with individuals, families, groups, organizations, communities, and policies for survey development and in conjunction with experimental research designs.

**LO 9.2** Differentiate between the various types of mixed-methods strategies.

**Sequential explanatory mixed-methods strategy** refers to the collection and analysis of quantitative data followed by collection and analysis of qualitative data. The purpose of this strategy is to use the qualitative data to assist in interpreting the results of a quantitative study.

**Sequential exploratory mixed-methods strategy** refers to the collection and analysis of qualitative data followed by collection and analysis of quantitative data. The purpose of this strategy is to provide insight about a phenomenon.

**Sequential transformative mixed-methods strategy** refers to either the qualitative or quantitative data being collected and analyzed first. The purpose of this approach is to use the best strategy that aligns with the theoretical perspective guiding the study.

**Concurrent triangulation mixed-methods strategy** refers to the collection of both qualitative and quantitative data simultaneously. The purpose of this strategy is to corroborate the study's findings.

**Concurrent nested mixed-methods strategy** refers to prioritizing one method over another, while the other one is embedded or nested. The purpose of this strategy is to address a different question than the main research question.

**Concurrent transformative mixed-methods strategy** refers to the collection of both qualitative and quantitative data simultaneously. The purpose of this strategy is to evaluate the theoretical perspective used.

**LO 9.3** Differentiate between the various sampling strategies used in mixed-methods research.

Four types of sampling strategies can be employed in mixed-methods research:

*Identical sampling* produces a sample where the same individuals are included in both the qualitative and quantitative samples.

*Parallel sampling* produces a sample where different individuals are included in both the qualitative and quantitative samples, but these individuals have been chosen from the same population.

*Nested sampling* involves selecting a subset of individuals, for example, who participated in the quantitative data collection, and including them in the qualitative sample.

*Multilevel sampling* involves selecting individuals from different populations for the qualitative and quantitative samples.

**LO 9.4** Identify the ethical and diversity issues associated with mixed-methods research.

Ethical issues associated with mixed-methods research are not fundamentally different than those associated with quantitative and qualitative research methods.

Diversity issues associated with mixed-methods research are not fundamentally different than those associated with quantitative and qualitative research methods.

## KEY TERMS

Mixed-methods research 171
Concurrent design 173
Sequential design 173
Exploratory design 173

Explanatory design 173
Inference quality 174
Identical sampling 175
Parallel sampling 175

Nested sampling 175
Multilevel sampling 175

## COMPETENCY NOTES

In this chapter, you were introduced to the competencies below:

Competency 1, *Demonstrate Ethical and Professional Behavior.* Social workers will be involved in ethical decision-making at every stage of the research process.

Competency 2, *Engage Diversity and Difference in Practice.* Social workers recognize that focusing on diversity in mixed-methods research will advance our understanding of the phenomenon under investigation.

Competency 4, *Engage in Practice-Informed Research and Research-Informed Practice.*

Social workers use mixed-methods research to inform and improve practice.

Competency 5, *Engage in Policy Practice.* Social workers use mixed-methods research designs to assess how policies affect the delivery of and access to social services.

Competency 9, *Evaluative Practice With Individuals, Families, Groups, Organizations, and Communities.* Social workers use mixed-methods research to evaluate practice with individuals, families, groups, organizations, and communities.

## ASSESSMENT QUESTIONS

1. How did the information in this chapter enhance your knowledge about mixed-methods research?

2. What specific content discussed in this chapter is still unclear to you? If there is

still content that is unclear, schedule an appointment with your instructor to gain more clarity.

## END-OF-CHAPTER EXERCISES

1. Find a qualitative or quantitative study and redesign it to be a mixed-methods research study. How do you think you improved upon the original study?

2. Propose a study where you would you use a mixed-methods research study. State your research question(s). Identify what you will use to collect both the qualitative and quantitative data. Indicate how you plan to analyze both the qualitative and quantitative data. Share this with a student in your class and have him or her provide you with feedback on what you wrote.

3. Read the article "Toward Transgender Affirmative Social Work Education," by Austin, Cray, and McInroy (2016; *Journal of Social Work Education, 52*, pp. 297–310). In reading the article, you will notice that the authors did not mention the specific mixed-methods strategy that was used. Identify the mixed-methods strategy used. Justify your response.

## ADDITIONAL READINGS

Creswell, J. W., Plano Clark, V. L., Gutmann, M. L., & Hanson, W. E. (2003). Advanced mixed-methods research designs. In A. Tashakkori & C. Teddlie (Eds.), *Handbook of mixed-methods in social and behavioral research* (pp. 209–240). Thousand Oaks, CA: Sage.

## $SAGE edge™

Get the tools you need to sharpen your study skills. SAGE Edge offers a robust online environment featuring an impressive array of free tools and resources.

Access practice quizzes at **edge.sagepub.com/farmer**

# CHAPTER 10

# Observational Research

## Learning Objectives

10.1 Identify the ways in which observational research can be used.

10.2 Differentiate between the various types of observational research designs.

10.3 Identify the diversity and ethical issues associated with observational research.

| Competencies Covered | Learning Objectives | Dimension |
|---|---|---|
| **Competency 1**<br>*Demonstrate Ethical and Professional Behavior* | 10.3 Identify the ethical issues associated with observational research. | Skills |
| **Competency 2**<br>*Engage Diversity and Difference in Practice* | 10.3 Identify the diversity issues associated with observational research. | Skills |
| **Competency 5**<br>*Engage in Policy Practice* | 10.1 Identify the ways in which observational research can be used.<br>10.2 Differentiate between the various types of observational research designs. | Skills |
| **Competency 9**<br>*Evaluate Practice With Individuals, Families, Groups, Organizations, and Communities* | 10.1 Identify the ways in which observational research can be used.<br>10.2 Differentiate between the various types of observational research designs. | Skills |

Master the content at
**edge.sagepub.com/farmer**

## Prenatal Opioid Exposure:
## Implications for Children and Their Families

By responding to the questions related to this case, you will be able to identify what type of observational research should be conducted.

With the increase in opioid use among pregnant women, there has been an influx of infants being born who are opioid exposed. Because of this, Dr. Mason Sharpe, the medical director of Morris Brown Medical Center (MBMC), is concerned about the future of these children. He calls a meeting with the medical social work staff to discuss his concerns. MBMC is located in an urban setting and is designated as a Level 1 Trauma Center. It is well-known for its gynecologic and obstetric services and pediatric care.

During the meeting, Priscilla Winstead, the medical social work director, states that she thinks a study needs to be conducted to understand the short- and long-term effects of prenatal opioid exposure on infants and their families. All persons in the room stated that Ms. Winstead's suggestion was excellent, as they had only been thinking about the need to look at the effects of opioid exposure on the infants. Dr. Sharpe agrees that Ms. Winstead's proposed study should be the one that is conducted, and he asks her to lead the team who will design the study.

You are doing your field placement at MBMC in the medical social work department, and your field supervisor is Ms. Winstead.

At this point, take a few minutes to think about the case example and do the following:

1. Identify the problem.

2. Determine what you already know about the problem.

3. Determine what information you need to solve the problem.

4. List the questions needed to be answered related to the information you need to solve the problem.

Please write down your responses to each item. You will need to refer to them while reading this chapter.

Ms. Winstead convenes a meeting with all the medical social work staff. She states that she thinks the study should examine the effects of prenatal opioid use on cognitive and language development, sensory processing, respiratory disorders, temperament, family stress, parental practices and social support. She further states she would like for you, Sherry, Carl, Jodi, and Marshall to work on determining what type of study should be conducted.

# Introduction

In this chapter, you will learn about the types of observational research designs and when they are appropriate to conduct. Threats to the internal and external validity are described.

# Observational Research Defined

**Observational research** is used to examine the effects of exposure to a variable of interest that is not under the control of the researcher. In other words, the researcher did not randomly assign the participants to the exposure. The exposure variable could potentially serve as the independent variable in a study examining a causal relationship. An observational research design is conducted when an experimental design might be unethical (e.g., exposing study participants to toxins or conditions that could cause them harm). Random assignment is unethical when one is interested in studying the association between secondhand smoke and the development of respiratory diseases in young children. The best way to study the association between secondhand smoke and the development of respiratory diseases in young children is to use an observational research design. To do this, you would review the charts of the children who came to a clinic for treatment for a respiratory disease. You would search these charts to see if they had a parent residing with them who smoked. Additionally, you would also check the charts to see if there were any other factors that could have attributed to their respiratory disease, as you want to rule other out variables that could have contributed to their condition besides residing with a parent who smoked. Because individuals are not randomly assigned to the exposure condition, as in an experimental research study, then causality cannot be inferred. You can only talk about there being an association or a relationship between the variables in the study. Observational research designs can be classified as prospective or retrospective. Researchers using a **prospective research design** start by first identifying the determinant or risk factor and then follow the participants over time until they develop the outcome. Referring to the case example, Dr. Sharpe would be using a prospective, observational research design if she followed the children who were opioid exposed at birth until they developed a respiratory disease. On the other hand, researchers using a **retrospective research design** start by first identifying the outcome and then looking backwards in time to see if they can find the determinant or risk factor that contributed to the outcome. Referring to the case example, Dr. Sharpe would be using a retrospective, observational research design if she reviewed the charts of all the children who received or were currently receiving medical services for respiratory diseases at MBMC to determine if they were exposed to opioids in utero. The unit of analysis in an observational research design study is usually individuals, except when one uses an ecological observational research design, where the unit of analysis is the population or community. An ecological (ecologic) research design is used when researchers initially suspect there is an association between exposure and outcome. As for this observational research design, the unit of analysis is the population or community. Observational research designs are useful for evaluating effectiveness of social work interventions with individuals, families, groups, organizations, and communities (Competency 9, *Evaluate Practice With Individuals, Families, Groups, Organizations, and Communities*). For example, Boyd, Baker, and Reilly (2019), using a respective, observational cohort design, examined the association between depression and anxiety and service delivery models (i.e., stratified step care and progression model). Data were collected by reviewing the charts of individuals who had completed treatment. Their depression and anxiety scores at the first and last session of treatment were used as the dependent variables in the study. The results of their study revealed that the progression model was more appropriate for persons with severe depression and anxiety scores than the stratified step model. Observational research designs are also appropriate for evaluating the effects of policy (Competency 5, *Engage in Policy Practice*). Cohen et al. (2018), using an observational cohort design, evaluated the impact of the Healthy, Hunger-Free Kids (HHFK) Act (2010) and the Massachusetts Competitive Food (MCF) Law of 2010 (105 CMR 225.000) on school meal and snack selection and nutrients consumption. These policies went into effect in 2012. Data were collected on all the above-mentioned variables prior to and after the implementation of these policies. The results demonstrated that after the implementation of these policies there was a reduction in the amount of sugar and unhealthy snacks consumed and an increase in the selection of school meals.

---

### Critical Thinking Question 10.1

Thinking about the case example, should Ms. Winstead propose Dr. Sharpe use an experimental or observational research design? Justify your response.

---

## Types of Observational Research Designs

There are seven types of observational research designs: *case report (case series), ecological (ecologic), cross-sectional, cohort, case-control, nested case-control,* and *case cohort*. In this chapter, you will only learn about the ecological, cross-sectional, cohort, and case-control observational research designs. Table 10.1 presents differentiating characteristics of these research designs.

### Ecological Research Design

An **ecological (ecologic) research design** is used when researchers initially suspect there is an association between exposure and outcome at the population, community, or country level. For this design, either the exposure or outcome variable

**Table 10.1** Differentiating Characteristics of Observational Research Designs

| Observational Research Designs | Level of Observation | Participants Identified Based on Exposure or Outcome | Measure of Association |
|---|---|---|---|
| Ecological | Population, community, or country | Not applicable | Correlation |
| Cross-sectional | Individual | Not applicable | Prevalence |
| Cohort | Individual | Exposure | Relative risk |
| Case-control | Individual | Outcome | Odds ratio |

is measured at the group level and not at the individual level. An example of an exposure variable measured at the group level would be consumption of sugar per capita while an outcome variable measured at the group level would be the incidence rate of cancer. An appropriate research question for this type of study would be as follows: "Is there an association between poverty and child maltreatment in cities in England?" Ecological designs are good for generating a hypothesis to be tested using a case-control, cohort, or experimental research design to determine if what was found can be confirmed at the individual level (Lu, 2009). An ecological research design is typically used for a retrospective study. A **correlational analysis** is often used to measure the association in an ecological research study, despite existing literature questioning the appropriateness of this statistical procedure (Ojha, Offutt-Powell, Evans, & Singh, 2011). Lu (2009) recommends that ecological research design studies only be undertaken when individual-level data are unavailable. An example of a study where a researcher would use an ecological research design is one where a researcher suspects there is an association between eating pickled vegetables and throat cancer in a rural town. In this study, pickled vegetable consumption would be measured as per capita consumption (measured at the population level) because it is the average measure of exposure for the persons who live in the town. It does not mean that everyone consumed the same amount of pickled vegetables. The rate of throat cancer is measured as the amount of throat cancer in the rural town (measured at the population level) and not as an individual's experience with throat cancer. Researchers using an ecological research design may make an ecological fallacy if they do not carefully interpret their findings. An **ecological fallacy** is the assumption that the relationship that exists for groups is assumed to also be true for individuals.

## Cross-Sectional Research Design

A **cross-sectional research design** is used when a researcher is determining simultaneously the exposure and outcome for everyone in the study. Because data are collected on the exposure and outcome simultaneously at one point in time, causality cannot be established. In other words, you cannot determine if the exposure led to the outcome. Therefore, the results may be due to some other variables. These other variables are referred to as confounding variables. **Confounding variables** are related to both the exposure variable and the outcome variable, causing a spurious relationship. A **spurious relationship** is one in which the relationship between the exposure variable and outcome variable is due to a third variable, which is referred as a confounding variable. An example of a spurious relationship is one where a researcher finds a relationship between the sales of ice cream and heat strokes. That is, the sales of ice cream are the highest when the number of heat strokes is the highest. Based on this association, it would be wrong for the researcher to conclude that the sales of ice cream led to the heat strokes or vice versa, because there is a third variable that could account for the relationship found. This third variable, referred to as confounding variable, would be a heat wave. A heat wave would account for the number of ice cream sales and the number of persons having heat strokes. A cross-sectional research design is good for establishing an association between the exposure and outcome, generating hypotheses to be tested in future studies, and determining the prevalence of the exposure. **Prevalence** is the number of cases in a population in a specific time period, expressed as the proportion of the total population at risk for the condition. Prevalence can be calculated using the following formula:

$$\text{Prevalence} = \frac{\text{Number of people with the condition at a specific time}}{\text{The number of people in the population at risk at a specific time period}}$$

The prevalence can be reported as a number or as a percentage. These are both descriptive statistics. An example of a cross-sectional research design study is one conducted by O'Dwyer et al. (2018). Using this design, they determined the prevalence and pattern of anti-epileptic medication prescribing in the treatment of epilepsy in older adults with intellectual disabilities.

## Example of a Study Using a Cross-Sectional, Observational Research Design

Hyland et al. (2014) used a cross-sectional, observational research design to examine the association between active and passive (secondhand smoke exposure [SHS]) lifetime tobacco exposure on self-reported spontaneous abortions, stillbirths, and ectopic pregnancies. Data for the study were derived from the Women's Health Initiative Observational Study (WHIOS), which included 93,676 women ages 50–79 years of age who had completed a questionnaire between 1993 and 1998. Of the 93,676 women, only 80,762 met the inclusion criteria for the study, which was the women needed to have reported at least one pregnancy. The women were coded by the researchers into four categories: (1) ever smoked; (2) never smoked; (3) never smoked, no SHS exposure; and (4) never smoked, SHS exposure.

The findings of the study were as follows: (1) childhood-only SHS was not associated with any of the outcomes; (2) women who ever smoked had a greater risk of having one or more spontaneous abortions, stillbirths, and ectopic pregnancies compared to women who never smoked; and (3) women who never smoked with the highest levels of lifetime SHS exposure had a greater risk of having spontaneous abortions, stillbirths, and ectopic pregnancies than women who never smoked with no SHS exposure.

## Application Checkpoint 10.1

Thinking about the case example, identify a potential confounding variable that would make the relationship between prenatal opioid exposure and respiratory disorders a spurious relationship.

## Cohort Research Design

In using a **cohort research design**, both individuals who have and who have not been exposed are followed over time until the outcome of interest occurs. A cohort research design can be used to assess causality because the exposure has been identified before the outcome and can be prospective or retrospective. According to Carlson and Morrison (2009), an observational cohort research design is appropriate when

1. there is good evidence to suggest an association between the exposure and an outcome (prior cross-sectional studies),

2. the interval between exposure and development of the outcome is relatively short to minimize loss to follow-up, and

3. outcome is not too rare (so that the size of the cohort is reasonable) (p. 79).

This type of design is good for identifying **incidents**—the occurrence of new cases of the outcome. An **incidence rate** is the number of new cases arising in a given period in a specified population and is usually expressed as number of cases per 1,000. Incidence rates can be calculated using the following formula:

$$\text{Incidence Rate} = \frac{\text{Number of people who get the disease given a specific time period}}{\text{Sum of time each person remained under observation and at risk for becoming a case}}$$

**Relative risk** (RR) is used to measure the association in a cohort research design study. RR is the ratio of the probability of an outcome in the exposed group to the probability of an outcome in an unexposed group. RR is a descriptive statistic and cannot be used to determine if there is a statistically significant probability of one group developing the outcome compared to the other. RR can be calculated using the following formula:

$$\text{Relative Risk} = \frac{\text{Probability of an event occurring in Group 1}}{\text{Probability of an event occurring in Group 2}}$$

RR greater than 1 means there is a positive association between exposure and the outcome; RR less than 1 means there is a negative association between exposure and the outcome; and RR equal to 1 means there is no association between exposure and the outcome. Let say, for example, that Dr. Sharpe conducted the study and had a total of 200 participants. There are 100 children in the prenatal opioid exposed group, with 45 who developed a respiratory disease at age 2 and there are 100 children in the non-exposed group, with 25 who developed a respiratory disease at age 2. Table 10.2 shows the number of children who developed a respiratory disease at age 2 along with the number of children in each group.

In looking at Table 10.2, you will see that there are 100 children in the prenatal opioid exposed group, with 45 who developed a respiratory disease at age 2 and there are 100 children in the non-exposed group, with 25 who developed a respiratory disease at age 2. The probability for the exposed group was calculated

| Table 10.2 | Hypothetical Cohort Data for Study Examining the Association Between Prenatal Opioid Exposure and Respiratory Disease at Age 2 | | |
| --- | --- | --- | --- |
| **Respiratory Disease at Age 2** | **No Respiratory Disease** | **Total in Each Group** | |
| Prenatal Opioid Exposed | 45 | 55 | 100 |
| Non-Exposed | 25 | 75 | 100 |

by dividing the number of children who developed a respiratory disease by the number of participants in that group. In this case, $45 \div 100 = .45$. The probability for the non-exposed group was calculated by dividing the number of children who developed a respiratory disease by the number of participants in that group. In this case, $25 \div 100 = .25$. We then divided .45 by .25 and got 1.8. The results suggest that children who were exposed to opioids in utero were 1.8 times more likely to have developed a respiratory disease by age 2 as compared to children who were not exposed to opioids in utero.

An example of a cohort research design study is one conducted by Sarna et al. (2018), where they determined the timing of first respiratory infection in infants until the age of 2. The infants in the sample were born between September 2010 and October 2012.

Threats to the internal validity of an observational cohort research design are attrition and selection bias. Attrition occurs as a result of persons dropping out of the study. With this type of design, researchers need to be concerned about differential attrition. This is where the drop-out rate differs in the exposed group compared to the non-exposed group, which introduces bias into the study. Selection bias could occur when there are systematic differences between the exposed group compared to the non-exposed group on factors related to the outcome (Lu, 2009).

## Case-Control Research Design

In using a **case-control research design**, individuals are selected based on the outcome and are compared to individuals who do not have the outcome (controls), according to past history of exposure to a disease, toxin, or an event. According to Carlson and Morrison (2009), "case-control designs are appropriate when: (1) the outcome is rare and (2) there is reliable evidence of past exposure" (p. 80). There needs to be reliable evidence of past exposure; if not, then the results of the study may be biased. A case-control research design is usually retrospective. Data for the case-control can be obtained from the individuals themselves or by reviewing charts, registries, medical records, or other types of archival records. Researchers must ensure that the controls are similar to the cases in all respects other than what they were exposed to. Matching can be used to ensure that the cases and controls are similar on demographic variables such as age, gender, race/ethnicity, or socioeconomic background. **Matching** refers to the selection of persons to include to serve as controls that are similar to the cases. Referring to the case example, let us say that Ms. Winstead and the social work interns recommend that opioid-exposed babies born at MBMC between 2018 and 2019 whose parents reside in rural areas be included in the study. Therefore, the comparison group should include non-exposed babies born at MBMC between 2018 and 2019 whose parents reside in rural areas.

**Odds ratio** (OR) is used to measure the association in a case-control research design study. An OR that equals 1 means exposure does not affect the odds of developing the outcome; an OR greater than 1 means exposure is associated with higher odds of developing the outcome; and an OR of less than 1 means the exposure is associated with lower odds of developing the outcome. To learn more about the statistical procedures that produce an OR, please refer to Szumilas (2010). An example of study using a case-control research design is one conducted by Sánchez-Sellero, San-Román-Rodríguez, Santos-Pérez, Rossi-Izquierdo, and Soto-Varela (2018). They examined the association between caffeine intake and Menière's disease. There were three groups in the study: (1) those who had Menière's disease, (2) those who had vertigo but was not due to Menière's disease, and (3) those who had other hearing diseases (the case-controls). The findings of the study indicated that those who had Menière's disease had higher caffeine intake than those in the other two groups.

Threats to the internal validity of case-control studies are recall and selection bias. Recall bias may occur because the cases may be more likely to recall the past exposure than the controls (Carlson & Morrison, 2009). Selection bias could occur if the controls were drawn from a different geographical location than the cases, whereby they were less likely to be exposed to the variable of interest (Morrow, 2010).

**External validity** refers to the extent to which the researcher can generalize the study's findings beyond those persons included in the study. The cross-sectional, cohort, and the case-control observational research designs do not allow researchers to generalize their findings beyond the persons in the sample. These research designs are used with small sample sizes, which are not representative samples, and are normally conducted at a single site.

## Ethics and Observational Research

Ethical issues associated with observational research are not fundamentally different than those associated with experimental and quasi-experimental designs (Competency 1, *Demonstrate Ethical and Professional Behavior*). Please re-read Chapters 6 and 7 to re-familiarize yourself with these ethical issues. Oftentimes researchers use person's medical records as a source of collecting data in observational research. The Health Insurance Portability and Accountability Act (HIPAA) of 1996 was enacted to protect the privacy of medical patients and their records. The "Privacy Rule" went into effect in 2000, as mandated by HIPAA; the Privacy Rule outlines how covered entities (e.g., health care groups, businesses) can use and/or disclose protected personal health information (PPHI), including for research purposes. The Privacy Rule requires that individuals sign an authorization form for their PPHI to be used for a specific research study. The form will inform the individuals about why, how, and to whom their information will be used and/or disclosed for research purposes. Besides signing the authorization form, individuals still need to sign an informed consent form. For more information about the Privacy Rule and its implications for research, go to https://privacyruleandresearch.nih.gov/pr_08.asp#8b. We recommend that prior to conducting an observational research study where you are doing your field placement that you speak with your supervisor to determine the guidelines for conducting research in this agency.

## Diversity and Observational Research

Diversity issues associated with observational research are not fundamentally different than those associated with experimental and quasi-experimental designs (Competency 2, *Engage in Diversity and Differences*). Please re-read Chapters 6 and 7 to re-familiarize yourself with these diversity issues.

---

### Critical Thinking Question 10.2

Mrs. Winstead convenes a meeting with all the medical social work interns. She informs everyone that Dr. Sharpe, the medical director, will be meeting with her staff next week to hear about what type of research design will be used to conduct the proposed study. Prior to the meeting, Ms. Winstead would like you, Sherry, Carl, Jodi, and Marshall to do a presentation at the next medical social work staff meeting. She would like for the following to be included in the presentation:

1. Purpose of the study
2. Proposed research question(s)
3. Hypothesis
4. Research design (i.e., ecological observational, cross-sectional observation, cohort observational, or case-control observational); rationale for the choice of the design must be provided.
5. Type of observational research design (prospective or retrospective); rationale for the choice of the type of observational design must be provided.
6. Identify the unit of analysis
7. Inclusion and exclusion criteria
8. Identify the potential ethical issues and the strategy that will be used to address these concerns.

---

# SUMMARY, REVIEW, AND ASSIGNMENTS

## CHAPTER SUMMARY ORGANIZED BY LEARNING OBJECTIVES

LO 10.1 Identify the ways in which observational research can be used.

Observational research can be used to evaluate practice with individuals, families, groups, organizations, communities, and policies.

LO 10.2 Differentiate between the various types of observational research studies.

An *ecological study* is an observational research study that one initially conducts when a researcher suspects there is an association between exposure and an outcome. This type of study is conducted when either the exposure or outcome variable is measured at the group level and not at the individual level.

A *cross-sectional study* is an observational research study in which exposure and outcome are determined simultaneously for everyone in the study.

A *cohort study* is an observational research study in which both

individuals who have and who have not been exposed to a disease, toxin, or an event are followed over time until the outcome of interest occurs.

A *case-control study* is an observational research study in which the individuals are selected based on the outcome and are compared to individuals who do not have the outcome (controls), according to past history of exposure to a disease, toxin, or an event.

LO 10.3 Identify the diversity and ethical issues associated with observational research.

Ethical issues associated with observational research are not fundamentally different than those associated with quantitative and qualitative research methods.

When conducting observational research in a health care setting, the Privacy Rule applies to your being able to conduct research in covered entities.

## KEY TERMS

Observational research   183
Prospective research design   183
Retrospective research design   183
Ecological (ecologic) research design   184
Correlational analysis   185

Ecological fallacy   185
Cross-sectional research design   185
Confounding variables   186
Spurious relationship   186
Prevalence   186
Cohort research design   187
Incidents   187

Incidence rate   187
Relative risk   188
Case-control research design   189
Matching   189
Odds ratio   190
External validity   190

## COMPETENCY NOTES

In this chapter, you were introduced to the competencies below:

Competency, 1 *Demonstrate Ethical and Professional Behavior*. Social workers will be involved in ethical decision-making at every stage of the research process.

Competency 2, *Engage Diversity and Differences*. Social workers recognize that focusing on diversity in observational research will advance our understanding of the phenomenon under investigation.

Competency 5, *Engage in Policy Practice*. Social workers should use observational research designs to evaluate policies.

Competency 9, *Evaluate Practice With Individuals, Families, Groups, Organizations, and Communities*. Social workers should use observational research designs to evaluate practice with individuals, families, groups, organizations, and communities.

## ASSESSMENT QUESTIONS

1. How did the information in this chapter enhance your knowledge about observational research?

2. How did the information in this chapter enhance your knowledge about when one should conduct a cross-sectional study as opposed to a case-control study?

3. What specific content discussed in this chapter is still unclear to you? If there is still content that is unclear, schedule an appointment with your instructor to gain more clarity.

## END-OF-CHAPTER EXERCISES

1. Choose a topic where you would use an observational research design. Discuss why you chose to use an observational research design as opposed to an experimental research design.

2. Referring back to Critical Thinking Question 10.2, develop an outline of the presentation.

3. Find a case-control study and describe how the authors ensured that the participants only differed on the exposure variable of interest.

## ADDITIONAL READINGS

National Institute of Health. (2004). Protecting personal health information in research: Understanding HIPAA Privacy Rule, Publication Number 03-5388. https://privacyrule andresearch.nih.gov/pdf/HIPAA_Booklet_4-14-2003.pdf

Szumilas, M. (2010). Explaining odds ratio. *Journal of Canadian Academy of Children and Adolescent Psychiatry, 19*(3), 227–229.

These, M. S. (2014). Observational and interventional study design types: An overview. *Biochemia Medica, 24*(2), 199–210. doi:10.11613/BM.2014.022

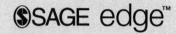

Get the tools you need to sharpen your study skills. SAGE Edge offers a robust online environment featuring an impressive array of free tools and resources.

Access practice quizzes at **edge.sagepub.com/farmer**

## Learning Objectives

11.1   Define sampling.

11.2   Differentiate between the various types of sampling strategies.

11.3   Differentiate between the various types of sampling errors.

11.4   Identify how to assess the quality of a sample.

11.5   Identify the ethical and diversity issues associated with sampling.

| Competencies Covered | Learning Objectives | Dimension |
|---|---|---|
| Competency 1<br>*Demonstrate Ethical and Professional Behavior* | 11.5   Identify the ethical issues associated with sampling. | Skills |
| Competency 2<br>*Engage Diversity and Difference in Practice* | 11.5   Identify the diversity issues associated with sampling. | Skills |
| Competency 3<br>*Engage in Policy Practice* | 11.2   Differentiate between the various types of sampling strategies.<br><br>11.4   Identify how to assess the quality of a sample. | Skills |

*(Continued)*

Master the content at
**edge.sagepub.com/farmer**

(Continued)

| Competencies Covered | Learning Objectives | Dimension |
|---|---|---|
| Competency 4<br>*Engage in Practice-Informed Research and Research-Informed Practice* | 11.2 Differentiate between the various types of sampling strategies.<br>11.4 Identify how to assess the quality of a sample. | Skills |
| Competency 9<br>*Evaluate Practice With Individuals, Families, Groups, Organizations, and Communities.* | 11.2 Differentiate between the various types of sampling strategies.<br>11.4 Identify how to assess the quality of a sample. | Skills |

## PBL Case 11

### Predictors of Bullying Behaviors: Variations Across Gender

By responding to the questions related to this case example, you will be able to determine what type of sampling strategy is appropriate.

The principal of Eastside Elementary School called a meeting with all the teachers, school social workers, and student interns at the beginning of the school year. At the meeting, the principal spoke about a national conference she attended on bullying and victimization in schools. She learned that in order to address this issue, schools first needed to collect data on the factors that contribute to bullying and other forms of victimization. These factors include characteristics of the individuals who are being bullied; the persons who are doing the bullying; the school, including school policies and the quality of instruction; and the community in which the school is located. Eastside Elementary School is located in a suburban area and currently there are 750 students enrolled, with 20% receiving free lunch and 30% having an individualized educational plan (IEP). The population of the school is 56% male. The children who attend this school are from diverse backgrounds.

At the end of the meeting, the principal asked attendees to be part of a work group to help determine the contributing factors to bullying and other forms of victimization at her school. Ms. Pauline Patterson, a school social worker, tells the principal that she and her interns are volunteering to be a part of the work group. You are doing your field placement at the Eastside Elementary School.

At this point, take a few minutes to think about the case example and do the following:

1. Identify the problem.

2. Determine what you already know about the problem.

3. Determine what information you need to solve the problem.

4. List the questions needed to be answered related to the information you need to solve the problem.

Please write down your responses to each item. You will need to refer to them while reading this chapter.

**Your field supervisor, Ms. Patterson, calls a meeting with you and the other social work interns. She wants to discuss how to assist the principal in gathering information about the characteristics of the individuals who are being bullied; the persons who are doing the bullying; the school, including school policies and the quality of instruction; and the community in which the school is located. She states that the principal is interested in knowing if the predictors of bullying and other forms of victimization differ by gender.**

**You tell Ms. Patterson that you are taking a research course and this week you are discussing sampling strategies, and you may be able to let the work group know what sampling strategy may be appropriate to use for recruiting the participants for this study.**

# Introduction
...................................................................................

In this chapter, you will learn about the different types of sampling strategies. The reasons why samples may be different from the population are provided. A brief discussion of how to assess the quality of a sample is presented. Ethical and diversity issues associated with sampling are discussed.

# Terminology
...................................................................................

**Sampling** refers to the strategies used to select a given number of individuals or things (e.g., cities, neighborhoods, or schools) from a population. For a graphic depiction of sampling, see Figure 11.1. The **population** is all the individuals or things the researcher is interested in for the study being undertaken. Let us say a researcher is interested in examining the factors that contribute to stress

Figure 11.1  Graphic Depiction of Sampling

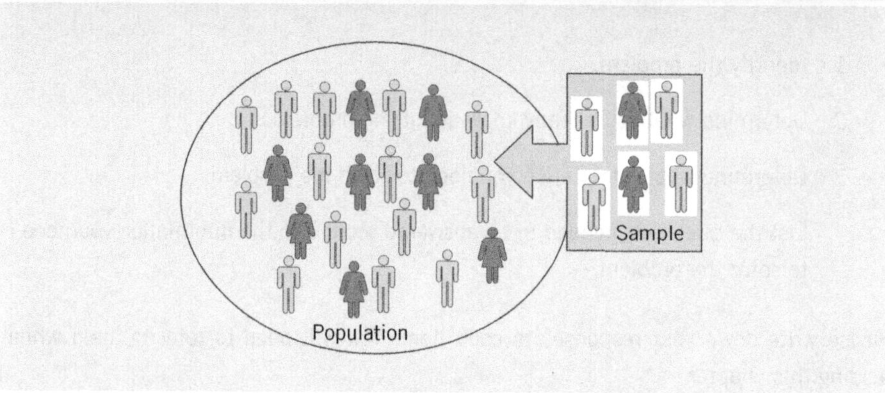

Population

Sample

in immigrants and refugees. Such a study would be hard to conduct because there is not a list that has all the names of all those in the population of interest. Additionally, it might be too time-consuming or expensive to identify and collect information from all of the members of the population. Thus, the researcher needs to focus on selecting the sample from an accessible population. An **accessible population** is one that the researcher can potentially access. The researcher may have access to this population because he or she works in the agency where services are provided to the population or lives in close proximity to where the population is located geographically. Once the accessible population has been identified, then the researcher needs to think about the unit of analysis. The **unit of analysis** is what you are comparing in the study. For example, are you comparing individuals, families, communities, or nations? Many times, studies conducted by social work researchers focus on comparing individuals; therefore, the unit of analysis is individuals. Referring to the case example, the unit of analysis could be individual students or classrooms. Individual students as the unit of analysis would be in a study that focuses on gathering data about an individual student's experiences of being bullied. On the other hand, we could focus on students' perceptions of the culture of their classrooms as it relates to bullying. In this study, the unit of analysis would be the classroom. Once the unit of analysis has been identified, then you need to obtain a list of all those in the accessible population—this is referred to as the **sampling frame**. The sampling frame is used to select those who will be included in the sample. For a graphic depiction of the sampling frame, see Figure 11.2. Referring to the case example, let us say that the work group decided to collect data from the students about their experiences of being bullied, then the sampling frame would be the students in the school. On the other hand, if the work group decided to collect data from the students about their perceptions about the culture of their classroom as it relates to bullying, then the sampling frame is the classrooms in the school.

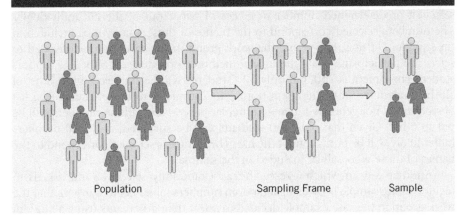

**Figure 11.2  Graphic Depiction of Sampling Frame**

Population          Sampling Frame          Sample

## Types of Sampling Strategies

There are two types of sampling strategies—probability and nonprobability sampling. With **probability sampling**, we can determine the probability that any individual in the sampling frame can be selected. For example, the selection of individuals can be done to make sure that each individual has an equal probability of being selected. Probability sampling is used to produce a representative sample. A **representative sample** is one that closely matches the population from which it was drawn. Probability sampling allows the results of a researcher's study to be generalized to the population from which the sample was drawn. With **nonprobability sampling**, it is unknown what the chance was that an individual was selected. Typically, researchers using nonprobability sampling use their judgment regarding the characteristics of the sample that are needed to address their study's aim. For example, Tweneboah and Owusu (2013) used a convenience-based nonprobability sampling method to study the use of condoms among commercial drivers in Ghana.

### Types of Probability Sampling

There are four types of probability sampling strategies: random sampling, systematic random sampling, stratified random sampling, and cluster sampling. **Random sampling**, also referred to as *simple random sampling* (SRS), uses a procedure that seeks to select participants randomly from the population or sampling frame. When SRS is used, each member of the sampling frame has an equal probability of being selected. Random selection is based on three methods. One method is known as a **lottery**. Using this method, a researcher assigns a number to everyone who is on the list compiled from the sampling frame and puts this number on a piece of paper and then puts the paper in a hat. The researcher then selects a predetermined number of pieces of paper out of the hat individually. The numbers selected correspond to the names of those who will be included in the sample. Let us suppose that the work group in the case example decided to select the participants using the lottery method to produce an SRS. The school's student enrollment is 750, but only 300 students will be surveyed. First, a list of all the students, numbering them from 1 to 750 needs to be generated. The list of students is not generated in any particular order. Next, all the numbers will be put in a hat. Given that only 300 students will be surveyed, only 300 numbers individually will be pulled out of the hat. The numbers selected correspond to the names of those who will be included in the sample.

Another way in which a researcher can randomly select the individuals to include in the sample is by using a random numbers table. Let us suppose that the work group in the case example decided to select the participants using a random numbers table. The school's student enrollment is 750, but only 300 students will be surveyed. First, a list of all the students, numbering them from 1 to 750, needs to be generated. The list of students is not generated in any particular order. Mr. Barry, who is a member of the work group, would then go to the Internet to get a copy of a random number table (see Table 11.1).

The numbers in the table were randomly generated and are in random order. Since the school has a population of 750 students and this is a three-digit number, Mr. Barry needs to use the first three digits of the numbers listed in the table. Next, he would close his eyes and randomly point to a spot on the table. For this example, we will assume that he selected 03002 in the seventh column. The first three digits are "030" or "30," therefore the student assigned the number 30 will be selected to receive the survey. Mr. Barry then goes to the next number below 03002, which is "53608" or "536"; therefore, the student assigned the number 536 would be selected to receive the survey. He then goes to the next number. Mr. Barry would continue this process until he had selected 300 students.

Another method used to produce an SRS is to use software to generate the random numbers that will be used to randomly select persons to be in the sample. For example, Microsoft Excel can be used to generate random numbers. The formula to generate the random numbers in Excel is as follows: =Randbetween (1,100). Once you have entered the formula, then you hit "Enter." A number will appear in the first line of the first column. After the number appears, then you can scroll down or over and then more numbers will appear. This formula will generate random numbers between 1 and 100. By changing the number after the comma, you change the sample size. If, for example, you want your sample size to be 200, the formula would be =Randbetween (1,200). To see a demonstration of how to use Excel to generate random numbers, you can simply do a "how to generate random numbers in Excel" Google search.

There are two subtypes of random sampling—sampling with replacement and sampling without replacement. **Sampling with replacement** involves, for example, selecting a number from a hat, including the participant associated

## Table 11.1 Table of Random Numbers

| | | | | | | | | | | | | |
|---|---|---|---|---|---|---|---|---|---|---|---|---|
| 36518 | 36777 | 89116 | 05542 | 29705 | 83775 | 21564 | 81639 | 27973 | 62413 | 85652 | 62817 | 57881 |
| 46132 | 81380 | 75635 | 19428 | 88048 | 08747 | 20092 | 12615 | 35046 | 67753 | 69630 | 10883 | 13683 |
| 31841 | 77367 | 40791 | 97402 | 27569 | 90184 | 02338 | 38318 | 54936 | 34641 | 95525 | 86316 | 87384 |
| 84180 | 93793 | 64953 | 51472 | 65358 | 23701 | 75230 | 47200 | 78176 | 85248 | 90589 | 74567 | 22633 |
| 78435 | 37586 | 07015 | 98729 | 76703 | 16224 | 97661 | 79907 | 06611 | 26501 | 93389 | 92725 | 68158 |
| 41859 | 94198 | 37182 | 61345 | 88857 | 53204 | 86721 | 59613 | 67494 | 17292 | 94457 | 89520 | 77771 |
| 13019 | 07274 | 51068 | 93129 | 40386 | 51731 | 44254 | 66685 | 72835 | 01270 | 42523 | 45323 | 63481 |
| 82448 | 72430 | 29041 | 59208 | 95266 | 33978 | 70958 | 60017 | 39723 | 00606 | 17956 | 19024 | 15819 |
| 25432 | 96593 | 83112 | 96997 | 55340 | 80312 | 78839 | 09815 | 16887 | 22228 | 06206 | 54272 | 83516 |
| 69226 | 38655 | 03811 | 08342 | 47863 | 02743 | 11547 | 38250 | 58140 | 98470 | 24364 | 99797 | 73498 |
| 25837 | 68821 | 66426 | 20496 | 84843 | 18360 | 91252 | 99134 | 48931 | 99538 | 21160 | 09411 | 44659 |
| 38914 | 82707 | 24769 | 72026 | 56813 | 49336 | 71767 | 04474 | 32909 | 74162 | 50404 | 68562 | 14088 |
| 04070 | 60681 | 64290 | 26905 | 65617 | 76039 | 91657 | 71362 | 32246 | 49595 | 50663 | 47459 | 57072 |
| 01674 | 14751 | 28637 | 86980 | 11951 | 10419 | 41454 | 48527 | 53868 | 37846 | 85912 | 15156 | 00865 |
| 70294 | 35450 | 39982 | 79503 | 34382 | 43186 | 69890 | 63222 | 30110 | 56004 | 04819 | 05138 | 57476 |
| 73903 | 98066 | 52136 | 85925 | 50000 | 96334 | 30773 | 80511 | 31178 | 52799 | 41050 | 76298 | 43995 |
| 87789 | 56408 | 17107 | 88452 | 80975 | 03406 | 36114 | 64549 | 19244 | 82044 | 00202 | 45727 | 35709 |
| 92320 | 95929 | 58545 | 70699 | 07679 | 23296 | 03002 | 63885 | 54677 | 55745 | 52540 | 62154 | 33314 |
| 46391 | 60276 | 92061 | 43591 | 42118 | 73094 | 53608 | 58949 | 42927 | 90993 | 46795 | 05917 | 01934 |
| 67090 | 45063 | 84584 | 66022 | 48268 | 74971 | 94861 | 61749 | 61085 | 81758 | 89640 | 39437 | 90044 |
| 11666 | 99916 | 35165 | 29420 | 73213 | 15275 | 62532 | 47319 | 39842 | 62273 | 94980 | 23415 | 64668 |
| 40910 | 59068 | 04594 | 94576 | 51187 | 54196 | 17411 | 56123 | 66545 | 82163 | 61868 | 22752 | 40101 |
| 41169 | 37965 | 47518 | 92180 | 05257 | 19143 | 77486 | 02457 | 00985 | 31960 | 39033 | 44374 | 28352 |
| 76418 | | | | | | | | | | | | |

with the number in the sample, and then putting the number back in the hat so that it can be selected again. **Sampling without replacement** involves, for example, selecting a number from a hat, including the participant associated with the number in the sample, and not putting the number back into the hat. For the bullying case example, we would use sampling without replacement. An advantage of using random sampling is that it seeks to reduce selection bias in the sample being studied. Selection bias can reduce the validity of the inferences you want to draw from inferential statistical tests you have conducted to analyze the data. An assumption of inferential statistics (see Chapter 13) is that the sample is obtained via SRS. A disadvantage of random sampling is that when the population is heterogeneous and particular subgroups have a larger presence in the population, it is possible that SRS will not result in their representation in the sample. Another disadvantage is that there may not be a list that contains everyone in the population from which to draw the sample. There are five steps that need to be conducted to create a random sample: (1) define the target population, (2) identify an existing sampling frame of the target population or develop one, (3) assign numbers to each individual (unit of analysis) in the sampling frame, (4) determine the desired sample size, and (5) randomly select the participants (by lottery, use of a random numbers table, or Excel-generated random numbers) until you reach the desired sample size.

Systematic random sampling involves the researcher selecting the first person to be in the sample based on a random starting point and then selecting the remainder of the sample based on a fixed sampling interval. The **sampling interval** is calculated by dividing the entire population by the desired sample size. Let us say, for example, a researcher wants a sample size of 100 and the entire population includes 1,000 individuals. To calculate the sampling interval, the researcher would divide 1,000 by 100, which is equal to 10. Therefore, the researcher would select every 10th individual to be in the sample. Let us say that the researcher selects a random starting point of 5—the fifth individual on the list would be the first case selected to be in the sample. After this, then the researcher would select every 10th person past the random starting point (15, 25, 35, 45, etc., until there were 100 persons in the sample). An advantage of systematic random sampling is that it is appropriate for use when the researcher has budget constraints. A disadvantage of systematic random sampling is that it could produce a biased sample if the list of names was organized in some type of pattern. Let us say a social worker who is working for child protective services decides to study the parenting practices of foster parents. The social worker decides she would look at the cases she had in the past year and only wants to interview 25 of the 200 parents. The names of the parents are in alphabetical order; hence, those whose names start with letters early in the alphabet or more likely to be selected to participate in the study than those whose names start with letters later in the alphabet. There are seven steps that need to be conducted to create a systematic random sample: (1) define the target population, (2) determine the sample size, (3) identify an existing sampling frame of the target population or develop one, (4) assign numbers to the cases (unit of analysis), (5) select the random starting point, (6) calculate the sampling interval, and (7) select the nth case until you obtain the desired sample size.

**Stratified random sampling** is used when a researcher is interested in comparing two or more subgroups (or strata) of the population. In using this sampling strategy, the researcher must decide if the sample size for each subgroup will be proportional or disproportional in its representation to the population. If the researcher wants the sample size of each subgroup to be proportional in its representation to the population, then a **proportional stratified sampling** strategy would be employed. An example of a study where a proportional stratified sampling would be appropriate would be if a social work researcher is interested in studying the effects of stress, burnout, and social support on social workers' well-being. The research question is, "Will the effects of stress, burnout, and social support be different for male and female social workers?" The researcher would contact the NASW Chapter in the state he or she resides and purchase its membership list. Once the list has been obtained, the researcher will assign each member a number. Because the researcher is interested in examining the differences by gender, the sample would be stratified by gender (male and female). The social work researcher chose to stratify the sample by gender because she knows by looking at the membership list that women are three or four times more likely to be social workers than men. The use of a proportional stratified sample will result in a sample that accurately represents the population of the membership of the NASW Chapter in the state in which the researcher resides. An advantage of proportional stratified sampling is that it reduces sampling error when the variance between the stratified groups is large. A disadvantage is that you need to have complete data on the variable used to stratify the sample on everyone in the population.

## Example of a Study Using Stratified Random Sampling

Kim and Dymond (2012) used a proportional stratified random sample in their study investigating the effects of the type of residence and hours of in-home support on community participation of individuals with severe disabilities. The sample was stratified by type of residence (i.e., group home and supported apartment). A proportional stratified random sampling was used to select 500 group homes and 500 supported apartments. These facilities were selected from each state. The percentage of group homes and supported apartments from each state was calculated by dividing the number of persons living in the state by the total U.S. population, using the 2008 Census data and then multiply that number by 500 (i.e., the total sample size for each residence type).

*(Continued)*

(Continued)

After the 500 group homes and 500 supported apartments were selected, the residential specialists (i.e., the participants in the study) were randomly selected from each group home in each state. The same procedure was used to select the residential specialists from the group homes, except for in four states, where executive directors at the regional office were asked by the researchers to randomly select the case manager to participate. The modification to the selection procedure was warranted because the supported homes in these four states are under the auspices of the regional offices.

Because there is not a national list of residential specialists, the researchers e-mailed the director of residential services for each state asking for the names and mailing addresses of the director for each group home and supported apartments.

If the researcher wants the sample size of each subgroup to be disproportional in its representation to the population, then a **disproportional stratified sampling** strategy would be employed. Elliott, Golinelli, Hambarsoomian, Perlman, and Wenzel (2006) demonstrated how a disproportional stratified sampling strategy could be used to collect data from sheltered homeless and low-income housed women. The population consisted of facilities where homeless women and low-income women reside. The sample was stratified by type of facility (shelters and housing units). Next, a simple random sampling strategy was used to select the participants from the shelters and housing units, with higher numbers of women being selected from small shelters and low-income housing sites than large shelters and low-income housing sites.

There are seven steps that need to be conducted to create a stratified sample: (1) define the target population; (2) identify the variable that will be used to stratify the sample and the number of strata to be used; (3) identify an existing sampling frame or develop one, including the information on the variable used to stratify the sample; (4) divide the sampling frame into strata, creating a sampling frame for each stratum; (5) assign a number to each unit of analysis; (6) determine the desired sample size for each stratum; and (7) randomly select the target number of units of analysis from each stratum by random sampling or systematic random sampling.

**Cluster sampling** (or area sampling) involves selecting a cluster of participants from the population. The sampling clusters may be space based (e.g., states, counties, census tracts), organizational based (e.g., school district, grade levels, classes), or telephone based (e.g., area codes). For example, let us say a researcher is interested in the effects of a campaign to reduce opioid use in persons who reside in low-income neighborhoods. Let us say the researcher uses the U.S. Census data to identify the low-income neighborhoods in the county in which she resides. She would assign each neighborhood a number. Let us say there are 32 neighborhoods and her desired sample size for her study is 12 neighborhoods. She would then randomly select 12 of the 32 neighborhoods. Members of the households in these 12 neighborhoods would be included in her sample.

There are two subtypes of cluster sampling: one stage and two stage (multi-stage sampling). In the **one-stage cluster** sampling, the sample is obtained by selecting the cluster. **Two-stage cluster** sampling involves selecting clusters at the first stage and then selecting who will be in the sample from every selected cluster (second stage). Random sampling is used to select the participants at the second stage. An advantage of cluster sampling is that it is appropriate for use when the target population is widely dispersed geographically. A disadvantage of cluster sampling is that the clusters may not produce a sample as representative of the population as one would have obtained by using a random sample, given the same sample size. There are five steps that need to be conducted to create a cluster sample: (1) define the target population, (2) determine the sample size, (3) identify an existing sample frame of clusters or develop one, (4) determine the number of clusters to be selected, and (5) randomly select the target number of clusters.

---

### Critical Thinking Question 11.1

The chair of the work group convenes the first meeting of the group. The agenda items are: (1) discuss the purpose of the study, (2) develop the research question(s), (3) identify the sampling strategy (i.e., random sampling, systematic random sampling, stratified random sampling, or cluster sampling), (4) define the target population, (5) identify the sampling frame, and (6) identify the unit of analysis. Prior to discussing the agenda items, the Chair reminds the group that the principal is interested in knowing if the predictors of bullying and other forms of victimization differ by gender.

Write down your responses to the agenda items and justify your response for your choice of sampling strategy.

---

## Types of Nonprobability Sampling

There are four commonly used types of nonprobability sampling strategies: convenience, purposive, snowball, and quota.

**Convenience sampling**, also referred to as *accidental* or *availability sampling*, involves selecting persons from the target population because they are accessible to the researcher. The participants may be accessible to the researcher because the researcher works in a facility where he or she has access to the target population, for example. Let us say a social worker is interested in the effects of social isolation on substance use among adolescents. The social worker works in a facility that provides mental health services to adolescents. Therefore, the adolescents who can potentially participate in the study are readily accessible and would be selected to participate in the study via convenience sampling.

Four steps are conducted to create a convenience sample: (1) define the target population, (2) identify ways to recruit individuals in the target population, (3) determine the sample size, and (4) select the targeted number of individuals (unit of analysis). An advantage of using convenience sampling is that it less time-consuming than using random sampling. A disadvantage is persons from hard-to-reach populations may not be included in the sample.

**Purposive sampling** involves selecting persons from the target population because of their fit with the purpose of the study and inclusion criteria. Referring to the case example, let us say that the principal developed the following inclusion criteria: only students who have been bullied will be surveyed. The type of purposive sampling strategy that would be appropriate to ensure that only the persons that meet the inclusion criteria are selected for the study is criterion sampling. **Criterion sampling** involves selecting participants based on a criterion established by the researcher. There are 14 types of purposive sampling strategies, and they are outlined in Table 11.2. An advantage of purposive sampling is that it can be used in both quantitative and qualitative research. A disadvantage of purposive sampling is that it may take time to get the sample size you desire. There are five steps that need to be conducted to create a purposive sample: (1) define the target population, (2) identify the inclusion and exclusion criteria for the sample, (3) identify ways to recruit individuals in the target population who meet the inclusion criteria for the sample (unit of analysis), (4) determine the sample size, and (5) select the targeted number of individuals.

**Snowball sampling** first involves selecting participants from the target population because of their fit with the purpose of the study and inclusion criteria. Once the researcher finishes surveying or interviewing the participant, he or she will ask the participant to tell others about the study. If someone the participant spoke with is interested in participating in the study, he or she is instructed to call the researcher. In conversation with the researcher, he or she will determine if the person is eligible to participate in the study. An advantage of snowball sampling is that it can be used to recruit persons from hard-to-reach populations. A disadvantage of this approach is that it may produce a homogeneous sample—that is, the sample may not consist of persons from diverse backgrounds. There are eight steps that need to be conducted to create a snowball sample: (1) define the target population, (2) identify the inclusion and exclusion criteria for the sample, (3) identify ways to recruit individuals in the target population who meet the inclusion criteria for the sample (unit of analysis), (4) determine the desired sample size, (5) recruit individuals and survey or interview them, (6) ask participants to refer others to be included in the study, (7) potential participants who have been referred contact the researcher, so he or she can determine if they meet the study's eligibility criteria, and (8) continue to ask your participants to identify potential participants until the desired sample size has been obtained.

**Quota sampling** involves obtaining a sample that is as representative as possible in relation to potentially confounding variables and of a specific size (quota). **Confounding variables** are unusually demographic variables that are related to both the independent and dependent variable causing a spurious association.

## Table 11.2  Purposive Sampling Strategies

| Types of Purposive Sampling Strategies | Characteristics of the Sample |
| --- | --- |
| Homogeneous | Participants share many similarities to one another (used in both qualitative and quantitative research) |
| Maximum variation | Participants share many differences from one another (used in both qualitative and quantitative research) |
| Random purposeful sampling | Participants are randomly selected from a purposeful sample (used in both qualitative and quantitative research) |
| Stratified purposeful sampling | Participants are selected based on a specific characteristic (e.g., race/ethnic background, gender) the researcher is interested in making a comparison on (used in both qualitative and quantitative research) |
| Comprehensive sampling | The entire group of participants is selected based on a set of criteria established by the researcher (e.g., researcher selects entire group of students because they had a specific course; used in both qualitative and quantitative research) |
| Typical case sampling | A case is selected to demonstrate the average example of the focus of the study (used specifically for qualitative research) |
| Intensity sampling | Cases selected to intensely demonstrate the phenomenon of investigation (used specifically for qualitative research) |
| Critical case sampling | A case that serves as a "benchmark" with which to compare other cases (used specifically for qualitative research) |
| Politically important sampling | Cases that draw political attention to the phenomenon; cases that will draw the attention of the media (used specifically for qualitative research) |
| Extreme or deviant case sampling | Participants are selected based on having the most positive or most negative experiences (used in both qualitative and quantitative research). Please note if this sampling strategy is used in quantitative research, the study will be affected by the threat to internal validity statistical regression to the mean (see Chapter 13) |
| Opportunistic sampling | Participants are selected based on how the research evolves (used specifically for qualitative research) |
| Criterion sampling | Participants are selected based on a criterion established by the researcher (used in both qualitative and quantitative research) |
| Theoretical sampling | Theory derived from your data collection guides the sampling strategy (used specifically in qualitative research using grounded theory) |
| Confirming and disconfirming sampling | During the theoretical sampling, the researcher searches for cases to support or refute findings (used specifically in qualitative research) |

*Source:* Adapted from Hays, D. G. & Sigh, A. A. (2012). Qualitative inquiry in clinical and educational settings. New York, New York, Guilford Press.

A **spurious association** is one where the researcher thought there was a relationship between the independent and dependent variable; however, another variable explains away this relationship. There are two subtypes of quota sampling: proportional quota and nonproportional quota. In **proportional quota sampling**, the researcher wants the sample size of each subgroup of the confounding variable to be proportional in its representation to the population. In **nonproportional quota sampling,** the researcher wants the sample size of each subgroup to be disproportional in its representation to the population. Determining the number of individuals that should be selected for each quota category (i.e., subgroup) is based on noninterlocking or interlocking quotas. With **noninterlocking quota**, the researcher considers the quota separately. For example, a researcher needs 60 participants and the quota controls are gender and socioeconomic status (lower socioeconomic status, middle socioeconomic status, and upper-middle socioeconomic status). The researcher would need 30 males and 30 females. Of these, 20 must be from lower socioeconomic status, 20 must be from middle-class socioeconomic status, and 20 must be of upper-middle socioeconomic status. With **interlocking quota**, the researcher considers the quota jointly. For example, a researcher needs to take into consideration both gender category and age categories—how many males do you need in each of the following age categories: 18–24, 25–35, 36–46 and how many females do you need in each of the following age categories: 18–24, 25–35, 36–46? An advantage of quota sampling is that it includes subpopulations in the sample. A disadvantage of quota sampling is that it is time-consuming to create the sample. There are six steps that need to be conducted to create a quota sample: (1) define the target population; (2) identify the inclusion and exclusion criteria for the sample; (3) determine the quota (confounding variable) to be used, basing this determination on the empirically based literature; (4) determine the sample size; (5) determine the number of individuals that should be selected for each quota category based on noninterlocking or interlocking quotas; and (6) select the target number of individuals per the quota using convenience or purposive sampling.

## Critical Thinking Question 11.2

The chair of the work group convenes a second meeting of the group. The focus of this meeting is to discuss the concerns of several members of the group who have questioned the appropriateness of a probability sampling strategy (i.e., random sampling, systematic random sampling, stratified random sampling, or cluster sampling) to be used to select the respondents for the study. Prior to the discussion, the chair reminds the group that the principal is interested in knowing if the predictors of bullying and other forms of victimization differ by gender.

Given what you know about probability sampling, would a nonprobability sampling strategy be more appropriate? If you believe a nonprobability sampling strategy is more appropriate to be used than a probability sampling strategy, which nonprobability sampling strategy (i.e., convenience sampling, purposive sampling, snowball sampling, or quota sampling) would you recommend be used? Justify your response.

## Reasons Why Samples May Differ From the Population

The sample may differ from the population which it was drawn from because of sampling error, nonsampling error, and sampling bias. **Sampling error** is produced by using sampling strategies (e.g., stratified sampling and quota sampling) that overrepresent a portion of the study population. Sampling error generally decreases as the sample size increases. The use of random sampling can also reduce sampling error. **Nonsampling error** is due to the difference between those who responded to the survey/questionnaire and those who did not and how the survey/questionnaire was administered. **Sampling bias** is due to the methods used to select the sample. The methods used result in a sample that is not representative of the population.

## Criteria for Evaluating the Quality of a Sample

There are two criteria for evaluating the quality of a sample: representativeness and sample size. As mentioned earlier, a representative sample is one that closely matches the population from which it was drawn. Probability sampling allows the results of a researcher's study to be generalized to the population from which the sample was drawn. Another criterion used is determining if the sample size is adequate to produce valid results. Making sure that the sample size is adequate to produce valid results ensures that social workers can inform practice (Competency 4, *Engage in Research-Informed Practice and Practice-Informed Research*) and policy (Competency 3, *Engage in Policy Practice*). Additionally, having an adequate sample size is important when social workers are evaluating the effectiveness of interventions (Competency 9, *Evaluate Practice With Individuals, Families, Groups, Organizations, and Communities*). We suggest that you conduct a statistical power analysis to determine your sample size. A **power analysis** allows researchers to determine the sample size required to produce a given effect size. The **effect size** is a way of quantifying the size of difference between two groups. Finding statistically significant results is dependent upon both the sample size and the effect size. There are several software packages and online calculators that can be used to calculate a power analysis, such as G*power, WebPower, and SPSS Sample Power.

To determine your sample size using any of the above-named power analysis software, you will need to know the following:

1. What is your study design? Is your research design experimental, non-experimental, or observational?

2. What are your research questions?

3. How many independent and dependent variables do you have?

4. What are the levels of measurements for the independent and dependent variables?

5. Is the dependent variable normally distributed?

6. What is the statistical analysis you plan to conduct?

7. What is the p-value you plan to use to test your hypothesis? Normally, a p-value of .05 is used.

8. What is the power level you plan to use? Normally, a power level of .80 or higher is used.

9. What effect size do you plan to use? Normally Cohen's d is used. For Cohen (1988), a small effect is .20, a medium effect is .50, and .80 is a large effect.

Sample size not only plays a role in the power analysis calculation, but it also impacts the representativeness of a sample. When samples are heterogeneous, larger sample sizes and/or more complex sampling strategies may be needed in order to capture that heterogeneity in the sample.

## Application Checkpoint 11.1

Download one of the online calculators that can be used to calculate a power analysis to determine the sample size for the case example, for a power level of .80.

## Ethics and Sampling

Social work researchers must take into consideration how the sampling strategies used in their research might present ethical dilemmas (Competency 1, *Demonstrate Ethical and Professional Behavior*). For example, snowball sampling presents an ethical dilemma as it relates to remuneration of the participants. There are no standard guidelines for the remuneration of participants. You may recall that in snowball sampling the researcher asks the participants to identify potential participants. In this situation, the participant receives remuneration for his or her participation and for each person he or she recruits. Let us say that the participant was paid $15 to participate and was paid $15 for each person recruited. The participant recruits 25 individuals; therefore, the participant would receive $375 for recruiting persons to participate and $15 for his or her participation. Thus, the total received is $390. To address the issue of having participants recruit as many persons as they can and preventing the participant perceiving that the remuneration is a source of income, Semaan, Santibanez, Garfein, Heckathorn, and Des Jarlais (2008) recommend that a quota limit be set. They recommend that the participant only be asked to recruit three individuals. The participant should be given three coupons, with unique serial numbers, to distribute to these three individuals and these individuals should be instructed to bring their coupons with them when they come to their scheduled appointment to participate in the study.

In the above example, because there was not a quota limit set, there exists the possibility that the recruiter could have pressured the individuals to participate. The recruiter may have pressured the participants because he or she perceived the remuneration as a source of income. In thinking about how much remuneration participants should receive, Semaan et al. (2008) suggest that the amount should "be acceptable to recruiters, large enough to attract and sustain interest in participant-driven recruitment, and small enough to represent remuneration for time and effort associated with participant-driven recruitment" (p. 22).

Social work researchers must be truthful in how they explain the purpose, benefits, and potential risks of their research when recruiting participants. There are several examples of how researchers misled persons they had recruited for their research. For example, in the Lead-Based Paint Abatement and Repair and Maintenance Study from 1993 to 1995, the consent provided to the parents did not describe the purpose of the study, the harmful effects of lead-based paint on their children, and the three different methods of lead abatement (*Ericka Grimes v. Kennedy Krieger Institute, Inc. and Myron Higgins, a minor, etc., et al. v. Kennedy Krieger Institute*, 2000).

## Diversity and Sampling

In order for social workers to engage diversity and difference in practice, they must read studies that have persons from diverse backgrounds in their samples (Competency 2, *Engage Diversity and Difference in Practice*). By reading these studies, one will become aware of effective strategies that have been used to recruit persons from diverse backgrounds as research participants. The importance of having a diverse sample in one's research is well-documented.

Numerous studies have been conducted to determine the facilitators and barriers for participating in research studies for various diverse groups. We will mention in this chapter a few of the strategies that can be used to diversify your sample. Strategies that can be used to diversify your sample include conducting the interview in the participant's home, using trained bilingual interviewers, employing interviewers of the same ethnic/racial background as the participants, using formal ways of addressing the participants, making sure that the study has benefits for the community from which participants belong, and placing flyers and information about the study in places where the participants frequent in their communities (e.g., grocery stores, barber and beauty shops). Strategies to diversify the sample in conducting studies with older adults are described in a special issue of the *Gerontologist*, published in June 2011. The use of community-based participatory research (CBPR) and culturally tailored recruiting approaches have also been deemed effective in diversifying one's sample (Burlew et al., 2011). CBPR involves the community of interest in an equitable partnership with researchers, in all aspects of the research process (Israel, Schulz, Parker, & Becker, 1998).

## Application Checkpoint 11.2

Let us say that the work group recommends that the parents of the children in the school be surveyed to gather information about the characteristics of the individuals who are being bullied, the persons who are doing the bullying, the school, and the community in which the school is located. What strategies would you recommend be used to ensure the sample of parents is diverse?

## Critical Thinking Question 11.3

The chair of the work group convenes another meeting with the group. She mentions that she recently met with the principal to provide her with an update on the status of the work of the group. During the meeting, the principal mentioned she wants to ensure that the sample includes representation from all of the diverse groups in the school, as she is interested in if the predictors of bullying and other forms of victimization differ by racial/ethical background of the student. What sampling strategy would you recommend be used? Justify your response.

# SUMMARY, REVIEW, AND ASSIGNMENTS

## CHAPTER SUMMARY ORGANIZED BY LEARNING OBJECTIVES

**LO 11.1** Define sampling.

Sampling refers to the strategies used to select a given number of individuals or things (e.g., cities, neighborhoods, or schools) from a population.

**LO 11.2** Differentiate between the various types of sampling strategies.

Types of Probability Sampling

*Random sampling*, also referred to as simple random sampling, is used when everyone in the population has an equal chance of being selected.

*Systematic random sampling* involves the researcher selecting the first person to be in the sample based on a random starting point and then selecting the remainder of the sample based on a fixed sampling interval.

*Stratified random sampling* is used when a researcher is interested in comparing two or more subgroups (or strata) of the population.

*Cluster sampling* involves selecting a cluster of participants from the population. The sampling clusters may be space based (e.g., states, counties, census tracts), organizational based (e.g., school district, grade levels, classes), or telephone based (e.g., area codes).

Types of Nonprobability Sampling

*Convenience sampling*, also referred to as accidental or availability sampling, involves selecting persons from the target population because they are accessible to the researcher.

*Purposive sampling* involves selecting persons from the target population because of their fit with the purpose of the study and inclusion criteria.

*Snowball sampling* first involves selecting participants from the target population because of their fit with the purpose of the study and inclusion criteria. Once the researcher finishes surveying or interviewing the participant, he or she will ask the participant to tell others about the study. If someone the participant spoke with is interested in participating in the study, he or she is instructed to call the researcher.

*Quota sampling* involves obtaining a sample that is as representative as possible in relation to potentially confounding variables and of a specific size (quota).

**LO 11.3** Differentiate between the various types of sampling errors.

*Sampling error* is produced by using sampling strategies (e.g., stratified sampling and quota sampling) that overrepresent a portion of the study population.

*Nonsampling error* is due to the difference between those who responded to the survey/questionnaire and those who did not and to how the survey/questionnaire was administered.

*Sampling bias* is due to the methods used to select the sample.

LO 11.4  Identify how to assess the quality of a sample.

A representative sample is one that closely matches the population from which it was drawn.

Determine if the sample size is adequate to produce valid results.

LO 11.5  Identify the ethical and diversity issues associated with sampling.

Snowball sampling presents an ethical dilemma as it relates to remuneration of the participants.

It is unethical for researchers not to explain the purpose, benefits, and potential risks of their research when recruiting participants.

Recruitment strategies may be a barrier to producing a diverse sample.

## KEY TERMS

Sampling   197
Population   197
Accessible population   198
Unit of analysis   198
Sampling frame   198
Probability sampling   199
Representative sample   199
Nonprobability sampling   199
Random sampling   199
Lottery   199
Sampling with replacement   200
Sampling without replacement   202

Systematic random sampling   202
Sampling interval   202
Stratified random sampling   203
Proportional stratified sampling   203
Disproportional stratified sampling   204
Cluster sampling   204
One-stage cluster   205
Two-stage cluster   205
Convenience sampling   205
Purposive sampling   206
Criterion sampling   206

Snowball sampling   206
Quota sampling   206
Confounding variables   206
Spurious association   208
Proportional quota sampling   208
Nonproportional quota sampling   208
Noninterlocking quota   208
Interlocking quota   208
Sampling error   209
Nonsampling error   209
Sampling bias   209
Power analysis   209
Effect size   209

## COMPETENCY NOTES

In this chapter, you were introduced to the competencies below:

Competency 1, *Demonstrate Ethical and Professional Behavior.* Social workers must take into consideration how the sampling strategies used in their research might present ethical dilemmas. Social work researchers must be truthful in how they

explain the purpose, benefits, and potential risks of their research when recruiting participants

Competency 2, *Engage Diversity and Difference in Practice.* Social workers need to use strategies to diversify their samples.

Competency 3, *Engage in Policy Practice.* Social workers need to ensure that they have adequate sample sizes to produce valid results to inform policy.

Competency 4, *Engage in Practice-Informed Research and Research-Informed Practice.* Social workers need to ensure that they have adequate sample sizes to produce valid results to inform practice.

Competency 9, *Evaluate Practice With Individuals, Families, Groups, Organizations, and Communities.* Social workers need to have adequate sample sizes to effectively evaluate practice with individuals, families, groups, organizations, and communities.

## ASSESSMENT QUESTIONS

1. How did the information in this chapter enhance your knowledge about sampling?

2. How did the information in this chapter enhance your knowledge about when one should use a probability sampling strategy as opposed to a nonprobability sampling strategy?

3. What specific content discussed in this chapter is still unclear to you? If there is still content that is unclear, schedule an appointment with your instructor to gain more clarity.

## END-OF-CHAPTER EXERCISES

1. Develop a study using three of the sampling strategies described in this chapter. Discuss why you chose these sampling strategies.

2. Find an empirical study. Conduct a power analysis to determine if the researcher had an adequate sample size for the study. If you determine that the sample size was not adequate, what implications does this have for the researcher's findings?

3. Propose a study where you would you use a stratified random sample. What would be your strata? What would be your research question?

4. Find a study where the researcher used a convenience sample. Suggest an alternative sampling strategy you would use, if you had to conduct the study. Why do you think your sampling strategy is better than the original one selected?

## ADDITIONAL READINGS

Daniels, J. (2012). *Sampling essentials: Practical guidelines for making sampling choices.* Thousand Oaks, CA: Sage.

Wallace, S. P., Chadiha, L. A., Crowther, M., Nápoles, M., & Sood, J. R. (Eds.). (2011, June). The science of recruitment and retention among ethnically diverse older adults. *Gerontologist, 51*(Suppl 1), S142–S146.

# CHAPTER 12 — Survey Research

## Learning Objectives

12.1 Define survey research.

12.2 Differentiate between the types of errors that affect survey research.

12.3 Differentiate between the types of survey designs.

12.4 Differentiate between the various methods of data collection via surveys.

12.5 Identify the ethical and diversity issues associated with survey research.

| Competencies Covered | Learning Objectives | Dimension |
|---|---|---|
| Competency 1 *Demonstrate Ethical and Professional Behavior* | 12.5 Identify the ethical issues associated with survey research. | Skills |
| Competency 2 *Engage Diversity and Difference in Practice* | 12.5 Identify the diversity issues associated with survey research. | Skills |

## PBL Case 12

### Opioid Knowledge Among Older Adults

By responding to the questions related to this case example, you will be able to identify what method of data collection for survey research is appropriate.

Dr. Michelle Avery, the director of a senior center, recently read an article that said older adults (i.e., adults age 50 and above) were often overlooked when discussing the opioid epidemic. She was surprised to learn that between 2000 and 2013, the misuse of prescription

Master the content at
**edge.sagepub.com/farmer**

opioid use more than doubled for older adults. Opioid misuse in this population is associated with heart attacks, fall-related injuries, and suicide ideations. The article also mentioned the risk factors for opioid use, including previous illicit drug use in the past year, being bothered by pain, and posttraumatic stress disorder.

During a meeting Dr. Avery had with her staff, she raised the following question: "What should be the agency's long-term approach to addressing substance abuse?" As of a result of raising this question, others emerged:

- How knowledgeable are staff as it relates to substance abuse among older adults?

- In what ways is opioid use impacting members of the local community?

- What potential risk factors are present in the community that may contribute to opioid use among older adults?

- What are the ways in which the center can be involved in addressing substance abuse?

- Are older adults in the community aware of the nonpharmacologic approaches to the management of pain?

- What is the risk profile of those who participate in programs at the center for opioid use?

At this point, take a few minutes to think about the case example and do the following:

1. Identify the problem.

2. Determine what you already know about the problem.

3. Determine what information you need to solve the problem.

4. List the questions needed to be answered related to the information you need to solve the problem.

Please write down your responses to each item. You will need to refer to them while reading this chapter.

You are doing your field placement at this center. Dr. Avery is your field supervisor. During orientation for new student interns, Dr. Avery mentions that as a result of a meeting with her staff, she is interested in gathering information to answer the questions raised. She further states that she does not know the best way to gather such information and would like for you and the other student interns to assist her.

# Introduction

In this chapter, you will learn about the different methods of data collection for survey research. Ethical and diversity issues one needs to think about when conducting survey research are discussed. The stages of survey development and sources of errors affecting survey research are described.

# Survey Research Defined

**Survey research** is a type of observational research in which respondents are asked a series of questions. Information is collected about opinions, behaviors, attitudes, and beliefs from a specific group of persons. Additionally, survey research is a type of nonexperimental research design as there is no manipulation of the independent variable by the researcher. When conducting survey research, one refers to the individuals completing the surveys as respondents. The term *participant* is used when individuals are participating in an experimental, pre-experimental, or quasi-experimental study. Both probability and nonprobability sampling strategies are used in survey research. The scope of survey research can vary from use of survey instruments that collect data on a wide range of subjects to those that are more narrowly focused (Ruel, Wagner, & Gillespie, 2016a). Studies like the American Values Survey conducted by the Pew Research Center represents an example of a survey broadly focused on gathering data on Americans' values and basic beliefs on such topics as the social safety net, the environment, immigration, religiosity, and political engagement. The American Values Survey, which began in 1987, is an annual cross-sectional survey of adults nationwide. The American Values Survey was designed to provide data on Americans' attitudes about current issues. For example, the 2012 survey gathered data on individuals' beliefs regarding the government's responsiveness to the needs of people, the role of the government in providing a social safety net, and the overall effectiveness of governmental officials. Example items from the 2012 American Values Survey are presented in Table 12.1, along with information related to the number of persons who agreed or disagreed with the statement.

An example of a narrowly focused survey research study is the Fragile Families and Child Wellbeing Study (FFCWS). The FFCWS focuses on the impact of welfare reform, non-marital childbearing, and the role of fathers in economically challenged families (Garfinkel & Zilanawala, 2015), to name a few areas covered on the survey. This study has provided researchers with the opportunity to examine a variety of factors that may contribute to children's and adolescents' well-being, for example, neighborhood disorder (Pei, Wang, Yoon, & Tebbenm 2019), family socioeconomic status and school bonding (Assari, 2019), and contact with the police and the perceptions of the legal system (Geller & Fagan, 2019).

| Table 12.1 | Examples of Items From the 2012 American Values Survey | | |
|---|---|---|---|
| **Government Responsiveness** | | **Agree** | **Disagree** |
| People like me don't have any say about what the government does *(disagree = high)* [Q30a] | | 55 | 43 |
| Generally speaking, elected officials in Washington lose touch with the people pretty quickly *(disagree = high)* [Q30b] | | 81 | 16 |
| Most elected officials care what people like me think *(agree = high)* [Q30c] | | 35 | 62 |
| Voting gives people like me some say about how government runs things *(agree = high)* [Q30d] | | 69 | 29 |
| The government is really run for the benefit of all the people *(agree = high)* [Q30m] | | 41 | 57 |

*Source:* "The trends in American values: 1987–2012: Partisan polarization surges in the Bush, Obama years." Pew Research Center, Washington, DC (2012) https://www.people-press.org/values/.

## Sources of Errors Affecting Survey Research

In research studies, we are often using samples of individuals from a population to estimate values of variables in the population. Because of this, we have sampling error.

For example, in our case example, Dr. Avery is interested in the following question: "On a scale from 1 (not confident) to 10 (extremely confident), how confident are you that you know how to manage pain using strategies that do not involve the use of medication (prescriptions or over-the-counter medications)?" Dr. Avery would like to estimate the average level of confidence among the older adults in the community about their use of strategies to manage pain other than the use of drugs. She chose to gather data from a sample of older adults because in most cases it would not be feasible to collect data from the entire population of older adults in the community. Because of her choice, Dr. Avery needs to be concerned about sources of errors that will affect her survey research. There are six sources of errors that she needs to be concerned about: sampling, random, coverage, systematic, measurement, and non-response. These types of errors are described below.

**Sampling error** occurs when researchers survey a sample of the population instead of conducting a census. A **census** involves collecting data from everyone in the population. Sampling error can be reduced by increasing the sample size. The various sources of error can be divided into two broad categories—random error and systematic error. **Random error** results in chance variations in individual responses around the actual (or "true") values of what is observed for the group. For example, some of the study respondents might not have been wearing their reading glasses when completing the survey. This could result in a misreading of the question. Someone may have mistakenly circled a "3" when he or she might have really wanted to circle "5." There is no way for the researcher to predict who would have misread an item because of not wearing their reading glasses. Because someone was not wearing his or her glasses, this will impact the variability of the respondent's responses.

In Figure 12.1 (page 222), you see the responses to a question from 10 individuals—five from each of the separate samples. Random error did not have an impact on the average responses to the question for the two groups. The group averages were 5.4 for both groups. In order to determine if there is an impact of random error on the responses to the question, you need to assess for variability, which can be done by examining the range of responses and the standard deviations for each sample. Differences in the ranges of responses and the standard deviations between the samples would indicate variability between the groups. Random error is believed to be one of the factors contributing to variability. We can address the bias that random error introduces by using the average of repeating observations as an estimate of the true value.

**Systematic error** (also called systematic bias) is consistent, repeatable error associated with faulty measurement instruments or flawed procedures associated with the data collection. There are three types of systematic error: coverage, measurement, and nonresponse.

**Coverage error** occurs when researchers do not have a complete list of names of the individuals in the sampling frame from which the sample is drawn. Therefore, there are differences between the sampling frame and target population. Because of this, the sample may not be representative of the population. Coverage error leads to biased results. Coverage error can be reduced by making sure you have a complete list of names of those in the sampling frame.

**Measurement error** is error associated with the observation itself. Many aspects of the measure can contribute to this form of error. For example, the use of unclear phrasing of items, unfamiliar words or phrases, irrelevant items on a survey, and the interaction between the interviewer and respondent when conducting interview surveys can contribute to measurement error. To reduce measurement error that might be due to the lack of specificity of items when surveying older adults on their use of pain relievers, the National Survey of Drug Use and Health (NSDUH) included pictures of the pill in the questions (Schepis & McCabe, 2016). In order to ensure the items you develop for your survey do not lack specificity, during the early stages of the development of the survey you should seek the feedback from potential respondents and subject area experts to create questions that are clear, concise, and able to capture quality information.

**Nonresponse error** occurs when all the prospective respondents did not respond to the survey. Nonresponse error also occurs when there is nonresponse to specific questions, therefore limiting the generalizability of the responses to those questions. To decrease nonresponse error, researchers need to follow up with those who did not respond to the survey.

Figure 12.1    Illustration of the Impact of Random Error

## Sample #1

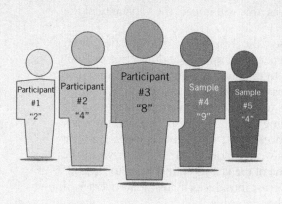

| Participants | Response |
|:---:|:---:|
| 1 | 2 |
| 2 | 4 |
| 3 | 8 |
| 4 | 9 |
| 5 | 4 |
| Average | 5.4 |
| Range | 2–9 |
| Standard Deviation | 2.97 |

## Sample #2

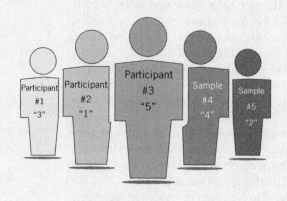

| Participants | Response |
|:---:|:---:|
| 1 | 4 |
| 2 | 5 |
| 3 | 8 |
| 4 | 4 |
| 5 | 6 |
| Average | 5.4 |
| Range | 4–8 |
| Standard Deviation | 1.67 |

# Design Phases of the Survey

Developing the survey instrument involves several stages: *Statement of Purpose, Literature Review, Survey Outline and Development of Items, Survey Draft, Draft Revision, Pilot Testing,* and *Survey Finalization.*

## Statement of Purpose

The process of designing the survey begins with considering the information or data that the survey needs to address. During this stage, one should ask the following questions: "What is the study's aim(s)?" and "What are the specific study questions that the survey intends to answer?" The purpose of the survey informs all stages of the survey design process. A survey can serve more than one purpose. For example, the National Survey on Drug Use and Health's purposes are to (1) provide up-to-date information on alcohol, tobacco, drug use, mental health and other health-related issues in the United States; (2) support prevention and treatment programs; (3) monitor substance use trends; (4) estimate the need for treatment facilities; and (5) assist with the creation of government policy.

Let us say, in the case example, that in discussion with her staff, Dr. Avery decided the purpose of the study was to determine older adults' knowledge of risk factors associated with opioid use. Additionally, she wanted the survey to provide information on older adults' knowledge of nonpharmacologic methods of pain management, along with documentation of their history of existing chronic pain. Given the above, Dr. Avery would have three purposes for her survey.

Besides thinking about the purpose of the survey, you need to think about how often you plan to administer the survey. If you plan to administer the survey only at one point in time, you will use a **cross-sectional survey design**. A disadvantage of a cross-sectional survey design is that it does not allow you to assess changes in the construct of interest. A cross-sectional survey only allows you to collect data that will give you a snap-shot of what is going on. If you plan to administer the survey at multiple points in time, you will use a **longitudinal survey design**. An advantage of a longitudinal survey design is that it allows you to assess changes in the construct of interest. The disadvantage is that it may be too time-consuming or costly to conduct a longitudinal survey design.

---

### Critical Thinking Question 12.1

Assume that a survey can provide Dr. Avery with the answers to the questions that were raised during the meeting with her staff. What information might Dr. Avery need to support the development of a survey? What type of survey design should she use? Justify your response.

---

## Literature Review

Based on the survey's purpose, a series of research questions can be developed that will guide a literature review focused on determining what needs to be included on the survey. Additionally, the review can determine if measures exist in the literature that could be used to collect the data needed for the study.

Reflecting on the case example, in order for Dr. Avery and her staff to move forward with developing a plan to address opioid use among the center's participants, Dr. Avery has to determine what information is needed to answer the following questions: *In general, what is known about older adults' knowledge of the risk factors for opioid use? What is known about their knowledge of nonpharmacologic approaches to the management of pain? Are there existing measures or surveys that have been used in previous studies to assess opioid use among older adults?*

Let us say that Dr. Avery had the social work interns conduct a literature review to answer the above-mentioned questions. When they conducted a search using online and electronic databases (for example, Google Scholar, PsychINFO and Medline), a number of useful publications were found. Below, is a brief list of these publications.

Han, B. H., Sherman, S. E., & Palamar, J. J. (2019). Prescription opioid misuse among middle-aged and older adults in the United States, 2015–2016. *Preventive Medicine: An International Journal Devoted to Practice and Theory, 121*, 94–98. doi:10.1016/j.ypmed.2019.02.018

Huang, A. R., & Mallet, L. (2013). Prescribing opioids in older people. *Maturitas, 74*(2), 123–129. doi:10.1016/j.maturitas.2012.11.002

Karp, J. F., Lee, C.-W., McGovern, J., Stoehr, G., Chang, C.-C. H., & Ganguli, M. (2013). Clinical and demographic covariates of chronic opioid and non-opioid analgesic use in rural-dwelling older adults: The MoVIES project. *International Psychogeriatrics, 25*(11), 1801–1810. doi:10.1017/S104161021300121X

Maree, R. D., Marcum, Z. A., Saghafi, E., Weiner, D. K., & Karp, J. F. (2016). A systematic review of opioid and benzodiazepine misuse in older adults. *The American Journal of Geriatric Psychiatry, 24*(11), 949–963. doi:10.1016/j.jagp.2016.06.003

Palamar, J. J., Han, B. H., & Martins, S. S. (2019). Shifting characteristics of nonmedical prescription tranquilizer users in the United States, 2005–2014. *Drug and Alcohol Dependence, 195,* 1–5. doi:10.1016/j.drugalcdep.2018.11.015

Park, J., Clement, R., & Lavin, R. (2011). Factor structure of Pain Medication Questionnaire in community-dwelling older adults with chronic pain. *Pain Practice, 11*(4), 314–324. doi:10.1111/j.1533-2500.2010.00422.x

Those articles providing information about risk factors are ones written by Han, Sherman, and Palamar (2019) and Maree, Marcum, Saghafi, Weiner, and Karp (2016). The article by Park, Clement, and Lavin (2011) provided them with information about an existing measure. The items on this measure could possibly be used on the survey that Dr. Avery, the staff, and social work interns plan to develop.

## Survey Outline and Development of Items

With the information from the existing literature and keeping the study's purpose in mind, Dr. Avery, the staff, and the social work interns developed an outline for the survey (see Table 12.2). Like a topical outline one might develop for a paper, their outline identified the topics covered in each section. From the outline, specification of the proposed data collection strategy will be identified. See Table 12.3 for the proposed strategies for collecting information for "Current Health Status" and "Risk for Substance Use" sections of the survey. In some cases, instruments that were found in the literature were recommended to be used (see the "Current Health Status" section). In other cases, Dr. Avery, the staff, and social work interns proposed to create their own measures (see the "Risk for Substance Use" section). During the stage of survey outline and development of items, Dr. Avery, the staff, and social work interns need to consider the sequencing of questions on the survey and general guidelines for developing items.

| Table 12.2   Outline of Survey Content and Objectives of the Questions |
|---|
| **Purpose of the Survey: To determine how much the center participants know about the consequences of and risk factors for opioid use.** |
| I   Informed Consent and Instructions |
| II   Current Health Status |
|    a.   Assessment of the overall quality of health |
|    b.   Current health problems |
|    c.   Current medication use |
| III   Risk for Substance Use |
|    a.   Pain management |
|       i.   Current practices |
|       ii.   Historical practices |

*(Continued)*

**Table 12.2** (Continued)

**Purpose of the Survey: To determine how much the center participants know about the consequences of and risk factors for opioid use.**

    b.  History of substance use

    c.  Family history of substance use

    d.  Support network

       i.  Formal

      ii.  Informal

IV  Background Information

    a.  Gender

    b.  Race/ethnicity

    c.  Marital status

    d.  Economic status

    e.  Education

    f.  Employment status

**Table 12.3** Illustration of the Identification of Data Collection Methods

| Sections | Data Required to Answer Questions | Methods for Collecting Data |
| --- | --- | --- |
| **Current Health Status** | Quantitative assessment of overall health | One item self-assessed health status scale will be used. The measure is based on one used in the 2002 World Health Survey (Subramanian, Huijts, & Avendano, 2010) |
| | Identification of current health problems | Standard checklist of chronic illness. A modified version of the Patient Assessment of Chronic Illness Care Questionnaire will be used (Glasgow et al., 2005) |
| | Identification of current medication use | Open-ended questions |

| Sections | Data Required to Answer Questions | Methods for Collecting Data |
|---|---|---|
| **Risk for Substance Use** | Pain management | |
| | Identification of current practices (categorical variable data) | Checklist of pain management strategies |
| | Identification of historical practices (categorical variable data) | Checklist of pain management strategies |
| | Identification of history of substance use (categorical variable data | Yes/No |
| | Identification of family history of substance abuse (categorical variable) | Yes/No |
| | Quantitative assessment of support network (ratio level variable) | Scale measuring the quality of participants' social network |

*Sequencing of Questions.* There are two types of questions that are typically found on surveys: open ended and closed ended. **Open-ended questions** are ones that require the respondents to respond to the question in their own words. A disadvantage of open-ended questions is that you need to code the data so that it can be analyzed. This may be time-consuming. **Close-ended questions** have a list of responses from which the respondents choose their response. An advantage of close-ended questions is that they are already coded. An example of a close-ended question is one where the respondents are asked to rate their attitude about something on a 5-point Likert scale, where 1 = disagree and 5 = agree.

The first question should be one that will result in making the respondent want to complete the survey. Questions should be ordered in a way that they do not influence how subsequent questions are interpreted. Avoid asking knowledge questions before attitude questions. You want to make sure that respondents are knowledgeable about the topic before you ask them about their opinion about the topic. If you include sensitive questions on your survey, they should be in the middle of the survey. If they are at the beginning or end of the survey, the respondents may not respond to them. Questions related to demographic information should be at the end of the survey. The section of the survey where the demographic information is included is referred to as "Background Information." There should be a question that asks respondents about their ethnic background and one that asks them about their racial background, as these two constructs are different. Make sure that you provide an open-ended question so the respondents can identify their ethnic and racial backgrounds.

*General Guidelines for Developing Items.* Ruel, Wagner, and Gillespie (2016b) provide guidelines for the development of survey items. For them, clarity and specificity are critical. This means that items and instructions given to the respondents should use simple, clear language and be free from professional jargon, vague terminology, and abbreviations. When possible, use terms that are commonly used by the respondents. For example, some older African American adults refer to having diabetes as having the *Sugar*. Therefore, on a checklist that includes diabetes as one of the chronic illnesses, the phrase "having the Sugar" should also be included.

*Comprehensiveness.* Response options should be as comprehensive as possible. For example, traditional gender options (i.e., male and female) do not reflect a comprehensive list of gender options. Recognizing the diversity of gender identities that exists, Facebook allows it users to select from 58 gender options (Goldman, 2014). While a researcher may not want to include all 58 options, she/he/they can use knowledge of the study sample to include those categories likely to have high frequency on the survey. If the respondent does not find a suitable category on the list, he/she/they is given the option to write in his/her/their response.

*Mutual Exclusivity.* The researcher must be clear about when categories are mutually exclusive. For example, the categories about how each member of the household is related to the person completing the survey are designed to be mutually exclusive.

See the following example (U.S. Census Bureau, 2010):

How is this person related to Person 1?

| | |
|---|---|
| ☐ Husband or wife | ☐ Parent-in-law |
| ☐ Biological son or daughter | ☐ Son-in-law or daughter-in-law |
| ☐ Adopted son or daughter | ☐ Other relative |
| ☐ Stepson or stepdaughter | ☐ Roomer or boarder |
| ☐ Brother or sister | ☐ Housemate or roommate |
| ☐ Father or mother | ☐ Unmarried partner |
| ☐ Grandchild | ☐ Other nonrelative |

Avoid creating *double-barreled* questions. **Double-barreled questions** are sometimes referred to as "two-in-one questions" as they ask multiple questions in a single question. "Do you receive support from family *and* friends?" is an example of a double-barreled question. The use of *and* in the sentence is often an indication that you have a double-barreled question. It would be better to make the above-mentioned question two separate questions: "Do you received support from family?" and "Do you receive support from friends?"

Avoid biased or offensive language. Being aware of language that is found to be biased or offensive to the respondent is critical. For example, some persons find it offensive when nonbinary pronouns are not used—when persons use the word *he/she*, when the word *they* should be used. Members of the transgender, genderqueer, and other gender-variant communities or members of the groups that you plan to survey should be consulted regarding construction of survey items and instructions to make sure the language used is not biased or offensive.

Keep in mind that underlying each item are assumptions that are being made about the respondents—assumptions about what experiences they have had and how they view those experiences. Knowing this is important when asking questions about sensitive issues. For example, asking women about their reproductive health and family planning and using terms like *pro-life* or *reproductive rights*, you are making assumptions about how particular groups view an issue. Developers of questions need to be aware of persons' cultural points of view underlying the words or phrases that are being used, as terms or words are rarely neutral.

*Response Biases.* Social desirability is one potential response bias that needs to be considered when developing items on the survey. **Social desirability** is the tendency to give socially acceptable responses. Items that ask about behaviors, attitudes, or beliefs that are controversial or stigmatizing may illicit socially desirable responses. In those situations when responses are not anonymous, social desirability is also an issue that needs to be addressed. Collecting data anonymously along with providing respondents with information that clearly indicates only aggregated responses will be published can reduce social desirability.

*Acquiescent Response Bias.* An **acquiescent response bias** is the tendency of persons to respond in a positive manner to a question regardless of the question being asked. Among those cultural or social groups where the social norms emphasize being polite or not to challenge authority, acquiescence response bias can be a threat to the validity of data collected. Researchers will often use multiple items to measure the same construct or variable as a way of reducing acquiescent response bias. For example, Lavrakas (2008) used a series of items where half were worded so that the "agree" response indicated one position and the other half worded so that the "agree" response indicated the opposite position.

## Survey Draft

Once the survey has been outlined and the items have been developed, you can begin drafting the survey. Before the respondents are presented with the actual items that they are to respond to, you need to provide them with a brief overview of the purpose of the survey, without revealing to them the hypotheses of your study; describe what they will be asked to do; indicate approximately how long it will take for them to complete the survey; and indicate the amount of compensation they will receive, if any, for completing the survey. It is important to thank the respondents for their filling out the survey in advance. Once the instructions have been drafted, you can begin drafting each section of the survey, keeping in mind how the items on the survey should be sequenced and the general guidelines for survey development, which were described earlier.

## Draft Revision

Once you have finished drafting your survey, you should share it with your colleagues and get their feedback about the questions, instructions, sequencing of the questions, and time it takes to complete the survey. You should ask them to indicate if there are any modifications they think should be made to the survey and to provide you with a rationale for these modifications. Once you have reviewed their feedback, you should revise your survey accordingly.

## Pilot Testing

Prior to administering the survey, you should administer it to a small sample of individuals from the target population. The purpose of pilot testing the survey is to get feedback about the questions, instructions, sequencing of the questions, and time it takes to complete the survey. Pilot testing the survey will give you an opportunity to find out if your questions are clear or ambiguous. You should ask the respondents to let you know if they think any of the questions will not be answered. They should provide you with a rationale for why they think the question will not be answered. You should ask them if any of the questions should be modified and how. Additionally, you should ask them to recommend additional questions and explain why they are making these recommendations. Based on the results of pilot testing, you may want to make modifications to your survey.

## Survey Finalization

Information from the pilot testing will be used to finalize the survey. The descriptive statistics results will be used to obtain estimates of the reliability of the scales and amount of variability in respondents' responses to items. This information will be used to identify items that need to be eliminated or modified. In addition to the quantitative data, the collection of qualitative data provides information on how respondents' experience the survey. The qualitative data can also be used to provide feedback on clarity of the items and the instructions for completing the survey. The use of qualitative interviews with respondents can be used to collect in-depth information on what persons are thinking when they are completing their responses to each item. The finalization process would also involve changes to the formatting of the survey to improve its aesthetics.

Table 12.4 presents information related to how Dr. Avery, the staff, and social work interns developed their survey based on the stages described earlier.

**Table 12.4** Application of the Design Phases of Survey Development to Dr. Avery's Survey to Assess Opioid Knowledge and Pain Management

**Stages of Survey Development**

| Stages/Objectives | Research Questions or Study Activity | Hypothesis or Purpose of the Activity | Conclusion/Product |
|---|---|---|---|
| 1. Statement of Purpose | What information needs and/or study questions will the survey address? | Development of study's purpose. | Description of the statement of purpose. |
| 2. Literature Review | What is known about the risk factors for opioid use?<br><br>What are the nonpharmacologic approaches to pain management?<br><br>Are there existing surveys or measures that could be used to address this study's purpose? | The existing literature identifies the risk factors and nonpharmacologic approaches to pain management.<br><br>These surveys or measures identified in the literature could be used to address this study's purposes. | Documentation of the knowledge obtained from the literature on the history of substance use, history of experience with chronic pain, knowledge of nonpharmacologic approaches to pain management among cancer patients and those with substance use history has been identified.<br><br>Surveys exist assessing risk factors and substance use history.<br><br>Qualitative interviews have been used to assess substance use history and knowledge of nonpharmacologic approaches to pain management. |

*(Continued)*

Table 12.4 (Continued)

**Stages of Survey Development**

| | | | |
|---|---|---|---|
| 3. Survey Outline and Development of Items | Outline each section of the survey. | How will each section contribute to the purpose of the study? What specific information will each section provide? What format will the information take? | Survey outline has been developed. |
| 4. Survey Draft | Constructing draft measure | Determine whether existing measures can be incorporated into the survey. Developing of original items or modification of existing items. | Draft version of the survey. |
| 5. Draft Revision | Review of draft survey | Review of each section of draft survey: Is the language in the items and instructions concise, simple, clear, and free from technical jargon and bias? Are there no leading questions? Are you using the words and phrases that are familiar to the respondents? | Revised draft |
| 6. Pilot Testing | Survey administration | Administer to the sample of respondents | Descriptive statistical information |
| 7. Survey Finalization | Final revisions to survey | Revision of the survey based on the results of the pilot testing | Final survey prepared for administration |

# Methods of Data Collection Used in Survey Research

In this section, we will describe the methods of collecting data from samples in survey research. These methods are mailed surveys, interview surveys, telephone surveys, and online surveys. There are two modes of administering surveys—self-administered and administered by trained personnel. Mailed and online surveys are referred to as self-administered surveys.

## Self-Administered Surveys

A **self-administered survey** is one in which the individual does not receive assistance from others when completing the survey. Interview surveys and telephone surveys are administered to the prospective respondents by trained personnel. In deciding which method of data collection will be used, researchers take into consideration the characteristics of the sample, the types of questions, and the cost and time associated with administering the survey.

## Mailed Surveys

**Mailed surveys** are ones that are mailed to the prospective respondents. A cover letter that explains the purpose of the survey and thanks the prospective respondents in advance for their participation should accompany the survey. There should not be any mention of the hypothesis being tested, if there is one. If persons are to receive a monetary incentive for their participation, this should be clearly stated in the letter. The monetary incentive should be acceptable to the prospective respondents for their participation and time. It should not make the prospective respondents feel like they are being coerced to respond to the survey. If there are sponsors of the survey (i.e., government agency, your specific university, nonprofit organization), this should be mentioned in the letter, as well as the names of your collaborators. The ways in which you plan to maintain the confidentiality and anonymity of the prospective respondents should be clearly described in the letter. The letter should mention how long the survey will take to complete and if the prospective respondents will be receiving other surveys; if so, note the time frame in which these surveys should be received. Along with the survey and cover letter, there should be two consent forms. The prospective respondents should be instructed to send back one of the consent forms along with the survey and to retain one for their records. The contents of what should be included in a consent form are described in Chapter 2, "Research Ethics." A self-addressed, stamped envelope for returning the survey should be provided, as this is a way to increase the response rate. A more detailed discussion about how to calculate the response rate and why this is important to do so is mentioned in the "Response Rate" section of this chapter. A disadvantage of mailed surveys is that you cannot ensure that the person whom the survey was sent actually completed the survey. The possibility exists that he or she could have gotten another member of their household to do so. Mailed surveys are more appropriate for gathering sensitive information than interview surveys, and if persons are highly literate then they are preferable (Fowler, 2009).

Upon its return, each survey should be assigned an identification number (ID). These numbers should be assigned serially as the surveys are returned. The date that the survey was received should be noted on each as well. According to Rubin and Babbie (2014), putting the date on the survey when it is received can help you determine if an extraneous event affected how the respondents responded to the survey. For example, let us say a researcher is interested in studying the effects of trauma on social functioning. During the third week of data collection a hurricane hits the area where the prospective respondents live. Knowing the date when the hurricane hit and when the survey was received will help you determine the effects of the extraneous event (i.e., the hurricane) on how the respondents responded to the survey.

It is important that another survey to be sent via the mail within 2 to 3 weeks after the original survey was sent. This is known as a **follow-up mailing**. The follow-up mailing is an effective way of increasing the response rate. Two follow-up mailings are deemed to be appropriate. For each follow-up mailing, you should include the cover letter, self-addressed stamped envelope, consent form, and survey.

## Interview Surveys

**Interview surveys** are ones where trained interviewers read the questions to the respondents and record their responses. Given that the interviewer's presence could potentially affect the respondent's responses, the interviewer must be trained to not respond in the affirmative or negative to the respondent's responses. Additionally, the interviewer should be trained on how to administer the survey. Prior to administering the survey to a prospective respondent, the interviewer should role-play administering the survey to his or her supervisor. The supervisor should give feedback to the interviewer. The interviewer should not be allowed to interview a prospective respondent until the supervisor thinks he or she is ready to do so. Prior to conducting the interview, the interviewer should provide the prospective respondents with a consent form to sign and urge them to retain one for their records. In conducting the interview, the interviewer should read the questions on the survey exactly as they are written. Any modifications to the questions could result in the respondent not interpreting the questions as they were intended. In recording the responses to the open-ended questions, it is important that the interviewer record those words verbatim. Research has demonstrated that an interview survey is the preferred method to collect survey data from persons who may not be proficient in English, those who are not familiar using a computer, and persons who are not well educated (Fowler, 2009).

## Telephone Surveys

**Telephone surveys** are ones in which prospective respondents are interviewed by a trained interviewer over the telephone. Prior to conducting the telephone survey, the interviewer should get the person's informed consent. The telephone numbers for the prospective respondents are selected via **random digit dialing** (RDD). RDD is a method of selecting individuals to participate in the telephone survey by generating telephone numbers at random. RDD can be used to select both landline and cell phone numbers and ensures that the sample includes those who have listed and unlisted numbers. RDD is used to produce a representative sample of residential households. An advantage of conducting telephone surveys is that it is cheaper than conducting interview surveys.

## Online Surveys

**Online surveys** are conducted via e-mail or websites. An advantage of online surveys is that they allow you to reach a large number of prospective respondents, and the administration of such surveys is relatively inexpensive. There are several online survey tools that can be used to design your survey, such as SurveyMonkey and Qualtrics. SurveyMonkey is a free online software and survey tool. It allows you to customize your survey, and templates of surveys are also available. You analyze the data using SurveyMonkey or export the data into other statistical software packages, such as Statistical Packages for the Social Sciences (SPSS) and STATA. SurveyMonkey allows you to use its mobile app (SurveyMonkey Genius) for designing, sending, and analyzing surveys. Once you have created your survey using SurveyMonkey, you need to enter the e-mail addresses of the prospective respondents, and they will receive an e-mail invitation to complete the survey. A consent form should be sent along with the survey. A disadvantage of sending an online survey is that individuals may not want to fill out the survey because they think it is spam e-mail. To prevent this from happening, you need to make sure you specify in the subject line who the survey is from. Online surveys are less costly compared to the other methods of survey data collection, and if persons are highly literate then they are preferable (Fowler, 2009).

Another online survey tool that can be used to design your survey is Qualtrics. Qualtrics is a subscription software for designing surveys, and collecting and analyzing data. Additional features include a Help Option on the menu bar in the right-hand corner of the screen; free training webinars; and a Qualtrics Community, an online community of Qualtrics users who are available to discuss their experiences with Qualtrics and provide you with help with your questions. Qualtrics can be accessed free of charge by students via their university, if the university has a subscription.

## Response Rate

After the time for the administration of the survey is over, it is important that you calculate the response rate. The **response rate** is calculated by dividing the number of completed surveys by the number of surveys that were sent. Then you multiple the number obtained by 100. Let us say, for example, a researcher sent out 200 surveys and 80 were returned. The response rate is 40%. A response rate of 70% has been deemed as acceptable (Johnson & Christensen, 2008). Mertens (2015) cautions researchers about accepting 70% as the acceptable response rate, as this response rate assumes the respondents and nonrespondents are similar. Therefore, she recommends that researchers determine if the respondents are representative of the target population. To determine if the respondents are different than the nonrespondents, one needs to assess if there are differences between the groups on demographic variables.

**Application Checkpoint 12.3**

Although the demographics of the persons who are receiving services at the center mentioned in the case example were not provided, think of some of the demographics in which respondents and nonrespondents may differ.

Increasing the response rate is a way of reducing the nonresponse bias. **Nonresponse bias** occurs when there is a significant difference between those who completed the survey and those who did not. There are several things that can be done to increase the response rate, including (1) contacting those who did not respond to the survey and inquiring if they received the survey—if they did not receive it, offer to send them another and remind them of when the survey is due; (2) avoiding sending the survey during the holidays, the beginning of school year, and at the end of the school year; (3) including a stamped self-address envelope so that the prospective respondents can return the survey; (4) offering monetary incentives; (5) making sure that your survey will not take too much time to be completed; and (6) offering to share the results of the survey with the respondents.

## Ethics and Survey Research

Ethical surveying means that you do not violate any of the NASW Code of Ethics related to research and evaluation (Competency 1, *Demonstrate Ethical and Professional Behavior*). It is important as with any other type of research that you obtain informed consent from the prospective respondents and maintain confidentiality and anonymity. If the results of the survey are to be disseminated, it is important the data be presented in an aggregate—that is, for the entire sample or subgroups within the sample, rather than for a particular individual, whereby his or her responses might be identified. Researchers need to have procedures in place to protect the names of the respondents. The ID numbers should be on a list separate from the names of the respondents. These should be kept in two separate locked file cabinets, to which only the principal investigator has access. Prior to conducting surveys in schools, the researcher must obtain informed consent from the parent or guardian and assent from the child or adolescents, if they are not of legal age. If you are conducting interview surveys and plan to record the respondents' responses, it is important that respondents be informed before the interview commences that he or she will be recorded. Mailed surveys, once returned, should be filed in a locked file cabinet, with only the principal investigator having access. All data derived from any method of survey collection must be destroyed according to your university's IRB-specified timeline. Analyzing any data after the IRB's specified timeline is unethical. Doing such may result in a researcher being terminated from his or her employment or the suspension of already approved studies.

## Diversity and Survey Research

When conducting research with respondents whose primary language is not English, it is important that the survey be translated into their language (Competency 4, *Engage Diversity and Difference in Practice*). In translating the survey, you need to be concerned about linguistic equivalence, which is the extent to which a measure is compatible with the language and culture to which it will be adapted.

Decentering is a process in which the original items are translated. After comparing the original and translated items, the original items may be revised and then another translation is produced. This process continues until equivalent items are obtained in both languages. Decentering allows the wording in the original language to be modified when the grammatical structures produce an awkward version in the target language or when the concepts in the original are inappropriate, unknown, or lack an equivalent in the second language. Decentering is the optimal method for producing linguistically equivalent and culturally appropriate surveys because it does not make the assumption that the original language of the existing survey is the authoritative version. Decentering should not be used when translating a standardized measure, if it is part of the survey, because the wording of the items in the original language should not be changed.

## SUMMARY, REVIEW, AND ASSIGNMENTS

## CHAPTER SUMMARY ORGANIZED BY LEARNING OBJECTIVES

LO 12.1  Define survey research.

Survey research involves collecting information from individuals about specific topics using e-mails, interviews, mail, questionnaires, or websites. Information is collected about opinions, behaviors, attitudes, and beliefs from a specific group of persons.

**LO 12.2**  Differentiate between the types of errors that affect survey research.

*Coverage error* occurs when researchers do not have a complete list of names of the individuals in the sampling frame from which the sample is drawn.

*Sampling error* occurs when researchers survey a sample of the population instead of conducting a census.

*Measurement error* occurs when the questions on the survey are vague or ambiguous or when the questions do not include a response that all the respondents could possibly choose.

*Nonresponse error* occurs when all the prospective respondents did not respond to the survey.

*Random error* results in chance variations in individual responses around the actual (or "true") values of what is observed for the group.

*Systematic error* is consistent, repeatable error associated with faulty measurement instruments or flawed procedures associated with the data collection.

**LO 12.3**  Differentiate between the types of survey designs.

A *cross-sectional survey design* is used when researchers want to collect data at one point in time.

A *longitudinal survey design* is used when researchers want to collect data at multiple points in time.

**LO 12.4**  Differentiate between the various methods of data collection via surveys.

*Mailed surveys* are ones that are mailed to the prospective respondents.

*Interview surveys* are ones where trained interviewers read the questions to the respondents and record their responses.

*Telephone surveys* are ones in which prospective respondents are interviewed by a trained interviewer over the telephone.

*Online surveys* are conducted via e-mail or websites.

**LO 12.5**  Identify the ethical and diversity issues associated with survey research.

If the results of the survey are to be disseminated, it is important the data be presented in an aggregate—that is, for the entire sample or subgroups within the sample, rather than for a particular individual, whereby his or her responses might be identified.

When conducting research with respondents whose primary language is not English, it is important that the survey be translated into their language.

## KEY TERMS

## COMPETENCY NOTES

In this chapter, you were introduced to the competencies below:

> Competency 1, *Demonstrate Ethical and Professional Behavior.* Social workers should disseminate the results of their survey research in the aggregate.

Competency 4, *Engage Diversity and Difference in Practice.* Social workers, when conducting survey research with respondents whose primary language is not English, should translate the survey items into the respondents' language.

## ASSESSMENT QUESTIONS

1. How did the information in this chapter enhance your knowledge about survey research?

2. What specific content discussed in this chapter is still unclear to you? If there is still content that is unclear, schedule an appointment with your instructor to gain more clarity.

## END-OF-CHAPTER EXERCISES

1. Write a cover letter for the study proposed in the case example. Share it with one of your classmates and ask him or her to provide you with feedback on your letter.

2. Describe a research problem for which a mail survey would be best to collect the data as opposed to an online or interview survey. Justify your response.

## ADDITIONAL READINGS

Baumgartner, H., & Steenkamp, J. E. M. (2001). Response styles in marketing research: A cross-national investigation. *Journal of Marketing Research, 38*(2), 143–156.

Blair, J., Czaja, R. F., & Blair, E. A. (2013). *Designing surveys: A guide to decisions and procedures.* Thousand Oaks, CA: Sage.

Dillman, D. A. (2007). *Mail and Internet surveys: The tailored design method* (2nd ed.). Hoboken, NJ: John Wiley.

Fink, A. (2017). *How to conduct surveys: A step-by-step guide* (6th ed.) Thousand Oaks, CA: Sage.

Ruel, E. (2019). *100 questions (and answers about) survey research.* Thousand Oaks, CA: Sage.

# $SAGE edge™

Get the tools you need to sharpen your study skills. SAGE Edge offers a robust online environment featuring an impressive array of free tools and resources.

Access practice quizzes at **edge.sagepub.com/farmer**

# Learning Objectives

**13.1**  Identify what type of analysis is appropriate for analyzing your data, depending on the level of measurement of the independent and dependent variables and the type of research question.

**13.2**  Differentiate between the various statistical analyses used to describe data.

**13.3**  Differentiate between the various statistical analyses used to assess the degree of relationship among variables.

**13.4**  Differentiate between the various statistical analyses used to assess significance of group differences.

**13.5**  Identify the ethical and diversity issues associated with analyzing quantitative data.

| Competencies Covered | Learning Objectives | Dimension |
|---|---|---|
| Competency 1<br>*Demonstrate Ethical and Professional Behavior* | 13.5  Identify the ethical issues associated with analyzing quantitative data. | Skills |
| Competency 2<br>*Engage Diversity and Difference in Practice* | 13.5  Identify the diversity issues associated with analyzing quantitative data. | Skills |
| Competency 3<br>*Advance Human Rights and Social, Economic, and Environmental Justice* | | |

*(Continued)*

Master the content at
**edge.sagepub.com/farmer**

| Competencies Covered | Learning Objectives | Dimension |
|---|---|---|
| **Competency 4**<br><br>*Engage in Practice-Informed Research and Research-Informed Practice* | 13.1 Identify what type of analysis is appropriate for analyzing your data, depending on the level of measurement of the independent and dependent variables and the type of research question.<br><br>13.2 Differentiate between the various statistical analyses used to describe data.<br><br>13.3 Differentiate between the various statistical analyses used to assess the degree of relationship among variables.<br><br>13.4 Differentiate between the various statistical analyses used to assess significance of group differences. | Skills |
| **Competency 5**<br><br>*Engage in Policy Practice* | 13.1 Identify what type of analysis is appropriate for analyzing your data, depending on the level of measurement of the independent and dependent variables and the type of research question.<br><br>13.2 Differentiate between the various statistical analyses used to describe data.<br><br>13.3 Differentiate between the various statistical analyses used to assess the degree of relationship among variables.<br><br>13.4 Differentiate between the various statistical analyses used to assess significance of group differences. | Skills |
| **Competency 9**<br><br>*Evaluate Practice With Individuals, Families, Groups, Organizations, and Communities* | 13.1 Identify what type of analysis is appropriate for analyzing your data, depending on the level of measurement of the independent and dependent variables and the type of research question.<br><br>13.2 Differentiate between the various statistical analyses used to describe data.<br><br>13.3 Differentiate between the various statistical analyses used to assess the degree of relationship among variables.<br><br>13.4 Differentiate between the various statistical analyses used to assess significance of group differences. | Skills |

## Is This Parenting Program Effective for Adolescent Fathers?

By responding to the questions related to this case example, you will be able to identify what type of data analysis is appropriate for the type of data you plan to analyze, and you will be able to support your choice by being able to identify the level of measurement of the variables you plan to use in your analysis.

Mary, Chris, Tamela, and Juan work in a community-based agency. The agency's mission is to provide services to all persons regardless of their ethnic/racial background, socioeconomic status, sexual orientation, or religious beliefs. Such services are age and culturally appropriate and are delivered by competent social service providers.

In recent months, the social service providers and clients have been asking about providing services for adolescent fathers. Mary, the director of the agency, has noticed an increase in the number of families being served at her agency where there is an adolescent father in the household.

Mary convened a meeting with Chris, Tamela, and Juan and told them she is interested in developing a parenting program for these adolescent fathers and she wants to evaluate its effectiveness. You are doing your field placement at this agency. Mary has asked you along with Chris, Tamela, and Juan to conduct a literature search to see what programs have been deemed to be effective with adolescent fathers.

Based on the findings of the literature review, Mary and her staff developed a parenting program for adolescent fathers who have children 2 to 5 years of age. The program focuses on enhancing fathers' knowledge of child's development, their quality time with their children, and their ability to engage in appropriate play. Given that Mary and her staff were interested in evaluating the effectiveness of the parenting program, they used a pretest-posttest control group experimental research design to assess the program's effectiveness. Fifty fathers were randomly assigned to the experimental group and fifty fathers were randomly assigned to the control group. Fathers in the experimental group participated in an interactive computer-based parenting group, while fathers in the control group participated in a didactic, in-person parenting group.

Mary and her staff are confident that they have selected the appropriate research design to evaluate the effectiveness of their program. She convenes a meeting with Tamela, Chris, Juan, and yourself and announces that the data collected from the program participants are now ready to be analyzed.

At this point, take a few minutes to think about the case example and do the following:

1. Identify the problem.

2. Determine what you already know about the problem.

3. Determine what information you need to solve the problem.

4. List the questions needed to be answered related to the information you need to solve the problem.

Please write down your responses to each item. You will need to refer to them while reading this chapter.

Mary and her staff have chosen a pretest-posttest control group experimental research design to evaluate the effectiveness of the parenting program for adolescent fathers that is being implemented in their agency. The program focuses on enhancing fathers' knowledge of child's development, their quality time with their children, and their ability to engage in appropriate play. Knowledge of a child's development was assessed pretest and posttest, using a 40-item measure. Fathers were asked to rate these items on a 6-point Likert scale, where 0 = do not know and 6 = strongly agree. A total score was derived by summing all the items on the scale. Quality of time was assessed pre- and posttest. Fathers were asked to indicate the amount of time they spent with their child engaging in the following activities: educational activities (reading to the child, teaching the child the alphabet or numbers), structured activities (playing, taking classes together), and unstructured activities (watching television, listening to music, doing nothing). Fathers were instructed to record the amount of time spent engaging in the above activities each time they visited the child or when the child was in their care. The pre- and post-measure to assess fathers' engagement in appropriate play was developed by one of the agency staff. This measure was completed by a trained rater who observed the father playing with his child. The rater was asked to rate the length of time the father engaged in appropriate play with his child. A father's engagement in appropriate play was measured using a 5-point Likert scale, with the following responses: 1 = did not engage in appropriate play, 2 = spent less than 30 minutes engaging in appropriate play, 3 = 30 minutes to 1 hour engaging in appropriate play, 4 = 1 hour to 1.5 hours spent engaging in appropriate play, and 5 = 1.5 hours or longer engaging in appropriate play. The rater was also asked to record what the father was doing when he did or did not engage in appropriate play.

## Introduction

In this chapter, you will learn about the statistical analyses that you can use to describe or summarize data; assess the degree of relationship among variables; and assess significance of group differences. The assumptions associated with each analysis will be discussed, and ways to deal with violating these assumptions will be presented. A brief discussion of what statistical packages are available to analyze quantitative data is presented. Ethical and diversity issued one needs to think about when conducting quantitative data analysis are discussed.

# What Type of Statistical Analysis
# Is Appropriate for Analyzing Your Data?

Competency 4, *Engage in Practice-Informed Research and Research-Informed Practice*, states social workers "apply critical thinking to engage in analysis of quantitative . . . research methods" (CSWE, 2015, p. 8). This suggests that *you* must know what type of analysis is appropriate for the data *you* plan to analyze. The type of analysis you use is dependent upon

1. the research question: description of the variables, degree of the relationship among the variables, and group differences;

2. the level of measurement of the independent and dependent variables;

3. the number of independent and dependent variables; and

4. the ability to satisfy the assumptions associated with the analysis (Mertens, 1998).

Knowing what factors determine what statistical analysis you should use is important because it will allow you to select and use appropriate methods for evaluating outcomes and practice effectiveness (Competency 9, *Evaluate Practice With Individuals, Families, Groups, Organizations, and Communities*), and assess how social welfare and economic policies impact the delivery of and access to social services (Competency 5, *Engage in Policy Practice*). Besides knowing what types of statistical analysis to conduct based on the level of measurement of the independent and dependent variables, the purpose of the research question, and the number of independent and dependent variables, social workers need to be able to interpret the results from these analyses. For all the statistical procedures discussed in this chapter, you will find information on how to interpret the results.

At the outset, we must state that we will not discuss all the statistical procedures researchers use to analyze their data. For those of you who are interested in learning more about other statistical procedures not discussed in this book, there are lots of books available that provide a comprehensive overview of these procedures. In this chapter, you will be introduced to two types of statistics—descriptive and inferential. **Univariate descriptive statistics** allow researchers to describe or summarize their data. A researcher would use descriptive statistics to answer the following research question: "What percentage of individuals participated in a particular program?" Descriptive statistics would not be appropriate to answer a research question where a researcher is interested in determining if parenting practices are associated with less substance use. The descriptive statistics you will learn about in this chapter are frequency distributions and measures of central tendency, and measures of variability (dispersion). Diagram 13.1 presents information about when these descriptive statistics should be used based on the level of measurement of the independent and dependent variables. Researchers use **inferential statistics** to estimate a parameter and to determine whether the results of statistical tests based on the sample drawn from a population can be generalized to that population. One type of inferential statistic that is used to estimate a parameter is a **confidence interval** (CI). CI is a statistic used to estimate a parameter based on the data from the sample to say something about a population parameter that is unknown. The CI gives you an interval (a range of values that likely includes the unknown population parameters) and an associated confidence, which quantifies the level of confidence a researcher can have that the parameter lies in the interval. The 95% confidence level is the most commonly used. A CI is normally formatted as follows: (98.000, 98.37), 95% confidence interval. In this chapter, you will be introduced to inferential statistics that are used to test the statistical significance of hypotheses. There are two categories of inferential statistics used to test the statistical significance of hypotheses. One type of inferential statistic is categorized as statistics used to assess the degree of relationship among variables (i.e., Pearson's correlation, chi-square test of independence, and multiple regression analysis). Diagram 13.2 presents information about when these statistics are to be used to assess the degree of relationship among variables based on the level of measurement of the independent and dependent variables. The other type of inferential statistics is categorized as statistics used to assess significance of group differences (i.e., independent and dependent *t*-tests, analysis of variance [ANOVA], and multivariate analysis of variance [MANOVA]). Diagram 13.3 presents information about when to use the independent *t*-test, dependent *t*-test (paired *t*-test), and ANOVA to assess significance of group differences based on the level of measurement of the independent and dependent variables.

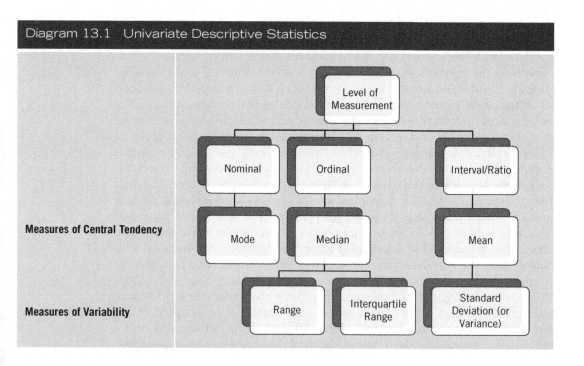

Diagram 13.1  Univariate Descriptive Statistics

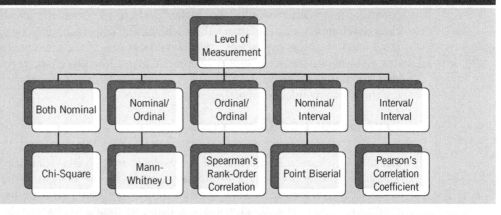

Diagram 13.2 Inferential Statistics Used to Assess the Degree of Relationship Among Variables

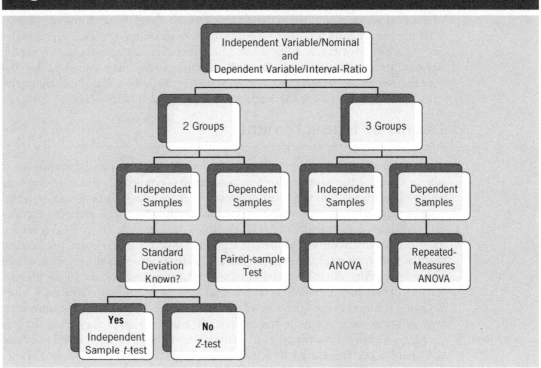

Diagram 13.3 Mean Differences

Referring to the case example, let us say that Mary and her staff hypothesized that fathers' posttest knowledge of a child's development score is associated with posttest quality of time fathers spent with the child engaging in educational activities. To test this hypothesis, Mary would use one of the inferential statistics that assess the degree of relationship among variables. She and her staff additionally hypothesized that adolescent fathers who received an interactive computer parenting intervention would have higher posttest scores on the knowledge of child development measure than fathers who had an in-person, didactic parenting program. To test this hypothesis, Mary would use one of the inferential statistics that assesses significance of group differences. By reading this chapter, you will be able to determine which inferential statistics test is appropriate for Mary to use to test the above-mentioned hypotheses.

## Key Statistics Concepts

*Statistical Significance.* To determine if the results of an analysis is statistically significant, one needs to look at the *p*-value associated with the analysis. If the *p*-value is less than .05, then the results are statistically significant. This means that the results have less than a .05 probability of being attributed to chance. The *p*-value only tells you if the results are statistically significant or not. It does not tell you the strength of association between the variables of interest or effect size. The measures of association one would use is dependent upon the level of measurement of your variables. Commonly reported measures of association are the Pearson's correlation, Cramer's V, or eta, to name a few. The **effect size** is a way of quantifying the size of difference between two groups. It is commonly used as a way of quantifying the effectiveness of an intervention in comparison to another. The effect size can be calculated using the Cohen's d, Hedges's g, or Glass's delta formulas.

## Levels of Measurement

You may recall from reading Chapter 5 that all variables can be measured at one or more of the four levels of measurement—nominal, ordinal, interval, or ratio—depending upon their nature or attributes. Nominal variables are assigned a numerical value, but the value is not meaningful. Nominal variables are also referred to as "categorical variables." Variables measured on an ordinal level are assigned numerical values that can be logically ranked. Variables measured on the interval level have intervals between the categories that are equal and do not have a true zero value. Variables at the ratio level of measurement have all the characteristics of variables measured at the interval level, in addition to a true zero value. Knowing the level of measurement of a variable is important for determining what type of statistical procedures researchers will use to analyze their data. In this chapter, you will learn what types of analysis should be conducted when you have data that has been measured at each of the levels of measurement described above.

## Coding of the Data

Before you start analyzing your data, it needs to be in a form in which it can be analyzed. This is done by coding the data. **Coding** involves assigning a numerical value to each category of each variable in your study. Let us say, for example, you have a question on your survey where you ask the respondents to indicate their favorite television show. In order for the answer to the question to be in a form in which it can be analyzed, you must assign each respondent's favorite show a numerical value. Let us say that one respondent indicated that *CBS Morning News* is his favorite television show. You would assign this show the number 1. Let us say another respondent indicated that her favorite television show is *Empire*. You would assign this show the number 2. Still another respondent indicated that his favorite television show is *Family Feud*. You would assign this show the number 3.

There are two instances where you do not need to code the respondent's responses in a form in which it can be analyzed. One is where the responses are already a numerical value. Examples of questions that would produce a response that would be a numerical value are "How old are you?," "What year were your born?," and "How old were you when you got married?" The other is where there are preassigned numerical values associated with the response. Referring to the case example, you will see that father's engagement in appropriate play was measured using a 5-point Likert scale, with the following responses: 1 = did not engage in appropriate play, 2 = spent less than 30 minutes engaging in appropriate play, 3 = 30 minutes to 1 hour engaging in appropriate play, 4 = 1 hour to 1.5 hours engaging in appropriate play, and 5 = 1.5 hours or longer engaging in appropriate play.

Once researchers have their data in a form ready for analysis, they are now ready to enter the data into a specialized computer program that analyzes quantitative data. There are several statistical software packages that can be used for conducting quantitative analyses. In this chapter, we will only mention four statistical software packages: Statistical Packages for the Social Sciences (SPSS), Statistical Analysis Software (SAS), Statistic Open for All (SOFA), and R. All allow you to manage, analyze, and graph your data and have a drop-down menu. Both R and SOFA can be downloaded for free. SOFA is available at http://sofastatistics.com/home.php and R is available at https://www.r-project.org. These statistical software packages have made analyzing data easy.

# Statistical Analyses Used to Describe Data

## Univariate Descriptive Analyses

**Univariate descriptive analyses** are used to describe or summarize the data related to a specific variable of interest. Researchers also conduct univariate descriptive analyses when they are interested in looking at the characteristics of a variable to determine if it meets the assumptions necessary to conduct analyses used to assess the relationship among variables or significance of group differences. Conducting descriptive univariate analyses is the first step in any data analysis plan. There are three main types of descriptive univariate analyses: frequency distributions, measures of central tendency, and measures of variability (dispersion).

*Frequency Distribution.* A **frequency distribution** shows the researcher the number of observations in each category of the variable of interest. The variable being described is being measured at the nominal/categorial level of measurement. Referring to the case example, the following question would be answered using information from a frequency distribution: "What were the number of fathers with boys and fathers with girls who participated in the study?" The nominal/categorical variable is gender of the child. A frequency distribution can be graphed as a bar chart, frequency polygon, histogram, or pie chart. A bar graph is appropriate when the data are measured on a nominal level (see Figure 13.1).

Most researchers prefer to graph the frequency distribution as a histogram with a superimposed normal curve, as this allows them to look at the shape of the distribution to determine if it is a normal curve (i.e., bell-shaped curve) or does the shape deviate from a normal curve (i.e., a skewed distribution; see Figure 13.2).

A normal curve is fairly symmetrical, with a high point in the middle and trailing off on the right and left (see Figure 13.3). Many of the analyses you will be introduced to in this chapter have the assumption that the distribution of the data is a normal curve (or close to a normal curve).

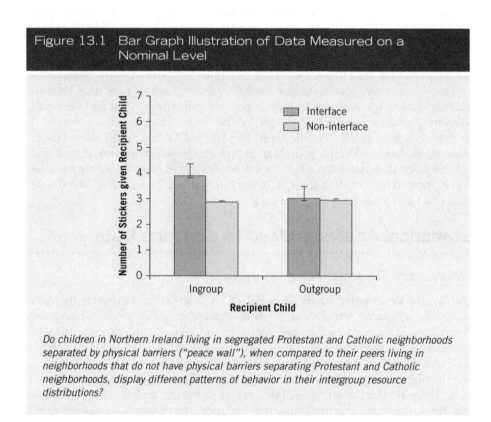

**Figure 13.1** Bar Graph Illustration of Data Measured on a Nominal Level

*Do children in Northern Ireland living in segregated Protestant and Catholic neighborhoods separated by physical barriers ("peace wall"), when compared to their peers living in neighborhoods that do not have physical barriers separating Protestant and Catholic neighborhoods, display different patterns of behavior in their intergroup resource distributions?*

Source: O'Driscoll, D., Taylor, L. K., & Dautel, J. B., Copyright 2018, American Psychological Association.

Figure 13.2   Graph of Frequency Distribution as a Histogram With
              Superimposed Normal Curve

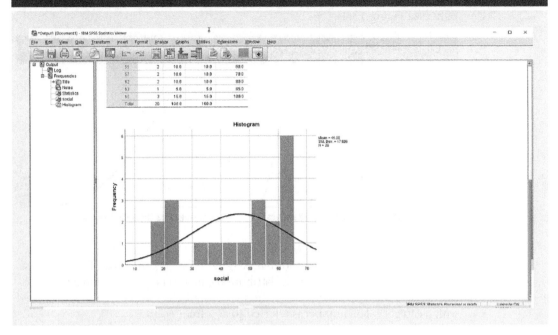

Figure 13.2   Graph of Frequency Distribution as a Histogram With
              Superimposed Normal Curve

Figure 13.3   Normal Distribution

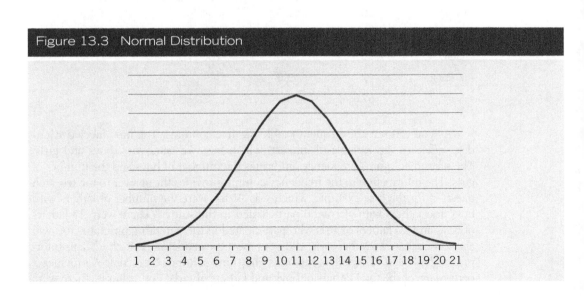

Skewed distributions have a tail on one side of the curve and not on the other. A negatively skewed distribution is one where the tail is skewed to the left, whereas a positively skewed distribution is one where the tail is skewed to the right (see Figure 13.4).

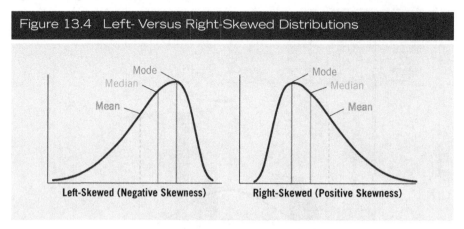

**Figure 13.4  Left- Versus Right-Skewed Distributions**

Left-Skewed (Negative Skewness)                    Right-Skewed (Positive Skewness)

The type of distribution (normal or skewed) affects the type of data analysis you can conduct. The frequency distribution can also be presented in a table (i.e., frequency table; see Table 13.1). A frequency table lists every number associated with a category. The number is referred to as a frequency.

**Table 13.1  Frequency Distribution Children's Gender**

| Gender | Frequency | Percentage | Valid Percentage | Cumulative Percentage |
| --- | --- | --- | --- | --- |
| Girls | 30 | 52.6 | 54.5 | 54.5 |
| Boys | 25 | 43.9 | 45.5 | 100 |
| Total | 55 | 96.5 | 100 | |
| Missing | 2 | 3.5 | | |
| | 57 | 100 | | |

As you can see, the frequency table has five columns. The first, labeled "Gender," refers to the variable of interest, which has two categories: boys and girls. The second column, "Frequency," indicates the number of boys and the number of girls. The information in the frequency column provides the answer to the research question for the case example, which was "What were the number of fathers with boys and fathers with girls who participated in the study?" There were 25 fathers of boys and 30 fathers of girls who participated in the parenting program. You will also notice that two fathers who did not report the gender of their child. This information has been assigned as missing. The third column, "Percentage" provides a percentage of the total fathers of boys and fathers of girls. For example, there were

25 fathers of boys. In order to get the percentage, you would divide 25 by (57 the number of cases) and then multiple the answer by 100. The answer is 43.9. The fourth column, "Valid Percentage," is a percentage that does not include missing cases. There are 25 fathers of boys and 30 fathers of girls for a total of 55 children. In order to get the valid percent for the number of girls, you would divide 30 by the number of cases with the missing data, which is 55 and the multiple the answer by the 100. The answer for the valid percent for the number of fathers of girls would be 54.5. The fifth column, "Cumulative Percentage," is a percentage based on the adding up of the percentage for each number from the top of the table to the bottom of the table, cumulating in 100%. A frequency table will be produced when you use any of the computer software packages discussed earlier to analyze your data.

## How to Conduct a Frequency Analysis in SPSS

A researcher, for example, would conduct a frequency analysis if he or she wants to know how many respondents have a particular score on a social support scale. In this analysis, score is the variable of interest, and every possible score one could receive serves as a category. For example, a score of 20 would be a category, a score of 21 would be a category, and so forth. In order to find out how many respondents have a particular score on a social support scale, the researcher would conduct the analysis described below.

Step 1: Go to the menu bar and click *Analyze*, then scroll down to Descriptive Statistics, and then highlight *Frequencies* (see Figure 13.5).

Figure 13.5   Demonstrating Step 1 of How to Conduct a Frequency Analysis in SPSS

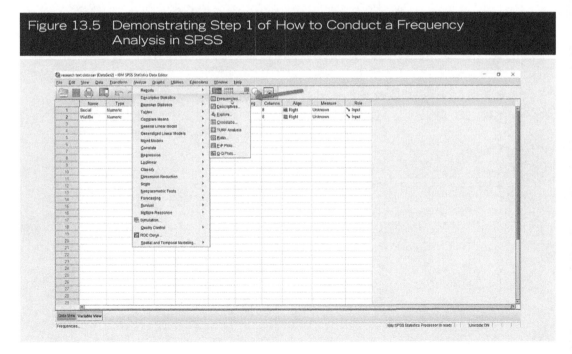

Step 2: Click on *Frequencies*. Once you have done this, the "Frequencies" dialogue box will appear (see Figure 13.6). You need to highlight the variable you want to include in the analysis then click the *Arrow* button, which will automatically place the variable in the "Variable(s) dialogue box. Make sure the box beside "Display frequencies tables" has been checked.

Figure 13.6 Demonstrating Step 2 of How to Conduct a Frequency Analysis in SPSS

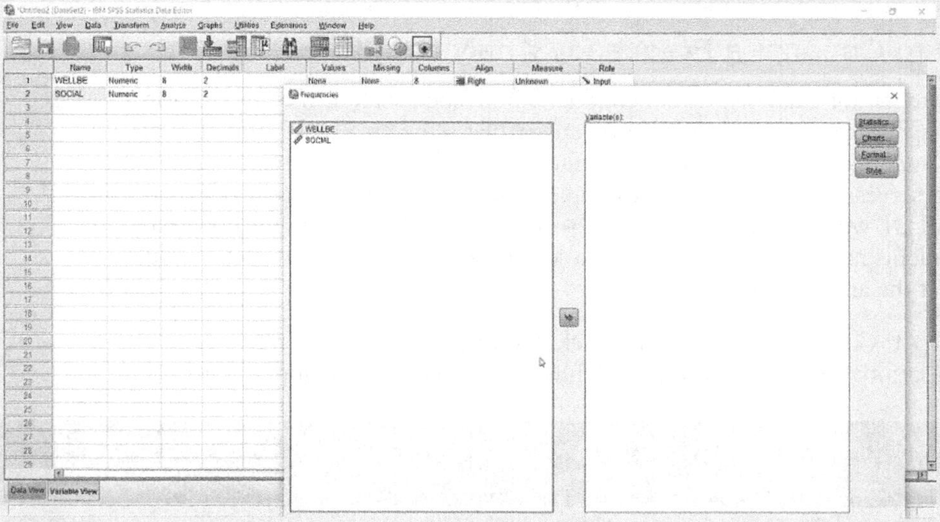

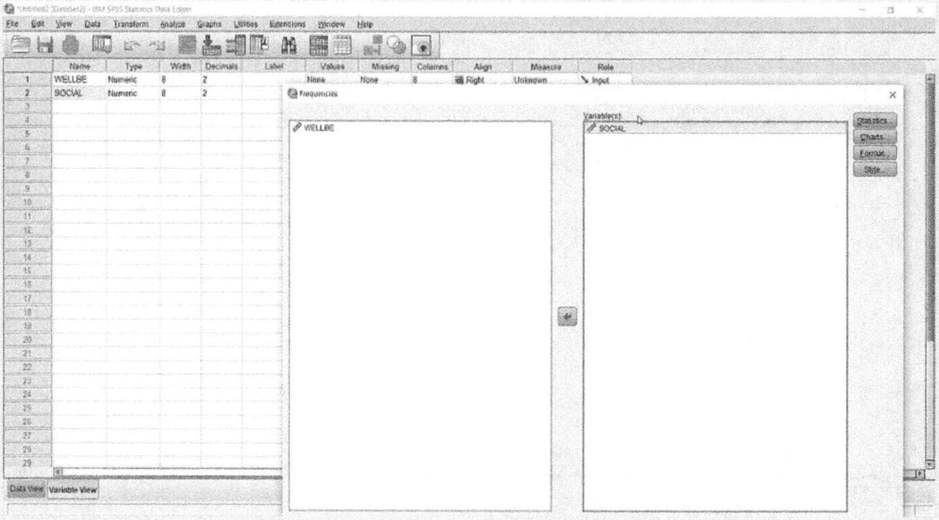

Step 3: Click on the *Statistics* button. Once you have done this, the "Frequencies: Statistics" box will appear (see Figure 13.7). Scroll down to the "Characterize Posterior Dispersion" area. Click on *Skewness* and *Kurtosis*. **Skewness** is a measure of symmetry or lack thereof, while **kurtosis** is a measure of whether the data are heavy tailed or light tailed relative to a normal distribution. Both skewness and kurtosis are referred to as "shape statistics" as they describe the shape of the distribution. A normal distribution has a skewness of 0 and a kurtosis of 3. A highly skewed distribution is one where the skewedness value is less than −1 or greater than 1. If the distribution is skewed, you will need to transform your data by using the log transformation function in SPSS to get a normal distribution (or close to a normal curve).

Figure 13.7 Demonstrating Step 3 of How to Conduct a Frequency Analysis in SPSS

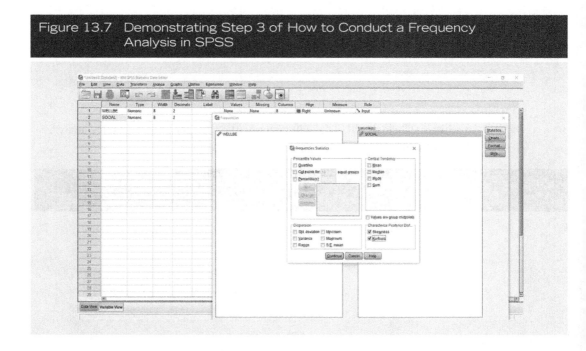

Step 4: Click *Continue*. Once you have done this, the "Frequencies: Charts" dialogue box will appear. Note: This was previously shown in Figure 13.5.

Step 5: Click on the *Charts* button. Once you have done this, the "Frequencies: Charts" box will appear (see Figure 13.8). Click on *Histograms*. Check the box beside "Show normal curve on histogram." Then click *Continue*.

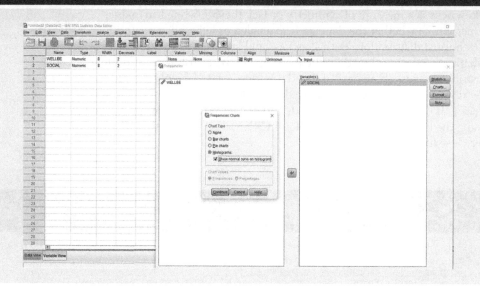

Step 6: Click on *OK*. This will generate the results of the frequency analysis (see Figure 13.9).

Figure 13.9  Demonstrating Step 6 of How to Conduct a Frequency Analysis in SPSS

(a)

**social**

| N | Valid | 20 |
|---|---|---|
| | Missing | 0 |
| Mean | | 46.55 |
| Median | | 53.50 |
| Mode | | 65 |
| Skewness | | -.543 |
| Std. Error of Skewness | | .512 |
| Kurtosis | | -1.311 |
| Std. Error of Kurtosis | | .992 |

**social**

| | | Frequency | Percent | Valid Percent | Cumulative Percent |
|---|---|---|---|---|---|
| Valid | 18 | 1 | 5.0 | 5.0 | 5.0 |
| | 19 | 1 | 5.0 | 5.0 | 10.0 |
| | 23 | 1 | 5.0 | 5.0 | 15.0 |
| | 25 | 2 | 10.0 | 10.0 | 25.0 |
| | 35 | 1 | 5.0 | 5.0 | 30.0 |
| | 36 | 1 | 5.0 | 5.0 | 35.0 |
| | 42 | 1 | 5.0 | 5.0 | 40.0 |
| | 50 | 1 | 5.0 | 5.0 | 45.0 |
| | 52 | 1 | 5.0 | 5.0 | 50.0 |
| | 55 | 2 | 10.0 | 10.0 | 60.0 |
| | 57 | 2 | 10.0 | 10.0 | 70.0 |
| | 62 | 2 | 10.0 | 10.0 | 80.0 |
| | 63 | 1 | 5.0 | 5.0 | 85.0 |
| | 65 | 3 | 15.0 | 15.0 | 100.0 |
| | Total | 20 | 100.0 | 100.0 | |

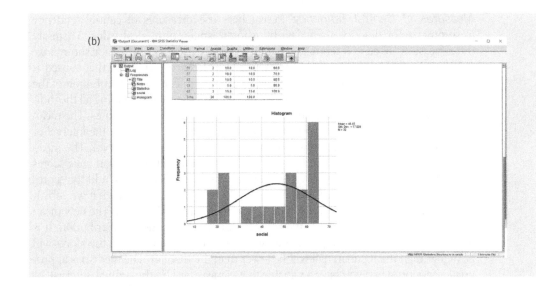
(b)

**Results:** The score on the social support scale with the highest frequency is 65. There are several scores (i.e., 18, 19, 23, 35, 36, 42, 50, 52, and 63) that have the lowest frequency. The distribution is negatively skewed as indicated by the value for skewness (−.543). The negative value for the kurtosis (−1.31) indicates a light-tailed distribution, which is consistent with a negatively skewed distribution. This can be seen in Figure 13.9.

You will see that there is additional information in the frequency table that we did not discuss in the results. We did not report the percentage of persons who received a particular score, as we were only interested in the actual number of individuals who received a particular score.

You will see that we did not mention the results from the histogram. The information from the histogram is used to assess the shape of the distribution. It is used to determine if the shape is normal or positively or negatively skewed. The information from the histogram should be consistent with the information from the shape statistics—skewness and kurtosis. In looking at the histogram (see Figure 13.9), you can see it shows that the distribution is negatively skewed (i.e., the tail of the distribution is skewed to the left). This finding is consistent with the results of the value for skewness (−.545), which indicated a negatively skewed distribution.

*Measures of Central Tendency.* Researchers use measures of central tendency to summarize or describe their data by using a single, numerical value. There are three measures of central tendency that are typically used to describe or summarize data: mean, median, and mode. Which measure of central tendency that is used is dependent upon the level of measurement of the variable and the distribution of the variable. The **mean**, the arithmetic mean, or average is derived by adding all the individual scores, and then dividing the answer by the total number of scores. The mean is appropriate to report when you have a variable that is measured on the interval or ratio level, and the distribution is a normal (or close to a normal curve). The mean is affected by extremely high or low scores. For example, let us say you have scores of 20, 50, and 60, and you wanted to calculate the mean. You would add the scores together and then divide by 3. The mean would be 43.33. Let us say that we substituted a score of 60 for the score of 20 and then recalculated the mean. The new mean would be 56.67. The **median** is the middle score in the frequency distribution. It is the score that divides the frequency distribution in half. That is, half of the scores will be higher than the median, half will be lower than the median. The median is appropriate to report when you have a variable that is measured on the ordinal, interval, or ratio level, and the distribution is positively or negatively skewed. The **mode** is the most frequently occurring score in the frequency distribution. The mode is appropriate to report when the variable is measured on a nominal level.

By looking at the mean, median, and mode, one can also determine the shape of the distribution. If the mean, median, and mode are equal, then you have a normal distribution (or close to normal distribution). If the mode is less than the median and the median is less than the mean, then the distribution is positively skewed. If the mean is less than the median and the median is less than the mode, then the distribution is negatively skewed.

## How to Obtain the Mean, Median, and Mode in SPSS

Let us say, for example, a researcher, would like to know the mean, median, and the mode for a social support scale. Social support is measured on an interval level. To obtain the above information, the researcher would conduct the analysis described below.

Step 1: Go to the menu bar and click *Analyze*, then scrolled down to "Descriptive Statistics," and then highlight *Frequencies*. Note: This was previously shown in Figure 13.5.

Step 2: Click on *Frequencies*. Once you have done this, the "Frequencies" dialogue box will appear. You need to highlight the variable you want to include in the analysis then click the *Arrow* button, which will automatically place the variable in the "Variable(s)" dialogue box. Make sure the box beside "Display frequencies tables" has been checked. Note: This was previously shown in Figure 13.6.

Step 3: Click on the *Statistics* box. Once you have done this, the "Frequencies: Statistics" box will appear. Scroll down to the "Central Tendency" area. Click the boxes for "Mean," Median," and "Mode" (see Figure 13.10).

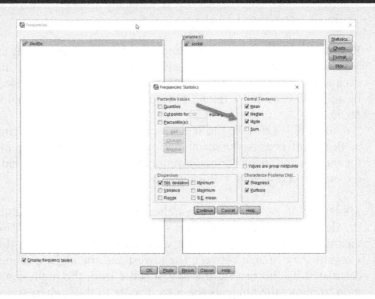

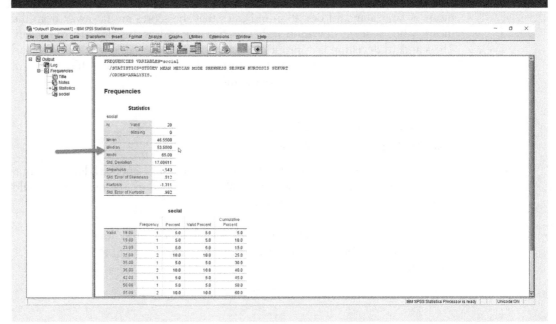

Step 4: Click *Continue*. Once you have done this, the "Frequencies" dialogue box will appear. Note: This was previously shown in Figure 13.6.

Step 5: Click on *OK*. This will generate the results for the mean, median, and mode (see Figure 13.11).

**Results:** The mean for the social support scale is 46.55. According to the *Publication Manual of the American Psychological Association* (7th ed., 2020), one should report decimals to two places, and as a general rule numbers, are rounded up if followed by a 5, 6, 7, 8, or 9. Therefore, a mean of score of 46.5500 would be reported as 46.55.

You will see that we did not report in our results the median (53.50) or the mode (65.00) because the social support scale is measured on an interval level and the median and mode are not appropriate to report. We only had SPSS compute the median and mode for illustrative purposes.

*Measures of Variability.* Researchers use measures of variability to describe the degree which the scores are spread around the mean. There are several measures of variability; however, we will only discuss two in this chapter. The **range** is the distance between the lowest and the highest scores. The range is calculated by subtracting the lowest score from the highest score. It is common to report the range as the lowest score to the highest score. The range is appropriate to report when the variable is measured on an ordinal, interval, or ratio level.

The **standard deviation** is a single, numerical value indicating how scores distribute themselves around the mean and the distance of the scores from the mean. A large standard deviation indicates that the scores are far away from the mean, while a small deviation indicates that the scores are close to the mean. The standard deviation is appropriate to report when the variable is measured on an ordinal, interval, or ratio level. In a normal distribution, 68% of the scores will be within one standard deviation of the mean.

## How to Obtain the Range and Standard Deviation in SPSS

A researcher, for example, would like to know the range and standard deviation for a social support scale. To obtain the above information, the researcher would conduct the analysis described below.

Step 1: Go to the menu bar and click *Analyze*, then scroll down to "Descriptive Statistics," and then highlight "Descriptives" (see Figure 13.12).

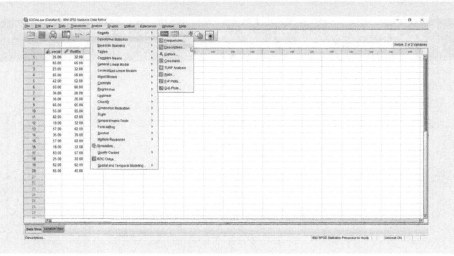

Step 2: Click on *Descriptives*. Once you have done this, the "Descriptives" dialogue box will appear. You need to highlight the variable you want to include in the analysis then click the *Arrow* button, which will automatically place the variable in the "Variable(s)" dialogue box (see Figure 13.13).

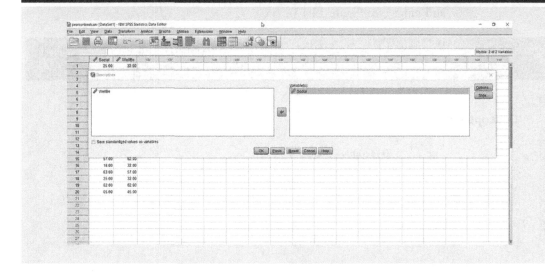

Step 3: Click on the "Options" button. Once you have done this, the "Descriptives: Options" box will appear (see Figure 13.14). Scroll down and click on "Std. deviation" and "Range."

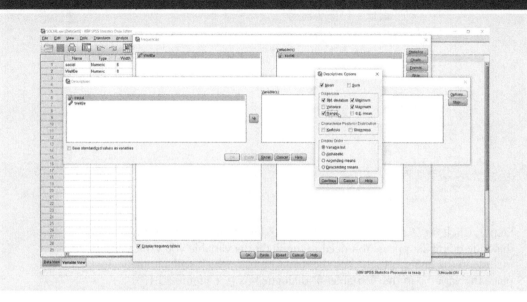

Step 4: Click *Continue*. Once you have done this, the "Descriptives" dialogue box will appear. Note: This was previously shown in Figure 13.13.

Step 5: Click *OK*. This will generate the results for the standard deviation and range (see Figure 13.15).

Figure 13.15    Demonstrating Step 5 of How to Obtain the Range and
                 Standard Deviation in SPSS

⇨ **Descriptives**

**Descriptive Statistics**

| | N | Range | Minimum | Maximum | Mean | Std. Deviation |
|---|---|---|---|---|---|---|
| social | 20 | 47.00 | 18.00 | 65.00 | 46.5500 | 17.00611 |
| Valid N (listwise) | 20 | | | | | |

**Results:** The standard deviation for the social support scale is 17.06, and the range is from 18.00 to 65.00.

You will notice that we did not report the number 47.00 as the range, as we mentioned earlier that most researchers report the range as the lowest score to the highest score.

Table 13.2 provides a brief overview of when you report the mean, median, mode, standard deviation, and range based on the level of measurement of the variable of interest.

**Table 13.2  When to Report the Mean, Median, Mode, Standard Deviation, and Range**

| Types of Statistics | Level of Measurement of Variable of Interest |
| --- | --- |
| Mean | Interval or ratio |
| Median | Ordinal, interval, or ratio |
| Mode | Nominal |
| Standard deviation | Ordinal, interval, or ratio |
| Range | Ordinal, interval, or ratio |

### Critical Thinking Question 13.1

Mary convenes a meeting with her staff and social work interns and states that she would like to know if the fathers who participated in the interactive computer-based parenting program had higher posttest scores on the knowledge of child development measure than fathers who participated in the didactic, in-person parenting program. What univariate descriptive statistics (i.e., mean, median, mode, standard deviation, or range) would you calculate to answer her question? Justify your response.

## Statistical Analyses Used to Assess the Degree of Relationship Among Variables

There are several statistical analyses that can be used to assess the degree of relationship among variables. We will briefly discuss three: Pearson's correlation, chi-square test of independence, and multiple regression analysis.

## Pearson's Correlation Analysis

Researchers conduct a correlation analysis when they are interested in examining the association between two variables. Referring to the case example, if Mary is interested in knowing if there is an association between the posttest knowledge of child development score and the posttest quality of time father spent with the child engaging in educational activities, then she would conduct a correlation analysis. The most commonly conducted correlation analysis is the **Pearson's correlation**. The Pearson's correlation is also referred to as the Pearson product-moment correlation. The Pearson's correlation is used to determine the association between an interval or ratio (a scale) independent variable and an interval or ratio (a scale) dependent variable. The Pearson's correlation measures the strength of the association between the independent and dependent variable. The Pearson's correlation produces a correlation coefficient, which indicates the strength and direction of the association. The closer the coefficient is to +1 and −1, the stronger the relationship is between the two variables. Researchers typically use this guideline to determine the strength of the correlation, see Table 13.3.

| Table 13.3 Determining the Strength of the Correlation | |
|---|---|
| **Value of the Correlation** | **Strength of the Relationship** |
| −1.0 to −0.5 or +1.0 to +0.5 | Strong |
| −0.5 to −0.3 or +0.3 to +0.5 | Moderate |
| −0.3 to −0.1 or +0.1 to +0.3 | Weak |
| −0.1 to +0.1 | None or very weak |

The direction of the correlation is indicated by the plus and minus sign. (Please note that you will not see a plus sign before a positive correlation on the SPSS printout; see section titled "How to Conduct a Pearson's Correlation Analysis in SPSS.") The correlation coefficient has a value between −1 and +1. A zero coefficient means that there is no association between the independent variable and the dependent variable, while a −1 coefficient means that there is a perfect negative correlation between the independent variable and dependent variable. A coefficient of +1 means that there is a perfect positive correlation. Figure 13.16 depicts a positive correlation, no/zero correlation, and negative correlation.

In looking at Figure 13.16, you can see when there is a positive correlation, there are high scores on the independent variable associated with high scores on the dependent variable. Although not depicted in the figure, a positive correlation also occurs when low scores on the independent variable are associated with low scores on the dependent variable. When there is a no/zero correlation, there is no

Figure 13.16 Correlations

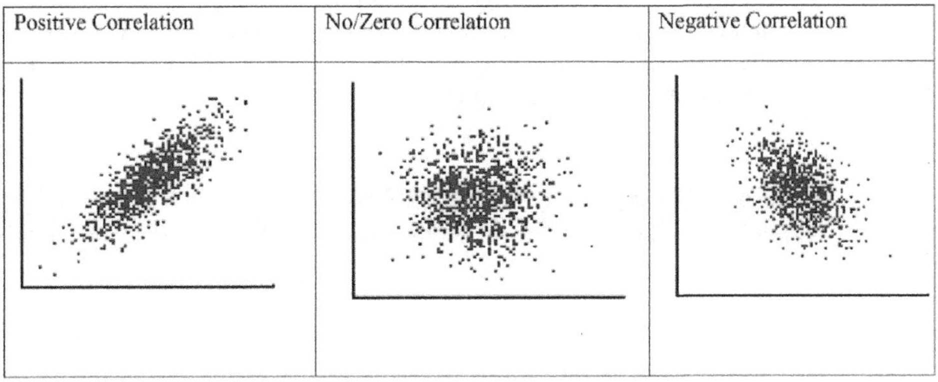

| Positive Correlation | No/Zero Correlation | Negative Correlation |
|---|---|---|
| | | |

relationship between the variables. You can see when there is a negative correlation there are high scores on the independent variable associated with low scores on the dependent variable.

Before conducting the Pearson's correlation, one must ensure that the assumptions required for this analysis are met. There are seven assumptions that must be met to produce valid results. These assumptions are as follows:

**Assumption 1:** Both the independent variable and the dependent variable should be measured on the interval or ratio level (a scale). Examples of variables that can meet this assumption are scores on a measure used to assess depression or anxiety, weight, and intelligence, to name a few.

**Assumption 2:** There needs to be related pairs. In other words, there needs to be data points for both the independent and the dependent variable.

**Assumption 3:** There should be no significant outliers. An **outlier** is a data point within your data that does not follow the usual pattern of all the other data points in your data. Including an outlier in your analysis affects the validity of your results. You can test for this assumption by using descriptive statistics (e.g., frequencies and the range of scores), along with the boxplot and histogram in SPSS for both the independent and the dependent variable. In SPSS an extreme outlier is denoted by an asterisk (*) in the boxplot. In looking at the histogram, the extreme outlier will be represented by the bar that is the farthest distance from all the other bars.

**Assumption 4:** There needs to be a linear relationship between the independent and the dependent variable. You can test this assumption by using the scatterplot in SPSS. The line drawn between all the dots going from left to right should form a straight line. In order to determine if this assumption has been met, you need to visually inspect the scatterplot. In looking at Figure 13.17 you will see a linear and a nonlinear relationship depicted.

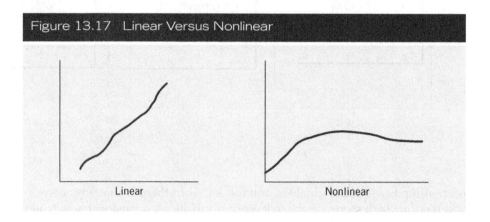

Figure 13.17   Linear Versus Nonlinear

Linear                    Nonlinear

**Assumption 5:** The scores on the independent and the dependent variable should be normally distributed. This is known as the **assumption of normality**. You can test for the assumption of normality by using the Shapiro-Wilk test of normality in SPSS. The Kolmogorov-Smirnov test can also be used and is also reported in SPSS. Other methods of testing the assumption of normality are by examining the skewness and kurtosis of the data, along with the histograms and normal Q-Q plots in SPSS. By looking at the histograms and normal Q-Q plots, one is looking to see if the distribution of the data looks like a normal distribution, a bell-shaped curve distribution.

**Assumption 6:** There needs to be **homoscedasticity**. The variance around the regression line is the same for all values of the independent variable. You can test to see if this assumption has been violated by examining a plot of the standard residuals regressed on the predicted values. If this assumption is violated, you are at risk of making a Type I error—that is, rejecting the null hypothesis when it should have been accepted.

**Assumption 7:** The data were derived by **simple random sampling**—that is, everyone in the population to whom you want to generalize the results had an equal chance of being included in the sample.

We recommend testing of these assumptions be done prior to conducting the Pearson's correlation analysis. Conducting the analysis without doing this will produce erroneous results. If Assumption 1 is violated (i.e., the independent or the dependent variable is measured on a nominal level, that is, a dichotomous variable), you can still conduct a correlation analysis, but it would be called a point-biserial correlation analysis instead of a Pearson's correlation. A Spearman's rank-order correlation would be appropriate if both the independent and dependent variables are measured on an ordinal level or if there is a monotonic relationship between two variables measured on an interval or ratio (a scale) level. A **monotonic relationship** is one where the independent and dependent variable change together but not at a constant rate. If Assumption 3 is violated, *no significant outliers*, we recommend that you carefully examine the data to determine if both the independent and the dependent variable have been coded correctly, as many times outliers are due to the data not being coded correctly. If the outliers are due to the data not being coded correctly, then the data points should not be included in the analysis. On the other hand, if the outliers are not due to the data not being coded incorrectly, then you should run the analysis with and without the outliers. If the results of your analysis changes from non-significant to significant, the outlier should be dropped from the analysis. If Assumption 5 is violated, the assumption of normality, you can transform the data by using the log transformation function in SPSS to get a normal distribution (or close to normal curve).

## How to Conduct a Pearson's Correlation Analysis in SPSS

A researcher, for example, is interested in knowing if there is an association between social support and well-being. More specifically, the researcher hypothesized that persons who report high social support report good well-being. To test this hypothesis, the researcher would conduct the analysis described below.

To conduct a Pearson's correlation in SPSS, assuming none of the assumptions have been violated, one would go through these four steps:

Step 1: Go to the menu bar and click *Analyze*, then scroll down to *Correlate*, and then highlight *Bivariate* (see Figure 13.18).

Step 2: Click on *Bivariate*. Once you have done this, the "Bivariate Correlations" dialogue box will appear (see Figure 13.19). You need to highlight the variable you want to include in the analysis then click the *Arrow* button, which will automatically place the variable in the "Variables" box. You need to repeat the above step to include the second variable you want in your analysis. Once you have done this, please check to ensure that in the "Correlation Coefficients" area that "Pearson" has been checked. Then look at the "Test of Significance" area; make sure the circle beside

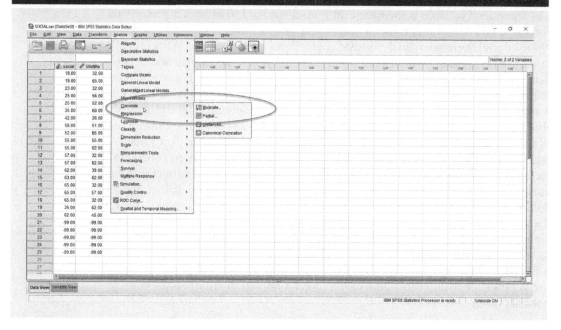

the one-tailed significance test has a blue dot in it. The one-tailed test is to
be used when you have a directional hypothesis. A directional hypothesis
predicts the direction of the relationship between the independent and the
dependent variable. If you read the researcher's hypothesis in our example,
you will see it is a directional hypothesis, as the researcher is predicting that
persons who have high social support will report good well-being. The two-
tailed test is to be used when you have a nondirectional hypothesis—that is,
a hypothesis that does not specify the relationship between the independent
and the dependent variable. Finally, make sure the "Flag significant
correlations" box is checked.

Step 3: Click the *Options* button. Once you have done this, the "Bivariate
Correlations Options" dialogue box will appear. Look at the "Statistics" box.
Make sure the "Means and Standard Deviations" box is checked. Look at the
"Missing Values" box. Make sure the circle beside Exclude cases pairwise has
a *blue dot* in it (see Figure 13.20). You need to exclude the cases pairwise
because one of the assumptions of the Pearson's correlation is that there
needs to be related pairs. In other words, there needs to be data points for
both the independent and the dependent variable.

**Figure 13.19  Demonstrating Step 2 to Conduct a Pearson's Correlation Analysis in SPSS**

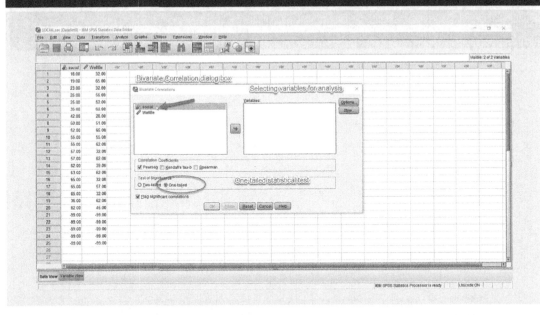

**Figure 13.20  Demonstrating Step 3 to Conduct a Pearson's Correlation Analysis in SPSS**

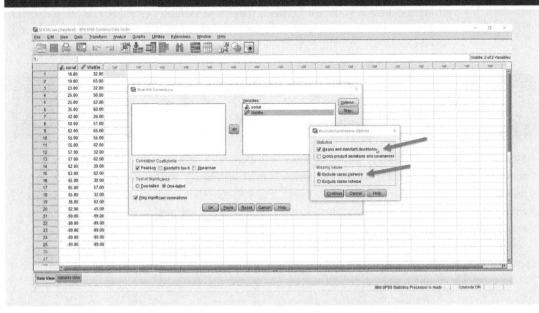

Step 4: Click *Continue* and then click *OK*. This will generate the results of the Pearson's correlation (See Figure 13.21).

Figure 13.21 Demonstrating Step 4 to Conduct a Pearson's Correlation Analysis in SPSS

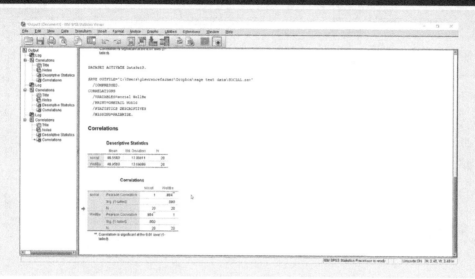

**Results:** A Pearson's correlation was conducted to determine if persons who perceive their social support is high report good well-being. The results revealed a strong, positive correlation between these two variables ($r = .88$, $n = 20$, $p < .001$). In other words, persons who have high social support reported good well-being. Based on the results, the hypothesis was supported.

## Example of a Study Using Pearson 's Correlation

Alorani and Alradaydeh (2017) examined the relationship between spiritual well-being, perceived social support, and life satisfaction among university students in Jordan. They used a cross-sectional descriptive-correlation research design. A total of 919 students participated in their study. Data were analyzed using a Pearson's correlation. The results indicated that there was a moderate, positive relationship between spiritual well-being and perceived social support ($r = .49$, $p < .001$) and a strong, positive relationship between spiritual well-being and life satisfaction ($r = .53$, $p < .001$). Additionally, there was a moderate, positive relationship between perceived social support and life satisfaction ($r = .46$, $p < .001$).

## Chi-Square Test of Independence

Researchers conduct a **chi-square test of independence** when they are examining the association between an independent and a dependent variable, where both are measured on a nominal level. For example, a researcher would conduct a chi-square test of independence if he or she is interested in knowing if gender is associated with exposure to community violence. The chi-square test compares the observed counts of the observations in each category with the expected count. Table 13.4 displays the observed and expected frequencies (counts) for exposure to community violence by gender.

| Table 13.4 | Observed and Expected Frequencies—Exposure to Community Violence by Gender | | Community Exposure | | Total |
| --- | --- | --- | --- | --- | --- |
| | | | Yes | No | |
| Gender Male | Count | | 40 | 15 | 55 |
| | Expected Count | | 20 | 18 | 38 |
| Gender Female | Count | | 20 | 30 | 50 |
| | Expected Count | | 15 | 10 | 25 |
| Total | Count | | 60 | 45 | 105 |
| | Expected | | 35 | 28 | 63 |

In looking at the above table, you will see that it was expected that 20 males and 15 females would indicate that have been exposed to community violence; however, it was found that 40 males and 20 females were exposed to community violence.

Before conducting the chi-square test of independence, one must ensure that the assumptions required for this analysis are met. There are four assumptions that must be met to produce valid results. These assumptions are as follows:

**Assumption 1:** Both the independent and the dependent variable should be measured at the nominal level. Examples of variables measured at the nominal level are age in categories (e.g., 1 = ages 1–5, 2 = ages 6–12, and 3 = ages 13–17), type of car driven (1 = Honda, 2 = Ford, 3 = Hyundai, 4 = other), and gender (1 = male, 2 = female), to name a few.

**Assumption 2:** If the data are to be displayed in a contingency table, each cell must have at least a frequency of 5. Violating this assumption will produce inaccurate results. A contingency table is "a frequency table that presents the observed frequencies of one categorical variable (dependent variable) as function of another categorical variable (independent variable)" (Abu-Bader, 2016, p. 286).

**Assumption 3:** The data were derived by simple random sampling —that is, everyone in the population to whom you want to generalize the results had an equal chance of being included in the sample.

**Assumption 4:** The data should not be correlated (i.e., data from matched pairs). This is known as the **assumption of independence**.

We recommend testing of these assumptions be done prior to conducting the chi-square test of independence, as conducting the analysis without doing this will produce erroneous results. If you violate Assumption 1 because both the independent and the dependent variable are not measured on the nominal level (but both are measured on the interval or ratio level), you should consider conducting a Pearson's correlation. If you violate Assumption 2, then you should consider conducting the Fischer exact test if the expected count in any of the cells in the contingency table is less than 5. It is also appropriate to use the Fischer exact test if greater than 20% of the cells have an expected count of less than 5. On the other hand, you should consider conducting the Yates corrected contingency test if the expected count in any of the cells in the contingency table is less than 10. If Assumption 4 is violated, you should conduct a McNemar's test. The McNemar's test is appropriate to use when one is interested in determining if there is a significant change in the nominal data before and after an intervention has been implemented.

Once the chi-square test of independence has been conducted, the next step is to determine the strength of the association. Determining the strength of the association is done by conducting the Cramer's V test. The Cramer's V test is interpreted the same way as the Pearson's correlation, because it is a form of a correlation. The Cramer's V will be reported when you conduct the chi-square test of independence using SPSS.

## How to Conduct a Chi-Square Test of Independence in SPSS

A researcher, for example, is interested in knowing if there is an association between taking college-level courses in a juvenile detention center and attending college. More specifically, the researcher hypothesized that juveniles who took college-level courses while in a juvenile detention center are more likely to attend college than those who did not take college-level courses while in a juvenile detention center. To test this hypothesis, the researcher would conduct the analysis described below.

To conduct a chi-square in SPSS, assuming none of the assumptions have been violated, one would go through these six steps:

Step 1: Go to the menu bar and click *Analyze*, then scroll down to "Descriptive Statistics," and then highlight *Crosstabs* (see Figure 13.22).

Figure 13.22  Demonstrating Step 1 on How to Conduct a Chi-Square Test of Independence in SPSS

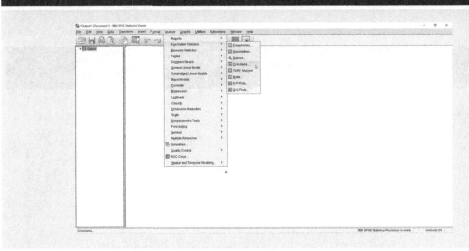

Step 2: Click on *Crosstabs*. Once you have done this, the "Crosstabs" dialogue box will appear (see Figure 13.23). You need to highlight the dependent variable you want to include in the analysis and then click the *Arrow* button and put it in the "Row(s)" box. You need to repeat the above step to include the independent variable you want to include in your analysis and put this variable in the "Column(s)" box.

Figure 13.23  Demonstrating Step 2 on How to Conduct a Chi-Square Test of Independence in SPSS

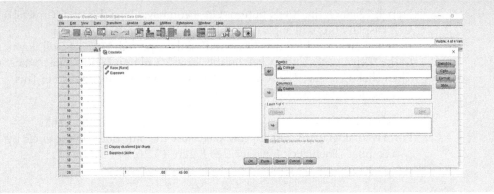

Step 3: Click on the "Statistics" button. Once you have done this, the "Crosstabs: Statistics" box will appear (see Figure 13.24). Click the box next to "Chi-square." Scroll down to the "Nominal" area and click on the "Phi and Cramer's V" box. Then click *Continue*. The "Crosstabs" dialogue box will appear.

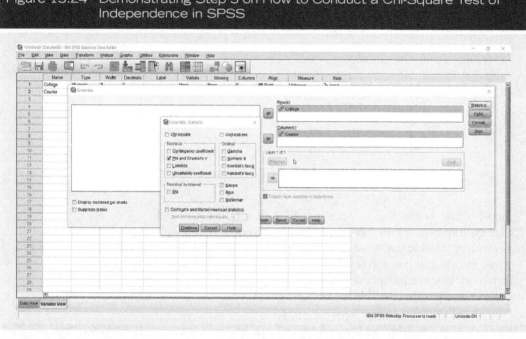

Figure 13.24   Demonstrating Step 3 on How to Conduct a Chi-Square Test of Independence in SPSS

Step 4: Click on the "Cells"button. Once you have done this, the "Crosstabs: Cell Display" box will appear (see Figure 13.25). Scroll down to the "Counts" area. Click on the "Observed" and "Expected" boxes. Scroll down to the "Percentages" area. Click on the "Row," "Column," and "Total" boxes. Then click *Continue*. The "Crosstabs" dialogue box will appear. Note: This was previously shown in Figure 13.23.

Step 5: Click *Format*. Once you have done this, the "Crosstabs: Table Format" dialogue box will appear. Make sure the blue dot is in the circle by "Ascending." Then click *Continue* (see Figure 13.26).

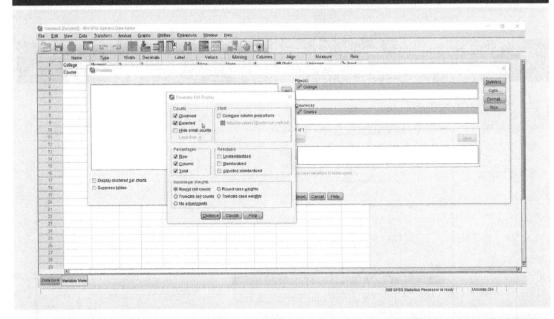

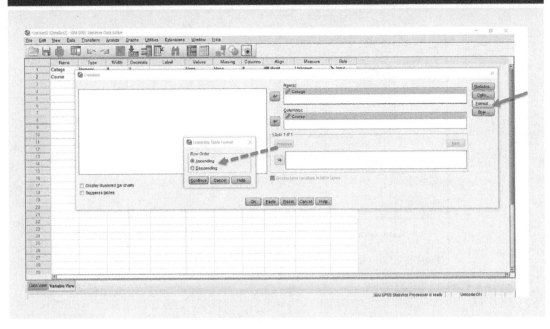

Step 6: Click on *OK*. This will generate the results of the chi-square test of independence (see Figure 13.27).

**Figure 13.27** Demonstrating Step 6 on How to Conduct a Chi-Square Test of Independence in SPSS

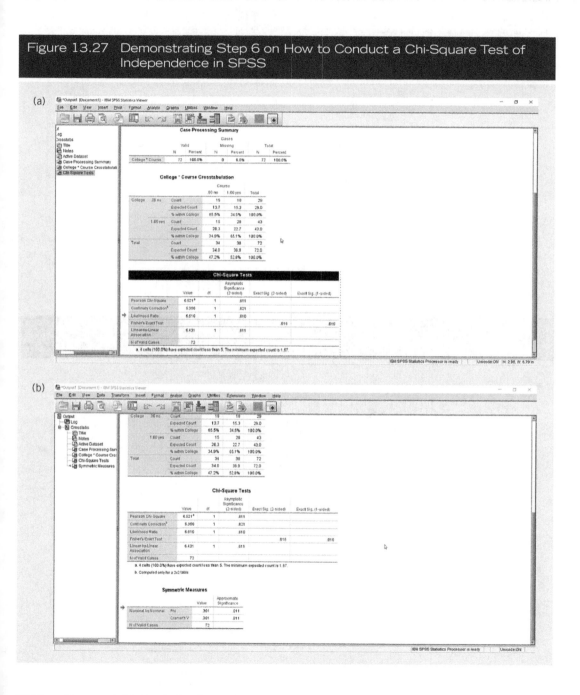

**Results:** The chi-square test of independence was used to examine the association between taking college-level courses in a juvenile detention center and attending college, among a sample of 72 youth. Inspection of the 2 × 2 contingency table shows no cells had an expected frequency of less than five. Therefore, the chi-square test will be reported.

The results of the chi-square test showed a statistically significant association between taking college-level courses in a juvenile detention center and attending college ($X^2_{(df = 1)} = 6.52$, $p < .05$). In other words, the two variables are related in the population.

The results of the contingency table showed the number of juveniles who took college-level courses in a juvenile detention center and attended college ($n = 28$) is statistically significantly greater than expected ($n = 23$). Therefore, the hypothesis was supported.

The results of the Cramer's V measure of symmetry showed a significant positive association between taking college-level courses and going to college (Cramer's $V = .30$, $p < .05$). In other words, juveniles who took college-level courses while in a detention center were more likely to go to college than those who did not take college-level courses. The strength of the association between taking college courses in a juvenile detention center and attending college is moderate.

---

### Critical Thinking Question 13.2

As mentioned earlier, Mary is interested in knowing if there is an association between the fathers' posttest score on the knowledge of child's development measure and the posttest quality of time spent with their child engaging in educational activities. What type of correlation analysis (i.e., Pearson's correlation or chi-square test of independence) would you recommend she conduct? Justify your response.

---

## Multiple Regression Analysis

A **multiple regression analysis** is appropriate to use when you have more than one independent variable (nominal, ordinal, interval, or ratio) and one dependent variable (interval or ratio). The purpose of a multiple regression analysis is to predict the unknown value of the dependent variable from the known values of the independent variables. There are other types of multiple regression analysis, but we will only discuss the simultaneous multiple regression analysis in this chapter. In the simultaneous multiple regression analysis, all the independent variables—also referred to as predictors or regressors—are entered at the same time as predictors of the dependent variable. The purpose of a simultaneous multiple regression analysis is to determine which independent variable predicts the dependent variable(s). In other words, this type of analysis helps the researcher determine which independent variable is associated with the dependent variable. An appropriate research question to be answered using a simultaneous multiple regression analysis would be as follows: "Does parental monitoring and social support predict community violence exposure?" For the above example, the researcher hypothesized that adolescents whose parents monitor their behavior and provide them with social support will report low levels of community violence exposure. The null hypothesis would be that parental monitoring and social support are not predictive of community violence exposure.

Before conducting a simultaneous multiple regression analysis, one must ensure that the assumptions required for this analysis are met. There are nine assumptions that must be met to produce valid results. These assumptions are as follows:

**Assumption 1:** Each independent variable should be measured on an interval or ratio level (a scale).

**Assumption 2:** The dependent variable should be measured on an interval or ratio level (a scale).

**Assumption 3:** The errors/residuals associated with each observation of the dependent variable are not associated with any other observation of the dependent variable. This assumption is known as the assumption of independence of observations (i.e., independence of residuals). This assumption is tested by using the Durbin-Watson statistics using SPSS.

**Assumption 4:** There should be no significant outliers, high leverage points, or highly influential points. An outlier is value that has a large residual. A high leverage point is an extreme value of the independent variable that is far from the mean, whereas a highly influential point is a data point that has an extreme effect on the regression coefficient and standard errors, compared to the other data point. Outliers, high leverage points, and highly influential points have a negative effect on the ability of the multiple regression analysis to accurately predict the value of the dependent variable. Outliers can be detected by using the Mahalanobis distance test, casewise diagnostics, and studentized deleted residuals in SPSS. The Cook distance test using SPSS can be used to check for highly influential points.
A scatterplot can be used to detect high leverage points.

**Assumption 5:** The relationship between each independent variable and the dependent variable is linear. To determine if the relationship is linear, you would create a scatterplot and partial regression plot using SPSS.

**Assumption 6:** The variances along the line of best fit remains similar as you move along the line. This is the assumption of homoscedasticity. To test this assumption, you need to plot the studentized residuals against the unstandardized predicted values.

**Assumption 7:** The independent variables should not be too highly correlated. This is known as the assumption of the **absence of multicollinearity**. Tabachnick and Fidell (2007) recommend that the correlations between the independent variables not be higher than .90. To detect for multicollinearity, you can exam the correlation between the independent variables and the dependent variable by conducting a Pearson's correlation and by looking at the tolerance and variance inflation factor (VIF), which is obtained by conducting the multiple regression analysis. Tolerance values range from 0 to 1; a value less than .01 for the independent variable, indicating multicollinearity, is an issue (Abu-Bader, 2016). A VIF value greater than 10 indicates multicollinearity is an issue (Stevens, 1992).

**Assumption 8:** The errors/residuals should be normally distributed. This assumption can be tested by creating a histogram with superimposed normal curve and a normal P-P plot or a normal Q-Q plot of the studentized residuals.

**Assumption 9:** The data were derived by simple random sampling—that is, everyone in the population to whom you want to generalize the results had an equal chance of being included in the sample.

We recommend testing of these assumptions be done prior to conducting the multiple regression analysis, as conducting the analysis without doing this will produce erroneous results. If Assumptions #1 and #2 are violated, then automatically one knows that the multiple regression analysis cannot be conducted. If Assumption 5 is violated, one needs to conduct a nonlinear regression analysis or transform the data so this assumption is no longer violated. If Assumption 7 is violated, one needs to consider combing the two independent variables into one variable that assesses a single construct (Stevens, 1992) or delete one of the independent variables, and use the one that best assesses the construct of interest (Sprinthall, 2000) in the analysis.

Earlier, it was mentioned that an independent variable measured on a nominal level can be used in a multiple regression analysis; however, this variable must be dummy coded prior to being used in the analysis. **Dummy coding** is a way of turning categories associated with a nominal variable into something a regression can treat as having a high and low score. By dummy coding the nominal variable, it takes on the variable of 0 or 1, indicating the absence or presence of some categorical effect.

Referring to the case example, let us say that participation in the interactive computer parenting problem is coded as 1 and participation in the didactic, in-person parenting program is coded as 2. To dummy code this variable, you would recode "1" to "0" (participation in the interactive computer parenting program) and "2" to "1" (participation in the didactic, in-person parenting program). The nominal variable is now referred to as a dummy variable.

A significant F-value associated with the simultaneous multiple regression analysis only tells you that there is a linear relationship between the dependent variable and at least one independent variable. It does not tell you which independent variable is a significant predictor of the dependent variable. To determine which of the independent variables is a significant predictor of the dependent variable, one needs to look at the $t$-value associated with the $t$-test. If the $t$-test is significant for the regression coefficient, it indicates that the independent variable of interest is predictive of the dependent variable, controlling for the other independent variables. Besides looking at the F- and $t$-values, it is important to look at the coefficient of determination ($R^2$). The coefficient of determination is the proportion of the dependent variable that can be explained by the independent variables. In order to determine the percentage of explained variance, one would multiply the value of $R^2$ by 100. The value for $R^2$ is always between 0 and 1. The closer $R^2$ is to 1 the better the model fit and its prediction. It is also important to look at the tolerance value. If the value is greater than .1, you can interpret the results of the analysis. If it is not, you need to redo the analysis without one of the independent variables or combine the two independent variables into a single variable assessing the construct of interest.

## How to Conduct a Simultaneous Multiple Regression Analysis in SPSS

A researcher, for example, is interested in determining if both parental monitoring and social support predict community violence exposure. The researcher hypothesized that adolescents whose parents monitor their behavior and provide them with social support will report low levels of community violence exposure. To test this hypothesis, the researcher would conduct the analysis described below.

Step 1: Go to the menu bar and click *Analyze*, then scroll down to *Regression*, and then go across to *Linear* (see Figure 13.28).

Step 2: Click on *Linear*. Once you have done this, the "Linear Regression" dialogue box will appear. You need to highlight the variable you want to include in the analysis then click the *Arrow* button and put it in the "Dependent" box. Repeat the above step to include the variable you want in the analysis in the "Independent" box. For the purpose of this analysis, you will not click on the *Previous* or *Next* buttons (see Figure 13.29).

**Figure 13.28** Demonstrating Step 1 of How to Conduct a Simultaneous Multiple Regression Analysis in SPSS

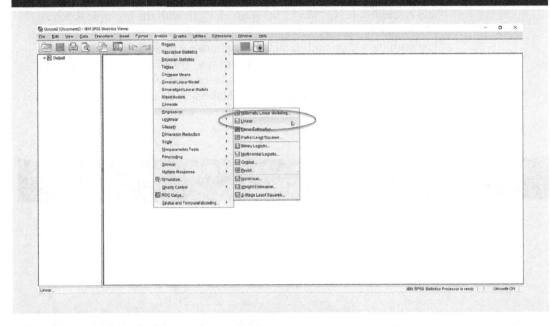

**Figure 13.29** Demonstrating Step 2 of How to Conduct a Simultaneous Multiple Regression Analysis in SPSS

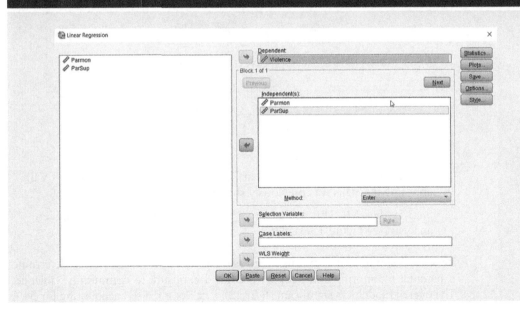

Step 3: Click *Statistics*. Once you have done this, the "Linear Regression Statistics" dialogue box will appear (see Figure 13.30). Make sure "Estimates" (provides you with the B and beta weights, standard error, and *t*- and *p*-values), "Model fit" (provides you with the multiple R, $R^2$, an ANOVA table, and corresponding F- and *p*-value), "Descriptives" (provides you with the means and standard deviations for each variable, and the correlation matrix), "Collinearity diagnostics" (provides tolerance value for each independent variable) and "Confidence intervals" in the "Regression Coefficients" area have been selected. Make sure 95 is indicated in the "Level %" field.

**Figure 13.30** Demonstrating Step 3 of How to Conduct a Simultaneous Multiple Regression Analysis in SPSS

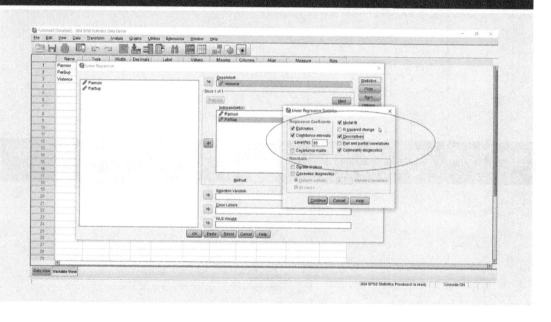

Step 4: Click *Continue*. The "Linear Regression Statistics" dialogue box will appear. Note: This was previously shown in Figure 13.30.

Step 5: Click *OK*. This will generate the results of the multiple regression analysis (see Figure 13.31).

**Results:** A simultaneous multiple regression analysis was conducted to determine if parental monitoring and support predicted exposure to community violence. The overall model was significant, $F(2, 22) = 12.96$, $p < .001$, accounting for 54%

of the variance. Only parental monitoring emerged as a significant predictor of exposure to community violence (B = −54, $p < .05$), indicating that adolescents who reported high levels of parental monitoring reported low exposure to community violence (see Figure 13.31).

**Figure 13.31** Demonstrating Step 5 of How to Conduct a Simultaneous Multiple Regression Analysis in SPSS

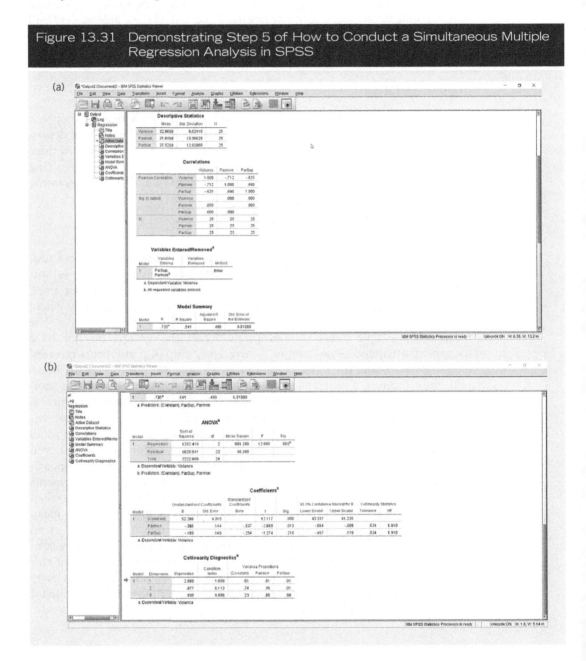

# Statistical Analyses Used to Assess Significance of Group Differences

There are several statistical analyses that can be used to assess for significance of group differences. We will briefly discuss three: *t*-tests (i.e., independent and dependent), analysis of variance (ANOVA), and multivariate analysis of variance (MANOVA).

## Types of *t*-Tests

There are two types of *t*-tests you need to be able to conduct. Both are appropriate when the independent variable is nominal, with two categories, and the dependent variable is interval or ratio (a scale); however, when you use either of these *t*-tests is dependent upon the type of samples you have and research design. The types of *t*-tests are the **independent-sample *t*-test** and the **dependent-sample *t*-test**.

### Independent-Sample *t*-Test

The independent-sample *t*-test—also referred to as the two-sample *t*-test, independent-samples *t*-test, the unpaired *t*-test, the unrelated *t*-test, or student's *t*-test—is an inferential statistical test that determines whether there is a statistical significant difference between the mean in two groups, where both the means and standard deviations are estimated from the data. The independent-sample *t*-test is appropriate when the groups do not have the same participants—for example, where one group of participants received the intervention and the other group of participants did not receive the intervention or received a different intervention. Moreover, the independent-sample *t*-test is appropriate when you have one independent variable, which is measured on a nominal level, with two categories, and one dependent variable, which is measured on an interval or ratio level (a scale). You may recall from Chapter 6 that the independent-sample *t*-test is appropriate when you have a posttest-only design with nonequivalent groups (static-group comparison design) or experimental research designs, when two groups of participants receive a different intervention. An independent *t*-test is also appropriate when a researcher has a research question such as, "Is there a difference in the mean scores on the exposure to community violence scale between African American and Hispanic males?" The researcher hypothesized that African American males would have a higher mean score on the exposure to community violence scale than Hispanic males. The null hypothesis would be that there is no difference in the mean scores on the exposure to community violence scale for African American and Hispanic males.

Before conducting the independent-sample *t*-test, one must ensure that the assumptions required for this analysis are met. There are eight assumptions that must be met to produce valid results. These assumptions are as follows:

**Assumption 1:** The independent variable should be measured on the nominal scale and should consist of two categories. Examples of a variable that can meet this assumption include group status (experimental or control), employment status (employed or unemployed), and racial/ethnic background (Hispanic or Non-Hispanic), to name a few.

**Assumption 2:** The dependent variable should be measured on the interval or ratio level (a scale).

**Assumption 3:** The scores or observations of the dependent variable should be independent of each of other. In other words, the scores for one participant are not systematically related to the scores of the other participants. This assumption is known as the assumption of independence. This assumption cannot be checked by examining the data, but by looking at the study's design. Research designs where the assumptions of independence are met are the posttest-only design with nonequivalent groups (static-group comparison design), and experimental research designs, when two groups of participants receive a different intervention.

**Assumption 4:** There should be no significant outliers.

**Assumption 5:** The scores on the dependent variable should be normally distributed within each group of the independent variable. This is known as the assumption of normality. The same procedures described for assessing normality when you conduct a Pearson's Correlation analysis can be used.

**Assumption 6:** The variances for the dependent variable should be equal within each group of the independent variable, when the standard deviation for each group is approximately equal. This is known as the assumption of homogeneity of variances. This assumption can be tested by using the Levene's test for homogeneity also referred to as the Levene's F test for equality of variances in SPSS. If the results of this test are not significant, *p*-value greater than .05, then the assumption of homogeneity of variances has been met.

**Assumption 7:** The data were derived by simple random sampling—that is, everyone in the population to whom you want to generalize the results had an equal chance of being included in the sample.

We recommend testing of these assumptions be done prior to conducting the independent-sample *t*-test, as conducting the analysis without doing this will produce erroneous results. If Assumption 3 is violated, the assumption of independence, then automatically one knows that the independent-sample *t*-test cannot be conducted. If Assumptions 4, 5, or 6 are violated, there are things you can do to the data so that these assumptions are no longer violated. For instance, if Assumption 4 (no significant outliers) is violated, the same procedures described for detecting outliers when you conduct a Pearson's correlation analysis can be used so this assumption is no longer violated. If Assumption 5 (the assumption of normality) is violated, you can transform your data by using the log transformation function in SPSS to get a normal distribution (or close to normal curve). If the transformation of the data does not produce a normal distribution, then a Mann-Whitney U test can be used, which is a nonparametric statistic to analyze the data instead of the independent-sample *t*-test.

## How to Conduct an Independent-Sample *t*-Test in SPSS

A researcher, for example, is interested in determining if African American males have a higher mean score on the exposure to community violence scale than the Hispanic males. The researcher hypothesized that African American males will have a higher mean score on the exposure to community violence scale than Hispanic males. To test this hypothesis, the researcher would conduct the analysis described below.

To conduct an independent-sample *t*-test, assuming none of the assumptions have been violated, one would go through these five steps:

Step 1: Go to the menu bar and click *Analyze*, then scroll down to "Compare Means," and then go across to "Independent-Samples T Test" (see Figure 13.32).

**Figure 13.32   Demonstrating Step 1 How to Conduct and Independent-Sample *t*-Test in SPSS**

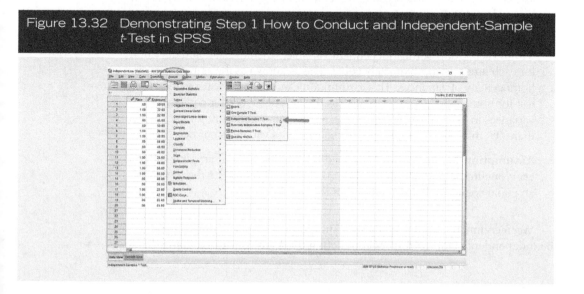

Step 2: Click on *Independent-Samples T Test*. Once you have done this, the "Independent-Samples T Test" dialogue box will appear (see Figure 13.33). You need to highlight the variable you want to include in the analysis then click the *Arrow* button and put it in the "Test Variable(s)" box. The variable you put in this box should be the one where you want the mean to be produced. It is also the variable that is measured on an interval or ratio measurement level, using a scale. You need to repeat the above step to include the second variable you want in your analysis and put this variable in the "Grouping Variable" field. The variable you put in the "Grouping Variable" field should be the one that is measured on the nominal scale.

Figure 13.33    Demonstrating Step 2 How to Conduct and Independent-Sample *t*-Test in SPSS

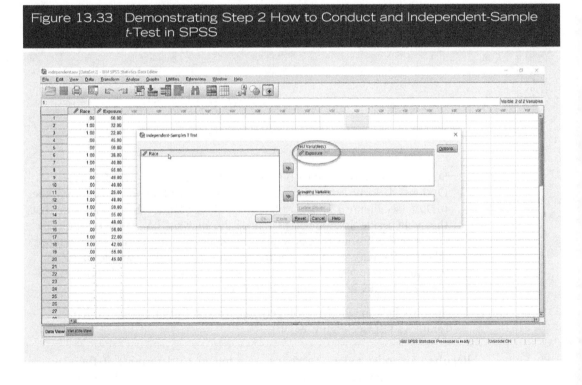

Step 3: Scroll down to "Define Groups." Click on *Define Groups*. The "Define Groups" dialogue box will appear. Enter the number associated with the first group in the "Group 1" field. Enter the number associated with the second group in the "Group 2" field (see Figure 13.34).

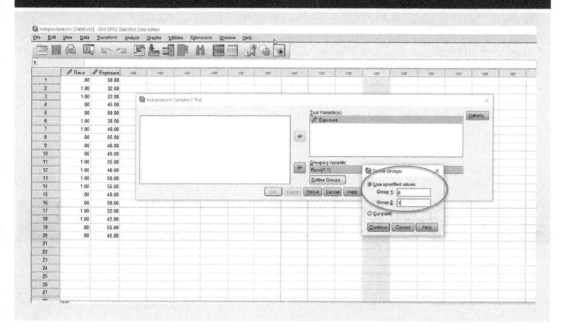

**Figure 13.34** Demonstrating Step 3 How to Conduct and Independent-Sample *t*-Test in SPSS

Step 4: Click on the *Options* button. In the "Independent-Samples T Test: Options" dialogue box, make sure the "Confidence Interval Percentage" is set to 95% (see Figure 13.35). Look at the "Missing Values" box. Make sure that the circle beside "Exclude cases analysis by analysis" has a blue dot in it. By choosing the "Exclude cases analysis by analysis" option, each *t*-test will use all cases that have valid data for the tested variables. The sample size may vary from test to test. The "Exclude cases analysis by analysis" option is the most commonly used option. Click on *Continue*.

Step 5: Click on *OK*. This will generate the results of the independent-samples *t*-test (see Figure 13.36).

**Results:** An independent *t*-test was conducted to determine if there was a difference between African American males and Hispanic males in regard to their exposure to community violence. The Levene's test of equality of variances revealed that equal variances cannot be assumed, $p < .05$; therefore, the *t*-test associated with equal variances not assumed is reported. The results of the independent *t*-test revealed a statistically significant difference between African American males and Hispanic males in regard to their exposure to community violence ($t_{(df = 13)} = 2.91$, $p < .05$). African American males had a higher

**Figure 13.35** Demonstrating Step 4 How to Conduct and Independent-Sample *t*-Test in SPSS

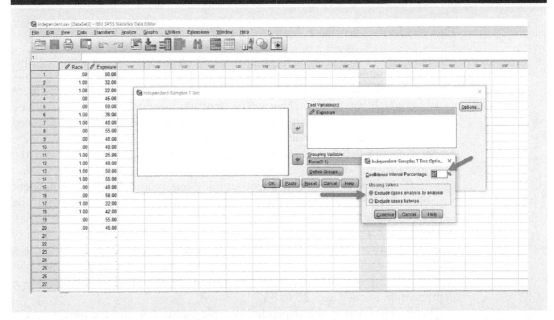

**Figure 13.36** Demonstrating Step 5 How to Conduct and Independent-Sample *t*-Test in SPSS

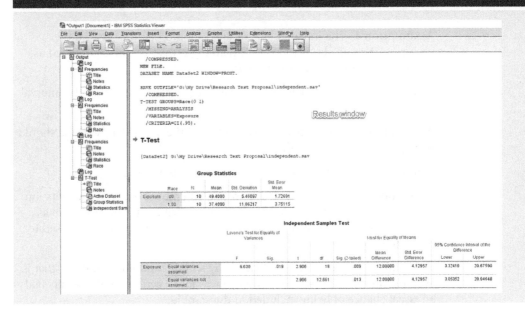

community violence exposure mean (mean = 49.40, SD = 5.46) than Hispanic males (mean = 37.40, SD = 11.86); a mean difference of 12. Based on the results, the hypothesis was supported (see Figure 13.36).

## Dependent-Sample *t*-Test

The dependent-sample *t*-test, also referred to as the paired *t*-test or paired sample *t*-test, is an inferential statistical test that determines whether there is a statistically significant difference between the means of the observations of the dependent variable, which was assessed twice. The dependent-sample *t*-test is appropriate when you have the same participants in both groups because you have assessed them on the dependent variable twice. For example, the same participants were assessed on the dependent variable prior to the intervention (pretest) and the same participants were assessed on the dependent variable after the intervention (posttest). Similar to the independent-sample *t*-test, you have one independent variable, which is measured on a nominal level, with two categories, and one dependent variable, which is measured on an interval or ratio level (a scale). A dependent *t*-test is also appropriate when a researcher has the following type of research question: "Is mindfulness effective in reducing depression in women ages 25 to 35?" The researcher hypothesized that mindfulness will reduce depression in women ages 25 to 35. The null hypothesis would be mindfulness will not reduce depression in women ages 25 to 35.

Before conducting the dependent-sample *t*-test, one must ensure that the assumptions required for this analysis are met. There are six assumptions that must be met for the dependent-sample *t*-test to be conducted to produce valid results. These assumptions are as follows:

**Assumption 1:** The independent variable should be measured on the nominal scale and should consist of paired groups (e.g., pretest [coded as group 1] and posttest [coded as group 2]).

**Assumption 2:** The dependent variable should be measured on the interval or ratio level (a scale).

**Assumption 3:** The scores or observations of the dependent variable should be dependent of each of other.

**Assumption 4:** There should be no significant outliers.

**Assumption 5:** The scores, which are the differences between the pairs, on the dependent variable should be normally distributed. This is known as the assumption of normality. The Kolmogorov-Smirnov test can be used to assess this assumption.

**Assumption 6:** The data were derived by simple random sampling—that is, everyone in the population to whom you want to generalize the results had an equal chance of being included in the sample.

We recommend testing of these assumptions be done prior to conducting the dependent-sample *t*-test, as conducting the analysis without doing this will produce erroneous results. If Assumption 5, the assumption of normality, is violated, you can transform the data by using the log transformation function in SPSS to get a normal distribution (or close to normal curve). If the transformation of the data does not produce a normal distribution, then you can use the Wilcoxon matched-paired signed ranks test, which is a nonparametric statistic test to analyze the data instead of the dependent *t*-test.

## How to Conduct a Dependent-Sample *t*-Test in SPSS

A researcher, for example, is interested in determining if mindfulness will reduce depression in women ages 25 to 35. The researcher hypothesized that mindfulness will reduce depression in women ages 25 to 35. To test the hypothesis, the researcher would conduct the analysis described below.

To conduct a dependent-sample *t*-test, assuming none of the assumptions have been violated, one would go through these four steps:

Step 1: Go to the menu bar and click *Analyze*, then scroll down to "Compare Means," and then go across to "Paired-Samples T Test" (see Figure 13.37).

Figure 13.37  Demonstrating Step 1 of How to Conduct a Dependent-Sample *t*-test in SPSS

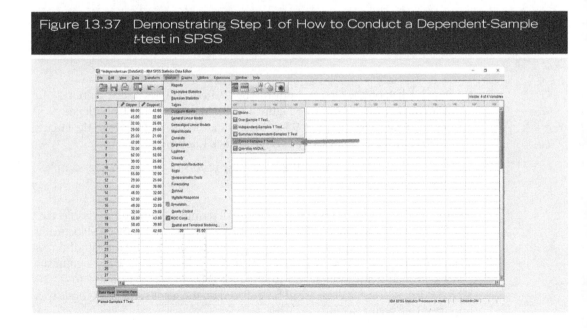

Step 2: Click on *Paired-Samples T Test*. Once you have done this, the "Paired-Samples T Test" dialogue box will appear (see Figure 13.38). You need to highlight the variable you want to include in the analysis then click the *Arrow* button, which will automatically place the variable in the "Paired Variables" dialogue box. You need to repeat the above step to include the second variable you want in your analysis.

**Figure 13.38  Demonstrating Step 2 of How to Conduct a Dependent-Sample *t*-Test in SPSS**

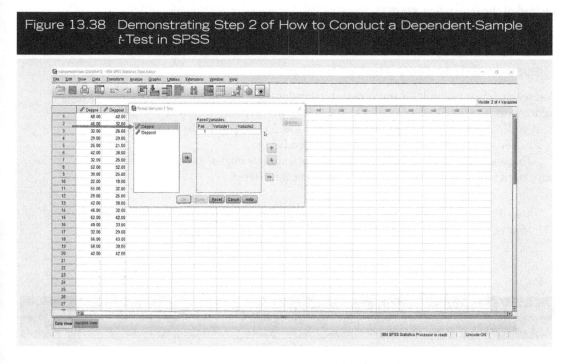

Step 3: Click on the *Options* button. The "Paired-Samples T Test Options" dialogue box will appear (see Figure 13.39). Make sure the "Confidence Interval Percentage" is set to 95%. Make sure there is a blue dot in the circle by "Exclude cases analysis by analysis." Click *Continue*.

Step 4: Click on *OK*. This will generate the results of the dependent-samples *t*-test (see Figure 13.40).

**Results:** A dependent *t*-test was conducted to determine if mindfulness is effective in reducing depression in women ages 25 to 35. The results showed statistically significant changes in depression among the women who received the mindfulness intervention ($t_{(df = 19)}$ = 5.58, $p < .001$). Participants had a statistically significant decrease in their depression scores from 41.95 (SD = 11.60) at pretest to 33.20 (SD = 8.60) at posttest, a decrease of 8.75. Based on the results, the hypothesis was supported (see Figure 13.40).

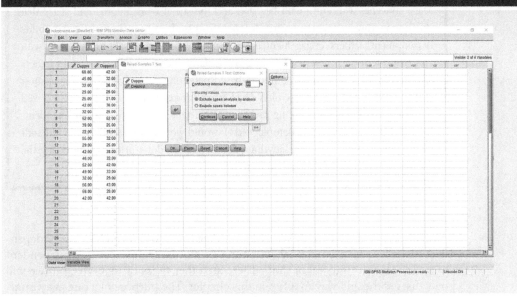

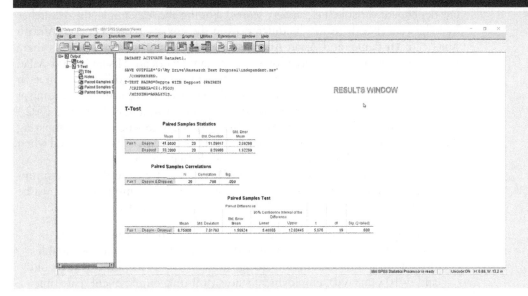

Mary convenes a meeting with her staff and the social work interns and states that she knows three dependent variables were assessed: fathers' knowledge of child's development, fathers' engagement in appropriate play, and quality time spent with child. Furthermore, she states that she is particularly interested in knowing if the fathers who received the interactive computer-based parenting program had higher posttest scores on knowledge of their child's development measure than fathers who received the didactic, in-person parenting program. What type of analysis (i.e., independent-sample *t*-test or dependent-sample *t*-test) would you recommend be conducted? Justify your response. Is there anything that should be done prior to conducting the analysis you recommended be conducted?

## Analysis of Variance

An analysis of variance (ANOVA) is appropriate to use when you have one independent variable, which is nominal, with three or more categories, and one dependent variable, which is interval or ratio. There are other types of ANOVAs, but we will only discuss the one-way ANOVA in this chapter. The purpose of a **one-way analysis of variance** is to assess for differences between the means for three or more groups. An appropriate research question to be answered using a one-way ANOVA would be as follows: "Are there differences in the anxiety scores between African American, Hispanic, and Asian females?" By reading this research question, you will see that there is one independent variable—race/ethnicity, which is divided into three categories (i.e., African American, Hispanic, and Asian American) and one dependent variable (i.e., anxiety scores). For the above example, the researcher hypothesized that there will be differences in the anxiety scores between African American, Hispanic, and Asian American females. The null hypothesis is there is no difference in the anxiety scores for African American, Hispanic, and Asian American females. There is no need to state which group is different from each other, because the alternative hypothesis only needs to be confirmed by finding at least one group mean that is different from the others (Mertler & Vannatta, 2002). It should be noted that a one-way ANOVA can also be used when one is comparing the means between two groups, and one will get the same p- value as you did when using the *t*-test and draw the same conclusion (Patten, 2004).

Before conducting the one-way ANOVA, one must ensure that the assumptions required for this analysis are met. There are seven assumptions that must be met to produce valid results. These assumptions are as follows:

**Assumption 1:** The independent variable should be measured on the nominal level and should consist of three categories. Examples of variables that can meet this assumption are age groups (1–5 years old, 6–8 years old, and 9–10 years old), employment status (full-time employment, part-time employment, and unemployed), and political party affiliation (democratic, libertarian, and republican), to name a few.

**Assumption 2:** The dependent variable should be measured on the interval or ratio level (a scale).

**Assumption 3:** The scores or observations of the dependent variable should be independent of each of other. In other words, the scores for one participant are not systematically related to the scores of the other participants. This assumption is known as the assumption of independence. This assumption cannot be checked by examining the data but by looking at the study's design. Research designs where the assumptions of independence are met are the experimental research designs, when three groups of participants receive a different intervention.

**Assumption 4:** There should be no significant outliers.

**Assumption 5:** The scores on the dependent variable should be normally distributed within each group of the independent variable. This is known as the assumption of normality. The same procedures described for assessing normality when you conduct a Pearson's correlation analysis can be used.

**Assumption 6:** The variances for the dependent variable should be equal within each group of the independent variable, when the standard deviation for each group is approximately equal. This is known as the assumption of homogeneity of variances. This assumption can be tested by using Levene's test for homogeneity, also referred to as Levene's F test for equality of variances in SPSS. If the results of this test are not significant, $p$-value greater than .05, then the assumption of homogeneity of variances has been met.

**Assumption 7:** The data were derived by simple random sampling—that is, everyone in the population to whom you want to generalize the results had an equal chance of being included in the sample.

We recommend testing of these assumptions be done prior to conducting the one-way ANOVA, as conducting the analysis without doing this will produce erroneous results. If Assumption 3, the assumption of independence, is violated, then automatically one knows that the one-way ANOVA cannot be conducted. If Assumptions 4, 5, or 6 are violated, there are things you can do to the data so that these assumptions are no longer violated. For instance, if Assumption 4, no significant outliers, is violated, the same procedures described for detecting outliers when you conduct a Pearson's correlation analysis can be used, so this assumption is no longer violated. If Assumption 5, the assumption of normality, is violated, you can transform the data by using the log transformation function in SPSS to get a normal distribution (or close to normal curve). If the transformation of the data does not produce a normal distribution, then a Welch ANOVA can be used, which is a nonparametric statistic, to analyze the data instead of the one-way

ANOVA. The appropriate post hoc test to be used with the Welch ANOVA is the Games-Howell test.

A significant F-value associated with the one-way ANOVA only tells you that the results of the analysis are significant. It does not tell you which group mean is different from another. To determine where the differences are among the groups, one needs to conduct a post hoc test. There are a variety of ones that can be conducted, such as Duncan's multiple range, Tukey's honestly significant differences test, the Newman-Keuls test, and the Scheffe test. These post hoc tests are to be conducted when equal variances among the groups are assumed. When the variances among the groups are not assumed to be equal, the following post hoc tests are appropriate: Dunnett's C, Dunnett's T3, Games-Howell, or Tamhane's T2.

## How to Conduct a One-Way ANOVA in SPSS

A researcher, for example, is interested in determining if there are differences between African American, Hispanic, and Asian American females on their anxiety scores. The researcher hypothesized that there would be differences between African American, Hispanic, and Asian American females on their anxiety scores. To test this hypothesis, the researcher would conduct the analysis described below.

To conduct a one-way ANOVA, assuming none of the assumptions have been violated, one would go through these five steps:

Step 1: Go to the menu bar and click *Analyze*, then scroll down to Compare Means, and then go across to One-Way ANOVA (see Figure 13.41).

Figure 13.41 Demonstrating Step 1 of How to Conduct a One-Way ANOVA in SPSS

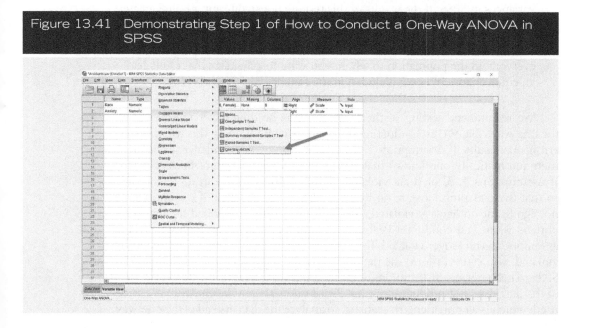

Step 2: Click on *One-Way ANOVA*. Once you have done this, the "One-Way ANOVA" dialogue box will appear (see Figure 13.42). You need to highlight the variable you want to include in the analysis then click the *Arrow* button

(a)

(b)

and put it in the "Dependent List" area. The variable you put in this area should be the one where you want the mean to be produced. It is also the variable that is measured on an interval or ratio measurement level, using a scale. You need to repeat the above step to include the second variable you want to be in your analysis and put this variable in the "Factor" field. The variable you put in this field should be the one that is measured on the nominal level, with three or more categories.

Step 3: Click the *Post Hoc* button. The "One-Way ANOVA Post Hoc Multiple Comparisons" box will appear (see Figure 13.43). You will see there are a lot of post hoc options. There are ones to be selected when the variances are assumed to be equal, and there are ones to be selected when the variances are not assumed to be equal. For the purpose of this analysis, we selected the "Tukey" option, which assumes that variances are equal. We did not select the options that assume the variances are not equal because we already stated in introducing how to conduct this analysis that the assumption of homogeneity of variances had not been violated. Look at the "Significance level" field and make sure *0.05* is indicated.

**Figure 13.43  Demonstrating Step 3 of How to Conduct a One-Way ANOVA in SPSS**

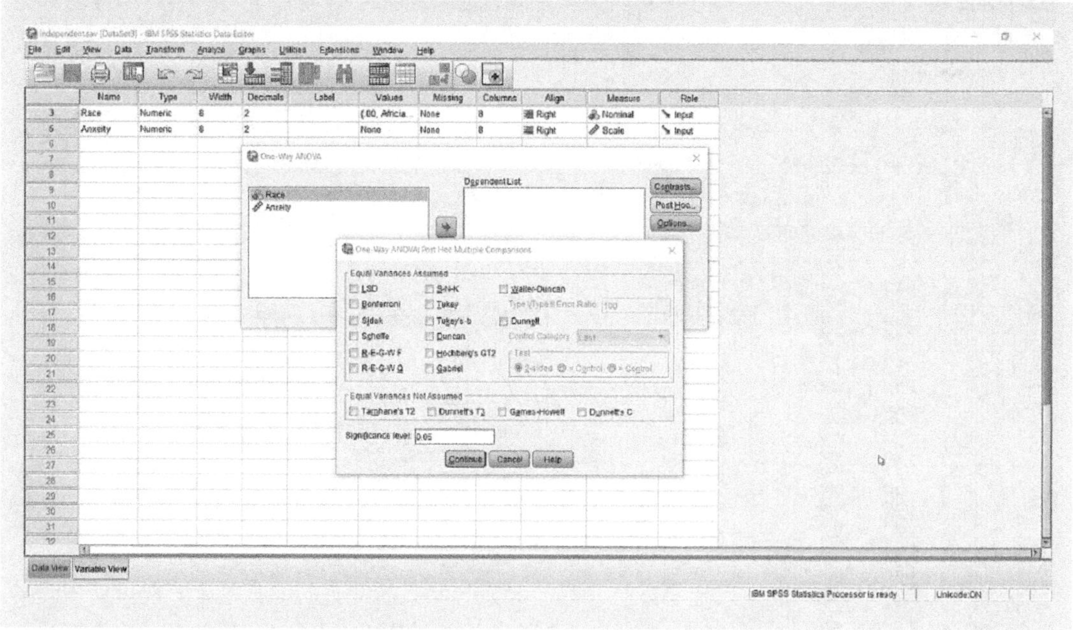

Step 4: Click on *Continue* and then Click *Options*. The "One-Way ANOVA: Options" box will appear (see Figure 13.44). Look at the "Statistics" area and check the box next to "Descriptive" (provides the means, standard deviations, and the number of participants in each group). Make sure there is a blue dot in the circle by "Exclude cases analysis by analysis."

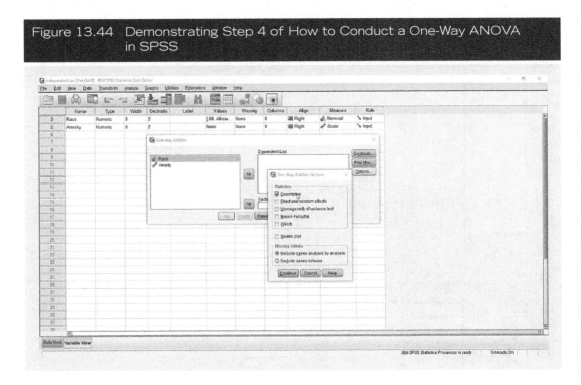

Figure 13.44 Demonstrating Step 4 of How to Conduct a One-Way ANOVA in SPSS

Step 5: Click *Continue* then *OK*. This will generate the results of the one-way ANOVA (see Figure 13.45).

**Results:** A one-way ANOVA was conducted to determine if there was a difference between African American, Hispanic, and Asian American females on their anxiety scores. The results revealed a statistically significant difference between the groups on their anxiety scores ($F (2, 21) = 5.551, p < .05$). The Tukey post hoc test revealed that Hispanic females had higher anxiety scores (mean = 43.6, SD =16.72) than African American females (mean = 23.9, SD = 9.89) and Asian American females (mean = 24.88, SD = 12.55). There was not a statistically significant difference in the anxiety scores between African American and Asian American females (see Figure 13.45).

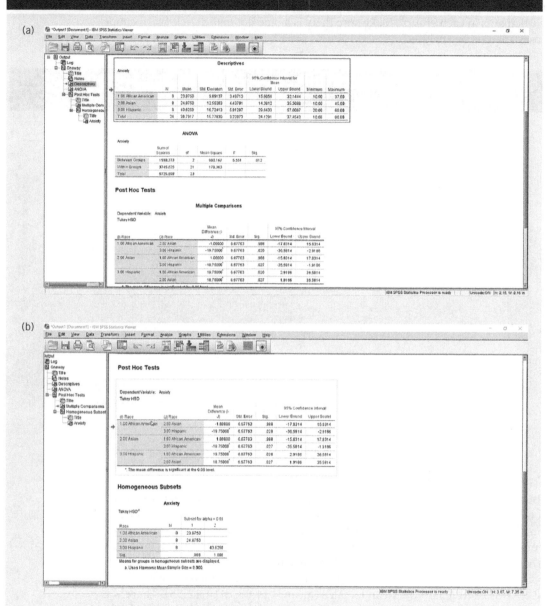

(a)

(b)

## Multivariate Analysis of Variance

A multivariate analysis of variance (MANOVA) is appropriate to use when you have one or more independent variables, which are measured on a nominal level, and two or more dependent variables, which are interval or ratio. For the purpose of this chapter, we will focus our discussion on the **one-way multivariate analysis of variance**, which is used when there is only one independent variable and two or more dependent variables. Similar to a one-way ANOVA, the purpose of a MANOVA is to assess for differences between the means for three or more groups. The only difference between these two procedures is the number of dependent variables that can be assessed. When conducting a one-way ANOVA, there is one dependent variable; however, for a MANOVA there is more than one dependent variable. An appropriate research question to be answered using a MANOVA would be as follows: "Will women ages 25 to 35 who received cognitive behavioral therapy plus stress management report more of a reduction in their depression and anxiety scores than women ages 25 to 35 who received cognitive behavioral therapy only or stress management only?" By reading this research question, you will see that there is one independent variable—type of therapy, which is divided into three categories (i.e., cognitive behavioral therapy plus stress management, cognitive behavioral therapy only, and stress management only) and two dependent variables (i.e., anxiety and depression scores). For the above example, the researcher hypothesized that women ages 25 to 35 who received cognitive behavioral therapy plus stress management will have lower posttest anxiety and depression scores than women ages 25 to 35 who received cognitive behavioral therapy only or stress management only. The null hypothesis is there is no difference in the posttest anxiety and depression scores for women ages 25 to 35 regardless of the intervention they received.

Before conducting the one-way MANOVA, one must ensure that the assumptions required for this analysis are met. There are nine assumptions that must be met to produce valid results. These assumptions are as follows:

**Assumption 1:** The independent variable should be measured on the nominal scale and should consist of three categories.

**Assumption 2:** Each dependent variable should be measured on the interval or ratio level (a scale).

**Assumption 3:** The scores or observations of the dependent variable should be independent of each of other. In other words, the scores for one participant are not systematically related to the scores of the other participants. This assumption is known as the assumption of independence. This assumption cannot be checked by examining the data but by looking at the study's design. Research designs where the assumptions of independence are met are the experimental research designs, when three groups of participants receive a different intervention.

**Assumption 4:** There should be no significant univariate or multivariate outliers. Multivariate outliers are cases where there is a combination of usual scores on the dependent variables. Multivariate outliers can be detected by using the Mahalanobis distance test.

**Assumption 5:** The scores on the dependent variables should be multivariate normally distributed within each group of the independent variable. This is known as the assumption of multivariate normality. It is hard to test for this assumption (Mertler & Vannatta, 2002), but most persons test for this assumption using the Shapiro-Wilk test of normality.

**Assumption 6:** The covariance matrices for the dependent variables must be equal within each group of the independent variable. This is known as the assumption of homogeneity of variance-covariance matrices. This assumption can be tested by Box's M test of equality of covariance in SPSS. If the result of this test is not significant, $p$-value greater than .05, then the assumption of homogeneity of variance-covariance has been met, and the Wilks' $\lambda$ associated with the multivariate F statistic would be reported. If the result of the Box's M test of equality of covariance is significant, then the Pillai's test would be reported.

**Assumption 7:** The dependent variables should not be too highly correlated. This is known as the assumption of the absence of multicollinearity. Tabachnick and Fidell (2007) recommends that the correlations between the dependent variables not be higher than .90.

**Assumption 8:** The relationships among the pairs of dependent variables for each of the independent variables must be linear.

**Assumption 9:** The data were derived by simple random sampling—that is, everyone in the population to whom you want to generalize the results had an equal chance of being included in the sample.

We recommend testing of these assumptions be done prior to conducting the one-way MANOVA, as conducting the analysis without doing this will produce erroneous results. If Assumption 3, the assumption of independence, is violated, then automatically one knows that the one-way MANOVA cannot be conducted. If Assumptions 4, 5, or 6 are violated, there are things you can do to the data so that these assumptions are no longer violated. For instance, if Assumption 4 (no significant outliers) is violated, the same procedures described for detecting outliers when you conduct a Pearson's correlation analysis can be used, so this assumption is no longer violated. If Assumption 5 (the assumption of multivariate normality) is violated, you can transform the data by using the log transformation function in SPSS to get a normal distribution (or close to normal curve).

To determine if the one-way MANOVA is statistically significant, rather than using F-value you would look at the multivariate F statistic value, such as the Pillai's trace, Wilks' $\lambda$, Hotelling's trace, and the Roy's largest root. Of these, the most commonly reported multivariate F statistics is the Wilks' $\lambda$, assuming that the variances across the groups are equal (Mertler & Vannatta, 2002). When the variances across the groups are not assumed to be equal, the Pillai's trace multivariate F statistics should be reported. The multivariate F statistics value only tells you that the results of the analysis are significant. It does not tell you which group mean is different from another. To determine where the differences are among the groups, one needs to conduct a one-way ANOVA followed by a post hoc comparison test. Such post hoc comparison tests are the Tukey, the Newman-Keuls test, and the Scheffe test, to name a few.

## How to Conduct a One-Way MANOVA in SPSS

A researcher, for example, is interested in determining if women ages 25 to 30 who received cognitive behavioral therapy plus stress management report more of a reduction in their depression and anxiety scores than women ages 25 to 35 who received cognitive behavioral therapy only or stress management only. The researcher hypothesized that women ages 25 to 35 who received cognitive behavioral therapy plus stress management will have lower posttest anxiety and depression scores than women ages 25 to 35 who received cognitive behavioral therapy only or stress management only. To test this hypothesis, the researcher would conduct the analysis described below.

To conduct a one-way MANOVA, assuming none of the assumptions have been violated, one would go through these 12 steps.

Step 1: Go to the menu bar and click *Analyze*, then scroll down to "General Linear Model," and then go across to "Multivariate" (see Figure 13.46).

Figure 13.46   Demonstrating Step 1 of How to Conduct a One-Way MANOVA in SPSS

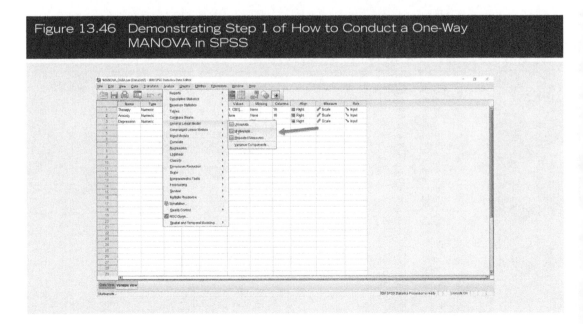

Step 2: Click on *Multivariate*. Once you have done this, the "Multivariate" dialogue box will appear (see Figure 13.47). You need to highlight the variable you want to include in the analysis then click the *Arrow* button

Figure 13.47   Demonstrating Step 2 of How to Conduct a One-Way
MANOVA in SPSS

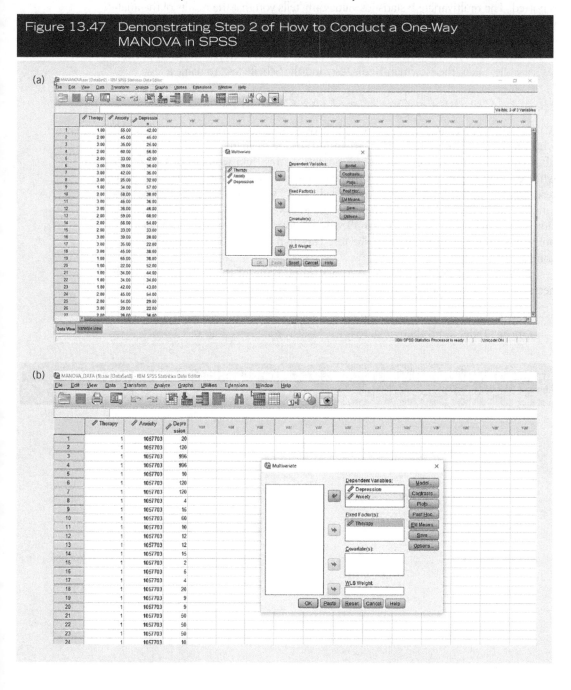

and put it in the "Dependent Variables" box. The variables you put in this box should be the one where you want the means to be produced. These variables are measured on an interval or ratio measurement level, using a scale. You need to repeat the above step to include the independent variable you want to be in your analysis and put this variable in the "Fixed Factor(s)" box. The variable you put in this box should be the one that is measured on the nominal scale. For the purpose of this analysis, you will not put any variables in the "Covariate(s)" or the "WLS Weight" boxes (see Figure 13.47).

Step 3: Click the *Plots* button. The "Multivariate Profile Plots" dialogue box will appear (see Figure 13.48). You need to highlight the variable in the "Factor(s)" box you want in the analysis. Click the *Arrow* button and put the highlighted variable in the "Horizontal Axis" box.

Figure 13.48   Demonstrating Step 3 of How to Conduct a One-Way MANOVA in SPSS

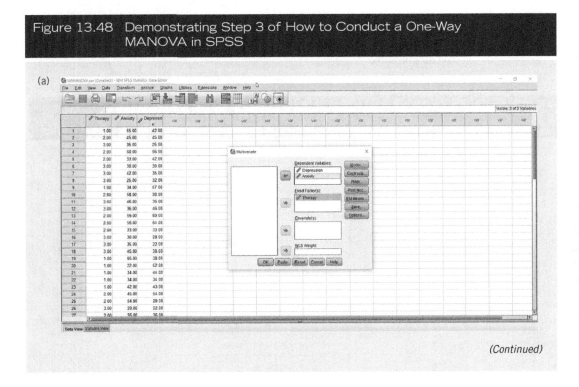

*(Continued)*

(Continued)

(b)

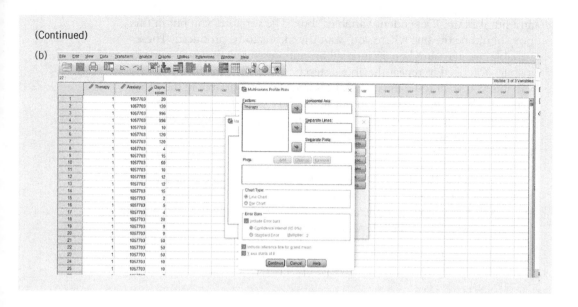

Step 4: Click the *Add* button (see Figure 13.49). You will see that the variable in the "Factor(s)" box also appears in the "Multivariate Profile Plots" dialogue" box.

**Figure 13.49** Demonstrating Step 4 of How to Conduct a One-Way MANOVA in SPSS

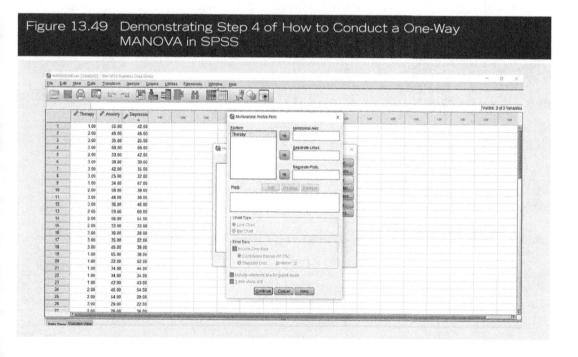

Step 5: Click the *Continue* button. The "Multivariate" dialogue" dialogue box will appear. Note: This is previously shown in Figure 13.47.

Step 6: Click the *Post Hoc* button. The "Multivariate: Post Hoc Multiple Comparison for Observed Means" dialogue box will appear (see Figure 13.50). You will see that the independent variable is in the "Factor(s)" box.

Figure 13.50 Demonstrating Step 6 of How to Conduct a One-Way MANOVA in SPSS

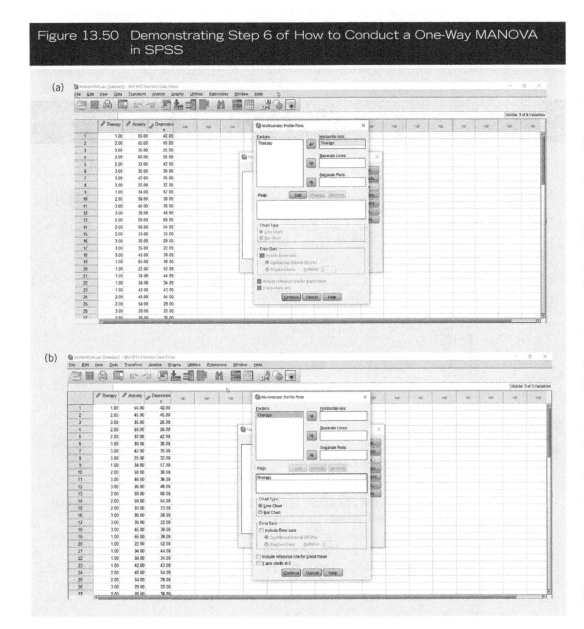

Step 7: Highlight the variable in the "Factor(s)" box. Click the *Arrow* button and put the highlighted variable in the "Post Hoc Test for" box (see Figure 13.51). You will see there are a lot of post hoc options. There are ones to be selected when the variances are assumed to be equal, and there are ones to be selected when the variances are not assumed to be equal. For the purpose of this analysis, we selected the "Tukey" option, which assumes that variances are equal. We did not select the options that assume the variances are not equal, because we already stated in introducing how to conduct this analysis that the assumption of homogeneity of variances had not been violated.

Figure 13.51 Demonstrating Step 7 of How to Conduct a One-Way MANOVA in SPSS

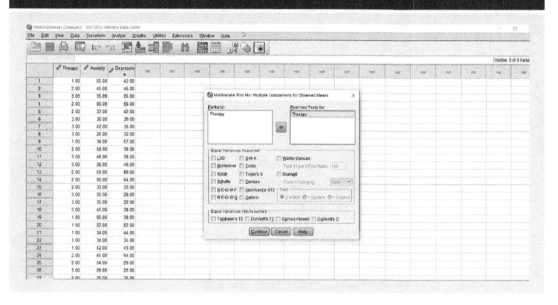

Step 8: Click the *Continue* button. The "Multivariate" dialogue box will appear. This was previously shown in Figure 13.47.

Step 9: Click the *EM Means* button. The "Multivariate Estimated Marginal Means" box will appear (see Figure 13.52). The "(OVERALL)" and independent variable will appear in the "Factor(s) and Factor Interactions" box. The "(OVERALL)" option will give you the overall mean for the dependent variables. Highlight the "(OVERALL)" and independent variable and then click the *Arrow* button. Put the highlighted variables in the "Display Means for" box.

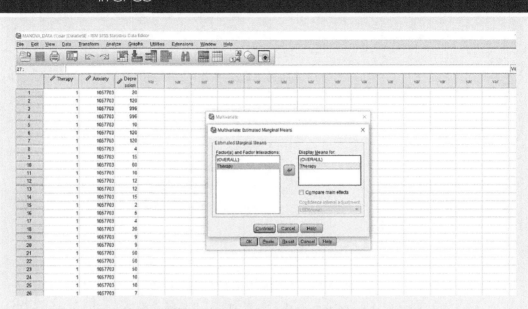

Figure 13.52   Demonstrating Step 9 of How to Conduct a One-Way MANOVA in SPSS

Step 10: Click the *Continue* button. The "Multivariate" dialogue box will appear (see Figure 13.53). Click the "Multivariate Options button. the "Multivariate Options" dialogue box (see Figure 13.53), check the following boxes: "Descriptive statistics" (provides you with the means and standard deviations for each variable, and the number of participants in each group), "Estimates of effect size" (provides the eta squared value; represented the amount of the total variance explained by the independent variable), and "Homogeneity tests" (provides the Levene statistics for testing the equality of variance for each group). Look at the "Significance level" field and make sure .05 is indicated.

Step 11: Click the *Continue* button. The "Multivariate" dialogue box will appear. Note: This was previously shown in Figure 13.46.

## Figure 13.53 Demonstrating Step 10 of How to Conduct a One-Way MANOVA in SPSS

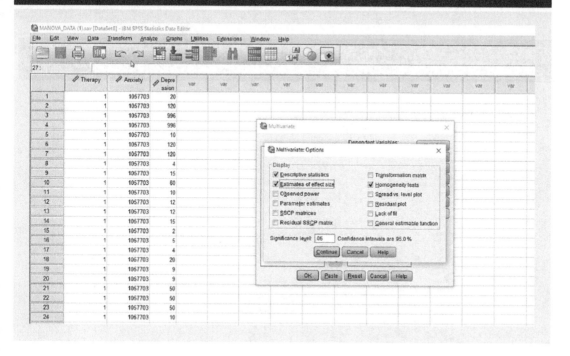

Step 12: Click *Continue* then *OK*. This will generate the results of the one-way MANOVA (see Figure 13.54).

**Results:** A one-way multivariate of variance (MANOVA) was conducted to determine if women ages 25 to 35 who received cognitive behavioral therapy plus stress management would report more of a reduction in their anxiety and depression scores than women who received cognitive behavioral therapy only or stress management only. The Box's test revealed that equal variances can be assumed, $F(6, 80975) = 1.51$, $p = .170$; therefore, Wilks' lambda ($\lambda$) will be used as the test statistic. The Wilks' $\lambda$ revealed significant differences between the type of treatment received, Wilks' $\lambda = .771$, $F(4, 112)$, $= 3.90$ $p < .01$, multivariate $= (\eta = .12)$. Univariate ANOVA results revealed that treatment differences were significant for depression, $F(2,60) = 5.15$, $p < .01$, partial $\eta^2 = .15$ and anxiety, $F(2,60) = 4.72$, $p < .05$, partial $\eta^2 = .14$. The Tukey post hoc analysis revealed that women who received cognitive behavioral therapy plus stress management had statistically significantly lower depression scores (mean $= 34.30$, SD $= 8.44$) than women who received cognitive behavioral therapy only (mean $= 43.35$, SD $= 8.76$). There was no statistically significant difference in the depression scores for women who received cognitive behavioral therapy only

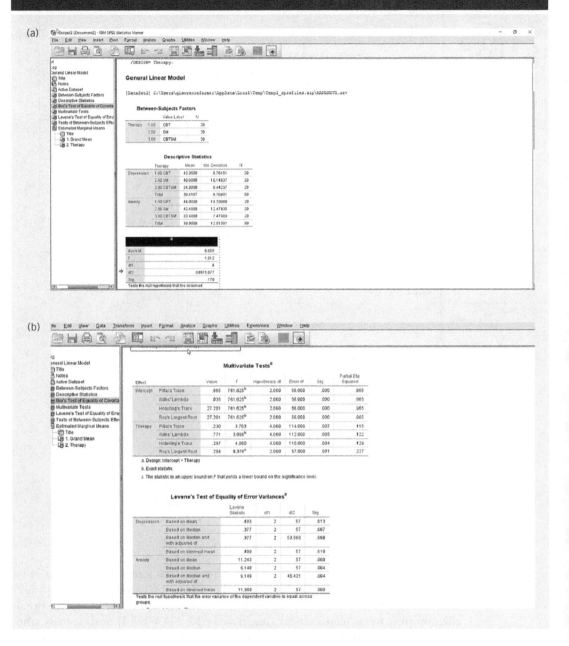

(c)

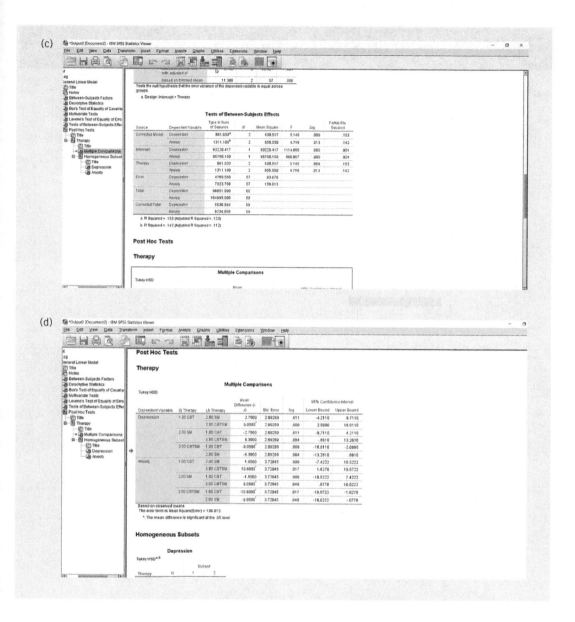

(d)

(mean = 43.35, SD = 8.76) and women who received stress management only (mean = 40.60, SD = 10.15). Moreover, there was not a statistically significant difference in the depression scores for women who received cognitive behavioral therapy plus stress management (mean = 34.30, SD = 8.44) and women who received stress management only (mean = 40.60, SD = 10.15). Additionally, the Tukey post hoc analysis revealed that women who received cognitive behavioral therapy plus stress management had statistically significantly lower anxiety scores (mean = 33.40, SD = 7.48) than women who received cognitive behavioral therapy only (mean = 44.00, SD = 14.33). There was no statistically significant difference in the anxiety scores for women who received cognitive behavioral therapy only (mean = 44.00, SD = 14.33) and women who received stress management only (mean = 42.45, SD = 12.48). Moreover, there was not a statistically significant difference in the anxiety scores for women who received cognitive behavioral therapy plus stress management (mean = 33.40, SD = 7.48) and women who received stress management only (mean = 42.45, SD = 12.48). Therefore, the researcher's hypothesis was partially supported, because the women who received stress management did not have statistically significant lower depression and anxiety scores than women who received cognitive behavioral therapy plus stress management (see Figure 13.54).

---

### Critical Thinking Question 13.4

Mary convenes a meeting with her staff and social work interns to discuss what analysis should be used to determine if the fathers who received the interactive computer-based parenting program had higher posttest scores on the knowledge of a child's development measure and quality of time spent with their child in educational and structured activities than fathers who received the didactic, in-person parenting program. Given your knowledge about the various statistical procedures discussed in this chapter that can be used to assess for significance of group differences (i.e., independent-sample $t$-test, dependent-sample $t$-test, one-way ANOVA, one-way MANOVA), what type of statistical analysis would you recommend Mary conduct. Justify your response.

---

## Ethics and Quantitative Data Analysis

It is important when analyzing your data that you conduct the correct analysis (Competency 1, *Demonstrate Ethical and Professional Behavior*), as conducting the incorrect analysis could result in one making a Type I or Type II error. **Type I error** produces results indicating that there are true differences between groups when no such differences exists. **Type II error** produces results indicating that there are no differences between study groups when really there are true group differences. The publication or dissemination of results based on incorrect data analysis has implications for providing adequate care, especially if these results are used to develop interventions or policies. Interventions or policies developed on incorrect analyses could result in harm to clients. Moreover, it is important that you report the correct measure of central tendency, depending on the level of measurement of your variables. As mentioned earlier, you would report the mode for a variable measured on a nominal level and not the mean. Making up or removing data to make the results seem better is unethical. The making up of data is referred to as "cooking" your data, while removing is referred to as "trimming." As a social worker, it is mandatory that you report your research findings accurately (see NASW Code of Ethics, 2017). Developing your hypothesis based on your results is unethical. This practice is known as HARKing (hypothesizing after the results are known; Kerr, 1998). Your hypothesis must be stated at the outset of your research. The statistical procedures you plan to use should be identified early on in the research process. Ignoring the assumptions associated with any statistical procedure is unethical. If any of the assumptions are violated, you should not conduct that analysis but should analyze the data using the nonparametric equivalence of that analysis. According to Maroof (2013), "violating statistical assumptions can often yield untenable results, rendering the inferences based on the primary analysis equally precarious" (p. 275). Inferring causality from results derived from statistical procedures assessing relationships among variables or group differences not in the context of an experimental research design is unethical. It is unethical to check the level of statistical significance before all the data has been collected to determine if more data needs to be collected to obtain a statistical significance. Engaging in any of the above is known as "P-harking." Failure to not report relationships that are not statistically significant is unethical. This practice is known as "cherry picking."

## Diversity and Quantitative Data Analysis

Although Competency 2, *Engage Diversity and Difference in Practice*, does not specifically mention anything about data analysis, it is important that issues related to diversity be taken into consideration. This competency emphasizes that "the dimensions of diversity are understood as the intersectionality of multiple factors including but not limited to age, class, color, culture, disability and ability, ethnicity, gender, gender identity and expression, immigration status, marital status, political ideology, race, religion/spirituality, sex, sexual orientation, and tribal sovereign status" (CSWE, 2015, p. 7). Based on this conceptualization of the dimensions of diversity, it implies that an intersectionality approach should be used in analyzing one's data. Cole (2009) defines intersectionality as "analytic approaches that simultaneously consider the meaning and consequences of multiple categories of identity, difference, and disadvantage" (p. 170). If you plan to use an intersectionality approach to analyze your data, we recommend that you incorporate this framework in the planning stage of your research process. Cole (2009) proposed three questions that researchers should use when using an intersectionality framework to analyze their data. The first question is, "Who is included in the category?" By asking oneself this question, one is addressing the issue of intersectionality. In other words, one is interested in knowing, for example, how race, gender, and sexual orientation shapes one's perception of the phenomenon under investigation. The second question is, "What role is inequality playing? This question requires the researcher to think about what contextual factors shaped one's perception of the phenomenon under investigation. The third question is, "Where are the similarities?" This question requires the researcher to think about the similarities across the groups being studied. Let us say a researcher is conducting a study examining the experiences of African American and Hispanic women who have experienced interpersonal violence. The commonality between these women is that they all have experienced interpersonal violence, but their experiences may differ based on their race/ethnicity, sexual orientation, or religious beliefs.

There are many advanced statistical procedures that can be used to conduct an intersectional analysis. For example, ANOVA or multiple regression, which were discussed in this chapter, can be used. An example of a study where an intersectionality approach was used to analyze the data is Cage, Corley, and Harris' (2018) study on the educational attainment of maltreated youth involved with the child welfare system. Using logistic regression, Cage et al. examined the effects of race and gender, separately, and the intersection of these two variables. They found that race nor gender predicted educational attainment; however, they did find that Black males were less likely to complete their education, compared to White males and females and Hispanic females. From an intersectionality framework, their results indicated that both gender and race together are predictors of educational attainment.

### Application Checkpoint 13.2

In reading the case example, you will notice that there is no mention of the ethnic/racial backgrounds of the fathers. Suppose you were conducting the study with African American, Native American, and Hispanic adolescent fathers. What type of analysis would you conduct to determine if these groups differ on knowledge of child development? Why is conducting such an analysis important?

When you have diverse groups in your study, it is important that you conduct separate descriptive analyses for each group and test for differences between the groups before combining the groups. The reason why you should conduct descriptive analyses separately for each group before combining the groups is because the mean you get by combining the groups may be different from the mean for each group. If the mean for each group is statistically significantly different from each other, this indicates that the groups should not have been combined. If the means are statistically significantly different, you need to look at the distributions for each group to see if they are close to normal curve and the skewness and kurtosis value. If the distributions are not close to normal or skewed, you can transform the data by using the procedures discussed in this chapter. Not only is it important to conduct separate univariate descriptive analyses, but it is important to conduct separate analysis to assess group differences. The results from such analysis may be used to promote social justice, as they may be used to develop interventions or policies for specific groups of individuals. Competency 3, *Advance Human Rights and Social, Economic, and Environmental Justice*, "clearly states that social workers engage in practices that advance social, economic, and environmental justice" (CSWE, 2015, p. 9).

# Sample Study: Write-Up of Quantitative Analysis (Academic Example)

**Research Problem:** Empirical evidence has demonstrated that providing parenting programs for fathers is important and such programs can improve fathers' knowledge of child development. Moreover, studies have shown that fathers' involvement in parenting programs has an effect on child outcomes. What we know about the effectiveness of parenting programs for fathers is based on studies of older fathers. Research on the effectiveness of parenting programs for adolescent fathers is sparse, and the rigor of the research designs used to evaluate parent programs for adolescent fathers vary (Bronte-Tinkew, Burkhauser, & Metz, 2008). Therefore, one must carefully consider the results of these studies. Bronte-Tinkew and her colleagues identified 10 aspects of promising teen fatherhood programs, and they found that an interactive program was more effective than a didactic one. The purpose of this study is to determine if an interactive computer-based parenting program is more effective than an in-person, didactic parenting program for adolescent fathers.

**Research Question:** Is an interactive computer-based parenting program more effective than an in-person, didactic parenting program for adolescent fathers?

**Hypothesis:** Fathers who received the interactive computer-based parenting program will have higher posttest scores on the knowledge of child development measure than the fathers who receive the in-person, didactic parenting program.

**Method:** A pretest-posttest control group experimental design was employed. African American adolescent fathers caring for their 5-year-olds were randomly assigned to an experimental or control group. Fathers in the experimental group received an interactive computer-based parenting program, while fathers in the control group received an in-person, didactic parenting program.

**Participants:** Participants were African American adolescent fathers caring for their 5-year-olds. There were 50 participants who were randomly assigned to the experimental group and 50 participants who were randomly assigned to the control group, for a total of 100 participants. Each group had 15 sessions, and after each they received $15.

**Measure:** Knowledge of child development was assessed pre- and posttest, using a 40-item measure. Fathers were asked to rate these items on a 6-point Likert scale, where 0 = do not know and 6 = strongly agree. A total score was derived by summing all the items on the scale. A high score means high knowledge of child development.

**Data Analysis:** Univariate descriptive statistics were computed to describe the characteristics of the sample and summarize the variables of interest. A Pearson's correlation was conducted to examine the interrelationships among the variable of interest, age of the father, and income. An independent-sample *t*-test was conducted to determine if fathers who received the interactive computer-based parenting program differed on age and income from fathers who received the in-person, didactic parenting program. For hypothesis testing, an independent-sample *t*-test was conducted. All statistical analyses were conducted using SPSS version 25.

**Results:** Ages of the fathers ranged from 15.5 to 19. 5. The mean age of the fathers who received the computer-based parenting program was 16.5, SD = 2.3, while the mean age of the fathers who received the in-person, didactic parenting program was 15.0, SD = .25. The mean posttest knowledge of child development score for the fathers who received the interactive computer-based parenting program was 160.82 (SD = 12.5). While the mean posttest knowledge of child development score for the fathers who received the in-person, didactic parenting program was 130.50 (SD = 18.88). The median income was $10,000 for the fathers who received the interactive computer-based parenting program, and the median income was $6,000 for the fathers who received the in-person, didactic parenting program. The results of the Pearson's correlation indicated that fathers who reported having a high income level had high knowledge of child development ($r = .50$) and older fathers reported having high knowledge of child development ($r = .30$). Meanwhile, older fathers had higher incomes ($r = .40$). A *t*-test indicated that there was no statistically significant difference between the two groups on age and income. An independent-sample *t*-test was conducted to determine if there was a difference between fathers who received the interactive computer-based parenting program and those who received the in-person, didactic parenting program in regard to their posttest knowledge of child development. Levene's test of equality of variances revealed that equal variances can be assumed to be equal. The results of the independent-sample *t*-test revealed a statistically significant difference between fathers who received the interactive computer-based parenting program and those who received the in-person didactic parenting program in regard to their posttest knowledge of child development ($t_{(df=98)} = 3.52, p < .01$). Fathers who received the interactive computer-based parenting program had a higher posttest knowledge of child development mean (160.82, SD = 12.5) than fathers who participated in the in-person didactic, parenting program (mean = 130.50, SD = 18.88)—a mean difference of 1.3. Based on the results, the hypothesis was supported.

**Discussion:** The purpose of this study was to determine if an interactive computer-based parenting program is more effective than an in-person, didactic parenting program for adolescent fathers. The findings of this study indicated that the interactive computer-based intervention was more effective than the in-person, didactic parent training program in increasing fathers' knowledge about child development. One limitation of this study is that the results cannot be generalized to White and Hispanic adolescent fathers. Future studies need to determine what components of the interactive computer-based intervention were effective.

# Sample Study: Write-Up of Quantitative Analysis (Non-Academic Example—Presentation)

**Target Audience:** Mary calls a meeting and informs her staff and social work interns that she has been asked to make a presentation to her advisory board about the evaluation of the parenting program for the adolescent fathers. She has asked you to write up the results and assist her with the presentation. Below is an example of how you could present the findings from the evaluation for this targeted audience.

## Story Identification

It is best to build the presentation of the research findings around the story that you believe the findings tell. The story should highlight the implications of the findings in a manner relevant to the targeted audience. When possible, try to provide illustrations of the findings along with the numerical data. For example, let us consider the finding that the interactive computer-based parenting program was more effective than the in-person, didactic parenting program. You would say the following: "We appreciate the opportunity to present to the board members of this agency. Approximately one year ago the staff and clients began to ask us to provide services to adolescent fathers. Mary, the director of the agency, reviewed the data pertaining to the number of adolescent fathers in our clients' households, and she indeed noticed an increase in this number over a two-year period. Mary held meetings with her staff and the social work interns on a weekly basis, where we reviewed the literature to determine what intervention would be appropriate and what outcomes the intervention should target. Based on the research by Bronte-Tinkew et al. (2008), we found that an interactive parenting program was more effective than an in-person, didactic one. Therefore, we decided that we would use an interactive computer-based parenting program. We were interested in assessing the effectiveness of this intervention; therefore, we randomly assigned the adolescent fathers to the interactive computer-based intervention parenting program and the in-person, didactic intervention parenting program. Prior to and after receiving the intervention, we assessed their knowledge of child development. We chose to assess knowledge of child development because research has demonstrated that the lack of knowledge of child development is linked to child maltreatment. We found that the interactive computer-based intervention parenting program was effective in increasing the father's empathy toward the children's needs, decreasing their inappropriate expectations of their children, and decreasing their belief that corporal punishment is effective in reducing children's problematic behaviors.

# CHAPTER SUMMARY ORGANIZED BY LEARNING OBJECTIVES

**LO 13.1** Identify what type of analysis is appropriate for analyzing your data, depending on the level of measurement of the independent and dependent variables and the type of research question.

The *Pearson's correlation* is used to determine the association between an interval or ratio (a scale) independent variable and an interval or ratio (a scale) dependent variable.

The *chi-square test of independence* is used to determine the association between a nominal independent variable and a nominal dependent variable.

A *multiple regression analysis* is appropriate to use when you have one or more independent variables, which are interval or ratio, and one dependent variable, which is interval or ratio.

The *independent-sample t-test* is appropriate to use when you have a nominal independent variable, with two categories, and the dependent variable is interval or ratio (a scale).

The *dependent-sample t-test* is appropriate to use when you have a nominal independent variable, with two categories, and the dependent variable is interval or ratio (a scale), which has been assessed twice.

A *one-way analysis of variance* (ANOVA) is appropriate to use when you have one independent variable, which is nominal, with three or

more categories, and one dependent variable, which is interval or ratio.

A *multivariate analysis of variance* (MANOVA) is appropriate to use when you have one or more independent variables, which are nominal, and two or more dependent variables, which are interval or ratio.

**LO 13.2** Differentiate between the various statistical analyses used to describe data.

A *frequency distribution* shows the researcher the number of observations in each category of the variable of interest or the number of respondents who have a certain score.

The *mean*, the arithmetic mean, or average is derived by adding all the individual scores, and then dividing the answer by the total number of scores. The mean is appropriate to report when you have a variable that is measured on the interval or ratio level, and the distribution is a normal curve (or close to a normal curve).

The *median* is the middle score in the frequency distribution. The median is appropriate to report when you have a variable that is measured on the ordinal, interval, or ratio level, and the distribution is positively or negatively skewed.

The *mode* is the most frequently occurring score in the frequency distribution. The mode is appropriate to report when the variable is measured on a nominal level.

The *range* is the distance between the lowest and the highest score. It is commonly reported as the lowest and the highest score. The range is appropriate to report when the variable is measured on an ordinal, interval, or ratio level.

The *standard deviation* is a single, numerical value indicating how scores distribute themselves around the mean and the distance of the scores from the mean. The standard deviation is appropriate to report when the variable is measured on an ordinal, interval, or ratio level.

**LO 13.3** Differentiate between the various statistical analyses used to assess the degree of relationship among variables.

The *Pearson's correlation* is used to determine the association between an interval or ratio (a scale) independent variable and an interval or ratio (a scale) dependent variable.

The *chi-square test of independence* is used to determine the association between a nominal independent variable and a nominal dependent variable.

A *multiple regression analysis* is appropriate to use when you have one or more independent variables, which are interval or ratio, and one dependent variable, which is interval or ratio.

**LO 13.4** Differentiate between the various statistical analyses used to assess significance of group differences.

The *independent-sample* t-*test* is appropriate to use when you have a nominal independent variable, with two categories, and the dependent variable is interval or ratio (a scale).

The *dependent-sample* t-*test* is appropriate to use when you have a nominal independent variable, with two categories, and the dependent variable is interval or ratio (a scale), which has been assessed twice.

A *one-way analysis of variance* (ANOVA) is appropriate to use when you have one independent variable, which is nominal level, with three or more categories, and one dependent variable, which is interval or ratio.

A *multivariate analysis of variance* (MANOVA) is appropriate to use when you have one or more independent variables, which are nominal, and two or more dependent variables, which are interval or ratio.

**LO 13.5** Identify the ethical and diversity issues associated with analyzing quantitative data.

It is important that you conduct the appropriate analyses based on the level of measurement of the independent and dependent variables. Disseminating or publishing results based on conducting the incorrect analysis may result in persons receiving inadequate care, especially if the results were used to develop interventions or policies.

It is unethical to (1) make up or remove data to make your results better, (2) report inaccurate findings, (3) develop your hypothesis based on your results, (4) ignore the assumptions associated with any statistical procedure, and (5) infer causality from statistical procedures assessing the relationship between variables or group differences not in the context of an experimental research design.

An intersectionality approach should be used in analyzing one's data, whenever possible. This approach allows one to simultaneously consider the meaning and consequences of multiple categories of identity, difference, and disadvantage.

Before combining samples, it is important that separate descriptive analyses be conducted for each group and analyses testing for group differences be conducted.

# KEY TERMS

# COMPETENCY NOTES

In this chapter, you were introduced to the competencies below:

Competency 1, *Demonstrate Ethical and Professional Behavior*. Social workers must be ethical in the way they analyze their data.

Competency 2, *Engage Diversity and Difference in Practice*. Social workers should consider the dimensions of diversity described by CSWE when analyzing their data, so they can have a more accurate picture of the participants' experiences.

Competency 3, *Advance Human Rights and Social, Economic, and Environmental Justice*. Social workers should analyze their data

to gain insights about how what they are studying can advance social, economic, and environmental justice.

Competency 4, *Engage in Practice-Informed Research and Research-Informed Practice*. Social workers can apply critical thinking to engage in analysis of quantitative data, by knowing what type of analysis is appropriate for the type of data they plan to analyze.

Competency 5, *Engage in Policy Practice*. Social workers must know what factors determine what statistical analysis they should use, as this allows them to select and use appropriate methods for assessing how social welfare and economic policies impact the delivery of and access to social services.

Competency 9, *Evaluate Practice With Individuals, Families, Groups, Organizations, and Communities.* Social workers know what factors determine what statistical analysis they should use, as this allows them to select and use appropriate methods for evaluating outcomes and practice effectiveness.

## ASSESSMENT QUESTIONS

1. How did the information in this chapter enhance your knowledge about when one should use Pearson's correlation as opposed to a chi-square test of independence?

2. How did the information in this chapter enhance your knowledge about when one should use an independent-sample *t*-test as opposed to a one-way ANOVA?

3. In what ways did the case example enhance your ability to determine what type of quantitative analysis should be conducted based on level of measurement of the variables?

4. What specific content discussed in this chapter is still unclear to you? If there is still content that is unclear, schedule an appointment with your instructor to gain more clarity.

## END-OF-CHAPTER EXERCISES

1. Propose a study where it would be appropriate to analyze the data using a one-way ANOVA.

2. Find an empirical article to bring to class. Before you bring the article to class, identify the alternative and null hypothesis, the measurement of each variable, and statistical tests used. Come prepared to discuss the above.

3. Propose a study where you would use an intersectional framework. Why would this approach be appropriate?

4. Come to class prepared to discuss how you would advise Alorani and Alradaydeh on how they could develop their research to focus on group differences.

## ADDITIONAL READINGS

Adedokun, O., & Burgess, W. D. (2012). Analysis of paired dichotomus data: A gentle introduction to the McNemar test in SPSS. *Journal of Multidisciplinary Evaluation, 8*(17), 125–131.

Faud Faud, M. D., Lye, M. S., Ibrahim, N., Kar, P. C., Ismail, S. I., & Nasir Al-Zufi, B. M. (2015). *t*-test using STATA software. *Education in Medicine Journal, 7*(2), pe 64–pe 70. doi:10.5959/eimj.v7i2.330.

Marco, C. A., & Larkin, G. L. (2000). Research ethics: Ethical issues using data reporting and the quest for authenticity. *Academic Emergency Medicine, 7*(6), 691–694.

McHugh, M. L. (2013). The chi-square test of independence. *Biochemical Medicine, 23*(2), 143–149. doi:10.11613/BM.2013.018

Osborne, J. W., & Waters, E. (2002). Four assumptions of multiple regression that researchers should always test. *Practical Assessment, Research and Evaluation, 8*(2), 1–5. Retrieved from http://pareonline.net/getvn.asp?v=8&n=2

Panter, A. T., & Sterba, S. K. (Eds.). (2011). *Handbook of ethics in quantitative methodology*. New York, NY: Routledge Academic.

Simpson, S. H. (2015). Creating a data analysis plan: What to consider when choosing statistics for a study. *Canadian Journal of Hospital Pharmacy, 68*(4), 311–317. doi:10.4212/cjhp.v68i4.1471

Sterba, S. K. (2006). Misconduct in the analysis and reporting of data: Bridging methodological and ethical agendas for change. *Ethics & Behavior, 16*(4), 305–318. doi:10.1207/s15327019eb1604_3

Wasserman, R. (2013). Ethical issues and guidelines for conducting data analysis in psychological research. *Ethics & Behavior, 23*(1), 3–15. doi:10.1080/10508422.2012.72847

# $\circledS$SAGE edge™

Get the tools you need to sharpen your study skills. SAGE Edge offers a robust online environment featuring an impressive array of free tools and resources.

Access practice quizzes at **edge.sagepub.com/farmer**

## Learning Objectives

**14.1** Differentiate between the various qualitative coding strategies.

**14.2** Differentiate between the different types of qualitative analysis.

**14.3** Identify the ethical and diversity issues associated with analyzing qualitative data.

| Competencies Covered | Learning Objectives | Dimension |
|---|---|---|
| **Competency 1**<br>*Demonstrate Ethical and Professional Behavior* | 14.3 Identify the ethical issues associated with analyzing qualitative data. | Skills |
| **Competency 2**<br>*Engage Diversity and Difference in Practice* | 14.3 Identify the diversity issues associated with analyzing qualitative data. | Skills |
| **Competency 3**<br>*Advance Human Rights and Social, Economic, and Environmental Justice* | | |
| **Competency 4**<br>*Engage in Practice-Informed Research and Research-Informed Practice* | 14.2 Differentiate between the different types of qualitative analysis. | Skills |
| **Competency 7**<br>*Assess Individuals, Families, Groups, Organizations, and Communities* | | |

Master the content at
**edge.sagepub.com/farmer**

## What Are the Perceptions of African American Adolescent Males About Police Brutality?

By responding to the questions related to this case example, you will be able to code the data so it can be analyzed by conducting a content analysis.

You are employed as a graduate research assistant for Dr. Booker, whose research focuses on juvenile justice, and community policing and organizing. Dr. Booker received a $250,000 grant from the National Institute of Justice (NIJ) to conduct a qualitative study examining the perceptions of African American adolescent males about police brutality. He conducted focus groups with African American adolescent males ages 13 to 18. The adolescents resided in urban, suburban, and rural communities. There were 50 adolescents who participated in the focus groups. Participants were recruited via snowball sampling. They were paid $25 for their participation.

Dr. Booker meets with you, two graduate research assistants, and two doctoral students he has hired to work on this grant. During the meeting, he announces that all the focus groups have been conducted and now the data are ready to be analyzed.

At this point, take a few minutes to think about the case example and do the following:

1. Identify the problem.

2. Determine what you already know about the problem.

3. Determine what information you need to solve the problem.

4. List the questions needed to be answered related to the information you need to solve the problem.

Please write down your responses to each item. You will need to refer to them while reading this chapter.

Dr. Booker convenes another meeting with you, the graduate research assistants, and the doctoral students who conducted the focus groups. He explains that the reasons for his study was the high-profile cases in several states where there was police brutality involved. He states that he has observed that after such cases are discussed in the media, the police are perceived in a negative light and they are not respected by persons in the communities they serve. He goes on to say that previous research has demonstrated that persons' perceptions of the police are shaped by a person's age, race/ethnicity, social class, personal experience, and type of community in which he or she resides. Dr. Booker goes on to share the questions that were asked of the participants. They are as follows:

1. What are your general impressions of the police in your community?

2. How would you describe the current relationship between the police and adolescents in your community?

3. Why do you think police brutality occurs?

4. What do you think can be done to stop police brutality?

5. Have you had any experiences with the police? If so, can you describe these experiences?

6. What role, if any, has the media played in shaping your perceptions about police brutality?

## Introduction

In this chapter, you will learn about qualitative data analysis. The purpose of qualitative data analysis is to examine the meaning and symbolic content of qualitative data. This chapter will provide you with information about the various interpretive coding strategies that can be used to code data derived from interviews, focus groups, field notes, and documents. Strategies to use in analyzing qualitative data are described. A brief discussion of which qualitative data software packages are available to analyze qualitative data is presented. Ethical and diversity issues you need to think about when conducting qualitative data analysis are also discussed.

## Qualitative Data Analysis Defined

Competency 4, *Engage in Practice-Informed Research and Research-Informed Practice*, states that social workers "apply critical thinking to engage in analysis of . . . qualitative research methods" (CSWE, 2015, p. 8). This suggests that *you* must know how to analyze qualitative data. Unlike quantitative data analysis, one is not analyzing numerical data but textual data. Qualitative analysis involves an inductive reasoning process. This means that the interpretation of qualitative data is used to generate hypotheses and theories.

At the outset, we must state that we will not discuss all the various types of qualitative analysis researchers use to analyze their data. In this chapter, you will be introduced to four types of qualitative data analysis: content, narrative, critical discourse, and grounded theory.

## Phases of the Qualitative Data Analysis Process

The analysis of qualitative data consists of a series of phases. The first phase involves organizing the data for analysis. Because computer software is generally used to analyze the data, it is important to make sure that all of the data are in an electronic format that the computer software can access. This will involve ensuring that interview notes, audiotapes, field notes, and other documents are converted into software-readable data files. These data files must be read for accuracy. Once the data have been verified for their accuracy, you can then begin to code the data.

## Coding of the Data

Analysis of qualitative data can be for the purposes of understanding

- persons' interpretation of their experiences,
- factors that have shaped persons' point of view, and
- how persons view their interactions with those in their environment.

Data derived for qualitative data analysis can come from interviews, focus groups, field notes, and other documents. If the information from the interviews and focus groups were audio-recorded, these recordings need to be transcribed. All transcriptions and other textual materials need to be read and reread thoroughly, so that one is very familiar with the content. You will use the above-mentioned materials as the data to be analyzed. Similar to quantitative data analysis, the data derived from qualitative research needs to be in a form in which it can be analyzed. The coding process for qualitative analysis is quite different than what is done for quantitative data analysis, where you assign a number to a variable or you use a preassigned code. Unlike the coding process for quantitative data where you code the data after it has been collected, the coding of qualitative data is ongoing. Coding in qualitative analysis

> involves reviewing all data line-by-line, identifying key issues or themes (codes) and then attaching segments of text (either original text or summarized notes) to those codes. New codes are added as additional themes or issues emerge in the data. (Neale, 2016, p. 1097)

In this chapter, you will learn about three ways of coding qualitative data, which Strauss and Corbin (1990) have identified as steps in the grounded theory analytic process: open coding, axial coding, and selective coding. You may recall from reading Chapter 8 that grounded theory is a research method that allows you to develop a theory based on data systematically gathered and analyzed (Strauss & Corbin, 1994).

**Open coding** is the process of developing codes and categories through the close examination of the qualitative data. It is the initial step in analyzing qualitative data. During this process, a paragraph, phrase, sentence, or word is examined and given a name or label that represents a phenomenon. Strauss and Corbin (1990) suggest that researchers, while examining the data, should ask themselves the following questions of the data:

1. *What?*—Identify the underlying issue and the phenomenon.

2. *Who?*—Identify the actors involved and the roles they play.

3. *How?*—Identify the aspects of the phenomenon.

4. *When? How long? Where?*—Time, course, and location.

5. *How much? How long?*—Identify the intensity.

6. *Why?*—Identify the reasons attached to the phenomenon.

7. *What for?*—Identify intention or purpose.

8. *By which?*—Strategies and tactics to achieve the goal.

Let us say a researcher is interested in understanding the experiences of mothers taking care of their adult sons who are living with complications of HIV/AIDS. The researcher conducts individual interviews with 12 mothers. Participants were asked the following question: "What has been your experience caring for your son?" The researcher reads the transcripts from the individual interviews and codes the data, using open coding. Table 14.1 presents a sample of the researcher's open coding.

| Table 14.1 Open Codes for Research Question | | |
| --- | --- | --- |
| **Open Codes** | **Subcategories** | **Examples of Participant's Words** |
| Not being able to socialize<br><br>Friends do not call<br><br>Isolated | How the illness has affected the caregiver<br><br>Not doing what she wants to do at her stage in life | I can't socialize with my friends when I want to<br><br>Some of my friends who know I am taking care of my son no longer call me. This has led me to become depressed and isolated. |

*(Continued)*

**Table 14.1** (Continued)

| Open Codes | Subcategories | Examples of Participant's Words |
|---|---|---|
| Depressed<br><br>Wish she was not caring for son<br><br>Not fair<br><br>Frustrated | | I wish I was not caring for my son at this stage of my life. I thought he would be taking care of me during my illness, but instead I found myself taking care of him. This is not fair. My health is failing, and I do not have anyone to take care of me. I would not say I am angry at him, but sometimes I am just frustrated. |
| Son's wife is not helping out<br><br>Angry<br><br>No control over situation<br><br>Rollercoaster<br><br>Do not know what to expect | How the illness has affected the individual | Why should I have to take care of him? He has a wife, and she is not doing a thing. This makes me angry, and there is nothing I can do to change this situation.<br><br>Well, I really do not know how to describe my situation, but if I have to I will. It has been like a rollercoaster. Some days are better than others. Like yesterday, my son was feeling really well. He even walked to the park. Two weeks ago, he was very down and would not get out of bed. I had to do everything for him—feed him, wash him, and so on. From week to week, I do not know what to expect. |
| Part of one's role<br><br>Glad for the opportunity | Gratitude<br><br>How others are cared for | I have had a good experience taking care of my son. I have no complaints. Mothers are supposed to take care of their children. I am thankful I have the strength to do this at my age. I am thankful that I can take care of my son.<br><br>I am glad I am able to care for my son. I have heard about so many people who have HIV/AIDS needing to be cared for by strangers or nonfamily members. |

---

### Critical Thinking Question 14.1

Examining the participants' responses presented in Table 14.1, answer the questions Strauss and Corbin (1990) suggest that researchers ask when examining the data.

---

**Axial coding** is the process of making connections among the categories and subcategories that were identified during the open coding process. During the axial coding process, you attempt to understand under what conditions the phenomenon occurs or does not occur or the consequences of engaging or not engaging in the phenomenon. Strauss and Corbin (1990) suggest that researchers ask themselves the following question: "What are the relationships between the categories?" According to Strauss and Corbin, axial coding is the final step in the coding process if one is not interested in developing a theory.

Going back to our example, the researcher has finished coding the data via open coding. The researcher is now ready to do the axial coding. Table 14.2 presents a sample of the researcher's axial coding.

**Critical Thinking Question 14.2**

Review the axial codes presented in Table 14.2. Are there other connections among the codes and subcategories identified during the open coding process that were not noted in the table? If so, what are these connections?

**Table 14.2  Axial Coding for Research Question**

| Open Codes | Axial Coding | Examples of Participant's Words |
|---|---|---|
| Not being able to socialize<br><br>Friends do not call<br><br>Isolated<br><br>Depressed<br><br>Wish she was not caring for son<br><br>Not fair<br><br>Frustrated | Negative caregiving experience | I can't socialize with my friends when I want to<br><br>Some of my friends who know I am taking care of my son no long call me. This has led me to become depressed and isolated.<br><br>I wish I was not caring for my son at this stage of my life. I thought he would be taking care of me during my illness, but instead I found myself taking care of him. This is not fair. My health is failing, and I do not have anyone to take care of me. I would not say I am angry at him, but sometimes I am just frustrated. |
| Son's wife is not helping out<br><br>Angry<br><br>No control over situation<br><br>Rollercoaster<br><br>Do not know what to expect | | Why should I have to take care of him? He has a wife, and she is not doing a thing. This makes me angry, and there is nothing I can do to change this situation.<br><br>Well, I really do not know how to describe my situation, but if I have to I will. It has been like a rollercoaster. Some days are better than others. Like yesterday, my son was feeling really well. He even walked to the park. Two weeks ago, he was very down and would not get out of bed. I had to do everything for him—feed him, wash him, and so on. From week to week, do not know what to expect. |
| Part of one's role<br><br>Glad for the opportunity | Positive caregiving experience | I have had a good experience taking care of my son. I have no complaints. Mothers are supposed to take care of their children. I am thankful I have the strength to do this at my age. I am thankful that I can take care of my son.<br><br>I am glad I am able to care for my son. I have heard about so many people who have HIV/AIDS needing to be cared for by strangers or nonfamily members. |

**Selective coding** is the final stage of the coding process and is completed after categories and subcategories have been identified via open and/or axial coding. It is the process of selecting one core category (the storyline) and relating the other categories/subcategories to it. Researchers use the data to support the core category and generate theory about the phenomenon.

Going back to our example, the researcher reviews the codes derived from the open coding and axial coding processes, and comes up with one core category, which is caregiving experience.

As you code your data, it is important that you write memos or notes to yourself and others involved in the research. Strauss and Corbin (1990) recommend three types of memos that should be written: code notes, theoretical notes, and operational notes. **Code notes** are used to document the code labels and their meaning. **Theoretical notes** are used to record ideas that will help you interpret the data. **Operational notes** are used to document issues related to data collection or other methodological issues.

---

### Application Checkpoint 14.1

Pretend that you are the researcher who collected the data in Table 14.1. What would you record in your theoretical notes that would help you interpret the data?

---

### Critical Thinking Question 14.3

Dr. Booker convenes a meeting with you, the graduate assistants, and the doctoral students and asked that you all begin coding the data to Question #3, "Why do you think police brutality occurs?" Using the sample responses to the question in Table 14.3, please code the data and give your open, axial, and selective codes to your instructor.

---

### Table 14.3 Examples of Responses to Question #3, "Why do you think police brutality occurs?"

P1: Police brutality occurs because persons do not respect others because of their race/ethical and socioeconomic backgrounds. They think they are better than we are, just because of our skin color and where we live.

P2: I think it occurs because they have stereotypes about us. I heard that someone did a study where they found that police officers mistake African American males as being older than they really are. I was surprised to hear this. I asked some of my friends had they heard about this study and they said no. Well, this study lets me know that young African American males are being killed because the police cannot tell the difference between a 12-year-old and a grown man.

P3: I think it happens because the police are under a lot of stress and they bring their stress into the situation. They take out their stress on the person they are interacting with. I do not think this is right.

P4: Police brutality occurs because there are some people who do not comply with the police's request. The police see that the situation is getting out of hand, so they need to think quickly about how to handle the situation. If they cannot think quickly, they could be killed. So, to ensure that they do not get killed, they may result to using tactics that may be aggressive in nature.

P5: It occurs because the police are poorly trained to deal with people from different ethnic/racial backgrounds.

P6: There are several reasons why police brutality occurs. First, police officers are not properly trained to interact with young African American males. When they see us, they look at our clothes and hair. They do not say, "hello, young man, what are you doing?" I think they look at our clothes and hair, because they have stereotypes about us. Why can't a young African American male wear a suit and have braided hair? Second, I think they get into situations where immediate action needs to be taken, so they use aggressive tactics as way to handle the situation.

P7: They do not know how to deal with people from different ethnic/racial backgrounds.

P8: They are poorly trained.

## Types of Qualitative Analyses

### Content Analysis

**Content analysis** is defined "as a research method for the subjective interpretation of the content of textual data through the systematic classification process of coding and identifying themes or patterns" (Hsieh & Shannon, 2005, p. 1278). There are three types of content analysis: conventional, direct, and summative.

**Conventional content analysis** is typically used when the aim of the study is to describe the phenomenon under investigation. The codes and categories are derived from the textual data. Data analysis starts with the researcher reading all the transcripts to become familiar with the content of the documents. The textual data are then read again word by word to derive codes. This is followed by reading the textual data again, noting general impressions and thoughts about the initial codes. The textual data are read again to determine if the codes can be merged into categories based on similarities and differences. Next, the definitions for each category and code is developed.

In **direct content analysis**, the researcher uses theory or prior research to develop the initial codes and operational definitions of the codes. In reading the textual data, the researcher looks to see what text relates to the predetermined codes. The text that cannot be categorized with the predetermined codes are given new codes. This type of analysis is useful in trying to find supportive and not supportive evidence related to the theory. A disadvantage of this approach is that researchers may overlook counter evidence found because they are whetted to the theory.

**Summative content analysis** "starts with identifying and quantifying certain words or content in the text with the purpose of understanding the contextual use of the words or content" (Hsieh & Shannon, 2005, p. 1283). In reading the textual data, the researchers look for the occurrence of a particular word or content in the text and then quantifies how many times the word was mentioned in the text. This is known as **manifest content analysis**. On the other hand, in **latent content analysis**, the researchers read the textual data to determine underlying meanings of the word or the content.

## Example of a Study Using Content Analysis

Syme, Yelland, Cornelison, Poey, Krajicek, and Doll (2017) examined the public opinion of sexual expression and dementia within nursing homes. A qualitative study was conducted where the authors reviewed all publicly available comments (N = 1,194) made online in response to the *New York Times* article "Sex and Dementia and a Husband on Trial at 78" posted on April 13, 2015. Their research question was as follows: "How does the public view sexual consent in the context of dementia in long-term care?"

A content analysis was conducted. Four researchers reviewed the posts, identifying categories and subcategories separately. They met with each other to discuss the codes that had emerged. The reliability of their coding was examined, and there was 80% agreement among the four coders.

The results of the content analysis revealed one theme: conditions necessary to be sexual and six related categories: (1) "Is marriage enough?," (2) "What about consent?," (3) "Is consent all-or-nothing?," (4)"What about intimacy needs?," (5) "Is it inappropriate/appropriate?," and (6) "Who gets to be sexual?"

### Critical Discourse Analysis

**Critical discourse analysis** (CDA) is "a qualitative analytical approach for critically describing, interpreting, and explaining the ways in which discourses construct, maintain, and legitimize social inequalities" (Mullet, 2018, p. 116). This analytic approach involves a seven-step process (Mullet, 2018):

1. Selecting a discourse related to social inequalities;

2. Searching for sources to be analyzed, such as books, song lyrics, or videos;

3. Exploring the background of the text—examining the text to determine the historical and social context, the characteristics of the writer of the text, and the intended audience and purpose of the text;

4. Identifying overarching themes via the coding of the data;

5. Analyzing external relations—examining the text to look for different discourses within specific texts;

6. Analyzing internal relations—examining patterns or words in the text that represent power relations or social context; and

7. Interpreting the themes, internal relations, and external relations identified.

Using critical discourse analysis, Hoffman, Rodriguez, Yang, and Ropers-Huilman (2018) examined the construction of college students of color experiences in relation to resources the institutions provide to them.

## Grounded Theory Analysis

**Grounded theory analysis** is a qualitative analytic approach to analyzing textual data using open, axial, and selective coding. During the coding process, memos are written to the researcher or members of the research team. These memos are used to document the meaning of codes, issues related to data collection, and thoughts about how the data will be interpreted.

## Thematic Analysis

**Thematic analysis** involves identifying, analyzing, and reporting patterns (themes) within the data (Braun & Clarke, 2006). For these researchers, "a theme captures something important about the data in relation to the research question, and represents some level of patterned response or meaning within the data set" (p. 82). Themes are identified via an inductive or a deductive approach. Using an inductive approach, the themes are derived from the data and are not coded using a preexisting coding scheme. On the other hand, with a deductive approach, researchers look at the data to find themes that support the theoretical perspective that is being used. Data analysis starts with the researcher reading all the transcripts to become familiar with content of the documents. The textual data are then read again word by word to generate initial codes. This is followed by analyzing the codes that have emerged to determine if there is one overarching theme, several main themes, or sub-themes. Next, the themes are reviewed again for the purpose of refining them. This process is followed by defining and naming the themes. Once you have gone through all of the above steps, you are now ready to write up the results of the analysis.

# Criteria for Ensuring the Trustworthiness of the Data

In Chapter 8, we introduced you to the ways in which researchers ensure the trustworthiness for qualitative research. In this chapter, we will focus specifically on how to ensure trustworthiness as it relates to the data analysis process. Therefore, we will discuss strategies related to creditability, transferability, authenticity, and confirmability. **Creditability** refers to the "believability" of the study. To ensure the credibility of your data, you should have more than one person involved in the coding of the data. These persons should code the same transcript separately and then meet to discuss the similarities and differences in the coding. During the meeting, they revise codes, develop new codes, and clarify the research findings. Another way to ensure the creditability of your data is to have your participants review the transcripts to make sure that their words, descriptions, and comments are accurate.

**Dependability** focuses on demonstrating the consistency of the research process, where both research and phenomenon appear to be unstable. Researchers may inadvertently render their research process unstable by some of the decisions they make while conducting the research. Therefore, researchers need to track their decision-making process. Dependability can be established by creating a dependability audit, in which a third-party auditor is employed to check the researcher's work by reviewing the audit trail. Dependability can also be established by using a reflexive journal. The journal is used to document why certain methodological decisions were made, such as how codes were created and research questions were developed, and why specific sampling decisions were made.

**Transferability** refers to providing enough detailed description of the data so the readers of the findings can make decisions about whether the findings are applicable to the individuals with whom they work with or settings in which they work. To establish transferability, examples of the raw data should be provided in presentations and publications so readers can consider their interpretation or alternative interpretations (Houghton, Casey, Shaw, & Murphy, 2013; Popay, Rogers, & Williams, 1998). These data should be presented in quotations so that readers will know that the data are actually from the participants. Moreover, excerpts from memos and journals about how the data were coded can be used as part of the presentation or included in the appendix of the publication (Houghton et al., 2013). The method described above can also be used to established authenticity. **Authenticity** is the degree to which the researcher fairly and completely shows a range of the lived experiences or realities of the participants (Polit & Beck, 2014).

**Confirmability** refers to demonstrating that the findings are derived from the data. Inclusion of the participants' quotes in the write-up of the findings is a way to establish confirmability.

## Ethics and Qualitative Data Analysis

It is important that when analyzing your data that you correctly interpret the results (Competency 1, *Demonstrate Ethical and Professional Behavior*). Incorrect interpretation of the data produces erroneous conclusions, which could potentially harm clients. It is unethical not to analyze all data that has been collected. The unanalyzed data could have information that is consistent or not consistent with your findings. According Boeije (2010), unanalyzed data also could produce erroneous conclusions, which could potentially harm clients. It is unethical to base one's conclusions on selective interpretation of the data and not take into consideration counter evidence (Haverkamp, 2005). The quotes used to illustrate the themes should be verbatim, as it is unethical to use quotes that have been modified to change the original intent of the participants.

In obtaining the participant's consent to participate in the study, he or she should have been informed that his or her information will be confidential and/or anonymous. To violate what you have told the participant is unethical. To safeguard the participant's confidentiality, no identifying information should be associated with the transcripts or audiotapes. You should assign a code number to identify the participant. To ensure anonymity, you should use pseudonyms instead of the participant's real name when coding the data, if you are linking a specify quote with a participant. Information that might reveal the identification of the participants needs to be disguised.

## Diversity and Qualitative Data Analysis

Competency 2, *Engage Diversity and Difference in Practice*, does not specifically mention anything about data analysis; however, it is important that issues related to diversity be taken into consideration. Finding ways for persons from diverse backgrounds to participate in the qualitative data analysis process demonstrates one's willingness to see them as experts about their own experiences. Competency 2 clearly states, "social workers present themselves as learners and engage clients and constituencies as experts of their own experiences" (CSWE, 2015, p. 7). Lyons, Bike, Johnson, and Bethea (2012) suggest that when conducting qualitative research with persons of African American descent, it is important that they be involved in the post hoc identification of themes. The post hoc identification of themes involves having the participants review the transcripts to identify themes after they have been coded and the themes have been identified by the researcher. For Lyons et al., having persons involved in the post hoc identification of themes process allows for the researcher to become aware of his or her own biases and for multiple worldviews to be compared and contrasted, ultimately leading to the discovery of one objective truth, which is the goal of qualitative research (Guba & Lincoln, 2005). Additionally, it allows a way of promoting social justice, as many times persons from diverse groups feel that they are exploited by researchers because they are not involved in the research process. It is important that social workers engage in practices that advance social, economic, and environmental justice when analyzing qualitative data (Competency 3, *Advance Human Rights, and Social, Economic, and Environmental Justice*).

Although member checking should be employed systematically when analyzing qualitative data, it is critically important when analyzing data from diverse groups as it may allow the researcher to become aware of his or her biases (Mertens, 2015) and enhance the quality of the interpretation of the data (Lyons et al., 2012). Member checking is an opportunity for social workers to demonstrate critical thinking when interpreting qualitative data (Competency 7, *Assess Individuals, Families, Groups, Organizations, and Communities*), as it allows them to take others' worldviews under consideration.

When the data have been gathered from participants whose language is different from the researcher, it may be important that the researcher employ persons who speak the same language as the participants to help with the coding of the data. Hsin-Chun Tsai et al. (2004) found that employing coders who spoke Chinese, the same language as the participants in their study, provided them with the opportunity to develop deeper and richer codes and helped contextualize the responses provided.

## Computer Programs for Qualitative Data

There are several qualitative data analysis software packages that can be used for storing, coding, analyzing, and retrieving textual material. Such programs are NVivo, MAXqda, Atlas.ti, QDA Minerlite, and CAT. QDA Minerlite and CAT can be downloaded for free. CAT can be found by searching "CAT textifier" and QDA can be found by searching "QDA Miner Lite."

### Application Checkpoint 14.2

Download one of the free software packages for analyzing qualitative data. Enter the data from Table 14.3 and attempt to analyze it.

### Critical Thinking Question 14.4

Dr. Booker convenes a meeting with you, the graduate assistants, and the doctoral students to discuss the data analysis strategy. What type of data analysis strategy (i.e., content analysis, critical discourse analysis, grounded theory analysis, or thematic analysis) would you recommend be used to analyze the data from the focus groups? Justify your response. Identify two criteria that Dr. Booker should consider to ensure the trustworthiness of the qualitative data analysis and the strategies he should use to do so.

## Sample Study: Write-Up of Qualitative Data Analysis (Academic Example)

<u>Research Problem</u>: Most of our knowledge about the experiences of African American males with the police have been derived from studies of adult African American males. Few, if any, have been conducted with adolescents, despite the fact that this group is increasingly at risk for having contact with the police. The purpose of this study was to examine the experiences of African American males, ages 13 to 18, with the police in their communities. It is hoped that the results of this study can be used to develop training programs for police officers so that their interactions with this population will not escalate to the point where someone is harmed.

<u>Research Question</u>: Have you had any experiences with the police? If so, can you describe these experiences?

<u>Method</u>: A qualitative study was conducted to examine the experiences of African American males, ages 13 to 18, with the police in their communities. Focus group interviews were conducted with 10 participants each, using an interview guide developed by the lead investigator. Prior to participating in the focus groups, participants were advised of confidentiality of the information and signed consent forms, and each participant completed a demographic data form.

The lead investigator and two doctoral students facilitated the focus groups. When necessary, they used probes and prompts to facilitate the discussion. The lead investigator had a PhD and the two doctoral students, both with master's in social work degrees, had prior experience with qualitative data collection. All focus group interviews were audio-recorded, and one doctoral student took notes during the focus groups. On average, the focus groups lasted 1½ hours.

<u>Participants</u>: The participants were 50 African American adolescent males ages 13 to 18, who were recruited using snowball sampling. Hence, this is a convenient sample. The participants resided in urban, suburban, and rural areas. Each person received $15 for their participation.

<u>Measure</u>: An interview guide was developed by the lead investigator. The question on the interview guide was as follows: "Have you had any experiences with the police? If so, can you describe these experiences?"

<u>Data Analysis</u>: A professional transcriptionist transcribed the audio-recorded focus group interviews verbatim. The transcripts were reviewed by the research team. NVivo 12 was used to analyze and categorize the data. Open coding was initially used to code the data through line-by-line examination

of the textual data. This was followed by axial and selective coding. Content analysis was used to analyze the data. Codes emerged into categories, and themes emerged from these categories. Member checking was conducted to confirm findings with the participants, and the participants were also involved in post hoc identification of themes.

Results: The theme experience with police emerged in response to the question, "Have you had any experiences with the police? If so, can you describe these experiences?" Two categories emerged for this theme: positive experiences and negative experiences.

*Positive Experience With the Police.* At least 20 participants indicated that they had a positive experience with the police. For example, Participant 05 explained: "My experience with the police has always been positive. I think this is because most of the police in my community grew up in this town, so they know my family members very well. My uncle and the chief of police were roommates in college."

Participant 12 described his interaction with the police as great. He expressed his opinion in this manner: "Several years ago, some of my friends were hanging out, and the police pulled up to where we were. We were afraid, and the police officer noticed our reaction." He said, "Boys, there is no need for you to be afraid. You have not done anything wrong. I just want to let you know that we heard that some people in the neighborhood have been complaining that your music is too loud. I just want you to turn it down a little bit. I know young people like to listen to loud music. I did too when I was your age. This is just a warning, but I do not want to come back out here again."

This participant went on to say he thought his interactions were great because the police officer knew what young people like to do, and he was not taken to jail.

*Negative Experience With the Police.* More than half of the sample reported negative experiences with the police. Many contributed these negative experiences to being African Americans and the police having stereotypes about them. Participant 32 stated, "I am tired of the police always pulling me over. I always give them what they ask for. You know—driver's license, car insurance, and registration. After I give these things, they all say, 'Does this car really belong to you?' Somehow I believe they think an African American man should not be driving this type of car or may be not a car at all." Participant 50 described his experience as follows: "I was walking down the street. My pants were hanging down and the police officer came up beside me and said, 'Don't you have a belt to put on? I am tired of seeing young African American males walking down the street with their pants hanging down. I wish someone would pass a law saying it is prohibited to wear your pants hanging down.'"

Discussion: The purpose of this study was to examine the experiences of African American males, ages 13 to 18, with the police in their communities. The findings of this study indicated that African American males had both positive and negative experiences with police in their communities, which is consistent with previous research. One limitation of this study is that the findings of this study cannot be generalized to the larger population of African American males, ages 13 to 18, because a random sampling strategy was not employed. Further research is needed to determine how to improve the experiences African American males have with the police.

## Sample Study: Write-Up of Qualitative Data Analysis (Non-Academic Example)

Let us say that Dr. Booker decides to disseminate the findings from his study via a podcast. Prior to recording his podcast, he should think about the duration of the podcast. It has been recommended that the podcast be no longer than 45 minutes. Next, he should be thinking about how he can use his personal experience to connect with the topic of discussion. This is referred to as positionality. Let us say, for example, that Dr. Booker had some experience with the police when he was an adolescent. Dr. Booker would start the podcast by talking about both the positive and negative experiences he had with the police. This should be followed by a brief overview of the study he conducted, highlighting the research questions that were asked, the number of participants, and the funding that was provided to conduct the study. After Dr. Booker has finished his overview of the study, he should then interview two or three of the participants in his study. After these persons have been interviewed, Dr. Booker would talk about how the findings from his research study have implications for how police should interact with African American adolescents and how African American adolescents should interact with the police. Following this, Dr. Booker would then interview someone who trains police on how to interact with African American adolescents and someone who works with African American adolescents on how to interact with the police. After these interviews, Dr. Booker would then speak about how what was presented by these two individuals has implications for further research. Following this, he would speak with the participants to solicit their opinions about what was mentioned by the person who trains police to interact with African American adolescents and the person who trains African American adolescents to interact with the police. After this, Dr. Booker would discuss what insights he gained about his research based on the interviews he conducted for the podcast and his final thoughts.

# SUMMARY, REVIEW, AND ASSIGNMENTS

## CHAPTER SUMMARY ORGANIZED BY LEARNING OBJECTIVES

**LO 14.1** Differentiate between the various qualitative coding strategies.

*Open coding* is the process of developing codes and categories through the close examination of the qualitative data.

*Axial coding* is the process of making connections among the categories and subcategories that were identified during the open coding process.

*Selective coding* is the process of selecting one core category (the storyline) and relating the other categories to it.

**LO 14.2** Differentiate between the different types of qualitative analysis.

*Conventional content analysis* is typically used when the aim of the study is to describe the phenomenon under investigation.

*Direct content analysis* is where the researcher uses theory or prior research to develop the initial codes and operational definitions of the codes.

*Summative content analysis* "starts with identifying and quantifying certain words or content in the text with the purpose of understanding the contextual use of the words or content" (Hsieh & Shannon, 2005, p. 1283).

*Critical discourse analysis* (CDA) is "a qualitative analytical approach for critically describing, interpreting, and explaining the ways in which discourses construct, maintain, and

legitimize social inequalities" (Mullet, 2018, p.116).

*Grounded theory analysis* is a qualitative analytic approach to analyzing textual data using open, axial, and selective coding.

**LO 14.3** Identify the ethical and diversity issues associated with analyzing qualitative data.

It is unethical to (1) not analyze all the data that has been collected; (2) base one's conclusions on selective interpretation of the data, (3) modify the quotes so that it changes the original intent of the participants, and (4) violate the participant's anonymity and confidentiality.

Whenever possible, involve the participants in post hoc identification of themes as a way of making the researcher aware of his or her biases and for multiple worldviews to be compared and contrasted when interpreting the data.

Member checking is a way of making the researcher aware of his or her biases and enhancing the quality of the data interpretation.

When conducting research with participants whose language is different from your own, you may want to employ persons to code the data who speak the same language as the participants so that your codes and themes are well developed.

# KEY TERMS

Open coding   329

Axial coding   330

Selective coding   332

Code notes   332

Theoretical
  notes   332

Operational notes   332

Content analysis   333

Conventional content
  analysis   333

Direct content analysis   333

Summative content
  analysis   334

Manifest content analysis   334

Latent content analysis   334

Critical discourse analysis   334

Grounded theory analysis   335

Thematic analysis   335

Creditability   336

Dependability   336

Transferability   336

Authenticity   336

Confirmability   336

# COMPETENCY NOTES

In this chapter, you were introduced to the competencies below:

Competency 1, *Demonstrate Ethical and Professional Behavior*. Social workers must be ethical in the way they analyze their qualitative data.

Competency 2, *Engage Diversity and Difference in Practice*. Social workers should engage the participants in post hoc identification of themes. Social workers demonstrate their willingness to see their participants as experts about their own experiences when they involve them in the qualitative data analysis process.

Competency 3, *Advance Human Rights and Social, Economic, and Environmental*

*Justice*. Social workers should engage the participants in post hoc identification of themes as a way of advancing human rights and social, economic, and environmental justice.

Competency 4, *Engage in Practice-Informed Research and Research-Informed Practice*. Social workers should apply critical thinking to engage in analysis of qualitative data analysis.

Competency 7, *Assess Individuals, Families, Groups, Organizations, and Communities*. Social workers apply critical thinking when interpreting qualitative data by employing membership checking, as this process may help the social worker become aware of their biases and help them see another worldview.

# ASSESSMENT QUESTIONS

1. How did the information in this chapter enhance your knowledge about qualitative data analysis?

2. In what ways did answering Critical Thinking Question 14.3 enhance your ability to do open and axial coding?

3. What specific content discussed in this chapter is still unclear to you? If there is still content that is unclear, schedule an appointment with your instructor to gain more clarity.

# END-OF-CHAPTER EXERCISES

1. Look at the Facebook postings or Twitter feed of 15 of your friends. Conduct a content analysis to determine what themes in these postings/feeds are the most prevalent.

2. Find a published qualitative study and explain what the researchers did to establish credibility, transferability, dependability, confirmability, and authenticity.

3. Select one of the questions that Dr. Booker proposed in his research study. Ask 10 adolescent males this question. Analyze the data using any of the methods described in this chapter. Share your results with your classmates.

# ADDITIONAL READINGS

Erlingsson, C., & Brysiewicz, P. (2017). A hands-on guide to doing content analysis. *African Journal of Emergency Medicine, 7*(3), 93–99. doi.org/10.1016/j.afjem.2017/08.001

Eysenbach, G., & Till, J. E. (2001). Ethical issues in qualitative research on Internet communities. *British Medical Journal, 323*(7321), 1103–1105. doi.org/10.1136/bmj.323.7321.1103

Friese, S. (2012). *Qualitative data analysis with ATLAS.ti.* Thousand Oaks, CA: Sage.

Oxhandler, H. K., & Giardina, T. D. (2017). Social workers' perceived barriers to and sources of support for integrating clients' religion and spirituality in practice. *Social Work, 62*(4), 323–332. doi:10.1093/sw/swx036

Sanjari, M., Bahramnezhad, F., Fomani, F. K., Shoghi, M., & Cheraghi, M. A. (2014). Ethical challenges of researchers in qualitative studies: The necessity to develop a specific guideline. *Journal of Medical Ethics and History of Medicine, 7,* 7–14.

Thumboo, J., Ow, M. Y. L, Uv, E. J. B., Xin, X., Chan, Z. Y. C., Sung, S. C., et al. (2018). Developing a comprehensive, culturally sensitive conceptual framework of health domains in Singapore. *PLoS, 136,* 1–14. doi.org/10.1371/journal.pone.0199881

Tong, A., Sainsbury, P., & Craig, J. (2007). Consolidated criteria for reporting qualitative research (COREQ): A 32-item checklist or interviews and focus groups. *International Journal for Quality in Health Care, 19*(6), 349–357. doi.org/10.1093/intqhc/mzm042

Windsong, E. A. (2018). Incorporating intersectionality into research design: An example using qualitative interviews. *International Journal of Social Research Methodology, 21*(2), 135–147. doi:10.1080/13645579.2016.1268361

# ⑤SAGE edge™

Get the tools you need to sharpen your study skills. SAGE Edge offers a robust online environment featuring an impressive array of free tools and resources.

Access practice quizzes at **edge.sagepub.com/farmer**

# CHAPTER 15

# Single-Case Design Evaluation

## Learning Objectives

**15.1** Identify what needs to be done prior to conducting a single-case design evaluation.

**15.2** Differentiate between the different phases of the single-case design evaluation.

**15.3** Differentiate between the various types of single-case design strategies.

**15.4** Identify the ethical and diversity issues associated with single-case design evaluation.

| Competencies Covered | Learning Objectives | Dimension |
|---|---|---|
| **Competency 1**<br>*Demonstrate Ethical and Professional Behavior* | 15.4 Identify the ethical issues associated with single-case design evaluation. | Skills |
| **Competency 2**<br>*Engage Diversity and Difference in Practice* | 15.4 Identify the diversity issues associated with single-case design evaluation. | Skills |
| **Competency 4**<br>*Engage in Practice-Informed Research and Research-Informed Practice* | 15.3 Differentiate between the various types of single-case design strategies. | Skills |
| **Competency 7**<br>*Assess Individuals, Families, Groups, Organizations, and Communities* | 15.2 Differentiate between the different phases of the single-case design evaluation. | Skills |
| **Competency 9**<br>*Evaluate Practice with Individuals, Families, Groups, Organizations, and Communities* | | |

Master the content at
**edge.sagepub.com/farmer**

345

## Is Peer Mentoring Effective?

By responding to the questions related to this case example, you will be able to identify what type of single-case design is appropriate for evaluative research purposes, and you will be able to justify your choice by critically analyzing the strengths and weaknesses of the single-case designs described in this chapter.

Ellen is employed as a school social worker in a middle school. Recently, she has spoken with several teachers who have told her that over the years they have seen an increase in the number of students who have behavioral problems. One of the teachers, Ms. Paulson, stated that two of her students in her class get into verbal arguments every day. Ms. Paulson also stated that she has spoken to the students' mothers and was told that these students also get into verbal arguments with their siblings as well.

You are doing your field placement at this school. Ellen is supervising you and she tells you that she would like for you to find an intervention that could address the students' behavior. She further states that she would like for you to evaluate its effectiveness.

At this point, take a few minutes to think about the case example and do the following:

1. Identify the problem.

2. Determine what you already know about the problem.

3. Determine what information you need to solve the problem.

4. List the questions needed to be answered related to the information you need to solve the problem.

Please write down your responses to each item. You will need to refer to them while reading this chapter.

You scheduled a meeting with Ellen to inform her that you have reviewed the literature and determined that peer mentoring is effective in increasing conflict resolution and social skills. You tell her that you plan to recruit two seventh graders to serve as the mentors for these two students. They will be trained to teach the students conflict resolution and social skills. They will meet with the students for 20 minutes each day before and after school. The session before school is when the mentors will teach the students conflict resolution and social skills and have them role play how they should handle various situations. The session after school is when the mentors will review with the students how they handled different situations that occurred during the day. If they used the skills learned to deal with a difficult situation, they will be given five tokens, which they can use to purchase a prize. If they did not handle the situation appropriately, then they will not earn any tokens for the day. The mentors will discuss how they could have handled the situation and role play with them the appropriate way to handle the situation.

## Introduction

In this chapter, you will learn about the various types of single-case design evaluations. A brief discussion of what software packages are available to analyze data derived from single-case design evaluations is presented. Ethical and diversity issues one needs to think about when conducting a single-case design evaluation are discussed.

## Single-Case Design Evaluation Defined

**Single-case design evaluation**, also referred to a single-system designs or single-subject designs, involves using a time-series design to evaluate the effectiveness of an intervention or the effects of policies on an individual client, a family unit, or individual case, be it a community or group (Competency 9, *Evaluation Practice With Individuals, Families, Groups, Organizations, and Communities*). A **time-series design** is one where there is repeated measurement (observation) of the dependent variable prior to the implementation of the intervention (independent variable) and after the intervention has been implemented. The standard notation for this design, based on the work of Campbell and Stanley (1963), is as follows:

OOOOOO X OOOOOO

The X stands for the intervention and O stands for observation. The observation refers to the measurement of the dependent variable. In the above example, you will see that there were six observations of the dependent variable made before the intervention was implemented and there were six observations of the dependent variable made after the intervention was implemented. Treatment effectiveness is evaluated by looking at the observations during the intervention phase and comparing them with the observations during the baseline phase. The observations from both the baseline and interventions are graphed, and by looking at the graphed data (see graph below, Figure 15.1), you will see that after the intervention was introduced there was improvement in the client's behavior.

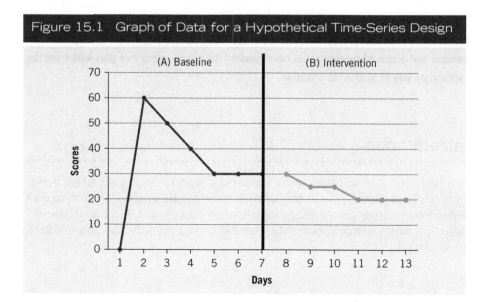

Figure 15.1 Graph of Data for a Hypothetical Time-Series Design

In social work, single-case design evaluation has primarily been used to determine the effectiveness of social work practice. Using single-case design evaluation is a way of social workers engaging in practice-informed research and research-informed practice (Competency 4, *Engage in Practice-Informed Research and Research-Informed Practice*). Single-case design evaluation allows social workers to answer the research questions (1) "What intervention is effective?," (2) "For whom?," and (3) "Under what conditions?"

## What Needs to Be Done
## Prior to Conducting a Single-Case Design

There are three things one must do before engaging in a single-case design evaluation. You must decide: (1) what client behavior to target for the intervention, (2) how to measure the target behavior, and (3) where to collect the data on the target behavior.

### Operationalizing the Target Behavior

When conducting a single-case design evaluation, the dependent variable is referred to as the target behavior. The **target behavior** is the behavior that both you and the client agree to work on during treatment. Whenever possible, the target behavior should be operationalized in a positive manner. For example, if you are working with a parent who says her child is not listening, the goal of your intervention would be to increase the number of times the child listens to the parent. Therefore, you would operationalize listening as carrying out a command given by the mother within five minutes of the request. Operationalizing of the target behavior occurs during the assessment phase of treatment, as this is the phase where you determine why the client is seeking services (Competency 7, *Assess Individuals, Families, Groups, Organizations, and Communities*). The target behavior must be amenable to being measured repeatedly as repeated measurement of the target behavior is a requirement for single-case design evaluation. Referring to the case example, let us say that the target behavior is arguing. The goal of the mentoring program would be to reduce the arguing behavior of the two students.

In working with the client to determine the target behavior, he or she may identify several behaviors that are causing him or her difficulties. You need to ask the client to prioritize which one to work on. You need to ask the client the following questions: "Which one of the behaviors you have identified is of most concern to you?," "How often does the behavior occur?," "What is the duration of the behavior?," and "When does the behavior occur?" The answer to some of the above questions will help you determine how the problem behavior will be measured and when the measurement will occur. For example, if a client states the behavior occurs in the evening, you want the client to measure the behavior during that time period.

## Measuring the Target Behavior

The target behavior you plan to intervene on must be one that can be measured repeatedly. Therefore, you must help the client think of a behavior that occurs on a daily basis. Additionally, it should be one that can be measured at the same time and in the same place every day, so that changes in the target behavior can be attributed to the intervention and not to outside factors. Once you and the client have agreed on the target behavior, you need to identify how it will be measured, who will measure it, and where it will be measured.

*How Will the Target Behavior Be Measured?* You will need to determine if the behavior will be measured using a standardized measure or individualized rating scales. **Individualized rating scales (IRS)** are tailor-made for each client and specifically measures how the client operationalized the target behavior. These measures are sometimes referred to as self-rating scales or self-anchored scales, because the client does the ratings. A disadvantage of using an IRS is that they are not reliable and only have face validity. Standardized measures are also appropriate for measuring the target because they are both reliable and valid and have instructions on how to administer and score them. A disadvantage of these measures is that they may not reflect how the client has operationalized the target behavior.

Prior to developing an IRS or selecting a standardized measure, you need to decide what characteristic or dimension of the target behavior you plan to measure. Characteristics or dimensions of the behavior are, for example, the intensity, frequency, duration, or presence or absence. To determine what characteristics or dimensions you plan to assess, you need to ask your client the following questions: "How often does the behavior occur?," "How long does the behavior last?," and "How intensive is the behavior?" Also consider what dimensions or characteristics of the target behavior you chose to measure have implications for the goal of the intervention. For example, if you chose to measure how often the behavior occurs, then your intervention should focus on decreasing the occurrence of the behavior. In working with the client, it is important to only assess one characteristic or dimension of the target behavior of the client. Referring to the case example, the teacher could measure the arguing behavior by frequency or duration. When measuring the target behavior by frequency, the teacher would simply count how often the target behavior occurred. If the teacher wanted to know the duration of the arguing, she would time how long the students argued with one of their classmates.

If you decide to use an IRS with your client, you need to decide how many response categories you will use. Too few response categories will not allow one to document changes in the target behavior. On the other hand, too many will make it too difficult for your client to distinguish among response categories. It has been recommended that no less than four response categories and no more than seven response categories be used (Bloom, Fischer, & Orme, 2006).

Once you have decided how many response categories to use, then you must decide along with your client what will be the rating scale anchors. The anchors consist of the behaviors, thoughts, and feelings that a client would be experiencing at each response category. Each anchor is associated with a response category. Examples of a rating scale with associated anchors are displayed in Table 15.1.

### Table 15.1 Examples of Scale Anchors for Individualized Rating Scales

1. How depressed are you today, compared to yesterday?

| 1 | 2 | 3 | 4 | 5 |
|---|---|---|---|---|
| Not at all depressed | A little more depressed | Somewhat more depressed | About the same | More depressed |

2. I feel depressed

| 1 | 2 | 3 | 4 | 5 |
|---|---|---|---|---|
| Strongly disagree | Disagree | Not sure | Agree | Strongly agree |

3. How often do you feel depressed?

| 1 | 2 | 3 | 4 | 5 |
|---|---|---|---|---|
| Never feel depressed | Rarely feel depressed | Not sure | Often feel depressed | All the time |

*Who Will Measure It?* You need to decide if the client or someone else will measure the problem. The client may be a good choice to measure the target behavior because he or she knows when the behavior occurs. If the client measures the target behavior, you need to be concerned about reactivity. **Reactivity** refers to changes in the target behavior that are due to the client recording his or her behavior and is a threat to internal validity. It is a threat to internal validity if you see changes in the target behavior prior to the implementation of the intervention. A parent or teacher may be a good choice to measure the target behavior depending on if the target behavior is observable or not and where the behavior is occurring. For example, a parent would be a good person to measure the number of times the child has a temper tantrum, while a teacher would be a good person to measure how often the child is off task in the classroom. If you choose to have someone other than the client measure the behavior, you need to be concerned about the client being aware of his or her behavior being measured. This awareness, too, may make the client change his or her behavior. Therefore, the person measuring the behavior must be unobtrusive in the way he or she observes the person's behavior—that is, the person must observe the client's behavior without the client's awareness.

*Where to Collect the Data on the Target Behavior?* As a general rule, the data on the target behavior need to be collected in the setting where the target behavior occurs or occurs on a regular basis. For example, if your client states that her child has temper tantrums, you need to find out where the behavior occurs. If the parent says that the behavior occurs at both home and school, then you need to find out if the behavior occurs more frequently at school or at home. If it occurs more frequently at school, then this is where the data collection on the target behavior should occur.

---

### Critical Thinking Question 15.1

Thinking about the case example, how would you operationalize and measure the target behavior? If you chose to use an IRS to measure the target behavior, you need to develop it. If you chose to use a standardized measure to measure the target behavior, you need to discuss the types of reliability and validity that have been assessed. Identify who should collect the data and where the data should be collected. Justify your response.

---

## Phases of the Single-Case Design Evaluation Process

### Baseline Phase

There are two phases of the single-case design evaluation process. The first phase is referred to as the baseline. The **baseline phase**, symbolically referred to as the A phase, is where there are repeated measures (observations) of the dependent variable (target behavior) being taken prior to the implementation of the intervention. It serves as the control condition analogous to the control group in an experimental design. During the baseline phase, there is an opportunity for you to (1) "conduct an assessment to determine the targets of change (dependent variable)," (2) "specify corresponding relevant measures for evaluating change," (3) "evaluate the severity or frequency of the client's problem before implementing any . . . specific intervention," and (4) establish rapport (Lundervold & Belwood, 2000, p. 94). Conducting a baseline is a way for social workers to "collect and organize data and apply critical thinking to interpret information from clients and constituencies" (CSWE, 2015, p. 9; Competency 7, *Assess Individuals, Families, Groups, Organizations, and Communities*). All the measurements of the target behavior during the baseline will help you determine if an intervention is warranted. Competency 7, *Assess Individuals, Families, Groups, Organizations, and Communities*, states that social workers select appropriate interventions based on the assessment. The measurement of the dependent variable should continue until a stable pattern of the behavior is obtained. A **stable pattern** is one where there is a predictable pattern to the occurrence of the problem behavior. In order to determine if you have a stable pattern, you need to plot the data points chronologically on a graph, drawing a line between each data point. A stable baseline is indicated by a flatline usually across three to five data points (Ray, Minton, Schottelkorb, & Brown, 2010).

Looking at the graph below (see Figure 15.2), you will see that the baseline phase is designated by the letter A. You will also see that a stable pattern in the baseline emerged after the fourth data point—that is, there is a flat line between data points five through nine.

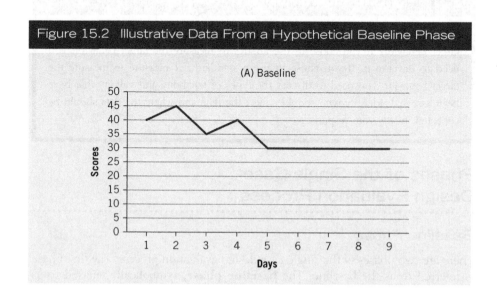

Figure 15.2 Illustrative Data From a Hypothetical Baseline Phase

The number of observations of the target behavior during the baseline is dependent upon when you obtained a stable pattern. Generally, it has been recommended that you have between five and 10 observations. In any case, it is important that you have enough observations to demonstrate that the intervention caused the change in the target behavior and not an extraneous event. If you can demonstrate that the intervention caused the change in the target behavior and not an extraneous variable, then you can infer causality. An **extraneous event** is one that occurs during the baseline phase resulting in a change in the target behavior that cannot be attributed to the intervention. Because it may take a while to get a stable baseline, one must ask oneself, "When can I start the intervention?" The answer to this question is that you need to start the intervention as soon as possible. Having a stable baseline prior to implementing the intervention is indeed important to demonstrate that your intervention is effective; however, it is not more important than you providing your client with the services he or she needs.

When you are in a situation where delaying the intervention is not an option, you need to consider constructing a retrospective/reconstructive baseline. A **retrospective/reconstructive baseline** is constructed from past data. The retrospective/reconstructive baseline can be constructed by asking the client to recall the occurrence of the target behavior (dependent variable). If you plan to use a retrospective/reconstructive baseline, you should ask the client to recall specific events, such as when did they curse, throw temper tantrum, that occurred within the last one or two weeks (Bloom, Fischer, & Orme, 2006). Having the client recall feelings or attitudes and events beyond a two-week time period may be too difficult.

Archival data can also be used to construct a retrospective/reconstructive baseline. For example, let us say a school social worker has been asked by a teacher to work with one of her students. She states that this particular student has been missing school. Instead of asking the student to tell her how many times he has missed school, she reviewed his school records. The information pertaining to how many days he missed school was used to construct a retrospective/reconstructive baseline.

## Application Checkpoint 15.1

Suppose that a retrospective/reconstructive baseline will be used for evaluating the behavior of the girls in the case example. Who should provide the data for the baseline? How reliable would you believe the data are from the person who provided it?

There are times when you are unable to conduct a baseline. One such situation is when a client is in crisis. When a client is in crisis, delaying the intervention is not an option. A retrospective/reconstructive baseline is appropriate in this case. Another situation in which you are unable to conduct a baseline is when the client is at risk of harming him- or herself or others. This type of situation requires that you intervene immediately.

The baseline phase normally occurs prior to the implementation of the intervention; however, there may be times when you need to conduct the baseline after the intervention has been implemented. You may want to reinstitute the baseline when the intervention appears not to be working.

## Intervention Phrase

Prior to implementing the intervention (independent variable), one should review the literature to determine what intervention is most effective in treating the targeted behavior. The second phase of the single-case design evaluation is known as the **intervention (treatment) phase**, symbolically referred to as the B phase. The intervention phase is where the clinician delivers the intervention aimed at changing the target behavior. The intervention, for example, could be cognitive behavioral therapy if you are treating the client for depression or a policy to improve access to services in the clinic where you are employed. The intervention phase is implemented after a stable baseline has been obtained. The reason for this is that introducing the intervention prior to obtaining a stable baseline could result in you erroneously concluding that the intervention made a difference, but really the client's behavior was getting better already (see Figure 15.3). During the intervention phase the measurement of the target behavior is ongoing. Observations of the target behavior during the intervention phase are compared to the observations taken during the baseline phase to determine if the intervention is effective.

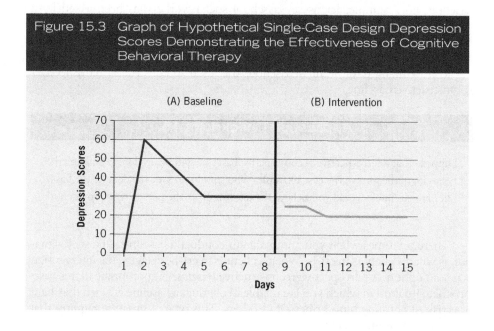

Figure 15.3 Graph of Hypothetical Single-Case Design Depression Scores Demonstrating the Effectiveness of Cognitive Behavioral Therapy

# Types of Single-Case Designs

There are four types of single-case designs that can be used for evaluation—case studies or predesigns, the basic single-case design, the experimental single-case design, and the multiple-baseline design. In this chapter, we will not discuss the experiment single-case design, as this design is the subject of much debate. The underlying assumption of this design is that introduction of the intervention results in a change in the target behavior. If this is true, then removing the intervention should result in the target behavior returning to its original state of occurrence. Many believe that withdrawing an intervention that the client has been responding to is unethical; therefore, some feel that experimental designs are not appropriate for social workers to use. Each of the strengths and weaknesses of these designs will be discussed. The sampling strategy used with these designs is purposive or convenience sampling, as the participants are usually clients receiving services in an agency.

## Types of Case Studies or Predesigns

*Case Studies or Predesigns.* **Case studies** or **predesigns** are ones where the researcher only conducts observations of the target behavior during the baseline phase, implements only the intervention without observations of the target behavior during the intervention phase, or implements the intervention with observations of the target behavior during the intervention phase. There are three types of case studies or predesigns: the observation only, labeled A; the intervention only, labeled B; and the simultaneous intervention and observation, also labeled B.

*Observation or Measurement-Only Design.* The **observation or measurement-only design** (Design A) is one where there is only measurement of the target behavior but there is no intervention implemented (Figure 15.4). This type of design is useful for determining if an intervention is warranted. For example, let us say a social worker is seeing a client who tells her that her mother recently died. The client further says that she does not feel that the death of her mother has affected her but notes that her friends stated that she does not seem like her jolly self. She tells you that she has come to see you today to appease her husband and her friends. The social worker asked her to monitor her behavior every morning at 9 a.m., as this is the time the client mentioned that her husband and friends state she is not like herself. This type of design does not allow one to study the effectiveness of an intervention because no intervention was implemented. If there are changes to the targeted behavior, then the changes must be attributed to an extraneous factor.

*Intervention-Only Design.* The **intervention-only design** (Design B) is one where there is implementation of the intervention but no observation of the

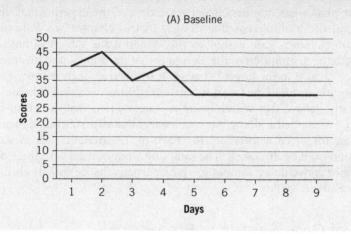

Figure 15.4 Graph of Hypothetical Data for the Observation or Measurement-Only Design

targeted behavior prior to its implementation or during the intervention phase. This type of design is appropriate when the client is at risk of harming one's self or others. This design does not allow one to study the effectiveness of an intervention because there was no measurement of the target behavior prior to the intervention implementation and while it was implemented.

*Simultaneous Intervention and Observation Design.* The **simultaneous intervention and observation design** (Case Study Design, Design B) is one where there is implementation of the intervention and observation of the target behavior during the intervention phase (see Figure 15.5).

This type of design is appropriate when the client is in a crisis and the researcher is interested in determining if the intervention is alleviating the distress the client is experiencing. Without there being an assessment of the target behavior prior to the implementation of the intervention, there is no baseline data for comparison. Therefore, one cannot conclude that the intervention led to changes in the outcome. Although one cannot conclude that the intervention led to changes in the target behavior, one can compare the scores on the outcome variable with the cut-off score for the measure used to assess the target behavior, if a standardized measure was used. A cut-off- score is a score that is used to indicate if someone's score puts him or her in a certain category. Let us say you are interested in seeing if your client who is being treated for depression is responding to the cognitive behavioral therapy. You used the Beck Depression Inventory-II (BDI-II; Beck, Steer, & Brown, 1996) to assess the client's depression. To determine if the

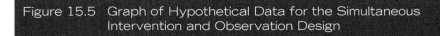

**Figure 15.5** Graph of Hypothetical Data for the Simultaneous Intervention and Observation Design

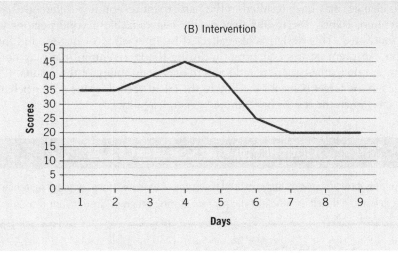

client responded to the treatment, you would compare his scores to the BDI-II cut-off scores, which are as follows: 0–13 minimal depression, 14–19 mild depression, 20–28 moderate depression, and 29–63 severe depression. Looking at the graph in Figure 15.5, you see that on day 7 the client has a score of 20; therefore, you would infer that she is responding to the treatment, because her score is in the range for moderately depressed, which is a score of 20 to 28. Because the simultaneous intervention and observation design does not control for extraneous variables, this design is considered to have weak internal validity. Internal validity refers to a researcher's ability to conclude that the change in the dependent variable is definitely attributed to the manipulation of the independent variable. This design fails to control for many of the threats to internal validity. Despite this, the simultaneous intervention and observation design helps researchers explore if the intervention is having or not having the intended effect. This design is affected by the following threats to internal validity:

1. **History:** History is a threat to this design if some event occurred at the same time the client received the intervention, which resulted in the outcome.

2. **Reactivity:** Changes in the target behavior are due to the client recording his or her behavior.

External validity refers to the researcher's ability to generalize the study's results beyond those persons included in the study. This design is affected by interaction of selection and X: A characteristic of the participant, such as motivation to change, may have resulted in the participant responding differently to the intervention. Hence, the results may not be generalizable beyond persons who were motivated. This design is also affected by interaction of history and intervention. An event occurs concurrently during the intervention that may not be present at other times, thereby reducing the generalizability of the results. If the changes in the target behavior are due to the client recording his or her behavior (reactivity), then the results have limited generalizability.

---

**Critical Thinking Question 15.2**

Thinking about the case example, would using any of the case studies or predesigns help you determine the effectiveness of the peer mentoring program? Justify your response.

---

## The Basic Single-Case Design

The **basic single-case design** is one that has both the baseline and intervention phase, where there is measurement of the target behavior in both phases. This design is referred to as the A-B design (Figure 15.6). The intervention is not implemented until there is a stable baseline.

This type of design allows one to evaluate the effectiveness of an intervention. Effectiveness of the intervention is determined by comparing the extent to which

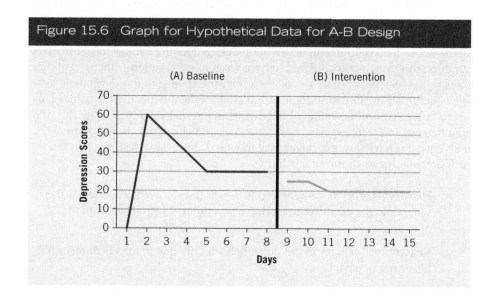

**Figure 15.6  Graph for Hypothetical Data for A-B Design**

the target behavior was occurring during the baseline with the extent to which the target behavior is occurring during the intervention phase. This design allows one to infer causality, if you can demonstrate that the intervention caused the change in the target behavior and not an extraneous variable. This design is affected by the following threats to internal validity:

1. **History:** History is a threat to this design if some event occurred at the same time the client received the intervention, which resulted in the outcome.

2. **Reactivity:** This threat was defined under the section titled "Simultaneous Intervention and Observation Design."

3. **Statistical Regression to the Mean:** If participants were selected to receive the intervention based on having extreme low or high scores on the pretest, when comparing the pretest scores with the posttest scores, you find the participants perform better on average on the posttest than the pretest.

Furthermore, this design is affected by the following threats to external validity:

1. **Interaction of testing and X:** As a result of the pretesting, the participants may become sensitized to the treatment. Therefore, the results of the study are only generalizable to the pretested population.

2. **Interaction of selection and X:** This threat was defined under the section titled "Simultaneous Intervention and Observation Design."

3. **Interaction of history and intervention:** This threat was defined under the section titled "Simultaneous Intervention and Observation Design."

4. **Reactivity:** This threat was defined under the section titled "Simultaneous Intervention and Observation Design."

## Example of a Study Using an A-B Single-Case Design

Callesen, Jensen, and Wells (2014) evaluated the effectiveness of metacognitive therapy (MCT) for depression, using an A-B single-case design. Four persons participated in their study. These individuals completed the Beck Depression Inventory-II (BDI-II) and the Major Depressive Disorder Scale (MDDS) on a weekly basis three weeks before the implementation of the

*(Continued)*

intervention (baseline phase) and weekly during the intervention phase at the start of their session. The MDDS was used to assess time spent ruminating. The intervention was delivered by a clinical psychologist and a psychologist. The four participants received anywhere from five to 11 sessions of treatment of 45–50 minutes in duration. The intervention ended when the participant scored 12 on the BDI-II for two or three consecutive sessions.

Visual analysis was used to analyze the graphed data. Two persons started to show improvement in their depression scores prior to treatment, and two showed improvement in their depression scores after the intervention was implemented. Similar findings were obtained for the MDDS.

## Multiple-Baseline Design

Earlier we mentioned that you should have your client prioritize which target behavior he or she would like to work on. We realize that you will be seeing clients that have more than one target behavior of concern. For these situations, you may want to use the multiple-baseline design. The **multiple-baseline design** has multiple baselines across target behaviors, clients, or settings and the intervention is staggered (starts at different times) across these entities. In other words, as soon as the baseline is stable for one target behavior, for example, the intervention begins while the baseline for the other target behaviors are continued. Once the second target behavior has a stable baseline, the intervention is started, while the baseline for the third target behavior is continued (Figure 15.7). The same intervention is used no matter when it is implemented. This design controls for the effects of extraneous variables by having more than one baseline. The underlying assumption of this design is that if some extraneous event coincides with the onset of the intervention and results in the improvement of the target behavior, for example, then that improvement will show up in the graph of each target behavior at the same time while the baseline is continuing for the target behavior not being intervene on. If the intervention results in the change in the target behavior, then the improvement in each target behavior should only occur when the intervention is introduced for that specific target behavior. It has been suggested that one should have at least three targeted behaviors to use the multiple-baseline design (Bloom, Fischer, & Orme, 2006). In essence, the more baselines you have the stronger evidence you have to demonstrate causality. The multiple-baseline design has strong internal validity. This design can be used to determine if the intervention is effective early, midway, or late in the process. Statistical regression to the mean would be a threat to this design, if participants were selected to receive the intervention based on having extreme low or high scores.

As mentioned earlier, the multiple-baseline design is applicable across target behaviors, clients, and settings. The multiple-baseline design across *target*

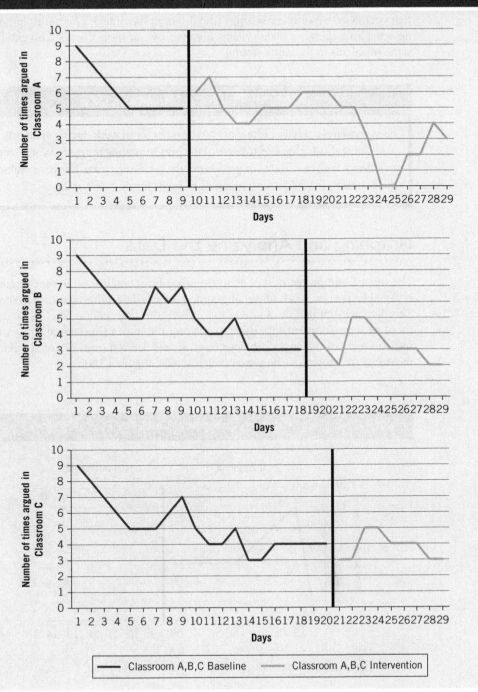

*behaviors* involves one client (or client system) with two or more target behaviors (the different baselines) that occur in one setting. The multiple-baseline design across *settings* involves one client (or client system) who has one target behavior that occurs in two or more settings (the different baselines). The multiple-baseline design across *clients or client systems* involves two or more clients who exhibit the same problems in the same setting.

## Critical Thinking Question 15.3

Ellen convenes a meeting with you and the other social work interns to discuss the plans for evaluating the effectiveness of the peer mentoring program. Which single-case design (i.e., case studies or predesigns, the basic single-case design, or multiple-baseline design) would you recommend be used? Justify your response.

## Graphing and Analyzing the Data

The most common method of analyzing data from single-case design evaluations is visual inspection (eyeballing) of graphed data to determine a pattern in the data. The data are graphed on a line graph, where the time period (e.g., days or time the data were recorded) are displayed along the *x*-axis (horizontal axis) and the measurement of the target behavior (e.g., scores derived from IRS or standardized measure) are shown on the *y*-axis (vertical axis; Figure 15.8).

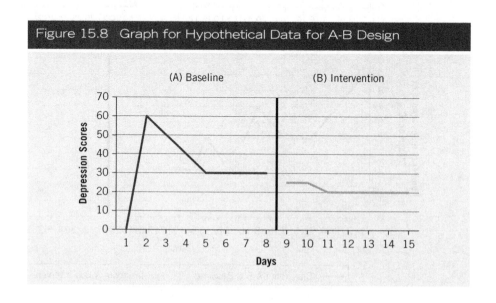

Figure 15.8 Graph for Hypothetical Data for A-B Design

In analyzing the data, there are five aspects that are examined: level, stability, trend, slope, and overlap. **Level** refers to the magnitude of change observed during the baseline and intervention phases. One is most interested in the magnitude of change in the level between the baseline and immediately after the intervention period. A large change between these two phases may indicate that the intervention is responsible for the change in the target behavior. **Stability** refers to a clear predictable pattern from the baseline to the intervention phase (usually represented by a flat line) and a clear predictable pattern within the baseline and intervention phases. A **trend** is a pattern in the data that indicates that the target behavior is improving, deteriorating, or staying the same (stability). The direction of the trend either upward or downward indicates if the target behavior is improving or deteriorating depending upon how the scores associated with the measure are interpreted. A flat line indicates that the target behavior is stable. **Slope** refers to the magnitude or steepness of the trend. **Overlap** is the extent to which the pattern in the data across phases overlap with each other. The less overlap across the phases the stronger evidence you have that the intervention resulted in the change in the target behavior. Visual analysis may increase Type I error—that is, the results may appear to indicate that the intervention was effective but it was due to how the data were graphed. For example, if the intervals between the data points are not the same, then the way the data have been graphed will account for the changes and not the intervention. To ensure that the data are interpreted correctly we recommend that you get some assistance from someone who is an expert at analyzing the data from single-case designs when using this method to evaluate your practice, so that the results are interpreted accurately. By doing this, you are demonstrating ethical and professional behavior (Competency 1, *Demonstrate Ethical and Professional Behavior*).

## Application Checkpoint 15.2

Suppose that the scores graphed in Figure 15.8 are from the Beck Depression Inventory-II. A high score means that the person is depressed. Looking at the graph, what would you say about the stability and the trend of the data?

There are a variety of software that can be used to graph the data from a single-case design evaluation. Such software includes Graph Pad Prism, Microsoft Excel, and Systat Sigma Plot. To read more about the use of Microsoft Excel, refer to Barton and Reichow (2012). R, which was discussed in Chapter 13, can also be used to analyze data from single-case design; to learn more, refer to Auerbach and Zeiltlin, (2014).

Statistical analysis is rarely used to analyze the data from single-case designs because most of the assumptions related to inferential statistics are not met (Morgan & Morgan, 2003). Additionally, there is no consensus about what statistical approach to use to analyze such data (Lundervold & Belwood, 2000). Recently, there has been a growing interest in the use of advanced statistical approaches to analyze data from single-case design; however, these will not be discussed in this chapter. For those interested in learning more about these approaches, please refer to Manolov and Moeyaert (2017) and Shadish (2014).

## Ethics and Single-Case Design Evaluation

It is unethical to remove an intervention especially if your client is responding to it (Competency 1, *Demonstrate Ethical and Professional Behavior*). Hence, we recommend that the experimental single-case design not be used in evaluating your clinical practice. If you are interested in knowing if your intervention did indeed cause a change in your client's behavior, we recommend that you use the basic-single case design or the multiple-baseline design.

It is good practice to evaluate the effectiveness of the intervention you use with your client. With any type of evaluation, it is important that you get the consent of your participant. We recommend you discuss with your field instructor what the policies and procedures are about obtaining consent from clients for the purposes of your evaluating the effectiveness of your work with them. You want to know if the consent form you get your client to sign for the provision of services also covers the client engaging in research projects or the evaluation of your work with the client. If the consent form does not, then you need to develop a consent form for this purpose. At a minimum, the consent form should describe the purpose of the evaluation, how many sessions will the client be meeting for, the benefits and risks associated with receiving the intervention, how confidentiality will be maintained, and what happens if the client does not want you to evaluate the intervention you are proposing to use. Besides reviewing the consent form you developed with your field instructor, you need to find out if the agency has an IRB or another entity that reviews requests for research or evaluation projects.

## Diversity and Single-Case Design Evaluation

The role of diversity needs to be taken into consideration when you are deciding to measure the target behavior (Competency 2, *Engage Diversity and Difference in Practice*). As mentioned earlier, you need to decide if you want to use an IRS, which is specifically designed to measure the target behavior based on how the client operationalized it or use a standardized measure. According to Sue and Sue (1990), using IRS with clients from diverse groups may be more appropriate than using standardized measures because many of them have been normed on White, middle-class respondents. Although standardized measures are reliable and valid, they may not have items that define the construct in the same manner as the persons who are filling out the measure. Therefore, the measure does not have conceptual equivalence. Conceptual equivalence is the extent to which the concepts represented by the items making up the measure are understood to have the same meaning across cultural groups. Additionally, measures that are valid and reliable for males may not be valid and reliable for females (Ibrahim, Scott, Cole, Shannon, & Eyles, 2001). The use of an IRS with diverse clients is a way of social workers presenting themselves as learners and engaging clients in the process of defining their own target behavior (Competency 2, *Engage Diversity and Difference in Practice*).

There are, however, standardized measures that are appropriate to use with diverse clients because they are reliable and valid for use with certain populations. For example, if one was interested in conducting a single-case evaluation to determine the effectiveness of cognitive behavioral therapy in reducing postpartum depression in Chinese women, the Chinese version of the Edinburgh Postnatal Depression Scale (Lee et al., 1998) could be used. A cut-off score of 10 or higher indicates the person is experiencing symptoms of minor or major depression. The measure has good internal consistency and has established criterion and concurrent validity (Lee et al., 1998).

# SUMMARY, REVIEW, AND ASSIGNMENTS

## CHAPTER SUMMARY ORGANIZED BY LEARNING OBJECTIVES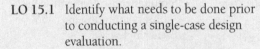

**LO 15.1** Identify what needs to be done prior to conducting a single-case design evaluation.

You must decide: (1) what client behavior to target for the intervention, (2) how to measure the target behavior, and (3) where to collect the data on the target behavior.

**LO 15.2** Differentiate between the different phases of the single-case design evaluation.

The baseline phase, symbolically referred to as the A phase, is where there are repeated measures (observations) of the target

behavior being taken prior to the implementation of the intervention.

The second phase of the single-case design evaluation is known as the intervention (treatment) phase, symbolically referred to as the B phase. The intervention phase is where the clinician delivers the intervention aimed at changing the target behavior.

**LO 15.3** Differentiate between the various types of single-case design strategies.

*Case studies or predesigns* are ones where the researcher only conducts observations of the target behavior during the baseline phase, and implements only the intervention without observations of the target behavior during the intervention phase or implements the intervention with observations of the target behavior during the intervention phase.

The *observation or measurement-only design* (Design A) is one where there is only measurement of the target behavior but there is no intervention implemented.

The *intervention-only design* (Design B) is one where there is implementation of the intervention but no observation of the targeted behavior prior to its implementation or during the intervention phase.

The *simultaneous intervention and observation design* (Design B) is one where there is implementation of the intervention and observation of the target behavior during the intervention phase.

The *basic single-case design* is one that has both the baseline and intervention phase, where there is measurement of the target behavior in the both phases.

The *multiple-baseline design* has multiple baselines across target behaviors, clients, or settings and the intervention is staggered (starts at different times) across these entities.

**LO 15.4** Identify the ethical and diversity issues associated with single-case design evaluation.

It is unethical to remove/withdraw an intervention especially if a client is responding to it.

Using individualized rating scales (IRS) with clients from diverse groups may be more appropriate than using standardized measures because many of them have been normed on White, middle-class respondents.

# KEY TERMS

# COMPETENCY NOTES

In this chapter, you were introduced to the competencies below:

Competency 1, *Demonstrate Ethical and Professional Behavior*. Social workers demonstrate ethical and professional behavior when they seek consultation about how to analyze data from single-case design evaluations. Moreover, social workers should not use single-case designs that require the removal of an intervention that is working for the client.

Competency 2, *Engage Diversity and Difference in Practice*. Social worker use individualized rating scales (IRS) with diverse clients as a way of presenting themselves as learners and engaging clients in the process of defining their own target behavior.

Competency 4, *Engage in Practice-Informed Research and Research-Informed Practice*. Social workers use single-case design evaluation as a way of engaging in practice-informed research and research-informed practice.

Competency 7, *Assess Individuals, Families, Groups, Organizations, and Communities*. Social workers select appropriate interventions based on the assessment.

Competency 9, *Evaluate Practice With Individuals, Families, Groups, Organizations, and Communities*. Social workers evaluate practice with individuals, families, groups, and organizations to advance practice, policy, and service delivery effectiveness.

# ASSESSMENT QUESTIONS

1.  How did the information in this chapter enhance your knowledge about single-case design evaluation?

2.  How did the information in this chapter enhance your knowledge about the ethical and diversity issues related to single-case design evaluation?

3.  What specific content discussed in this chapter is still unclear to you? If there is still content that is unclear, schedule an appointment with your instructor to gain more clarity.

# END-OF-CHAPTER EXERCISES

1.  Select an empirical study that is not a single-case design evaluation. Redesign it as a single-case design evaluation and list the strengths and weaknesses of your new study compared with the original study.

2.  You are employed as a school social worker and your school has a high rate of absenteeism. You have recently read an article about a program that is effective in reducing absenteeism in high school. You decided

that you would like to use it in your school. Discuss what type of single-case design you would use to evaluate the effectiveness of the program. Additionally, discuss why you selected this design.

3.  Construct a hypothetical graph of the results for the design you proposed for Exercise #2. In your analysis of the data, please describe the level, stability, trend, slope, and overlap.

## ADDITIONAL READINGS

Wong, S. E. (2010). Single-case evaluation for practitioners. *Journal of Social Service Research*, 36(3), 248–259. doi:10.1080/01488371003707654

# ⑤SAGE edge™

Get the tools you need to sharpen your study skills. SAGE Edge offers a robust online environment featuring an impressive array of free tools and resources.

Access practice quizzes at **edge.sagepub.com/farmer**

# CHAPTER
# 16

# Program Evaluation

## Learning Objectives

16.1  Define program evaluation.

16.2  Describe the components that are included in a logic model.

16.3  Differentiate between the various types of program evaluations.

16.4  Write an evaluation report.

16.5  Identify the ethical and diversity issues associated with program evaluation.

| Competencies Covered | Learning Objectives | Dimension |
|---|---|---|
| Competency 1<br>*Demonstrate Ethical and Professional Behavior* | 16.5  Identify the ethical issues associated with program evaluation. | Skills |
| Competency 2<br>*Engage Diversity and Difference in Practice* | 16.5  Identify the diversity issues associated with program evaluation. | Skills |
| Competency 9<br>*Evaluate Practice With Individuals, Families, Groups, Organizations, and Communities* | 16.3  Differentiate between the various types of program evaluations. | Skills |

## PBL Case 16

### Is Peer Mentoring Effective?

By responding to the questions related to this case example, you will be able to identify what type of program evaluation is appropriate for evaluative research purposes.

Master the content at
**edge.sagepub.com/farmer**

Ms. Paulson is convinced, based on the single-case design evaluation of the peer mentoring program used with the two students in her class, that peer mentoring is effective. She scheduled a meeting with the principal and the assistant principal to discuss the possibility of developing a peer mentoring program for all of the sixth-grade students. During the meeting, Ms. Paulson shows the principal and the assistant principal the data for each student she charted for the single-case design evaluation. Based on the data, both the principal and the assistant principal were convinced that a peer mentoring program is what they need to address the behavioral issues of the sixth graders in their school.

At this point, take a few minutes to think about the case example and do the following:

1. Identify the problem.

2. Determine what you already know about the problem.

3. Determine what information you need to solve the problem.

4. List the questions needed to be answered related to the information you need to solve the problem.

Please write down your responses to each item. You will need to refer to them while reading this chapter.

The principal and the assistant principal scheduled a meeting with Ellen, your supervisor, you, and the four sixth-grade teachers. She asks you to describe the peer mentoring program that will be used. You tell them about how the program was used with two students in Ms. Paulson's class and that the program was evaluated using a single-case design evaluation. You distribute the data from the charts for each student to show them the program's effectiveness. You go on to state that you plan to recruit 10 seventh graders to serve as the mentors to the sixth graders. Of these mentors, five will be males and five will be females. The male students will be assigned a male mentor and the female students will be assigned a female mentor. Each mentor will be responsible for mentoring five children. They will be trained to teach the students conflict resolution and social skills and will meet with the students for 20 minutes each day before and after school. The session before school is when the mentors will teach the children the skills and have them role play how they should handle various situations. The session after school is when the mentors will review with the children how they handled different situations that occurred during the day. If they used the skills learned to deal with a difficult situation, they will be given five tokens, which they can use to purchase a prize. If they did not handle the situation appropriately, then they will not earn any tokens for the day. The mentors will discuss how they could have handled the situation and role play with them the appropriate way to handle the situation.

Each teacher will fill out a social skills rating scale and a conflict resolution scale for each student prior to and after the implementation of the peer mentoring program. The ratings from these measures will be used to assess the effectiveness of the program.

---

## Introduction

In reading this chapter, you will learn about the different types of program evaluation. The logic model, which is used in most program evaluation, is presented. An overview of what should be included in an evaluation report is provided. Ethical and diversity issues associated with program evaluation are discussed.

## Program Evaluation Defined

**Program evaluation** refers to "the systematic scientific and rigorous evaluation of a program's effectiveness" (Shek, Lin, & Liang, 2018, p. 1311). The purpose of evaluation is to determine program efficacy and effectiveness, understand program delivery process and consumer experiences, ensure accountability, and build knowledge. **Efficacy evaluations** focus on demonstrating under experimentally controlled settings the ability of a program to achieve its stated outcomes. **Effectiveness evaluations** focus on the extent to which the impacts of the program can be demonstrated under authentic program settings. Together, they provide evidence that a program can be effective in real practice settings. Program evaluation is done using experimental, quasi-experimental, qualitative, and mixed-methods approaches. The purpose of program evaluation typically falls into two functional categories: *formative* and *summative* evaluation. **Formative evaluation**, also referred to as *process evaluation*, is used to determine the feasibility of the program's implementation and for monitoring the ongoing program. Examples of formative evaluations are a needs assessment and process evaluation. A **needs assessment** is used to determine the needs of the potential participants of the proposed program and the barriers and obstacles that may prevent persons from participating in the program. The results of the needs assessment can be used for program planning and development. Referring to the case example, let us say that the principal and the assistant principal decide to ask the teachers about some of the things affecting student learning and what they think can be done to address what they identified. By doing this, they would be conducting a needs assessment. **Process evaluation** is used to determine whether the program activities have been implemented as intended. Summative evaluation, also referred to as *outcome evaluation*, is used to evaluate the effectiveness of the program. Examples of summative evaluations are outcome evaluation, impact evaluation, cost-effectiveness evaluation, and cost-benefit analysis.

**Outcome evaluation** is used to determine if the program met its short-term goals. **Impact evaluation** is used to determine if the program met its long-term goals. **Cost-effectiveness evaluation** is used to compare two or more programs to determine the trade-offs between each program's cost and each program's outcome. **Cost-benefit analysis evaluation** is used to determine if the cost of the program outweighs the benefits of the program.

It is important for social workers to know how to conduct both formative and summative evaluations, as Competency 9 (*Evaluate Practice with Individuals, Families, Groups, Organizations, and Communities*) states that "social workers recognize the importance of evaluating processes and outcomes to advance practice, policy, and service delivery effectiveness" (CSWE, 2015, p. 9). There are several examples in the social work literature demonstrating how formative and summative evaluations are used to evaluate social service delivery. For example, Tandon, Parillo, Jenkins, and Duggan (2005) conducted a formative evaluation to determine the needs of low-income pregnant and parenting women for mental health, domestic violence, and substance abuse services. Additionally, they interviewed the home visitors working with these women about their perceptions about their training and ability to meet the identified needs of these women. An example of a summative evaluation is a study by Margolis et al. (2017). They examined how the Interprofessional Leadership Development Programme (ILDP) influenced parents' capacity to partner with health professionals and other parents.

## Program Logic Model

Development of a program evaluation begins with a researcher understanding the structure, processes, and procedures making up a program. According to Grinnell, Gabor, and Urau (2012), "program processes refer specifically to the activities and characteristics that describes how a program operates" (p. 144). A **program logic model** is a visual representation of the relationship between the program's core components. It represents a series of *"If–Then"* statements. If we have particular resources, and use them to delivery particular services, then particular outcomes for the program participants will be achieved. Moreover, the logic model also identifies contextual factors associated with the development and operation of the program. These contextual factors include the conditions of the current social problem or issues that the program is addressing, such as the need to promote the academic development of youth who attend public schools in the community. A program logic model can also be used to depict the elements of an intervention or program needed for its implementation. The program logic model also identifies the inputs, outputs, and expected outcomes associated with the program. Figure 16.1 depicts the program logic model for a mentoring program. The inputs, outputs, and outcomes may be similar to the mentoring program proposed in the case example.

Figure 16.1 Building the Future Mentor Program

Program: Building the Future Mentor Program

Situation: Early adolescent urban, minority boys living in low-income households and communities

Presence of environmental toxins (social, economic, and physical), health risk behaviors, diet/nutrition, academic failure)

| Inputs | Outputs | | Outcomes/Impacts | | |
|---|---|---|---|---|---|
| | Activities | Participation | Short | Medium | Long |
| FINANCIAL<br>Grant Funds<br><br>PERSONNEL<br>20 Mentors<br>Research Consultant<br>Secretarial Support<br><br>MATERIALS<br>Mentor training materials<br><br>FACILITIES<br>Office Space for workshops and training sessions | SUPPORT<br>Mentor screening<br>Mentor training<br>Mentee/parent orientation<br>Mentor supervision<br><br>DIRECT SERVICES<br>Bimonthly workshop series for mentors/youth: Focused on relationship and team building, promoting life skills, enhancing social problem-solving skills<br>One-to-one interactions between mentors and youth<br>Group sessions<br><br>EVALUATION<br>Outcome data collection: Student grades and attendance | DOSAGE<br>Mentors' workshop participation (5 during the academic school year)<br>Mentor selection/ orientation meeting (2 per year)<br>Boys ages 7–14 (age at entry into the program)<br>Mentee/parent selection/ orientation<br>Bimonthly meeting between mentor and mentees<br>Group meetings (3 times during the academic school year) | ↑ Knowledge of problem-solving skills<br>↑ Awareness of school-related strengths and areas for improvement<br>↑ Connect to mentor<br>↑ Development of academic and personal goals<br>↑ Identification of strategies to address personal goals | ↑ Self-efficacy<br>↑ Self-management skills<br>↑ Self-awareness<br>↑ Social competency<br>↑ Academic engagement | ↑ Academic performance<br>↑ Academic progress<br>↑ Graduation rate |

*Inputs.* The program's inputs are the material and human resources critical for the implementation of the program. For the mentoring program, the inputs include the grant funds, mentors, research consultants, and the office space.

*Outputs.* Outputs focus on the *activities* and *participation* of program participants that represent the implementation of the program with fidelity. Activities represent the essential deliverables of the program—for example, the specific activities of the mentors with their mentees. Additionally, the activities of program staff to provide training to mentors, parents, and mentees are also considered as outputs. Outputs also identify the nature and level of a program participant's participation, or *dosage*, that is needed to achieve the program outcomes. For example, the developers of the mentoring program have designed the program with the expectation that bimonthly meetings between the mentor and mentee are needed for the program outcomes to be achieved.

*Outcomes.* Outcomes represent the change in program participants that are expected to occur because of participation in the program. Outcomes can be characterized as short, medium, or long term. Like other aspects of the logic model, the outcomes are aligned in a causal, *"If–then"* fashion. For example, *if* youth improve their problem-solving skills, *then* their self-efficacy will improve. Improvements in self-efficacy will lead to improved academic performance. It is typical to think about short-term outcomes as those changes that can be achieved within short periods of time—for example, skill and knowledge development. Medium-term outcomes are those changes that follow short-term outcomes—for example, development of problem-solving skills is expected to lead to changes in how the youth manages conflict with peers. The long-term outcomes represent the ultimate goals of the program. Long term outcomes for social service programs typically focus on alleviating a social problem. The mentoring program ultimate outcomes would be to improve the high school completion rates of youth who attend schools in the community. It not uncommon for long-term outcomes to be identified as things the students will achieve after their participation in the program has been completed. For example, the mentoring program might have as a long-term outcome to increase college completion.

## Types of Program Evaluations

In this chapter, you will learn about effectiveness, efficacy, and formative and summative evaluations. Ethical and diversity issues are also discussed.

### Formative Evaluation

Formative or process evaluation is used to document the implementation of a program. It provides information about how various stakeholders experience the program, focusing on the *input* and *output* parts of the logic model and information needed to assess program fidelity and support ongoing program improvement. Conducting a formative evaluation is important because it allows you to determine if the program you are proposing is really needed and if there are barriers and facilitators of the program's implementation. A key to formative evaluation is that the stakeholders are involved in each phase of the process. **Stakeholders** are those persons who are involved in the decision-making process and they may include clients, and community, board and family members, and others.

<table>
<tr><td>**Application Checkpoint 16.1**</td></tr>
</table>

Thinking about the case example, who would be the stakeholders?

Formative evaluation is a three-step process. It is conducted prior to program implementation, during program implementation, and after program implementation. Formative evaluation is conducted prior to program implementation to determine if there is a need for the proposed program. During the program implementation, formative evaluation is conducted to determine if modifications are needed to be done to the program. After the program has been implemented, formative evaluation is conducted, for example, to determine if the participants were satisfied with the program. Table 16.1 presents examples of questions that can be asked at each phase of the formative evaluation process.

**Table 16.1  Examples of Formative Evaluation Questions**

| Questions | When the Question Should Be Asked |
|---|---|
| Is the program being implemented as planned? | During the program implementation |
| What are the barriers to and facilitators of successful program implementation? | After the program has been implemented |
| Is it feasible to implement the program with the intended population? | Before the program is implemented |
| What modifications need to be made to the evidence-based intervention before it can be implemented with the intended population? | Before the program is implemented |
| Is the program being implemented the same way across sites? | During the program implementation |
| How satisfied are the participants with the intervention? | After the program has been implemented |

Formative evaluation can be used to determine the barriers and facilitators of the program's implementation. When combined with outcome (summative evaluation), formative evaluation can be used to determine under what conditions and for whom a program works and how it needs to be adjusted. Formative evaluation focuses on monitoring the program's operations, understanding service delivery, fine-tuning what works, and identifying strengthens and weaknesses of the program.

Grinnell et al. (2012) outlined six steps for formative evaluation: (1) deciding on which questions to ask, (2) developing the data collection instruments, (3) developing a data collection monitoring system, (4) analyzing data, (5) developing a feedback system, and (6) communicating and disseminating results. Stakeholders should be involved at each of these steps.

1. *Deciding on which questions to ask.* During this step, it is important that the stakeholders be involved in determining what questions should be asked. Examples of questions to be asked are: "Who has the agency served?," "What types of services have been provided?," and "What is the staffing?"

2. *Developing the data collection instruments.* During this step, you are deciding what data needs to be collected. Some types of data you may want to collect are operational data, day-to-day administrative data, and enrollment data by service type. You also need to think about developing surveys to collect the data, if none exists.

3. *Developing a data collection monitoring system.* During this step, you need to think about a plan to collect the data.

4. *Analyzing the data.* During this step, you analyze the data, reflect on the findings, and draft the evaluation report. The stakeholders should be involved in reviewing the drafts of the evaluation report.

5. *Developing a feedback system.* You need to examine the results to see how they can be used to inform decisions and make changes to the program.

6. *Communicating and disseminating results.* Once the final report has been completed, its content should be discussed with the stakeholders. There must be an agreement between the stakeholders and the evaluator about further dissemination of the report.

### Critical Thinking Question 16.1

Thinking about the case example, using Steps 1–3, write up your plans for conducting a formative evaluation.

## Summative Evaluation

**Summative evaluation**, also referred to as *outcome evaluation*, is used to evaluate the effectiveness of a program. Summative evaluation is normally conducted after the program has been implemented. As mentioned earlier, there are four types of summative evaluations—outcome evaluation, impact evaluation, cost-effectiveness evaluation, and cost-benefit analysis. Table 16.2 presents examples of questions that can be asked when conducting a summative evaluation.

| Table 16.2 Examples of Summative Evaluation Questions |
| --- |
| How effective was the program? |
| Does the benefit of the program outweigh the cost of the program? |
| Were the overall goals of the program met? |
| Did some individuals respond better to the program than others? |

Summative evaluations are used to determine if the program met its short-term goals. The purpose of an outcome evaluation is to measure outcomes, assess changes over time, and generate knowledge.

Grinnell et al. (2012) outlined six steps for outcome evaluation: (1) specify the program objectives, (2) measure program objectives, (3) develop a data collection monitoring system, (4) analyze the data, (5) develop a feedback system, and (6) communicate and disseminate results. Stakeholders need to be involved at each of the above-identified steps.

1. *Specify the program objectives.* During this step, you need to conceptualize the program objectives. You need to be sure that you understand the program goals and objectives. You also need to think about how to measure change as it relates to the program objectives. Change is measured over time. For example, if you are assessing self-esteem, you would want to know if the program resulted in a change in the individual's self-esteem over the last two weeks.

2. *Measure program objectives.* During this step, you operationalize the variables and the objectives of the evaluations.

3. *Develop a data collection monitoring system.* During this step, you need to think about a plan to collect the data.

4. *Analyze the data.* During this step, you analyze the data, reflect on the findings, and draft the evaluation report. The stakeholders should be involved in reviewing the drafts of the evaluation report.

5. *Develop a feedback system.* You need to examine the results to see how they can be used to inform decisions and make changes to the program.

6. *Communicate and disseminate results.* Once the final report has been completed, the contents should be discussed with the stakeholders. There must be an agreement between the stakeholders and the evaluator about further dissemination of the report. The results can be used to make program modifications and for seeking additional funding for the program.

## Example of a Study Using Summative Evaluation

Margolis et al. (2017) conducted a summative evaluation to answer the following research questions: "(1) what influences did the Interprofessional Leadership Development Programme (ILDP) participation by parents have on their perceived capacity to partner both with health professionals and other parents?; and (2) what factors of the ILDP training facilitated the development of these vital partnership skills" (p. 498).

A qualitative evaluation was conducted. Semi-structured interviews were conducted with 17 of the 23 parents who participated in the ILDP. The data derived from the interviews were transcribed and then coded. The data were analyzed using a content analysis.

*Categories of Summative Evaluation.* There are two categories of summative evaluations—efficacy and efficiency. Efficacy summative evaluation is used to evaluate the effects of an intervention that was used in a random clinical trial (RCT). In an RCT, persons are randomly assigned to a treatment condition (i.e., the treatment under investigation) or a control condition, which usually is the standard form of treatment. RCT is a type of experimental research design. Efficacy summative evaluation is used to provide evidence of the impact of a program delivered in controlled settings. Efficacy summative evaluation studies maximize the effect size of the program by recruiting homogeneous, highly motivated samples. The implementation of the program is closely monitored by research staff, and the generalizability of the findings to real-practice settings is limited. Effectiveness summative evaluation is used to evaluate the effects of an intervention that was used in a quasi-experimental study. In a quasi-experimental design, persons are not randomly assigned to a treatment condition (i.e., the treatment under investigation) or control condition or there is no control group. Effectiveness summary evaluation is used to provide evidence of the impact of a program delivered in real-practice settings. The sample in effectiveness summary evaluation is heterogeneous.

## Critical Thinking Question 16.2

Thinking about the case example, using Steps 1–3, write up your plans for conducting a summative evaluation.

# Structure of an Evaluation Report

A final evaluation report is a written document that describes how you monitored and evaluated the program. It allows you to describe the *What*, *How*, and *Why it matters* for the program and demonstrates how the results can be used to improve the program and for decision-making purposes. The content that should be included in an evaluation report is presented in Table 16.3.

| Table 16.3  Structure of an Evaluation Report |
| --- |

1. Executive Summary

    A.  3- to 5-page brief overview of the evaluation purpose, project background, evaluation questions, methods, findings, and conclusions

2. Introduction

    A.  Description of the problems; its context and significance

    B.  Program description and questions addressed

    C.  Purpose of the evaluation

3. Literature Review

    A.  Theoretical/historical foundation of the program

    B.  A survey of relevant literature

4. Methodology

    A.  Evaluation design and data collection procedures clearly stated

    B.  Description of sampling plan, participants, and recruitment methods

    C.  Dependent variables operationalized; description of instruments

    D.  Procedures for data collection and data analysis

5. Results (Findings)

    A.  Factual information presented (including tables, charts)

    B.  Statistical and clinical or practical significance

6. Discussion

    A.  Explanation of findings

    B.  Application to agency, program, or practice

    C.  Limitations of the evaluation

# Ethics and Program Evaluation

Ethical issues associated with program evaluation are not fundamentally different than those associated with quantitative, qualitative, and mixed-methods approaches (Competency 1, *Demonstrate Ethical and Professional Behavior*). Please re-read Chapters 6, 7, and 9 to re-familiarize yourselves with these ethical issues. Moreover, you need to familiarize yourself with the NASW *Code of Ethics* (2017) standards for evaluation and research. These standards indicate that social workers engaged in evaluation or research should obtain informed consent from participants (Standard 5.02(e)), inform participants that they have the right to withdraw from the evaluation at any time (Standard 5.02 (i)), ensure anonymity and confidentiality (Standard 5.02 (m)), and report results accurately (Standard 5.02 (o)).

# Diversity and Program Evaluation

In 2011 the American Evaluation Association (AEA) released its *Public Statement on Cultural Competence in Evaluation*, stating the importance of considering culture across all phases of the evaluation process. According to the AEA (2011), a culturally competent evaluator is defined as one who is "prepared to engage with diverse segments of communities to include cultural and contextual dimensions important to the evaluation . . . and respects the culture represented in the evaluation throughout the process" (p. 1). This definition is consistent with the Competency 4, *Engage Diversity and Difference in Practice*. Additionally, the AEA identified the essential practices of culturally competent evaluators. They are as follows: acknowledge the complexity of culture (i.e., there is diversity within diversity, persons belong to more than one group, intersectionality), recognize the dynamics of power (i.e., be aware of marginalization, persons from marginalized groups need to be included as stakeholders), recognize and eliminate bias in language (i.e., use cultural-specific language in material that is disseminated), and employ culturally appropriate methods of evaluation (i.e., choose measures that have been vetted to be used with the population under investigation).

Competency 9, *Evaluate Practice With Individuals, Families, Groups, Organizations, and Communities*, states that "social workers understand that evaluation is an ongoing component of the dynamic and interactive process of social work practice with, and on behalf of, diverse individuals, families, groups, organizations, and communities" (CSWE, 2015, p. 9). Given the above, it is important that social workers are aware of evaluation strategies that can be used in evaluating programs for persons from diverse groups. **Culturally responsive evaluation** (CRE) has been identified as one approach that lets researchers take culture/diversity into consideration when they are doing their evaluation. CRE is an evaluation approach that stresses the importance of taking into consideration the historical, social, cultural, political, and economic contexts (Thomas & Parsons, 2017). CRE is a strengths-based approach to evaluation. Evaluators using this approach recognize the cultural strengths the individuals and communities in which they reside bring to the evaluand. They seek to promote social justice through the evaluation process. This is done, for example, by documenting who is not being served by the program and the barriers to their participation. Moreover, evaluators using CRE use a holistic way of thinking about evaluation—that is, they take into consideration how institutions, religion, and policies have an influence on the community in which the research is being conducted (Thomas & Parsons, 2017).

Another evaluation approach that takes into culture into consideration is the **culturally responsive indigenous evaluation** (CRIE). CRIE was developed by Nicole Bowman in 2005 and is based on the Stockbridge-Munsee/Lunaape's medicine wheel. Evaluation focuses on process, content, context, and community (Waapalaneexkweew [Bowman-Farell, Mohican/Lunaape], 2018). CRIE "uses traditional knowledge and contemporary Indigenous theory and methods to design and implement an evaluation study, so it is led by and for the benefit of Indigenous people and Tribal nations" (Waapalaneexkweew [Bowman, Mohican/Lunaape] & Dodge-Francis, 2018, p. 22).

# SUMMARY, REVIEW, AND ASSIGNMENTS

## CHAPTER SUMMARY ORGANIZED BY LEARNING OBJECTIVES

**LO 16.1** Define program evaluation.

*Program evaluation* refers to "the systematic scientific and rigorous evaluation of a program's effectiveness" (Shek et al., 2018, p. 1311).

**LO 16.2** Describe the components that are included in a logic model.

A *logic model* is a visual representation of the relationship between the program's inputs, activities, outputs, and identified outcomes.

**LO 16.3** Differentiate between the various types of program evaluations.

*Efficacy summative evaluation* is used to evaluate the effects of an intervention that was used in a random clinical trial (RCT).

*Effectiveness summative evaluation* is used to evaluate the effects of an intervention that was used in a quasi-experimental study.

*Formative evaluation*, also referred to as *process evaluation*, is used to determine the feasibility of the program's implementation and for monitoring the ongoing program.

*Summative evaluation*, also referred to as *outcome evaluation*, is used to evaluate the effectiveness of the program.

**LO 16.4**  Write an evaluation report.

A final evaluation report is a written document that describes how you monitored and evaluated the program.

**LO 16.5**  Identify the ethical and diversity issues associated with program evaluation.

Ethical issues associated with program evaluation are not fundamentally different than those associated with quantitative, qualitative, and mixed-methods approaches.

Persons who evaluate programs for diverse groups must be aware that they need to employ culturally appropriate methods of evaluation to ensure that programs are effective for the targeted populations.

# KEY TERMS

Program evaluation   371
Efficacy evaluations   371
Effectiveness evaluations   371
Formative evaluation   371
Needs assessment   371
Process evaluation   371
Outcome evaluation   372
Impact evaluation   372

Cost-effectiveness
   evaluation   372
Cost-benefit analysis
   evaluation   372
Program logic model   372
Stakeholders   375
Summative
   evaluation   377

Culturally responsive
   evaluation   380
Culturally responsive
   indigenous evaluation   381

# COMPETENCY NOTES

In this chapter, you were introduced to the competencies below:

Competency 1, *Demonstrate Ethical and Professional Behavior.* Social workers engaged in evaluation or research should obtain informed consent from participants (Standard 5.02(e)), inform participants that they have the right to withdraw from the evaluation at any time (Standard 5.02 (i)), ensure anonymity and confidentiality (Standard 5.02 (m)), and report results accurately (Standard 5.02 (o)).

Competency 2, *Engage Diversity and Difference in Practice.* Social workers

conducting evaluations must acknowledge the complexity of culture, recognize the dynamics of power, recognize and eliminate bias in language, and employ culturally appropriate methods of evaluation.

Competency 9, *Evaluate Practice With Individuals, Families, Groups, Organizations, and Communities.* Social workers need to know how to conduct both formative and summative evaluation. Social workers need to be aware of evaluation strategies that take into consideration culture/diversity.

## ASSESSMENT QUESTIONS

1. How did the information in this chapter enhance your knowledge about program evaluation?

2. How did the information in this chapter enhance your knowledge about when one should conduct a formative evaluation as opposed to a summative evaluation?

3. What specific content discussed in this chapter is still unclear to you? If there is still content that is unclear, schedule an appointment with your instructor to gain more clarity.

## END-OF-CHAPTER EXERCISES

1. Develop a logic model for the agency in which you are doing your field placement.

2. Write a 250-word executive summary and share it with one of your classmates. Ask the person to provide you with feedback on what you have written.

3. Find a program evaluation study published in a peer-reviewed journal. Based on the information presented in this chapter, write an evaluation report for the study you found.

4. Speak with your field instructor about the programs run by the agency. Are there any that could be evaluated using formative or summative evaluation? If so, propose two questions that can be used for the evaluation.

## ADDITIONAL READINGS

Community Toolbox. (2011). *Section 1. Developing a logic model or theory of change.* Retrieved from http://ctb.ku.edu/en/tablecontents/sub_section_examples_1877.aspx

Frierson, H. T., Hood, S., Hughes, G. B., & Thomas, V. G. (2010). A guide to conducting culturally responsive evaluations. In J. Frechtling (Ed.), *The 2010 user-friendly handbook for project evaluation* (pp. 75–96). Arlington, VA: National Science Foundation.

Julian, D. A., Smith, II, T., & Hunt, R. A. (2017). Ethical challenges inherent in the evaluation of an American Indian/Alaskan Native Circles of Care Project. *American Journal of Community Psychology, 60*(3–4), 336–345. doi:10.1002/ajcp.12192

Martin, J. I., & Meezan, W. (2003). Applying ethical standards to research and evaluations involving lesbian, gay, bisexual, and transgender populations. *Journal of Gay and Lesbian Social Services, 15*(1–2), 181–201. doi:10.1300/J041v15n01_12

Samuels, M., & Ryan, K. (2011). Grounding evaluations in culture. *American Journal of Evaluation, 32*(2), 183–198. doi:10.117/71098214010387657

W. K. Kellogg Foundation. (2004). *Logic model development guide.* Retrieved from https://www.wkkf.org/resource-directory/resource/2006/02/wk-kellogg-foundation-logic-modeldevelopment-guide

# Appendix

Guidelines for Writing a Research Proposal

## Research Proposal Guide

When writing a research proposal, it is preferable that you cite your references and in-text citations in the format prescribed in the *Publication Manual of the American Psychological Association* ([APA] 2020, 7th edition). Your research proposal will consist of the following: (1) title page, (2) an abstract, (3) introduction to the topic, (4) literature review, (5) method section, (6) limitations, (7) anticipated implications, and (8) references. Your research proposal should be double-spaced, with 1-inch margins on all sides and left justified margins, and it will include what is outlined above regardless if you are writing a research proposal for a quantitative or qualitative study.

## Structure of the Research Proposal

### Title Page

The title page consists of the title of the research proposal, author's name and affiliation, and the running head. The title of your research proposal gives the reader insight into what your paper is about. The title may include the names of the independent and the dependent variable that will be examined in the proposed study, the name of the population that will be sampled, the purpose of the study (i.e., descriptive, explanatory, exploratory), or the name of the theory or the conceptual framework that will guide your study. It is generally recommended that the title be no more than 12 words. There should not be any abbreviations used in the title. The title is centered, using both capital and lowercase letters, and can be up to two lines in length. An example of a title that contains both the independent variable and dependent is as follows: "The Relationship Between Community Violence and Self-Esteem." In this title, the independent variable is community violence and the dependent variable is self-esteem. A title with the name of the population mentioned is "The Relationship Between Community Violence and Self-Esteem among Asian American Adolescents." In reading this title, it is quite clear that the population under investigation was Asian American adolescents. The following is an example of a title that lets the reader know the purpose of the study: "A Descriptive Study of Opioid Use Among Older Adults." As the title suggests, the purpose of the study is to describe the opioid use among older adults. An example of a title that mentions the name of a theory is as follows: "An Application of Social Systems Theory in Examining the Relationship in Families." In reading the title, it is quite clear that social systems theory is being used to look at the construct of interest; however, it is not clear what population was sampled. Therefore, one would need to read the abstract to determine this.

It should be noted that if you are proposing to conduct a qualitative study, the title of the research proposal may indicate that it will be a qualitative study or specify the type of qualitative approach that will be used. For example, a title specifying the qualitative approach used would be as follows: "An Ethnographic Study of Workplace Interactions."

*Running head.* Each page of your research proposal should include a running head, which is a brief title. For example, the running head for the research proposal titled "A Descriptive Study of Opioid Use Among Older Adults" would be as follows: "Opioid Use and Older Adults." The running head should be in all caps, flushed left at the top of the title page. Therefore, the running head indicated above would be as follows:

Running head: OPIOID USE AND OLDER ADULTS

Throughout the rest of the paper the running head should be right-justified with paper number.

Opioid Use and Older Adults 2

*Author's Name and Affiliation.* You need to include your name (first name, middle initial(s), and last name) and affiliation, and the location where the author conducted the study, on the title page. For the purpose of your research proposal, your affiliation will be the university where you are obtaining your degree.

## Abstract

The second page of your research proposal will consist of an abstract. The word *abstract* should not be in bold, italicized, or enclosed within quotation marks. The abstract is a comprehensive summary of your research proposal and should be no more than 250 words in length. It will be written in future tense, as you have not yet conducted your study. The word *abstract* is centered on the page. The abstract is only one paragraph, formatted in block style (i.e., without paragraph indentation), and double-spaced. The first sentence of the abstract tells the reader the purpose of the study. The abstract should also include the number of persons who will be asked to participant in the study, along with their demographics; a statement about what they will be  asked to do; a statement about the type of analysis that will be performed; a statement about anticipated implications for practice, policy, and research; and a recommendation for future research. The abstract should be followed by keywords. These keywords are used in the electronic databases so that researchers looking for a particular topic can find the study. It is recommended that no more than five keywords be used. The word *keywords* is italicized. The abstract for the proposed study titled "A Descriptive Study of Opioid Use Among Older Adults" is shown in the box below.

## Abstract

The purpose of this study is to describe the prevalence and patterns of opioid use among adults age 50 and older. A total of 200 older adults will be surveyed about their opioid use via a self-administered questionnaire. Descriptive statistics (i.e., means along with their associated standard deviations, and percentages) will be used to analyze the data, along with independent-sample *t*-test analyses to assess for differences in prevalence rates between men and women and Whites and Non-Whites as it relates to their opioid use. Implications for developing interventions for older adults who use opioids will be discussed. Future research is warranted to determine why older adults engage in opioid use.

*Keywords*: Opioid Use, Older Adults, Substance Use, Prevalence Rates, Patterns of Opioid Use

## Introduction

Page three begins with the introduction of your study. There is no need to include the word *introduction* on this page. The introduction should include the following:

Problem statement: This describes the magnitude of the problem, who is affected by the problem, and the consequences of the problem. The terms used to describe the problem should be defined. Discuss the theories or conceptual frameworks used to explain the development of the problem.

Rationale for the study: You need to clearly articulate to the reader why you are conducting this study. For example, your rationale could be that your proposed study is filling a gap in the literature or you are testing a new intervention with a particular population, as interventions in the past have not been effective. Your rationale must justify why future research is needed on your topic.

Significance of the study: This is a description of why your study is important to be conducted. To determine the significance of your study you need to ask yourself, "By conducting this study, how will I be contributing to the existing literature?" and "What new insights about the phenomenon will emerge from my study?"

Purpose of the study: A description of the purpose of the study. In stating the purpose of your study, you need to state your research questions and or hypotheses.

## Literature Review

The literature review could be part of the introduction or a new section of the paper labeled "Literature Review." The literature review is written in past tense, as you are referring to studies that have already been conducted. The literature review provides the reader with insights about what previously has been done on the topic and should be a synthesis and not a detailed description of each study you read. Your literature review should be organized in a coherent manner. We suggest you organize your literature review by using subheadings. Definition of terms can also be included in the literature review, if you have not discussed them in the introduction. If your literature review is a separate section, we recommend that you include the rationale for your study, significance of your study, and the purpose of your study at the conclusion of your literature review.

## Method

The word *method* is centered on the page. The method section includes the following subheadings: (1) Sample and Procedures, (2) Statement About Getting IRB Approval, (3) Measures, and (4) Data Analysis Strategies.

*Sample and Procedures.* Information in this section is written in future tense. In regard to the sample, you need to provide information on the demographic characteristics of the sample, such as age, race/ethnicity, sexual orientation, income, social economic status, and so on. It is important that you provide as much information as possible about your sample, as this information can be used to compare results of your study with studies where the sample may have differed. You need to identify your inclusion and exclusion criteria. In other words, why did you select the individuals to participate in your study and why did you not select others to participate? You need to specify your sample size and justify choice of sample size.

If you are proposing a qualitative study, you need to identify how you plan to select your participants and in which setting will the study be conducted.

If you are proposing a mixed-method study, you need to identify what sampling strategy will be used for the quantitative and qualitative aspects of your study. Justify your sampling strategy choice.

In addition to describing the sample, you need to indicate what type of research design (i.e., experimental, non-experimental, or observational) will be used to answer the research question. You need to identify if you are conducting a cross-sectional or longitudinal study. You need to state the purpose (i.e., descriptive, explanatory, exploratory, or evaluative) of your study. You need to present a rationale for all of the above.

If you are proposing a qualitative research study, you should identify if you plan to conduct a case study, ethnographic research, grounded theory, or phenomenological research. You need to provide a rationale for your choice of qualitative approach.

If you are proposing a mixed-methods research study, you should identify what strategy you will be using—sequential explanatory mixed-method, sequential exploratory mixed-method, sequential transformative mixed-method, concurrent triangulation mixed-method, concurrent nested mixed-method, or concurrent transformative mixed-method. You need to provide a rationale for your choice of strategy for conducting a mixed-methods research study.

You need to provide a detailed description of the procedures you will use in your study so it is possible for someone to replicate what you plan to do. Describe how the data will be collected. For example, will the data be collected by surveys and indicate the type (self-administered, online, mailed, telephone) or will interviews or focus groups be conducted? Describe how informed consent and assent will be obtained and how the participants will be recruited. You need to indicate if the participants will be compensated for their participation and how much they will be compensated. You need to provide a detailed description of what the participants will be asked to do. You need to identify what type of sampling strategy will be used and provide justification for your choice of sampling strategy.

If you are proposing a qualitative study, you need to identify if you are going to be an observer, an observer as participant, a participant-observer, or full participant. You need to identify if you plan to conduct interviews, record the interviews, or review documents. You need to specify if the data will be transcribed and whom will be transcribing the data. You need to note the proposed period in which you plan to collect the data.

If you plan to conduct a mixed-methods research study, you should specify the procedures for both the quantitative and qualitative aspects of the study.

*Statement About Getting IRB Approval.* This statement should be as follows: "Prior to conducting this study, the researcher will be submitting the protocol to the university's IRB for their approval of this proposed study. The study will not commence until approval has been granted."

*Measures.* Describe the measures that will be used to assess each variable of interest. Identify who developed these measures, how the reliability and validity were assessed, how the measures were scored, what does a high score mean, number of items on each measure, and the number of subscales and their items, if applicable.

In a qualitative study, you are the data collection instrument, so think about your perceptions and values on the topic. Identify how you plan to establish the trustworthiness of the data—that is, indicate the strategies that will be used to establish authenticity, confirmability, creditability, dependability, and transferability.

If you plan to conduct a mixed-methods research study, you should specify the procedures for both the quantitative and qualitative aspects of the study. The method section for the proposed study titled "Descriptive Study of Opioid Use Among Older Adults" is shown in the box that follows.

## "A Descriptive Study of Opioid Use Among Older Adults"
### Method

**Method.** A descriptive, cross-sectional study will be conducted to describe the use of opioids among adults ages 50 and above. Prior to conducting this study, the researcher will be submitting the protocol to the university's IRB for their approval of this proposed study. This study will not commence until IRB approval has been granted.

**Sample.** The sample will be selected through random-digit dialing among older adults who own landline or cellular telephones, and the participants will be read the survey questions by a trained interviewer. This particular sampling strategy was chosen over other strategies because it is the least expensive.

The proposed sample is 200, which will consist of both men and women age 50 and above. This sample size was chosen based on conducting a power analysis, indicating that this sample size is significant to detect a statistically significant relationship between the variables of interest, using an alpha of .05, and a power of .08. The person who answers the phone will be asked their age and if they have used opioids within the last 30 days or within the last 12 months to determine if they are eligible to participate in the study. If they are eligible, the interviewer will ask them all of the questions on the survey. All participants will receive a $15 gift certificate, which will be mailed to their home. Demographic information will also be collected during the interview. If persons are not eligible to participate in the study, the interviewer will thank the person for his or her time.

**Measure.** The survey that will be used in this study was developed by the researcher and her research team. There is no known reliability for this measure. The measure does have face validity, which is the weakest type of validity.

*Data Analysis Strategies.* In this section, you are proposing the types of analysis you plan to use to analyze the data you plan to collect. You need to provide a rationale for every data analysis strategy you plan to use. If the data need to be coded or recoded, you need to note how this will be done.

If you are proposing a qualitative study, you need to indicate if you plan to use content analysis, critical discourse analysis, thematic analysis, or grounded theory to analyze the data. You should indicate how you plan to establish the trustworthiness of the data—that is, indicate the strategies that will be used to establish authenticity, confirmability, creditability, dependability, and transferability.

If you are proposing a mixed-methods research study, you should specify the procedures for both the quantitative and qualitative aspects of the study. The data analysis section for the proposed study titled "Descriptive Study of Opioid Use Among Older Adults" is shown in the box below.

## "A Descriptive Study of Opioid Use Among Older Adults": Data Analysis

Descriptive statistical analyses will be conducted. Means and their associated standard deviations will be reported for age and the number of times persons used opioids within the last 30 days and within the last 12 months. Percentages will be computed to indicate the percentage of males and females, persons from various ethnic/racial groups, and persons who use various types of opioids. An independent-sample *t*-test will be conducted to determine if there are differences between men and women as it relates to their opioid use, because the independent variable gender (men, women) will measured on a nominal level and the dependent variable (number of times they used opioids within the last 30 days and within the last 12 months will be measured on a ratio level). There will be separate analyses conducted for the last 30 days' and last 12 months' opioid use. In looking to determine if there are differences between Whites and Non-Whites as it relates to their opioid use, an independent-sample *t*-test will be conducted because the independent variable racial/ethnic background (White, Non-White) will be measured on a nominal level and the number of times they used opioids within the last 30 day and within the last 12 months will be measured on a ratio level. There will be separate analyses conducted for last 30 days' and 12 months' opioid use.

## Limitations

Note the limitations of your proposed study. If you are conducting a pre-experimental, experimental, or quasi-experimental research study, you need to identify the threats to internal and external validity. If there was no known reliability or validity for your measures, you need to indicate how this could have affected the data you collected. If the measures you selected were not previously used with the sample you plan to use in your study, you need to note how this may affect your data. Identify any limitations related to your sampling strategy. The box below contains an example from the limitation section of the opioid use study.

## "A Descriptive Study of Opioid Use Among Older Adults": Limitation

Several limitations of this proposed study need to be noted. Participants will be asked to report on their opioid use within the last 30 days and the past year. Because the participants may need

*(Continued)*

(Continued)

to recall this information, they may underreport or overreport their opioid use. Another factor that may contribute to underreporting is the way in which the survey will be administered. The participants will be read the survey over the phone by a trained interviewer. Because someone the respondents do not know is asking them about their opioid use, this may affect the truthfulness of information obtained. The survey was developed by the researcher and her research team. Therefore, the reliability of the measure is unknown. The measure only has face validity, which is the weakest type of validity. Still another limitation of this proposed study is that the anticipated findings cannot be generalized beyond those included in the sample, because a nationally representative sample will not be obtained.

## Anticipated Implications

You need to indicate the anticipated implications you can think of for social work practice, social work education/training of social workers, social policy, and research. The anticipated implications for the proposed study titled "Descriptive of Opioid Use Among Older Adults" are shown in the box below.

## "A Descriptive Study of Opioid Use Among Older Adults": Anticipated Implications

If it is found that persons tend to misuse opioids because they do not know about other pain management methods, then perhaps a pain management training program is warranted. If there are not enough persons from diverse backgrounds to conduct the analysis assessing for differences between Whites and Non-Whites, it is recommended that researchers conduct another study on this topic using a diverse sample. This will allow them to conduct the above-mentioned analysis.

## Timeline

You should include a proposed timeline, indicating when you anticipate a task related to your proposed study to start and be completed. The tasks you should include in your timeline are the writing of the literature review, developing measures, writing up the protocol for IRB, getting IRB approval, identifying respondents or participants, collecting the data, and coding and analyzing data. If you plan to actually conduct your proposed study, you need to include writing up the analysis and writing and revising your manuscript for publication on your timeline.

# References

Your references are listed on a separate page. The word *reference* is centered on the page. Each in-text citation must appear in the reference list and must be in APA format.

Reference

American Psychological Association. (2020). *Publication manual of the American Psychological Association* (7th ed.). Washington, DC: Author.

# References

## Preface

Albanese, M. A., & Mitchell S. (1993). Problem-based learning: A review of literature on its outcomes and implementation issues. *Academic Medicine, 68*(1), 52–81.

Barrows, H. S. (1985). *How do design a problem-based curriculum for the preclinical years.* New York, NY: Springer.

Barrows, H. S. (1996). Problem-based learning in medicine and beyond: A brief review. In L. Wilkerson & W. H. Gijselaers (Eds.), *Bringing problem-based learning to higher education: Theory and practice* (pp. 3–12). San Francisco, CA: Jossey-Bass.

Council on Social Work Education (CSWE). (2015). *Educational policy and accreditation standards.* Retrieved from http://www.cswe.org/File.aspx?id=81660.

Granić, A., Mifsud, C., & Ćukušić, M. (2009). Design, implementation and validation of a Europe-wide pedagogical framework for e-Learning. *Computers & Education, 53*(4), 1052–1081.

Greene, M., & Kirpalani, N. (2013). Using interactive whiteboards in teaching retail mathematics. *Marketing Education Review, 23*(1), 49–54.

Hung, W., Jonassen, D. H., & Liu, R. (2008). Problem-based learning. In M. Spector, D. Merrill, J. van Merrienböer, & M. Driscoll (Eds.), *Handbook of research on educational communications and technology* (3rd ed., pp. 485–506). New York, NY: Erlbaum.

Karantzas, G. C., Avery, M. R., Macfarlane, S., Mussap, A., Tooley, G., Hazelwood, Z., et al. (2013). Enhancing critical analysis and problem-solving skills in undergraduate psychology: An evaluation of a collaborative learning and problem-based learning approach. *Australian Journal of Psychology, 65*(1), 38–45. doi:10.1111/ajpy.12009

Kwan, A. (2009). Problem-based learning. In M. Tight, K. Mok, J. Huisman, & C. Morphew (Eds.), *The Routledge international handbook of higher education* (pp. 91–108). New York, NY: Routledge, The Taylor Francis Group.

Leon, J. S., Winskell, K., McFarland, D. A., & del Rio, C. (2015). A case-based, problem-based learning approach to prepare master of public health candidates for the complexities of global health. *American Journal of Public Health, 105*(S1), S92–S96. doi:10.2105/AJPH.2014.302416

Pearson, V., Wong, D. K. P., Ho, K., & Wong, K. (2007). Problem-based learning in an MSW programme: A study of learning outcomes. *Social Work Education, 26*(6), 616–631. doi:10.1080/02615470701456533

Stinson, J. E., & Milter, R. G. (1996). Problem-based learning in business education: Curriculum design and implementation issues. In L. Wilkerson & W. H. Gijselaers (Eds.), *Bringing problem-based learning to higher education: Theory and practice* (pp. 33–42). San Francisco, CA: Jossey-Bass.

Westhues, A., Barsen, C., Freymond, N., & Train, P. (2014). An outcome evaluation of a problem-based learning approach with MSW students. *Journal of Social Work Education, 50*(3), 472–489. doi:10.1080/10437797.2014.917897

Wong, D. K. P., & Lam, D. O. B. (2007). Problem-based learning in social work: A study of student learning outcomes. *Research on Social Work Practice, 17*(1), 55–65. doi:10.1177/1049731506293364

## Chapter 1

Akbaraly, T. N., Portet, F., Fustinoni, S., Dartigues, J.-F., Artero, S., Rouaud, O., . . . Berr, C. (2009). Leisure activities and the risk of dementia in the elderly: Results from the Three-City Study. *Neurology, 73*(11), 854–861.

Anderson, N. D., Damianakis, T., Kröger, E., Wagner, L. M., Dawson, D. R., Binns, M. A., . . . Cook, S. L. (2014). The benefits associated with volunteering among seniors: A critical review and recommendations for future research. *Psychological Bulletin, 140*(6), 1505–1533.

Bandura, A. (1986). *Social foundations of thought and action: A social cognitive theory.* Englewood Cliffs, NJ: Prentice Hall.

Bauminger, N., Shulman, C., & Agam, G. (2003). Peer interaction and loneliness in high-functioning children with autism. *Journal of Autism and Developmental Disorders, 33*(5), 489–507.

Bradt, L., Roose, R., Bouverne-De Bie, M., & De Schryver, M. (2011). Data recording and social work: From the relational to the social. *British Journal of Social Work, 41*(7), 1372–1382.

Burns, P. B., Rohrich, R. J., & Chung, K. C. (2011). The levels of evidence and their role in evidence-based medicine. *Plastic and Reconstructive Surgery, 128*(1), 305–310. doi:10.1097/PRS.0b013e318219c171

Cheung, S. O.-N. (2015). Pedagogical practice wisdom in social work practice teaching—A kaleidoscopic view. *Social Work Education, 34*(3), 258–274.

Chu, W. C. K., & Tsui, M.-S. (2008). The nature of practice wisdom in social work revisited. *International Social Work, 51*(1), 47–54.

Cline, R. J. W., & Haynes, K. M. (2001). Consumer health information seeking on the Internet: The state of the art. *Health Education Research, 16*(6), 671–692. doi:10.1093/her/16.6.671

Council on Social Work Education (CSWE). (2015). *2015 educational policy and accreditation standards for baccalaureate and master's social work programs*. Washington, DC: Council on Social Work Education.

Del Valle, R., Leahy, M. J., Sherman, S., Anderson, C. A., Tansey, T., & Schoen, B. (2014). Promising best practices that lead to employment in vocational rehabilitation: Findings from a four-state multiple case study. *Journal of Vocational Rehabilitation, 41*(2), 99–113. doi:10.3233/JVR-140708

Epstein, I. (2011). Reconciling evidence-based practice, evidence-informed practice, and practice-based research: The role of clinical data-mining. *Social Work, 56*(3), 284–288. doi:10.1093/sw/56.3.284

Epstein, I. (2015). Building a bridge or digging a pipeline? Clinical data mining in evidence-informed knowledge building. *Research on Social Work Practice, 25*(4), 499–506. doi:10.1177/1049731514536475

Feldman, D. B., & Crandall, C. S. (2007). Dimensions of mental illness stigma: What about mental illness causes social rejection? *Journal of Social and Clinical Psychology, 26*(2), 137–154. doi:10.1521/jscp.2007.26.2.137

Festinger, L. (1957). *A theory of cognitive dissonance.* Stanford, CA: Stanford University Press.

Fisher, M. (2012). Beyond evidence-based policy and practice: Reshaping the relationship between research and practice. *Social Work & Social Sciences Review, 16*(2), 20–36. doi:10.1921/903160201

Gambrill, E. (1999). Evidence-based practice: An alternative to authority-based practice. *Families in Society: The Journal of Contemporary Social Services, 80*(4), 341–350. doi:10.1606/1044-3894.1214

Gambrill, E. (2012). Obscure different views of knowledge and how to get it. In E. Gambrill (Ed.), *Propaganda in the helping professions* (pp. 199–234). New York, NY: Oxford University Press.

Gibbs, L. (2005). *Evidence-based practice for the helping professions: A practical guide with integrated multimedia.* Pacific Grove, CA: Brooks/Cole-Thomson Learning.

Hudson, J. D. (1997). A model of professional knowledge for social work practice. *Australian Social Work, 50*(3), 35–44. https://doi.org/10.1080/03124079708414096

Jaccard, J., & Jacoby, J. (2012). *Theory construction and model-building skills.* New York, NY: Guilford.

Jamal, F., Bonell, C., Harden, A., & Lorenc, T. (2015). The social ecology of girls' bullying practices: Exploratory research in two London schools. *Sociology of Health & Illness, 37*(5), 731–744. doi:10.1111/1467-9566.12231

Kolb, D. A., & Fry, R. E. (1974). *Toward an applied theory of experiential learning.* Cambridge, MA: MIT Press, Alfred P. Sloan School of Management.

Larsson, M., Pettersson, C., Eriksson, C., & Skoog, T. (2016). Initial motives and organizational context enabling female mentors' engagement in formal mentoring: A qualitative study from the mentors' perspective. *Children and Youth Services Review, 71*, 17–26. doi:10.1016/j.childyouth.2016.10.026

Mazzola, V. J. (2016). Fostering student connections: The hidden gems in our schools. *Children & Schools, 38*(4), 245–250. doi:10.1093/cs/cdw030

Mendoza, N. S., Resko, S., Wohlert, B., & Baldwin, A. (2015). "We have to help each other heal": The path to recovery and becoming a professional peer support.

*Journal of Human Behavior in the Social Environment, 26*(2), 137–148. doi:10.1080/10911359.2015.1052912

Mitchell, A., Gottfried, J., Barthel, M., & Shearer, E. (2016). *The modern news consumer: News attitudes and practices in the digital era*. Pew Research Center. Retrieved from https://www.issuelab.org/resource/the-modern-news-consumer-news-attitudes-and-practices-in-the-digital-era.html

Mullen, E. J., Bellamy, J. L., & Bledsoe, S. E. (2008). Best practices. In T. Mizrahi & L. Davis (Eds.), *Encyclopedia of social work* (20th ed.). New York, NY: Oxford University Press.

Mullen, E. J., & Shuluk, J. (2011). Outcomes of social work intervention in the context of evidence-based practice. *Journal of Social Work, 11*(1), 49–63. doi:10.1177/1468017310381309

National Association of Social Workers (NASW). (2017). *Code of ethics*. Washington, DC: Author. Retrieved from https://www.socialworkers.org/About/Ethics/Code-of-Ethics

Oates, J., Drey, N., & Jones, J. (2017). 'Your experiences were your tools': How personal experience of mental health problems informs mental health nursing practice. *Journal of Psychiatric and Mental Health Nursing, 24*(7), 471–479. doi:10.1111/jpm.12376

Parsons, W. (2002). From muddling through to muddling up: Evidence based policy making and the modernisation of British government. *Public Policy and Administration, 17*(3), 43–60. doi:10.1177/095207670201700304

Petr, C. G., & Walter, U. M. (2005). Best practices inquiry: A multidimensional, value-critical framework. *Journal of Social Work Education, 41*(2), 251–267. doi:10.5175/JSWE.2005.200303109

Plath, D., & Gibbons, J. (2010). Discoveries on a data-mining expedition: Single session social work in hospitals. *Social Work in Health Care, 49*(8), 703–717. doi:10.1080/00981380903520525

Porter, R. (1997). *The greatest benefit to mankind: A medical history of humanity*. New York, NY: W. W. Horton.

Pronin, E. (2007). Perception and misperceptions of bias in human judgment. *Trends in Cognitive Sciences, 11*(1), 34–43. https://doi.org/10.1016/j.tics.2006.11.001

Sanger, L. (2010). Individual knowledge in the Internet age. *EDUCASE Review, 42*(2), 14–24. Retrieved from https://er.educause.edu/articles/2010/4/individual-knowledge-in-the-internet-age

Scherder, E., Scherder, R., Verburgh, L., Königs, M., Blom, M., Kramer, A. F., & Eggermont, L. (2014). Executive functions of sedentary elderly may benefit from walking: A systematic review and meta-analysis. *The American Journal of Geriatric Psychiatry, 22*(8), 782–791. doi:10.1016/j.jagp.2012.12.026

Simons, H., Kushner, S., Jones, K., & James, D. (2003). From evidence-based practice to practice-based evidence: the idea of situated generalisation. *Research Papers in Education, 18*(4), 347–364. doi:10.1080/0267132032000176833

Sutherland, W. J., Pullin, A. S., Dolman, P. M., & Knight, T. M. (2004). The need for evidence-based conservation. *Trends in Ecology & Evolution, 19*(6), 305–308. doi.org/10.1016/j.tree.2004.03.018

Torres, R. T., & Preskill, H. (2002). Evaluation and organizational learning: Past, present and future. *American Journal of Evaluation, 22*(3), 387–395. doi:10.1016/S1098-2140(01)00170-9

Vicarioa, M. D., Bessi, A., Zollo, F., Petroni, F., Scala, A., Caldarellia, G. . . . Quattrociocchi, W. (2016). The spreading of misinformation online. *Proceeds of the National Academic of Science, 113*(3), 554–559. https://doi.org/10.1073/pnas.1517441113

Virues-Ortega, J., Julio, F. M., & Pastor-Barriuso, R. (2013). The TEACCH program for children and adults with autism: A meta-analysis of intervention studies. *Clinical Psychology Review, 33*(8), 940–953. doi.org/10.1016/j.cpr.2013.07.005

Zhang, A., Cui, L., Iyer, A., Jetten, J., & Hao, Z. (2014). When reality bites: Hopeful thinking mediates the discrimination-life satisfaction relationship. *Analyses of Social Issues and Public Policy, 14*(1), 379–393. doi:10.1111/asap.12034

Zickuhr, K., & Smith, A. (2012). *Digital differences*. Retrieved from https://www.pewinternet.org/wp-content/uploads/sites/9/media/Files/Reports/2012/PIP_Digital_differences_041312.pdf

# Chapter 2

Council on Social Work Education. (CSWE). (2015). *Educational policy and accreditation standards for baccalaureate and master's social work programs.* Alexandria, VA: Author. Retrieved from https://www.cswe.org/getattachment/Accreditation/Accreditation-Process/2015-EPAS/2015EPAS_Web_FINAL.pdf.aspx

Department of Health, Education, and Welfare (DHEW). (1979). Part 46—Protection of human subjects. Retrieved from https://www.govinfo.gov/content/pkg/CFR-2016-title45-vol1/pdf/CFR-2016-title45-vol1-part46.pdf

National Association of Social Workers (NASW). (2017). *Code of ethics.* Washington, DC: Author. Retrieved from https://www.socialworkers.org/About/Ethics/Code-of-Ethics

Office for Human Research Protection: Subpart A—Basic health and human services policy for protection of human research subject. Retrieved from https://www.ecfr.gov/cgi-bin/text-idx?m=05&d=19&y=2019&cd=20190219&submit=GO&SID=83cd09e1c0f5c6937cd9d7513160fc3f&node=pt45.1.46&pd=20180719#se45.1.46_1

National Institute of Health (NIH). (n.d.). *National Institute of Allergy and Infectious Diseases – Decision Trees for Human Subject requirements.* Retrieved from https://www.niaid.nih.gov/grants-contracts/decision-trees-human-subjects

*The Belmont Report: Ethical Principles and Guidelines for the Protection of Human Subjects of Research.* (1978). The National Commission for the Protection of Human Subjects of Biomedical and Behavioral Research. DHEW Publication No. (OS) 78-0012. Retrieved from https://repository.library.georgetown.edu/bitstream/handle/10822/779133/ohrp_belmont_report.pdf?sequence=1&isAllowed=y

Velasco, E. (2010a). Exclusion Criteria. In N. J. Salkind (Ed.), *Encyclopedia of research design* (pp. 438–439). Thousand Oaks, CA: Sage.

Velasco, E. (2010b). Inclusion criteria. In N. J. Salkind (Ed.), *Encyclopedia of research design.* Thousand Oaks, CA: Sage.

# Chapter 3

Bejerot, S., Edgar, J., & Humble, M. B. (2011). Poor performance in physical education—a risk factor for bully victimization. A case-control study. *Acta Paediatrica, 100*(3), 413–419. doi:10.1111/j.1651-2227.2010.02016.x

Council on Social Work Education (CSWE). (2015). *Educational policy and accreditation standards for Baccalaureate and Master's Social Work Programs.* Alexandria, VA: Author. Retrieved from https://www.cswe.org/getattachment/Accreditation/Accreditation-Process/2015-EPAS/2015EPAS_Web_FINAL.pdf.aspx

Dantchev, S., Zammit, S., & Wolke, D. (2018). Sibling bullying in middle childhood and psychotic disorder at 18 years: A prospective cohort study. *Psychological Medicine, 48*(14), 2321–2328. doi:10.1017/S0033291717003841

DeForge, B. R. (2010). Research design principles. In N. J. Salkind (Ed.), *Encyclopedia of research design.* Thousand Oaks, CA: Sage.

Evans, C. B. R., & Smokowski, P. R. (2016). Theoretical explanation for bullying in school: How ecological processes propagate perpetration and victimization. *Child and Adolescent Social Work Journal, 33*(4), 365–375. doi:10.1007/s10560-015-0432-2

Gallagher, E. E., O'Dulian, M., O'Mahony, N., Kehoe, C., McCarthy, F., & Morgan, G. (2017). Instructor-provided summary infographics to support online learning. *Educational Media International, 54*(2), 129–147. doi:10.1080/09523987.2017.1362795

Hays. D. G., & Singh, A. A. (2012). *Qualitative inquiry in clinical and educational settings.* New York, NY: Guilford.

Jamal, F., Bonell, C., Harden, A., & Lorenc, T. (2015). The social ecology of girls' bullying practices: Exploratory research in two London schools. *Sociology of Health & Illness, 37*(5), 731–744. https://doi.org/10.1111/1467-9566.12231

Madiba, S., & Mokgatle, M. (2015). "Students want HIV testing in schools" a formative evaluation of the acceptability of HIV testing and counseling at schools in Gauteng and North West provinces in South Africa. *BMC Public Health, 15,* 1–9. doi:10.1186/s12889-015-1746-x

Meyers, A. (2017). Lifting the veil: The lived experience of sibling abuse. *Qualitative Social Work, 16*(3), 333–350. doi:10.1177/147325015612143

Pardeck, J. T. (1988). An ecological approach for social work practice. *Journal of Sociology and Social Welfare, 15*(2), 133–142.

Rhodes, J. E., & Jason, L. A. (1990). A social stress model of substance use. *Journal of Consulting and Clinical Psychology, 58*(4), 395–401. doi:10.1037/0022-006X.58.4.395

Sahu, P. K. (2013). *Research methodology: A guide for researchers in agricultural science, social sciences, and related fields.* New Delhi, India: Springer.

Schmidt, P. W. (2019). An overview and critique of US immigration and asylum policies in the Trump era. *Journal of Migration and Human Security.* https://doi.org/10.1177/2331502419866203

Yegidis, B. L., Weinbach, R. W., & Myers, L. L. (2006). *Research methods for social workers* (7th ed.), Boston, MA: Allyn & Bacon.

# Chapter 4

Aloia, D. (2016). *Discover grey literature: Hidden health and science resources.* Retrieved from https://nyamcenterfor history.org/2016/10/18/discover-grey-literature-hidden-health-and-science-resources/

Alvesson, M., & Sandberg, J. (2013). *Constructing research questions: Doing interesting research.* Thousand, Oaks, CA: Sage.

Bellieni, C. V., & Buonocore, G. (2013). Abortion and subsequent mental health: Review of the literature. *Psychiatry and Clinical Neurosciences, 67*(5), 301–310. doi:10.111/pcn.12067

Boote, D. N., & Beile, P. (2005). Scholars before researchers: On the centrality of the dissertation literature review in research preparation. *Educational Researcher, 34*(6), 3–15.

Cohen, A. S., Fedechko, T., Schwartz, E. K., Le, T. P., Foltz, P. W., Bernstein, J., . . . Elvevåg, B. (2019). Psychiatric risk assessment from the clinician's perspective: Lessons for the future. *Community Mental Health Journal, 55*(15). doi:10.1007/s10597-019-00411-x

Denyer, D., & Tranfield, D. (2009). Producing a systematic review. In D. A. Buchanan & A. Bryman (Eds.), *The SAGE handbook of organizational research methods* (pp. 671–689). Thousand Oaks, CA: Sage.

Gibbs, L. (2003). *Evidence-based practice for the helping professions: A practical guide with integrated multimedia.* Pacific Grove, CA: Brooks/Cole.

Huang, L., Zhao, Y., Qiang, C., & Fan, B. (2018). Is cognitive behavioral therapy a better choice for women with postnatal depression. A systematic review and meta-analysis. *PLoS ONE, 13*(10), 1–16, doi:10.1371/journal.pone.0205243

Hughes, D., Seidman, E., & Williams, N. (1993). Cultural phenomena and the research enterprise: Toward a culturally anchored methodology. *American Journal of Community Psychology, 21*(6), 687–703.

Mertens, D. M. (2015). *Research and evaluation in education and psychology: Integrating diversity with quantitative, qualitative, and mixed-methods* (4th ed.). Thousand Oaks, CA: Sage.

Patten, M. L. (2004). *Understanding research methods: An overview of the essentials* (4th ed.). Glendale, CA: Pyrczak Publishing.

Pyrczak, P. (2014). *Evaluating research in academic journals: A practical guide to realistic evaluation* (6th ed.). Glendale, CA: Pyrczak Publishing.

Rodgers-Farmer, A. Y., & Potocky-Tripodi, M. (2001). Gender, ethnicity, and race matters. In B. A. Thyer (Ed.), *Handbook of social work research methods* (pp. 445–454). Thousand Oaks, CA: Sage.

Sackett, D. L., Richardson, W. S., Rosenberg, W., & Haynes, R. B. (1977). *Evidence-based medicine: How to practice and teach EBM.* New York, NY: Churchill Livingstone.

Williams, V. N., Ayele, R., Shimasaki, S., Tung, G. J., & Olds, D. (2019). Risk assessment practices among home visiting nurses and child protection caseworkers in Colorado, United States: A qualitative investigation. *Health & Social Care in the Community, 27*(5),1344–1352. doi:10.1111/hsc.12773

Willie, T. C., Powell, A., Callands, T., Sipsma, H., Peasant, C., Magriples, U., . . . Kershaw, T. (2019). Investigating intimate partner violence victimization and reproductive coercion victimization among young pregnant and parenting couples: A longitudinal study. *Psychology of Violence, 9*(3), 278–287. doi:10.1037/vio0000118

Youngstrom, E. A., Van Meter, A., Frazier, T. W., Hunsley, J. Prinstein, M. J., Ong, M. L., & Youngstrom, J. K. (2017). Evidence-based assessment as an integrative model for applying psychological science to guide the voyage of treatment. *Clinical Psychology: Science and Practice, 24*(4), 33–363. doi:10.1111/cpsp.12207

# Chapter 5

American Psychological Association (APA). (2002). Ethical principles of psychologists and code of conduct. *American Psychologist, 57*(12), 1060–1073.

American Psychological Association (APA). (2013). *Diagnostic and statistical manual of mental disorders* (5th ed.). Washington, DC: Author.

Babbie, E. (2010). *The practice of social research*. Belmont, CA: Wadsworth.

Barnette, J. J. (2000). Effects of STEM and Likert response option reversals on survey internal consistency: If you feel the need, there is a better alternative to using negatively worded STEMS. *Educational and Psychological Measurement, 60*(3), 361–370. doi:10.1177/00131640021970592

Beattie, P. (2001). Measurement of health outcomes in the clinical setting: Applications to physiotherapy. *Physiotherapy Theory and Practice, 17*(3), 173–185. doi:10.1080/095939801317077632

Beck, A. T., Steer, R. A., & Brown, G. K. (1996). *Manual for the Beck Depression Inventory-II*. San Antonio, TX: Psychological Corporation.

Burns, N., & Groves, S. (2009). *The practice of nursing research: Conduct, critique, & utilization* (6th ed.). Philadelphia, PA: W. B. Saunders.

Corcoran, K., & Fischer, J. (2013). *Measures for clinical practice and research: A sourcebook* (5th ed.), Volume I and II. New York, NY: Oxford University Press.

Corrigan, P. (2004). How stigma interferes with mental health care. *American Psychologist, 59*(7), 614–625. doi:10.1037/0003-066X.59.7.614

Council on Social Work Education (CSWE). (2015). *Educational policy and accreditation standards* for baccalaureate and master's social work programs. Alexandria, VA: Author. Retrieved from https://www.cswe.org/getattachment/Accreditation/Accreditation-Process/2015-EPAS/2015EPAS_Web_FINAL.pdf.aspx

Lin, C., Lee, C., & Huang, M. (2017). Cultural competence of healthcare providers: A systematic review of assessment instruments. *Journal of Nursing Research, 25*(3), 174–186. doi: 10.1097/jnr.0000000000000153

National Association of Social Workers (NASW). (2017). *Code of ethics*. Washington, DC: NASW Press. Retrieved from https://www.socialworkers.org/About/Ethics/Code-of-Ethics/Code-of-Ethics-English

Ungar, M., Liebenberg, L., Boothroyd, R., Kwong, W. M., Lee, T. Y., Leblanc, J., et al. (2008). The study of youth resilience across cultures: Lessons from a pilot study of measurement development. *Research in Human Development, 5*(3), 166–180.

Wolfer, L. (2007). *Real research: Conducting and evaluating research in the social sciences*. Boston, MA: Pearson Education.

# Chapter 6

Barrera, M., Castro, F. G., Strycker, L. A., & Toobert, D. J. (2013). Cultural adaptions of behavioral interventions: A progress report. *Journal of Consulting and Clinical Psychology, 81*(2), 196–205. doi:10.1037/a0027085

Beck, A. T., Steer, R. A., & Brown, G. K. (1996). *Manual for the Beck Depression Inventory-II*. San Antonio, TX: Psychological Corporation.

Bernal, G., Jimenez-Chafey, M. I., & Domenech Rodriguez, M. M. (2009). Cultural adaptation of treatments: A resource for considering culture in evidence-based practice. *Professional Psychology: Research and Practice, 40*(4), 361–368.

Campbell, D. T., & Stanley, J. C. (1963). Experimental and quasi-experimental designs for research on teaching. In N. L. Gage (Ed.), *Handbook of research on teaching* (pp. 171–246). Chicago, IL: Rand McNally. Reprinted in 1966 under the title Experimental and quasi-experimental designs for research.

Celik, S., Cosansu, S., Erdogan, S., Kahraman, A., Isik, S., Bayrak, G., Bektas, B., & Olgun, N. (2014). Using mobile phone text messages to improve insulin injection technique and glycaemic control in patients with diabetes mellitus: a multi-centre study in Turkey. *Journal of Clinical Nursing, 24*(11–12), 1525–1533. doi:10.1111/jocn.12731

Chambliss, D. E., & Schutt, R. K. (2006). *Making sense of the social world: Methods of investigation*. Thousand Oaks, CA: Sage.

Council on Social Work Education (CSWE). (2015). *Educational policy and accreditation standards for baccalaureate and master's social work programs.* Retrieved from http://www.cswe.org/File.aspx?id=81660

Epstein, I. (1996). In quest of a research-based model for clinical practice: Or, why can't a social worker be more like a researcher? *Social Work Research, 20*(2), 97–100. https://doi.org/10.1093/swr/20.2.67

Glass, G. V. (1965). Evaluating testing, maturation, and treatment effects in a pretest-posttest quasi-experimental design. *American Educational Research Journal, 2,* 83–87. https://doi.org/10.3102/00028312002002083

Hall, G. C. N. (2001). Psychotherapy research with ethnic minorities: Empirical, ethical, and conceptual issues. *Journal of Consulting and Clinical Psychology, 69*(3), 502–510. doi:10.1037//0022-006X.69.3.502

Hanrahan, D., et al. (2015). Linguistic and cultural challenge in communication and translation in US sponsored HIV prevention research in emerging economies. *PLos One, 10*(7). doi:10.371/journal.pone.10133394

Heyman, J. C., & Gutheil, I. A. (2010). Older Latinos' attitudes and comfort with end-of-life-planning. *Health and Social Work, 35*(1), 17–26. https://doi.org/10.1093/hsw/35.1.17

Hohmann-Marriott, B. E. (2001). Marriage and family therapy research: Ethical issues and guidelines. *The American Journal of Family Therapy, 29*(1), 1–11. doi:10.1080/01926180126081

Johnson, C. W. (1986). A more rigorous quasi-experimental alternative to the one-group pretest-posttest design. *Educational and Psychological Measurement, 46*(3), 585–591.

Knapp, T. R. (2016). Why is the one-group pretest-posttest design still used. *Clinical Nursing Research, 25*(5), 467–472. doi:10/1177/054773816666280

Marin, B. V., Marin, G., Perez-Stable, E. J., Otero-Sabogal, R., & Sabogal, F. (1990). Cultural differences in attitudes toward smoking: Developing messages using the theory of reasoned action. *Journal of Applied Social Psychology, 20*(6), 478–493.

Olsen, D. P., Wang, H., & Pang, S. (2010). Informed consent practices of Chinese nurse researchers. *Nursing Ethics, 17*(2), 179–187. doi:10.1177/0969733009355545

Radloff, L. S. (1977). The CES-D scale: A self-report depression scale for research in the general population. *Applied Psychological Measurement, 1,* 385–401. https://doi.org/10.1177/014662167700100306

Smith T., Domenech Rodríguez, M. M., & Bernal, G. (2010). Culture. *Journal of Clinical Psychology, 67*(2), 166–175. https://doi.org/10.1002/jclp.20757

Wolfer, L. (2007). *Real research: Conducting and evaluating research in the social sciences.* Boston, MA: Pearson Education.

# Chapter 7

Azeez, A. (2015). Positive mental health through life skill education: Empowering adolescents having psychological problems. *Journal of Psychosocial Research, 10*(1), 21–31.

Bender, K., Altschul, I., Yoder, J., Parrish, D., & Nickels, S. J. (2014). Training social work graduate students in evidence-based practice process. *Research on Social Work Practice, 24*(3), 339–348. doi:10.1177/1049731513506614

Campbell, D. T., & Stanley, J. C. (1963). Experimental and quasi-experimental designs for research on teaching. In N. L. Gage (Ed.), *Handbook of research on teaching* (pp. 171–246). Chicago, IL: Rand McNally. Reprinted in 1966 under the title Experimental and quasi-experimental designs for research.

Craig, P., Cooper, C., Gunnell, D., Haw, S., Lawson, K., Macintyre, S., Ogilive, D., et al. (2012). Using natural experiments to evaluate population health interventions: New MRC guidance. *Journal of Epidemiological Community Health, 66*(12), 1182–1186. doi:10.1136/jech-2011-200375

Kluve, J., & Tamm, M. (2013). Parental leave regulations, mothers' labor force attachment and fathers' childcare involvement: Evidence from a natural experiment. *Journal of Population Economics, 26*(3), 983–1005. doi:10.1007/s00148-012-0404-1

Leatherdale, S. T. (2019). Natural experiment methodology for research: a review of how different methods can support real-world research. *International Journal of Social Research Methodology, 22*(1), 19–35. doi:10.1080/13645579.2018.1488449

Meda, I. B., Dumont, A., Kouanda, S., & Ridde, V. (2018). Impact of fee subsidy policy on perinatal health in a low-resource setting: A quasi-experimental study. *PLoS ONE, 13*(11), 1–15. 10.1371/journal.pone.0206978

Thyer, B. A. (2012). *Quasi-experimental designs.* New York, NY: Oxford Press.

# Chapter 8

Baxter, P., & Jack, S. (2008). Qualitative case study methodology: Study design and implementation for novice researchers. *The Qualitative Report, 13*(4), 544–559.

Buch, E. D., & Staller, K. M. (2007). The feminist practice of ethnography. In S. N. Hesse-Biber & P. L. Leavy (Eds.), *Feminist research practice: A primer* (pp. 187–222). Thousand Oaks, CA: Sage.

Charmaz, K. (2006). *Constructing grounded theory: A practical guide through qualitative analysis.* Thousand Oaks, CA: Sage.

Creswell, J. W. (2003). *Research design: Qualitative, quantitative, and mixed methods approaches* (2nd ed.). Thousand Oaks, CA: Sage.

Creswell, J. W. (2006). *Qualitative inquiry and research designs: Choosing among five traditions* (2nd ed.). Thousand Oaks, CA: Sage.

Denzin, N. K., & Lincoln, Y. S. (Eds.). (2011). Introduction: The discipline and the practice of qualitative research in N. K. Denzin (Eds.), *The Sage handbook of qualitative research* (4th ed., pp. 1–20). Thousand Oaks, CA: Sage.

Glaser, B. G., & Strauss, A. L. (1967). *The discovery of grounded theory: Strategies for qualitative research.* Chicago, IL: Aldine.

Green, D., Creswell, J., Shope, R., & Clark, V. (2007). Grounded theory and racial/ethnic diversity. In A. Bryant & K. Charmaz (Eds.), *The SAGE handbook of grounded theory* (pp. 472–492). London, UK: Sage

Guba, E. G., & Lincoln, Y. S. (1994). *Competing paradigms in qualitative research.* In N. K. Denzin & Y. S. Lincoln (Eds.), *Handbook of qualitative research* (pp. 105–117). Thousand Oaks, CA: Sage.

Hadjistavropoulos, T., & Smythe, W. E. (2001). Elements of risk in qualitative research. *Ethics & Behavior, 11*(2), 163–174.

Haight, W., Kayama, M., & Korang-Okrah, R. (2014). Ethnography in social work practice and policy. *Qualitative Social Work, 13*(1), 127–143. doi:10:1177/1473325013507303

Hays. D. G., & Singh, A. A. (2012). *Qualitative inquiry in clinical and educational settings.* New York, NY: Guilford.

Hussein, M. E., Hirst, S., Salyers, V., & Osuji, J. (2014). Using grounded theory as a method of inquiry: Advantages and disadvantages. *The Qualitative Report, 19*, 1–15. Retrieved from https://nsuworks.nova.edu/tqr/vol19/iss27/3

Jobling, H. (2014). Using ethnography to explore causality in mental health policy and practice. *Qualitative Social Work, 13*(1), 49–68. doi:10:1177/1473325013504802

Kozinets, R. V. (2006). Netnography. In V. Jupp (Ed.), *The SAGE dictionary of social research methods* (p. 135). London: Sage.

Lincoln, Y. S., & Guba, E. G. (1985). *Naturalistic inquiry.* Thousand Oaks, CA: Sage.

Lyons, H. Z., Bike, D. H., Johnson, A., & Bethea, A. (2012). Culturally competent qualitative research with people of African descent. *Journal of Black Psychology, 38*(2), 153–171. doi:10.1177/0095798411414019

McLendon, T. (2014). Social workers' perspectives regarding the DSM: Implications for social work education. *Journal of Social Work Education, 50*(3), 454–471.

Miles, M. B., & Huberman, A. M. (1994). *Qualitative data analysis: An expanded source book* (2nd ed.). Thousand Oaks, CA: Sage.

Morse, J. M. (1995). The significance of saturation. *Qualitative Health Research, 5*(2), 147–149. https://doi.org/10.1177/104973239500500201

Patton, M. Q. (2015). *Qualitative research and evaluation methods* (4th ed.). Newbury Park, CA: Sage.

Polit, D. F., & Beck, C. T. (2014). *Essentials of nursing research: Appraising evidence for nursing practice* (8th ed.). Philadelphia, PA: Wolters Kluwer/Lippincott Williams & Wilkins.

Schneider, K. J. (1999). Multiple-case depth research. *Journal of Clinical Psychology*, 55(12), 1531–1540. doi:10.1002/(SICI)1097-4679(199912)55:123.3.CO;2-6

Singleton, R. A., & Straits, B. C. (2005). *Approaches to social research* (4th ed.). New York, NY: Oxford University Press.

Stake, R. E. (1995). *The art of case study research*. Thousand Oaks, CA: Sage.

Strauss, A., & Corbin, J. (1990). *Basics of qualitative research: Grounded theory and techniques*. Thousand Oaks, CA: Sage.

Tinker, C., & Armstron, N. (2008). From the outside looking in: How an awareness of difference can benefit the qualitative research process. *The Qualitative Report*, 13(1), 53–60. Retrieved from https://nsuworks.nova/tqr/vol13/iss1/5

Yin, R. K. (2018). *Case study research and applications: Design and methods* (6th ed.). Thousand Oaks, CA: Sage.

# Chapter 9

Austin, A. Craig, S. L., & McInroy, L. B. (2016). Toward transgender affirmative social work education. *Journal of Social Work Education*, 52(3), 297–310. doi:10.1080/1043 7797.2016.1174637

Brophy, L., & McDermott, F. (2013). Using social work theory and values to investigate the implementation of community treatment orders. *Australian Social Work*, 66(1), 72–85. doi.1080/031247X.2011.651727

Collins, K., M. T., Onwuegbuzie, A. J., & Jiao, Q. G. (2007). A mixed methods investigation of mixed methods sampling designs in social and health science research. *Journal of Mixed Methods Research*, 1(3), 267–294. doi:10.1177/1558689807299526

Creswell, J. W., Plano Clark, V. L., Gutmann, M. L., & Hanson, W. E. (2003). Advanced mixed-methods research designs. In A. Tashakkori & C. Teddlie (Eds.), *Handbook of mixed-methods in social and behavioral research* (pp. 209–240). Thousand Oaks, CA: Sage.

Hays. D. G., & Singh, A. A. (2012). *Qualitative inquiry in clinical and educational settings*. New York, NY: Guilford.

Mertens, D. M. (2015). *Research and evaluation in education and psychology: Integrating diversity with quantitative, qualitative, and mixed-methods*. Thousand Oaks, CA: Sage.

Teasley, M., Canifield, J. P., Archuleta, A. J., Crutchfield, J., & Chavis, A. M. (2012). Perceived barriers and facilitators to school social work practice: A mixed-method study. *Children & Schools*, 34(3), 145–152. doi:10.1093/csf/cdes014

Teddlie, C., & Tashakkori, A. (2009). *Foundations of mixed methods research*. Thousand Oaks, CA: Sage.

# Chapter 10

Boyd, L. Baker, E., & Reilly, J. (2019). Impact of a progressive stepped care approach in an improving access to psychological therapies service: an observational study. *PLos ONE*, 14(4), 1–16. doi:10.1371/journal.pone.0214715

Carlson, M. D. A., & Morrison, R. S. (2009). Study design, precision, and validity in observational studies. *Journal of Palliative Medicine*, 12(1), 77–82. doi:10.1089/jpm.2008.9690

Cohen, J. F. W., Gorski Findling, M. T., Rosenfeld, L., Smith, L., Rimm. E, B., & Hoffman, J. A. (2018). The impact of 1 year of healthier school food policies on students' diets during and outside of the school day. *Journal of the American Nutrition and Dietetics*, 118(12), 2296–2301. doi:10.1016/j.jand2018.07.009

*Healthy, Hunger-Free Kids Act of 2010*. Public Law 111-296, 124 Stat, 3183.

Hyland, A., et al. (2014). Associations of lifetime active and passive smoking with spontaneous abortion, stillbirth and tubal ectopic pregnancy: A cross-sectional analysis of historical data from the Women's Health Initiative. *Tobacco Control*, 24(4), 328–335. doi:10.1136/tobaccocontrol-2013-051458

Lu, C. Y. (2009). Observational studies: a review of study designs, challenges, and strategies to reduce confounding. *International Journal of Clinical Practice*, 63(5), 691–697. doi:10.1111/j.1742-1241.2009.02056.x

*Massachusetts Competitive Food (MCF) Law of 2010*. (105 CMR 225.000)

Morrow, B. (2010). An overview of case-control study designs and their advantages and disadvantages. *International Journal of Therapy and Rehabilitation, 17*(11), 570–574. doi:10.12968/ijtr.2010.17.11.79537

O'Dwyer, M., Peklar, J., Mulryan, N., McCallion, P., McCarron, M., & Henman, M. C. (2018). Prevalence and patterns of anti-epileptic medication prescribing in the treatment of epilepsy in older adults. *Journal of Intellectual Disability Research, 62*(3), 245–261. doi:10.1111/jir.12461

Ojha, R. P., Offutt-Powell, T. N., Evans, E. L., & Singh, K. P. (2011). Correlation coefficients in ecologic studies of environment and cancer. *Archives of Environmental and Occupational Health, 66*(4), 241–244. doi:1080/19338244.2010.539641

Sánchez-Sellero, I., San-Román-Rodríguez, E., Santos-Pérez, S., Rossi-Izquierdo, M., & Soto-Varela, A. (2018). Caffeine intake and Menière's disease. Is there a relationship? *Nutritional Neuroscience, 21*(2), 624–631. doi:10.1080/1028415X.2017.1327636

Sarna, M., Ware, R. S., Lambert, S. B., Sloots, T. P., Nissen, M. D., & Grimwood, K. (2018). Timing of first respiratory virus detections in infants: A community-based birth cohort study. *The Journal of Infectious Diseases, 217*(3), 418–427. doi:10.1093/infds/jix599

Szumilas, M. (2010). Explaining odds ratio. *Journal of Canadian Academy of Children and Adolescent Psychiatry, 19*(3), 227–229.

and low-income women. *Field Methods, 18*(1), 43–48. doi:10.1177/1525822X05284014

*Ericka Grimes v. Kennedy Krieger Institute, Inc. and Myron Higgins, a minor, etc., et al. v. Kennedy Krieger Institute.* (2000). Retrieved from https://caselaw.findlaw.com/md-court-of-appeals/1236870.html

Hays, D. G., & Singh, A. A. (2012). *Qualitative inquiry in clinical and educational settings.* New York, NY: Guilford.

Israel, B. A., Schulz, A. J., Parker, E. A., & Becker, A. B. (1998). Review of community-based research: Assessing partnership approaches to improve public health. *Annual Review of Public Health, 19*(1), 173–202. doi:10.1146/annurev.publhealth.19.1.173

Kim, R. K., & Dymond, S. K. (2012). A national study of community living: Impact of type of residence and hours of in-home support. *Research & Practice for Persons With Severe Disabilities, 37*(2), 116–129. doi:10.1177/154079691203700207

Semaan, S., Santibanez, S., Garfein, R. S., Heckathorn, D. D., & Des Jarlais, D. C. (2008). Ethical and regulatory considerations in HIV prevention studies employing respondent-driven sampling. *International Journal of Drug Policy, 20*(1), 14–27. doi:10.1016/j.drugpo.2007.12.006

Tweneboah, K. E. Y., & Owusu, F. N. (2013). Social marketing on AIDS: Using transtheoretical model to understand current condom usage among commercial drivers in Accra, Ghana. *International Journal of Nonprofit and Voluntary Sector Marketing, 18*(4), 241–260. doi:10.1002/nvsm.1470

# Chapter 11

Burlew, K., Larios, S., Suarez-Morales, L., Holmes, B., Venner, K., & Chavez, R. (2011). Increasing ethnic minority participation in substance abuse clinical trials: Lessons learned in the National Institute on Drug Abuse's Clinical Trials Network. *Cultural Diversity & Ethnic Minority Psychology, 17*(4), 345–356. doi:10.1037/2002668

Cohen, J. (1988). *Statistical power analysis for the behavioral sciences* (2nd ed.). Hillsdale, NJ: Lawrence Earlbaum Associates.

Elliott, M. N., Golinelli, D., Hambarsoomian, K. Perlman, J., & Wenzel, S. L. (2006). Sampling with field burden constraints: An application to sheltered homeless

# Chapter 12

Assari, S. (2019). Family socioeconomic position at birth and school bonding at age 15: Blacks' diminished returns. *Behavioral Sciences, 9*(3), 26.

Fowler, F. J. (2009). *Survey research methods* (4th ed.). Thousand Oaks, CA: Sage.

Garfinkel, I., & Zilanawala, A. (2015). Fragile families in the American welfare. *Children and Youth Services Review, 55,* 210–221. doi:10.1016/j.childyouth.2015.05.018

Geller, A., & Fagan, J. (2019). Police contact and the legal socialization of urban teens. *RSF: The Russell Sage*

Foundation Journal of the Social Sciences, 5(1), 26–49. doi:10.7758/rsf.2019.5.1.02

Glasgow, R. E., Wagner, E. H., Schaefer, J., Mahoney, L. D., Reid, R. J., & Greene, S. M. (2005). Development and validation of the Patient Assessment of Chronic Illness Care (PACIC). Med Care, 43(5), 436–444.

Goldman, R. (2014). Here's a list of 58 gender options for Facebook users. Retrieved from https://abcnews.go.com/blogs/headlines/2014/02/heres-a-list-of-58-gender-options-for-facebook-users/

Han, B. H., Sherman, S. E., & Palamar, J. J. (2019). Prescription opioid misuse among middle-aged and older adults in the United States, 2015–2016. Preventive Medicine: An International Journal Devoted to Practice and Theory, 121, 94–98. doi:10.1016/j.ypmed.2019.02.018

Huang, A. R., & Mallet, L. (2013). Prescribing opioids in older people. Maturitas, 74(2), 123–129. doi:10.1016/j.maturitas.2012.11.002

Johnson, B., & Christensen, J. (2008). Educational research (3rd ed.). Thousand Oaks, CA: Sage.

Karp, J. F., Lee, C.-W., McGovern, J., Stoehr, G., Chang, C.-C. H., & Ganguli, M. (2013). Clinical and demographic covariates of chronic opioid and non-opioid analgesic use in rural-dwelling older adults: The MoVIES project. International Psychogeriatrics, 25(11), 1801–1810. doi:10.1017/S104161021300121X

Keeter, S., McGeeney, K., & Weisel, R. (2015). Coverage error in internet surveys: Who web-only surveys miss and how that affect results. Pew Research Center. Retrieved from https://www.pewresearch.org/methods/2015/09/22/coverage-error-in-internet-surveys/

Lavrakas, P. J. (2008). Encyclopedia of survey research methods. Thousand Oaks, CA: Sage.

Maree, R. D., Marcum, Z. A., Saghafi, E., Weiner, D. K., & Karp, J. F. (2016). A systematic review of opioid and benzodiazepine misuse in older adults. The American Journal of Geriatric Psychiatry, 24(11), 949–963. doi:10.1016/j.jagp.2016.06.003

Mertens, D. M. (2015). Research and evaluation in education and psychology: Integrating diversity with quantitative, qualitative, and mixed methods (4th ed.). Thousand Oaks, CA: Sage.

Palamar, J. J., Han, B. H., & Martins, S. S. (2019). Shifting characteristics of nonmedical prescription tranquilizer users in the United States, 2005–2014. Drug and Alcohol Dependence, 195(1), 1–5. doi:10.1016/j.drugalcdep.2018.11.015

Park, J., Clement, R., & Lavin, R. (2011). Factor structure of pain medication questionnaire in community-dwelling older adults with chronic pain. Pain Practice, 11(4), 314–324. doi:10.1111/j.1533-2500.2010.00422.x

Pei, F., Wang, X., Yoon, S., & Tebben, E. (2019). The influences of neighborhood disorder on early childhood externalizing problems: The roles of parental stress and child physical maltreatment. 47(5),1105–1117. Journal of Community Psychology. doi:10.1002/jcop.22174

Pew Research Center. (2012). Trends in American values: 1987–2012: Partisan polarization surges in the Bush, Obama years. Retrieved from https://assets.pewresearch.org/wp-content/uploads/sites/5/legacy-pdf/06-04-12%20Values%20Release.pdf

Pew Research Center. (2019). Internet/broadband fact sheet. Retrieved from https://www.pewinternet.org/fact-sheet/internet-broadband/

Reichman, N. E., Teitler, J. O., Garfinkel, I., & McLanahan, S. S. (2001). Fragile families: sample and design. Children and Youth Services Review, 23(4), 303–326. doi.org/10.1016/S0190-7409(01)00141-4

Rubin, A., & Babbie, E. R. (2014). Research methods for social work (8th ed.). Belmont, CA: Brooks/Cole, Cengage Learning.

Ruel, E., Wagner, W. E., & Gillespie, B. J. (Eds.). (2016a). Types of surveys. In E. Ruel, W. E. Wagner, & B. J. Gillespie, The practice of survey research (pp. 13–24). Thousand Oaks, CA: Sage.

Ruel, E., Wagner, W., & Gillespie, B. (2016b). Survey question construction. In E. Ruel, W. E. Wagner, & B. J. Gillespie (Eds.), The practice of survey research: Theory and application (pp. 44–77). Thousand Oaks, CA: Sage.

SAMHSA Center for Behavioral Health Statistics and Quality. (2019). National survey on drug use and health (NSDUH). Retrieved from https://nsduhweb.rti.org/respweb/homepage.cfm

Schepis, T. S., & McCabe, S. E. (2016). Trends in older adult nonmedical prescription drug use prevalence: Results from the 2002–2003 and 2012–2013 National Survey on Drug Use and Health. *Addictive Behaviors, 60,* 219–222. doi:10.1016/j.addbeh.2016.04.020

Subramanian, S. V., Huijts, T., & Avendano, M. (2010). Self-reported health assessments in the 2002 World Health Survey: how do they correlate with education? *Bulletin of the World Health Organization, 88*(2), 131–138. doi:10.2471/BLT.09.067058

U.S. Census Bureau. (2010). 2010 census questionnaire. Retrieved from https://www.socialexplorer.com/data/C2010_PL94/documentation/670cbe35-2a2e-4e18-90dc-16d1f5c84734

# Chapter 13

Abu-Bader, S. H. (2016). *Using statistical methods in the social science research with a complete SPSS guide* (2nd ed.) New York, NY: Oxford Press.

Alorani, O. I., & Alradaydeh, M. F. (2017). Spiritual well-being, perceived social support, and life satisfaction among university students. *International Journal of Adolescence and Youth, 23*(3), 1–8.

American Psychological Association. (2020). *Publication manual of the American Psychological Association* (7th ed.). Washington, DC: Author.

Bronte-Tinkew, J., Burkhauser, M., & Metz, A. (2008). *Promising teen fatherhood programs: Initial evidence lessons from evidence-based research.* National Responsibilities Fatherhood Clearinghouse. U.S. Department of Health and Human Services Administration for Children and Families. Office of Family Assistance, Washington, DC.

Cage, J., Corley, N. A., & Harris, L. A. (2018). The educational attainment of maltreated youth involved with the child welfare system. Exploring the interaction of race and gender. *Children and Youth Services Review, 88,* 550–557. doi.org/10.1016.j. childyouth.2018.04.006

Cole, E. R. (2009). Intersectionality and research in psychology. *American Psychologist, 64*(3), 170–180. doi:10.1111/j.1467-9558.2010.01370.x

Council on Social Work Education (CSWE). (2015). *Educational policy and accreditation standards for baccalaureate and master's social work programs.* Retrieved from http://www. cswe.org/File.aspx?id=81660

Kerr, N. L. (1998). HARKing: Hypothesizing after the results are known. *Personality and Social Psychology Review, 2*(3), 196–217.

Maroof, D. A. (2013). Examining and reporting the status of statistical assumptions in neuropsychological research: A misbegotten ethical obligation? *Neurological Rehabilitation, 32*(2), 275–278. doi:10.3233/NRE-130844

Mertens, D. M. (1998). *Research methods in education and psychology: Integrating diversity with quantitative & qualitative approaches.* Thousand Oaks, CA: Sage.

Mertler, C. A., & Vannatta, R. A. (2002). *Advanced and multivariate statistical methods* (2nd ed.). Los Angeles, CA: Pyrczak Publishing.

Patten, M. L. (2004). *Understanding research methods: An overview of the essentials* (4th ed.). Glendale, CA: Pyrczak Publishing.

Sprinthall, R. C. (2000). *Basic statistical analysis* (6th ed.). Boston, MA: Allyn & Bacon.

Stevens, J. (1992). *Applied multivariate statistics for the social sciences* (2nd ed.). Hillsdale, NJ: Lawrence Erlbaum Associates.

Tabachnick, B. G., & Fidell, L. S. (2007). *Using multivariate statistics* (5th ed.). Needham Heights, MA: Allyn & Bacon.

# Chapter 14

Boeije, H. (2010). *Analysis in qualitative research.* London, England: Sage.

Braun, V., & Clarke, V. (2006). Using thematic analysis in psychology. *Qualitative Research in Psychology, 3*(2), 77–101. doi:10.1191/1478088706qp0630a

Council on Social Work Education (CSWE). (2015). *Educational policy and accreditation standards for baccalaureate and master's social work programs.* Retrieved from http://www. cswe.org/File.aspx?id=81660

Guba, E. G., & Lincoln, Y. S. (2005). Paradigmatic controversies, contradictions, and emerging confluences. In N. K. Denzin & Y. S. Lincoln (Eds.), *The SAGE handbook of qualitative research* (3rd ed., pp. 191–216). Thousand Oaks, CA: Sage.

Haverkamp, B. E. (2005). Ethical perspectives on qualitative research in applied psychology. *Journal of Counseling Psychology*, 52(2), 146–155. doi:10.1037/0022-0167.52.2.146

Hoffman, G. D., Rodriguez, F., Yang, M., & Ropers-Huilman, R. (2018). Assimilation and subversion on campus: A critical discourse analysis of students' experiences of race and institutional resources. *Journal of Diversity in Higher Education*, 12(3), 230–241. doi:10.1037/dhe0000093

Houghton, C., Casey, D., Shaw, D., & Murphy, K. (2013). Rigor in qualitative case-study research. *Nursing Researcher*, 20(4), 12–17.

Hsieh, H., & Shannon, S. (2005). Three approaches to qualitative content analysis. *Qualitative Health Research*, 15(9), 1277–1288. doi:10.1177/1049732305276687

Hsin-Chun Tsai, J., Choe, J. H., Mu Chen Lim, J., Acorda, E., Chan. N. L., Taylor, V., et al. (2004). Developing culturally competent health knowledge: Issues of data analysis of cross-cultural, cross-language qualitative research. *International Journal of Qualitative Methods*, 3(4), 16–27. doi.org/10.1177/160940690400300402

Lyons, H. Z., Bike, D. H., Johnson, A., & Bethea, A. (2012). Culturally competent qualitative research with people of African descent. *Journal of Black Psychology*, 38(2), 153–171. doi:10.1177/0095798411414019

Mertens, D. (2015). *Research and evaluation in education and psychology* (4th ed.). Thousand Oaks, CA: Sage.

Mullet, D. R. (2018). A general critical discourse analysis framework for educational research. *Journal of Advanced Academics*, 29(2), 116–142. doi:10.1177/1932202 × 18758260

Neale, J. (2016). Iterative categorization (IC): A systematic technique for analysing qualitative data. *Addiction*, 111(6), 1096–1106. doi:10.1111/add.13314

Polit, D. F., & Beck, C. T. (2014). *Essentials of nursing: Appraising evidence for nursing practice*. Philadelphia, PA: Wolters Kluwer Health/Lippincott Williams & Wilkins.

Popay, J., Rogers, A., & Williams, G. (1998). Rationale and standards for the systematic review of qualitative literature in health services research. *Qualitative Health Research*, 8(3), 341–351.

Strauss, A., & Corbin, J. (1990). *Basics of qualitative research: Grounded theory procedures and techniques*. Newbury Park, CA: Sage.

Strauss, A., & Corbin, J. (1994). Grounded theory methodology: An overview. In N. K. Denzin & Y. S. Lincoln (Eds.), *Handbook of qualitative research* (pp. 273–285). Thousand Oaks, CA: Sage.

Syme, M. L., Yellan, E., Cornelison, L., Poey, J. L., Krajicek, R., & Doll, G. (2017). Content analysis of public opinion on sexual expression and dementia: Implications for nursing home policy development. *Health Expectations*, 20(4), 705–713. doi:10.1111/hex.12509

# Chapter 15

Auerbach, C., & Zeitlin, W. (2014). *SSD for R: an R package for analyzing single-subject data*. New York, NY: Oxford University Press.

Barton, E. E., & Reichow, B. (2012). Guidelines for graphing data with Microsoft, Office 2007 and Office for MAC 2008 and 2011. *Journal of Early Intervention*, 34(3), 129–150. doi.org/10.1177/1053815112456601

Beck, A. T., Steer, R. A., & Brown, G. K. (1996). *Manual for the Beck Depression Inventory-II*. San Antonio, TX: Psychological Corporation.

Bloom, M., Fischer, J., & Orme (2006). *Evaluating practice: Guidelines for the accountable professional* (5th ed.). Boston, MA: Allyn & Bacon.

Callesen, P., Jensen, A. B., & Wells, A. (2014). Metacognitive therapy in recurrent depression: A case replication series in Denmark. *Scandinavian Journal of Psychology*, 55(1), 60–64. doi:10.1111/sjop.12089

Campbell, D. T., & Stanley, J. C. (1963). Experimental and quasi-experimental designs for research on teaching. In N. L. Gage (Ed.), *Handbook of research on teaching* (pp. 171–246). Chicago, IL: Rand McNally. Reprinted in 1966 under the title Experimental and quasi-experimental designs for research.

Council on Social Work Education (CSWE). (2015). *Educational policy and accreditation standards for baccalaureate and master's social work programs.* Alexandria, VA: Author. Retrieved from https://www.cswe.org/get attachment/Accreditation/Accreditation-Process/2015 -EPAS/2015EPAS_Web_FINAL.pdf.aspx

Ibrahim, S. A., Scott, F. E., Cole, D. C., Shannon, H. S., & Eyles, J. (2001). Job strain and self-reported health among working women and men: An analysis of the 1994–1995 Canadian National Population Health Survey. *Women's Health, 33*(1–2), 105–124.

Lee, D. T. S., Yip, S. K., Chiu, H. F. K., Leung, T. Y. S., Chan, K. P. M., Chau, I. O. L., et al. (1998). Detecting postnatal depression in Chinese women: Validation of the Chinese version of the Edinburg Postnatal Scale. *British Journal of Psychiatry, 172*(5), 433–437.

Lundervold, D. A., & Belwood, M. F. (2000). The best secret in counseling: Single-case (N = 1) experimental designs. *Journal of Counseling and Development, 78*(1), 92–102.

Manolov, R., & Moeyaert, M. (2017). How can single-case data be analyzed? Software resources, tutorial, and reflections on analysis. *Behavior Modification, 41*(2), 179–228. doi:10.1177/014545516664307

Morgan, D. L., & Morgan, R. K. (2003). Single-participant research design: Bringing science to managed care. In A. E. Kazdin (Ed.), *Methodological issues and strategies in clinical research* (3rd ed., pp. 635–654). Washington, DC: American Psychological Association.

Ray, D. C., Minton, C. A. B., Schottelkorb, A. A., & Brown, A. G. (2010). Single-case design in child counseling research: Implications for counselor education. *Counselor Education and Supervision, 49*(3), 193–208. doi:10.1002/j.1556-6978.2010.tb00098.x

Shadish, W. (2014). Statistical analysis of single-case designs: The shape of things to come. *Current Directions in Psychological Science, 23*(2), 139–146. doi:10.117/0963721414524773

Sue, D. W., & Sue, D. (1990). *Counseling the culturally different: Theory and practice* (2nd ed.) New York, NY: Wiley.

# Chapter 16

· · · · · · · · · · · · · · · · · · · · · · · · · ·

American Evaluation Association (AEA). (2011). *Public statement on cultural competence in evaluation.* Fairhaven, MA: Author. Retrieved from www.eval.org

Council on Social Work Education (CSWE). (2015). *Educational policy and accreditation standards for baccalaureate and master's social work programs.* Alexandria, VA: Author. Retrieved from https://www.cswe.org/get attachment/Accreditation/Accreditation-Process/2015 -EPAS/2015EPAS_Web_FINAL.pdf.aspx

Grinnell, R. M., Gabor, P. A., & Urau, Y. A. (2012). *Program evaluation for social workers: Foundations of evidence-based programs* (6th ed.). New York, NY: Oxford University Press.

Margolis, L. H., Steber, K. F., Rosenberg, A., Palmer, A., Rounds, K. & Wells, M. (2017). Partnering with parents in interprofessional leadership graduate education to promote family-professional partnerships. *Journal of Interprofessional Care, 31*(4), 497–504. doi:10.1080/1356 1820.2017.1296418

National Association of Social Workers (NASW). (2017). *Code of ethics.* Washington, DC: Author.

Shek, D. T. Lin, L., & Liang, J. (2018). Program evaluation. In B. Frey (Ed.), *The SAGE encyclopedia of education, research, measurement, and evaluation* (pp. 1131–1314). Thousand Oaks, CA: Sage.

Tandon, S. D., Parillo, K. M., Jenkins, C., & Duggan, A. K. (2005). Formative evaluation of home visitors' role in addressing poor mental health, domestic violence, and substance abuse among low-income pregnant and parenting women. *Maternal and Child Health Journal, 9*(3), 273–283. doi:10.1007/s10995-05-0012-8

Thomas, V. G., & Parsons, B. A. (2017). Culturally responsive evaluation meets systems-oriented evaluation. *American Journal of Evaluation, 38*(1), 7–28. doi:10.1177/1098214016644069

Waapalaneexkweew (Bowman-Farrell, N., Mohican/Lunaape). (2018). Looking backward but moving forward: Honoring the sacred and asserting the sovereign in indigenous evaluation. *American Journal of Evaluation, 39*(4), 543–568. doi:10.1177/1098214018790412

Waapalaneexkweew (Bowman, N., Mohican/Lunaape), & Dodge-Francis, C. (2018). Culturally responsive indigenous evaluation and tribal governments: Understanding the relationship. In F. Cram, K. A., Tibbetts, & J. LaFrance (Eds.), *Indigenous evaluation: New directions for evaluation, 159,* 17–31.

# Index

Hadjistavropoulos, T., 163
Haight, W., 151
Hambarsoomian, K., 204
Hanson, W. E., 172–173
Hao, Z., 12–13
Harden, A., 12, 46
Harris, L. A., 315
Hawthorne effect, 89
Hays, D. G., 163
Health Insurance Portability and Accountability Act (HIPAA ), 190
Heckathorn, D. D., 211
Heyman, J. C., 125
Histograms, 251 (figure)
History, definition of, 357
Hoffman, G. D., 335
Homogeneous sampling, 151 (table), 207 (table)
Homoscedasticity in Pearson's correlation, 266
Hsin-Chun Tsai, J., 338
Huang, L., 64
Huberman, A. M., 151
Hughes, D., 72
Human rights, 3
Humble, M. B., 51
Hyland, A., 186–187
Hypotheses, 11–12, 42–43
    experimental designs and, 122
    pre-experimental designs and, 111–112
    research design and, 50

Identical sampling, 175
Impact evaluation, 372
Incidence rate, 187–188
Incidents, 187
Inclusion criteria, 29
Independence in chi-square test of independence, 272
Independent-sample *t*-test, 284–290, 286–289 (figure)
Independent variables, 42, 107
Individualized rating scales (IRS), 349–350, 350 (table)
Inductive philosophy, 149
Inductive reasoning, 42–43, 42 (figure)
Inference quality, 174
Inferential statistics, 245–246, 248
Infographics, 52
Informed consent, 25, 26–28
Insider-researchers, 150

Institutional review board (IRB), 26–27, 30–33, 389
    CITI certification and, 33–34
    exempt review, 30–32
    vulnerable populations and, 33
    *See also* Ethics
Instrumentation
    in one-group pretest-posttest design, 116
    in time-series design, 141
Integration of scientific method with existing literature, 9 (figure), 14
Intensity sampling, 152 (table), 207 (table)
Interaction of history and intervention, 359
Interaction of selection and maturation, 118, 138
Interaction of selection and X, 114–115, 116, 139, 359
Interaction of testing and X, 116, 139, 359
Interactive feature of practice wisdom, 5–6
Interlocking quota, 208
Internal consistency, 91
Internal validity, 113–114, 143, 189, 357
Inter-observer reliability, 90
Interpretational analysis, 156
Interpretivism, 159
Interprofessional Leadership Development Programme (ILDP), 378
Inter-rater reliability, 90
Interrupted time-series design, 140
Interval measurement, 87
Intervention-only design, 355–356
Intervention phase in single-case design evaluation, 354, 354 (figure)
Interview guide, 156
Interviews, 156, 160
Interview schedule, 96
Interview surveys, 234
Intraclass correlation coefficient, 91
Introduction, research proposal, 387–388
Intuition in phenomenological research, 161
Iyer, A., 12–13

Jack, S., 155
Jamal, F., 12, 46
Jason, L. A., 44
Jenkins, C., 372
Jetten, J., 12–13
Jiao, Q. G., 175
Jobling, H., 151
Johnson, A., 337
Johnson, C. W., 116